The **Rough Guide** to

Amsterdam

written and researched by

Martin Dunford and Phil Lee

with additional contributions by

Karoline Densley and Malijn Maat

D0963642

GUIDES

NEW YORK • LONDON • DELHI

www.roughguides.com

Contents

3

◄◄ Leidseplein at night, ◄ Herengracht reflection

Introduction to

Amsterdam

Capital of The Netherlands, Amsterdam enjoys most of the advantages of a large city but not too many of the disadvantages: it's relatively small, it has a good transport system so it doesn't take forever to get from place to place, and, thanks to its canals, many parts of the centre are peaceful and relatively uncongested. The canals, too, make Amsterdam something special, lined with tall gabled houses reflected in their black-green waters. Above all it's a unique and beautiful city: whether you're touring its elegant waterways, sipping a beer in one of its old cafés, or dodging the trams on Dam Square, you'll know that you couldn't be anywhere else in the world.

Amsterdam is also defined by its people and culture, with a welcoming attitude towards visitors and a youthful orientation that has been shaped by the **liberal counterculture** of the last four decades. It's hard not to feel drawn by the buzz of open-air summer events, by the cheery intimacy of the city's cafés, and by the Dutch facility with languages: just about everyone you meet in Amsterdam will be able to speak good-to-fluent English, and often more than a smattering of French and German too.

The city was celebrated during the 1960s and 1970s for its radical permissiveness, and, despite the gentrification of the last twenty years, it retains a laid-back feel. It is, however, far from being as cosmopolitan a city as, say, London or Paris: despite the huge numbers of immigrants from the former colonies in Surinam and Indonesia, as well as Morocco and Turkey – to name but a few – almost all live and work outside the centre and can seem almost invisible to the casual visitor. Indeed, there is an ethnic and social homogeneity in the city centre that seems to run counter to everything you may have heard of Dutch integration. This apparent contradiction embodies much of the spirit of Amsterdam. The city is world-famous as a place where the possession and sale of **cannabis** are effectively legal – or at least decriminalized – and yet, for

Amsterdam is renowned for its tolerance towards all styles of behaviour

the most part, Amsterdammers themselves can't really be bothered with the stuff. And while Amsterdam is renowned for its **tolerance** towards all styles of behaviour (its policy on prostitution is also world-renowned), a primmer, more correct-thinking big city, with a more mainstream dress sense, would be hard to find. Behind the cosy cafés and dreamy canals lurks the suspicion that Amsterdammers' hearts lie squarely in their wallets, and while newcomers might see the city as a liberal haven, locals can seem just as indifferent to this as well.

In recent years, a string of hardline city mayors have taken this **conservatism** on board and have embarked on a generally successful – if unspoken – policy of squashing Amsterdam's image as a counterculture icon and depicting it

The Golden Age

Contrary to what you may think, the Dutch Golden Age wasn't during the 1960s, but three centuries earlier during the 1600s, when Holland's maritime strength and the canny commercial skills of the Dutch led to the establishment of a huge empire, with colonies and trading post all over the world. It's this era, perhaps more than any other, that has defined the city you see today: Amsterdam's major canals – Herengracht, Keizersgracht and Prinsengracht – were developed during this time; many of the city's most monumental buildings were built, for example, the Royal Palace and the numerous buildings of Henrik de Keyser; and many of the paintings and art that you find around Amsterdam date from this time, when the explosion in business activity funded an upsurge in the arts. Indeed, the careers of Rembrandt, Hals, Vermeer and other great Dutch seventeenth-century artists almost shadow the greatest years of the Golden Age itself.

▲ Huis Bartolotti, Herengracht

▲ East of Eden café-bar

instead as a centre for business and international high finance. Almost all of the inner-city squats, which once defined local people-power, are gone or legalized, and coffeeshops have been forced to choose between selling dope or alcohol – and, if only for economic reasons, many have switched to the latter. The cityscape, too, is changing, with large-scale **urban development** on the outskirts and regeneration within. Nevertheless, Amsterdam remains a casual and intimate place, and Amsterdammers themselves make much of their city and its attractions being *gezellig*, a rather overused Dutch

▲ Keizersgracht bridge

word roughly corresponding to a combination of "cosy", "lived-in" or "warmly convivial". Nowhere is this more applicable than in the city's unparalleled selection of **drinking** places, whether you choose a traditional brown café or one of a raft of newer, designer bars and grand cafés. The city boasts dozens of excellent **restaurants** too, with great Indonesian options and a host of increasingly adventurous Dutch establishments. As for **cultural attractions**, the city holds its own in contemporary European film, dance, drama and music; it has several top-rank jazz venues and the Concertgebouw concert hall is home to one of the world's leading orchestras. The club scene is relatively restrained, although the city's many **gay bars** and clubs partly justify Amsterdam's claim to be the "Gay Capital of Europe".

Where to go

◄ Kadinsky coffeeshop

The city's layout is determined by a web of canals radiating out from a historical core to loop right round Amsterdam's compact centre, which takes about forty minutes to stroll from one end to the other. Butting up to the River IJ, the **Old Centre** spreads south from **Centraal Station** bisected by Damrak and its continuation, Rokin, long the city's main drag; en route is the Dam, the main square. The Old Centre remains Amsterdam's commercial heart, with the best of its bustling street life. It also holds myriad shops, bars and restaurants, includes the **Red Light District**, just to the east of Damrak, and contains dozens of fine old buildings, most memorably the Oude Kerk, the Amstelkring and the Royal Palace. The Old Centre is bordered by the first of the major canals, the Singel, which is followed closely by the Herengracht, Keizersgracht and Prinsengracht – collectively known as the **Grachtengordel**, or "Girdle of Canals". These canals were part of a major seventeenth-century urban extension and, with the interconnecting radial streets, form the city's distinctive web shape. This is Amsterdam's most delightful area and the one you see on all the brochures – handsome seventeenth- and eighteenth-century canal houses, with their distinctive gables, overlooking narrow, dreamy canals; a familiar image perhaps, but one that is still entirely authentic. It's here you'll also find the city's most celebrated attraction, the **Anne Frankhuis**, where the young Jewish diarist hid away during the German occupation of World War II and now a poignant reminder of the Holocaust.

▲ Keizersgracht

Immediately to the west of the Grachtengordel lies the **Jordaan**, one-time industrial slum and the traditional heart of working-class Amsterdam, though these days almost entirely gentrified. The same applies to the adjacent **Westerdok**, though the origins of this district are very different. The artificial islands of the Westerdok were dredged out of the river to create extra wharves and shipbuilding space during the city's Golden Age and only in the last few decades has the shipping industry moved out. On the other side of the centre is the **Old Jewish Quarter**, which was once home to a thriving Jewish community until the German occupation of World War II. Post-war development has laid a heavy hand on the quarter, but nonetheless there are a couple of poignant survivors, principally the Portuguese synagogue and the Jewish Historical Museum. The adjacent Plantagebuurt is greener and more suburban, but it does possess one excellent museum, the Verzetsmuseum (Resistance Museum) – as does the neighbouring Oosterdok, another area of former dockland that is undergoing a rapid process of renewal and revival.

Amsterdam's **Museum Quarter** contains, as you might expect, the city's premier art museums, principally the **Rijksmuseum** with its wonderful collection of Dutch paintings, including several of Rembrandt's finest works, and the peerless **Van Gogh Museum**, with the world's largest collection of the artist's work. Both lie just a stone's throw from the city's finest park, the **Vondelpark**. Finally, the residential suburbs – or Outer Districts – spreading beyond Singelgracht are relatively short of attractions, notable exceptions being the wooded parkland of the Amsterdamse Bos and the Amsterdam ArenA, home to the city's celebrated football team, Ajax.

Talk to Amsterdammers about visiting other parts of their country and you may well be met with looks of amazement. Ignore them. The Netherlands is a small nation, and the Dutch have an outstanding public transport system, an integrated network of trains and buses that puts the city within easy grasp of a large and varied slice of the country. Consequently, the choice of possible **day-trips** is extensive: the towns of **Haarlem** and **Alkmaar**, the old Zuider Zee ports of **Marken** and **Volendam**, and the pretty village of **Edam** are all worth a visit – not to mention the much-touted Keukenhof Gardens, which are at their best, not surprisingly, during spring and summer.

When to go

A msterdam enjoys a fairly standard temperate climate, with warm summers and moderately cold and wet winters. The climate is certainly not severe enough to make very

> **Spring and autumn can be especially beautiful, with mist hanging over the canals**

▲ Skating in winter

much difference to the city's routines, which makes it an ideal year-round destination. That said, high summer – roughly late June to August – sees the city packed to the gunnels and parts of the centre almost overwhelmed by the tourist throng, whereas spring and autumn are not too crowded and can be especially beautiful, with mist hanging over the canals and low sunlight beaming through the cloud cover. At any time of the year, but particularly in summer, try to book your accommodation ahead of time.

Average daily temperatures (°C) and monthly rainfall (mm)

	Jan	Feb	Mar	Apr	May	June	July	Aug	Sept	Oct	Nov	Dec
Min°C	−0.2	−0.5	1.5	3.8	7.5	10.5	12.5	12.5	10.5	7.3	3.8	1.1
Max°C	4.3	4.9	8.1	11.6	16	19.1	20.5	20.5	18.3	14	8.8	5.7
mm	79.1	43.6	89.3	39.3	50.2	60.1	73.4	60	80.1	103.7	76.4	72.3

25

things not to miss

It's not possible to see everything Amsterdam has to offer on a short trip – and we don't suggest you try. What follows is a subjective selection of the city's highlights, from elegant canal-side architecture and vibrant markets to outstanding art collections and traditional bars – all arranged in colour-coded categories to help you find the very best things to see, do and experience. All entries have a page reference to take you straight into the guide, where you can find out more.

01 **Cycling** Page **32** • Get around the city like a local by renting a bike for the day.

03 The Heineken Experience Page 129 •
The former brewery, now converted to an imaginative, if self-publicising, museum.

02 Tuschinski Cinema Page 83 •
Opened in 1921, the Tuschinski has a superb Art Deco interior.

05 The Begijnhof Page 62 •
The fourteenth-century Begijnhof is one of the quietest and prettiest corners of the city centre.

04 Rijksmuseum Page 116 •
The city's greatest museum, featuring everything from paintings to furniture and applied arts. It's currently undergoing restoration but you can still see the best of its paintings in the Philips Wing.

06 Waterlooplein Page **101** • With every justification, Amsterdam is famous for its flea and antiques markets, and this is its oldest and best.

07 Herengracht Page **67** • The first of the seventeenth-century canals to be dug, and the one with the grandest buildings.

08 Amstelkring Page **56** • Once a clandestine church for the city's Catholics, the seventeenth-century Amstelkring is Amsterdam's most distinctive historic sight.

09 Van Gogh Museum Page **122** • The world's most comprehensive collection of the artist's work – simply unmissable.

10 **Queen's Day** Page **249** •
Amsterdammers let their tresses down on Queen's Day (Koninginnedag), the city's biggest and wildest municipal knees-up.

12 **Proeflokaaalen** Page **180** •
Served ice-cold, jenever, the Dutch version of gin, is the nation's favourite spirit, and these "tasting-houses" are the places where you traditionally sample it in its various flavours.

11 **Frans Hals Museum** Page **144** • Just a few minutes by train from Amsterdam, Haarlem is home to this outstanding collection of paintings by Hals and his contemporaries.

13 **Indonesian food** Page **178** • Fill up on Amsterdam's best ethnic food speciality.

13

15 Coffeeshops Page 186 •
Nowhere else in the world can you smoke high quality dope in such comfortable – and legal – surroundings.

14 Brouwersgracht Page 90 •
With its houseboats and gabled warehouses, Brouwersgracht is an especially charming canal.

16
Brown Cafés Page **180** • Amsterdam is famous for its brown cafés – dark, cosy and very traditional.

17
Museum Van Loon Page **82** • A handsome canal house complete with Rococo stucco work and Romantic murals.

18 Vondelpark Page **126** • The leafy Vondelpark, with its ponds, footpaths and colony of parrots, is the city's most attractive park.

20 The Jordaan Page **84** • The Jordaan holds many of the city's most diverting secondhand and bric-a-brac shops – and some of its prettiest canals.

19 Bloemenmarkt Page **62** • The place to come if you want tulips from Amsterdam.

21 The Royal Palace Page **51** • Co-opted by the Dutch royals but originally Amsterdam's town hall, this building speaks volumes about the city during the Golden Age.

23 Red Light District Page 54 • Too steeped in the art of titilation to be truly shocking these days, but Amsterdam's Red Light District is still the real thing – and a big attraction in its own right.

22 Oude Kerk Page 55 • The city's oldest and most venerable church, slap bang in the middle of the Red Light District.

24
Trams Page 31 • Rattling across the city, Amsterdam's fast and efficient trams are an enjoyable way to get around.

25
Anne Frankhuis
Page 70 • The secret annexe here (concealed by a bookcase) was home to Anne Frank and her family for two years during World War II. It's now the city's most moving sight.

Basics

Basics

Getting there

UK travellers are spoilt for choice when it comes to deciding how to get to Amsterdam (see below). From North America, the main decision is whether to fly direct – easy enough as Schiphol airport is a major European hub – or fly via another European city, probably London. From Australia and New Zealand, every flight to Amsterdam requires one or two stops on the way.

Booking online

Many airlines and travel websites offer you the opportunity to book tickets online, cutting out the costs of agents and middlemen. Good deals can often be found through discount or auction sites, as well as through the airlines' own websites – bear in mind, tickets are usually non-refundable and non-changeable. Students and those under 26 may be able to find even cheaper flights through specialist agents such as STA Travel (see below).

Online booking agents

ⓦ www.cheapflights.co.uk, ⓦ www .cheapflights.com Flight deals, travel agents, plus links to other travel sites.
ⓦ www.cheaptickets.com US discount flight specialists, also has deals on hotels and car hire.
ⓦ www.expedia.co.uk, ⓦ www.expedia.com Discount airfares, all-airline search engine and daily deals.
ⓦ www.hotwire.com US website with lots of last-minute deals, saving of up to forty percent on regular published fares.
ⓦ www.lastminute.com UK site that offers good last-minute holiday package and flight-only deals.
ⓦ www.opodo.com Pan-European site funded by the major European airlines that efficiently tracks down the cheapest and most convenient scheduled flight, and also offers accommodation, car rental and other services.
ⓦ www.skyauction.com US site that auctions tickets and travel packages.
ⓦ www.statravel.com. Worldwide specialists in low-cost flights with especially good discounts for students and under-26s.
ⓦ www.travelocity.co.uk, ⓦ www.travelocity .com Good web fares and deals on car rental, accommodation and lodging.

ⓦ www.travelshop.com.au Australian website offering discounted flights, packages, insurance, online bookings.

From the UK

There are flights direct to Amsterdam from London and a string of regional airports; Eurostar trains from London to Brussels, from where it's a little under three hours onwards by train; and ferries from Harwich to the Hook of Holland, Hull to Rotterdam and Newcastle (North Shields) to Ijmuiden, with all three Dutch ports within easy striking distance of the city. Other options include the Amsterdam Express rail and ferry link, driving via the Eurotunnel shuttle, or international buses from London.

Flights

Amsterdam is one of the UK's most popular **short-haul destinations**, and you'll find lots of choice in carriers, flight times and departure airports. KLM offers the widest range of flights, but British Airways and a hatful of budget airlines chip in too. Bear in mind also that competition is intense, so new routings appear and existing ones are abandoned on a regular basis.

Fares from the UK to Amsterdam begin at about £90 return and can climb to £350, but in most cases, providing you accept a non-exchangeable and/or non-refundable ticket and some limitations as to the length of your stay, you'll end up paying between £90 and £140. The best deals are usually for midweek travel and are available if you book well ahead of time, though last-minute bargains are relatively common too; there is usually a smallish premium for travelling from a regional (as distinct from London) airport. If there are no direct flights available, bear in mind you can try other Dutch aiports (such as Eindhoven or Rotterdam) or reach Amsterdam via Brussels (two and a half hours away by train).

Airlines and routings

bmi ☎0870/607 0555, 🌐www.flybmi.com. One-stop flights from Aberdeen, Belfast, Durham Tees Valley, Edinburgh, Glasgow, Inverness, Leeds/Bradford and Manchester to Amsterdam Schiphol via London Heathrow. Also London Heathrow direct to Amsterdam Schiphol.

bmibaby ☎0870/264 2229, 🌐www.bmibaby .com. Nottingham East Midlands Airport and Birmingham to Amsterdam Schiphol.

British Airways ☎0870/850 9850, 🌐www .britishairways.com. London Gatwick, London Heathrow & Manchester to Amsterdam Schiphol.

easyJet ☎0870/600 0000, 🌐www.easyjet .com. Belfast, Bristol, Edinburgh, Glasgow, Liverpool, London Gatwick, London Stansted and Luton to Amsterdam Schiphol.

Jet2 UK ☎0870/737 8282, 🌐www.jet2.com. Leeds-Bradford to Amsterdam Schiphol.

KLM ☎0870/243 0541, 🌐www.klmuk.com. Aberdeen, Birmingham International, Bristol, Cardiff, Durham Tees Valley, Edinburgh, Glasgow, Humberside, Leeds/Bradford, London City, London Heathrow, Manchester, Newcastle & Norwich direct to Amsterdam Schiphol.

Ryanair ☎0871/246 0000, 🌐www.ryanair.com. London Stansted to Eindhoven, in the Netherlands. Also Glasgow to Brussels (Charleroi). Eindhoven is a ninety-minute journey by train from Amsterdam.

Scotairways ☎0870/606 0707, 🌐www .scotairways.co.uk. Southampton to Amsterdam Schiphol.

SN (Brussels Airlines) UK ☎0870/735 2345, 🌐www.flysn.com. Birmingham, Bristol, London Gatwick, London Heathrow, Manchester and Southampton to Brussels international airport.

Thomson Fly ☎0870/1900 737, 🌐www .thomsonfly.com. Bournemouth and Coventry to Schiphol.

VLM London ☎020/7476 6677, Manchester ☎0161/493 3232. Jersey ☎01534/783 283; 🌐www.vlm-airlines.com. Jersey, Liverpool, London City and Manchester to Brussels; Guernsey, Jersey, Liverpool, London City and Manchester to Rotterdam. Most flights are routed via London City airport. Rotterdam is a one-hour journey by train from Amsterdam.

Specialist flight agents

Co-op Travel Care ☎0870/112 0085, 🌐www .travelcareonline.com. Flights and holidays to the Netherlands from the UK's largest independent travel agent.

ebookers ☎0870/010 7000, 🌐www.ebookers .com. Low fares on an extensive selection of scheduled flights and package deals to Amsterdam.

Flightcentre ☎0870/890 8099, 🌐www .flightcentre.co.uk. Rock-bottom fares.

North South Travel ☎01245/608 291, 🌐www .northsouthtravel.co.uk. Competitive travel agency, offering discounted fares. Profits are used to support projects in the developing world, especially the promotion of sustainable tourism.

Rosetta Travel ☎028/9064 4996, 🌐www .rosettatravel.com. Flight and holiday agent, specializing in deals from Belfast.

Travel Bag ☎0870/890 1456, 🌐www.travelbag .co.uk. Discount deals.

USIT Northern Ireland ☎028/9032 7111, 🌐www .usitnow.com. Specialists in student, youth and independent travel – flights, trains and study tours.

By rail

Eurostar trains running through the Channel Tunnel to Brussels put Amsterdam within reasonably easy striking distance of London's Waterloo and Kent's Ashford train stations. The same cannot be said if you're heading off to Amsterdam by rail from much of the rest of the UK, but at least it's possible to keep costs down by through-ticketing from your home station. More long-winded still are **train and ferry** routings, using the UK's three ferries to the Netherlands – Harwich to Hook of Holland, Hull to Rotterdam and Newcastle to Ijmuiden – even though all three of these Dutch ports are just a brief journey from Amsterdam (see box, p.21). Finally, if your visit to Amsterdam is just one part of a larger and longer rail itinerary, you might investigate a **pan-European rail pass** with **Rail Europe**, who sell every type of national and international rail ticket and pass.

Eurostar

There are normally seven or eight **Eurostar** train departures from London Waterloo to Brussels (Bruxelles-Midi station) every day, with a journey time of 2 hours 30 minutes. En route, most trains stop at Ashford in Kent and Lille in France. From Bruxelles-Midi station, Belgian Railways, Netherlands Railways and Thalys trains combine to operate a fast and frequent service to Amsterdam's Centraal station; this second train journey takes just under three hours.

As regards **fares**, the least expensive Eurostar ticket from London to Amsterdam (or any other Dutch station) is a Leisure fare of just £70. This requires either booking at least 21 days in advance or staying overnight on Saturday; it's available all year. Eurostar will also through-ticket passengers from any regional British train station to Amsterdam via Waterloo for a modest extra premium. On the other hand, a fully flexible and refundable Eurostar return ticket for travel any time or day of the week from Waterloo to Amsterdam will set you back about £300 in standard (as distinct from first) class.

Amsterdam Express – rail and ferry

A partnership between One Railways, Stena Line and Dutch Railways, the so-called **Amsterdam Express** "rail & sail" link connects central London (and One Railways stations in East Anglia) with Amsterdam's Centraal Station. From London there is a morning and afternoon departure from **Liverpool Street station** via Colchester to **Harwich** (journey time 1hr 25 mins). At Harwich passengers transfer to Stena Line's car ferry to the **Hook of Holland**. From the Hook, there are connecting trains to Amsterdam's **Centraal Station**. The whole journey from London to Amsterdam takes seven and a half hours, but note that the afternoon departure doesn't arrive in Amsterdam until (a pretty grim) 2.14am. **Prices** from London start at £50 return for a Special Apex fare, which must be booked at least a week in advance, with the return journey being made within one month. A standard open

return costs £85, or £68 if you are under 26. Book online at ⓦwww.amsterdamexpress .com, or, for travel from local stations in East Anglia contact **One Railways** (ⓣ0870/040 9090; ⓦwww.oneanglia.com).

Rail contacts

Amsterdam Express ⓦwww.amsterdamexpress .co.uk. London and East Anglia to Amsterdam via train and ferry.
Eurostar ⓣ0870/518 6186, ⓦwww.eurostar .com. London Waterloo to Brussels.
International Rail UK ⓣ0870/751 5000, ⓦwww.international-rail.com. Covers a wide range of options, including Eurostar, all European rail passes and tickets, plus ferry crossings.
NS (Dutch Railways) ⓦwww.ns.nl. Everything you ever wanted to know about Dutch railways – from timetables through to ticketing.
Rail Europe UK ⓣ0870/584 8848, ⓦwww .raileurope.co.uk. Umbrella company selling tickets and passes for European train travel, including Eurostar. Their comprehensive website is the most useful source of information on tickets and passes.
Thalys ⓦwww.thalys.com. Slick, international express trains to Amsterdam from Brussels and Paris.
Trainseurope UK ⓣ0900/195 0101 (60p/min, refundable against a booking), ⓦwww .trainseurope.co.uk. Sells all sorts of tickets and passes for European train travel.

Driving

To reach Amsterdam by **car** or **motorcycle**, you can either use the ferries or – preferable for its simplicity and hassle-free crossing – Eurotunnel's shuttle-train through the Channel Tunnel. Note that Eurotunnel only carries cars (including occupants) and motorbikes. Cyclists and foot passengers therefore need to take a ferry (invariably more expensive than a flight).

Dutch Railways

The Dutch train network, operated by **NS** (Nederlandse Spoorwegen – Dutch Railways), is one of the best in Europe: trains are fast, modern, frequent and very punctual, fares are relatively low, and the network of lines comprehensive. In particular, there is an excellent train service from the three ports – Hook of Holland, Rotterdam, and Ijmuiden – where the ferries from the UK dock. NS publishes mounds of information on its various services and fares. Full information is on its website (ⓦwww.ns.nl) and a comprehensive, inexpensive and easy-to-use timetable (*spoorboekje*) is sold at all major stations.

Eurotunnel

The easiest way to drive to Amsterdam is to head to Folkesone and drive on to one of **Eurotunnel** 's shuttle trains, then drive off at Calais for the straightforward run through Belgium. Trains run 24 hours a day between Folkestone and Coquelles, near Calais, with up to four departures per hour (only 1 hourly midnight–6am) and take around 35 minutes, though you must arrive at least half an hour before departure. Advance booking is advisable, though you can just turn up and buy your **ticket** at the toll booths (after exiting the M20 at junction 11a). From Calais, it's about 370km north to Amsterdam.

Eurotunnel **fares** depend on the time of year, time of day and length of stay: if, for instance, you travel between 10pm and 6am outside of the summer months, you could get a round-trip fare for just under £200 per vehicle; the highest fares apply on weekends and in July and August and can be as much as £415. Prices are charged per vehicle, with no additions for passengers. Call 0870/535 3535, or, for the lowest rates book at ⓦ www.eurotunnel.com.

Ferries

The speediest car ferry is the **Stena Line** service from **Harwich in Essex to the Hook of Holland** (daytime 3hr 40min; overnight 6hr 15min). On this route, a high-season, five-day period return costs costs £250 for a car with four passengers on daytime sailings, or around £450 travelling overnight, which includes (compulsory) cabin. Bargain rail and ferry deal are available on this route – see below. Alternatively, **P&O Ferries** operates from **Hull to Rotterdam** (11hr) and here, booking well in advance, a car plus four people, with a cabin and meals included, costs around £700 return. For foot passengers, P&O arrange onward coach transportation from the dock to Amsterdam, but note that this needs to be booked at the same time as the ferry ticket. The third possibility is the **DFDS Seaways** car ferry **from Newcastle (North Shields) to Ijmuiden**, on the North Sea coast to the west of Amsterdam. This crossing takes fourteen hours and fares are cheaper the earlier you book. As an example, a high-season, return fare for four adults including car and cabin and booked well ahead of time is in the region of £500. Foot passengers, again in high season and booked well ahead, pay around £100 return. DFDS provides a connecting coach service from the dock to Amsterdam Centraal station; make the coach booking at the same time as you pay for the ferry ticket.

DFDS Seaways UK ☎08705/333 000, ⓦ www .dfdsseaways.co.uk. Newcastle to Ijmuiden.
P&O Ferries UK ☎0870/600 0600 or 01304/864 003, ⓦ www.poferries.com. Hull to Rotterdam and Zeebrugge.
Stena Line UK ☎08704/00 67 98, Northern Ireland ☎028/9074 7747, Republic of Ireland ☎01/204 7777, ⓦ www.stenaline.co.uk. Harwich to the Hook of Holland.

By bus

Travelling by long-distance **bus from the UK** to Amsterdam is something of a last resort, given the number of bargain air fares, but it is still likely to be the least expensive way of getting there, if only by a few pounds.

Eurolines, the umbrella name for a number of bus companies, operates three or four services daily from London's Victoria Coach Station to Amsterdam's Amstel Station, southeast of the city centre; all use Eurotunnel. The standard fare is £55 return (under-26s and over-60s pay £49), though promotional return fares can be snapped up for as little as £17. The standard journey time is eleven and a half hours, but be sure to check times when you book as some routings take as many as nineteen.

The less well-known **Anglia Lines** also operates a bus service between London Victoria and Amsterdam, terminating just across from Centraal Station. This service leaves once daily (four weekly during the slacker parts of winter) and there's a standard fare of £43 return (under-26s and over-60s pay £35), though once again there are lots of special deals to look out for.

Anglia Lines ☎0870/608 8806, ⓦ www .anglia-lines.co.uk.
Eurolines ☎08705/143 219, ⓦ www.eurolines .co.uk. In the UK, Eurolines buses are operated by National Express (☎0870/580 8080, ⓦ www .nationalexpress.com).

Tour operators

Most high-street travel agents can fix you up with a city break in Amsterdam via one of the many large-scale **tour operators**. The list below details some of the more individual companies.

Brightwater Holidays ☎01334/657 155, ⓦwww.brightwaterholidays.com. Fife-based tour operator running trips to the Dutch bulb fields.

Exodus ☎020/8675 5550, ⓦwww.exodus.co.uk. Offer a five-day cycling tour beginning and ending in Amsterdam and taking in, amongst several destinations, Alkmaar, Enkhuizen and Edam.

Martin Randall Travel ☎020/8742 3355, ⓦwww.martinrandall.com. Small-group, architectural, musical and historical tours of Amsterdam and the Netherlands, led by an expert.

Prospect Music and Art Tours ☎020/7486 5704, ⓦwww.prospecttours.com. Interesting range of guided tours focusing on Dutch art and music – their six-day "Vermeer to Van Gogh" holiday is a cracker.

Saddle Skedaddle ☎0191/265 1110, ⓦwww.skedaddle.co.uk. Organizes eight-day cycling tours of the Netherlands, beginning and ending in Amsterdam, and visiting Alkmaar, Zaanse Schans, Edam and Enkhuizen on the way.

Travelscope ☎0871/222 0212, ⓦwww.travelscope.co.uk. Offers a variety of family-friendly packages to the Netherlands including coach tours, city breaks, river cruises and trips to flower festivals.

From Ireland

From the Republic of Ireland, the prime supplier of flights to **Amsterdam** is Aer Lingus, who fly six times daily to Amsterdam out of Dublin and twice daily from Cork. **Fares** are very reasonable, with the cost of a return working out at between €60 and €120 depending on the season and with some minor restrictions regarding length of stay and so forth; these discount tickets are, however, non-exchangeable and/or non-refundable. If you're **driving**, you have two choices: cross the Irish Sea and sail from an English port (see above), or travel from Ireland to France and then drive on to Amsterdam from there.

Airlines and routings

Aer Lingus ☎0818/365 000, ⓦwww.aerlingus.ie. Cork and Dublin to Amsterdam Schiphol.

British Airways ☎1-890/626 747, ⓦwww.britishairways.com. Dublin, Cork and Shannon to Amsterdam Schiphol via London or Manchester.

bmi ☎01/407 3036, ⓦwww.flybmi.com. From Dublin (and Belfast) to Amsterdam Schiphol.

Ryanair ☎0818/303 030, ⓦwww.ryanair.com. Shannon and Dublin to Brussels (Charleroi). Brussels is two and a half hours by train from Amsterdam; from Charleroi airport, it's about an hour by bus north to Brussels.

Ferry operators

Brittany Ferries ☎021/427 7801, ⓦwww.brittanyferries.ie. Cork to Roscoff.

Irish Ferries ☎1890/313 131, ⓦwww.irishferries.com. Rosslare to Cherbourg or Roscoff (March–Sept only).

Specialist flight agents and tour operators

Aran Travel First Choice ☎091/562 595, ⓦwww.firstchoicetravel.ie. Good-value flights.

CIE Tours International Republic of Ireland ☎01/703 1888, ⓦwww.cietours.ie. CIE offers a wide range of escorted bus tours, five of which flit through Amsterdam.

ebookers ☎01/241 5689, ⓦwww.ebookers.ie. Low fares on an extensive selection of scheduled flights and package deals.

Joe Walsh Tours ☎01/676 0991, ⓦwww.joewalshtours.ie. Long-established travel agent with a good line in discounted air fares.

McCarthys Travel ☎021/427 0127, ⓦwww.mccarthystravel.ie. Established Irish travel agent now part of the Worldchoice chain of travel shops. Features flights, short and city breaks, including breaks to Amsterdam.

Trailfinders ☎01/677 7888, ⓦwww.trailfinders.ie. One of the best-informed and most efficient travel agents for independent travellers with Amsterdam hotel and city break deals.

USIT ☎0818/200 020, ⓦwww.usit.ie. Specialists in student, youth and independent travel, including flights, trains and study tours.

World Travel Centre Republic of Ireland ☎01/416 7007, ⓦwww.worldtravel.ie. Excellent fares to many European cities, including Amsterdam.

From the US and Canada

Amsterdam's Schiphol airport is among the most popular and least expensive gateways to Europe from North America, and getting a convenient and good-value flight is rarely a problem. All that said, you may be able to save money by being routed via another European hub city, usually London. All the cheaper tickets come with restrictions regarding length of stay, refundability and so forth, and flying in the summer is, on average, about fifty percent more expensive than in the winter.

In the USA, KLM and Northwest, who operate a joint service, offer direct or one-stop flights to Amsterdam from a dozen or so US cities, and connections from many more. As regards **fares**, their high-season round-trip ticket to Amsterdam from New York (flight time 8hr 10min) comes in at around US$1100, low season US$600; from Chicago, it's US$1000/550 (11hr 15min flight); and from Los Angeles US$1300/700 (10hr 30min). By comparison, a high-season Continental return ticket from Newark, New Jersey, to Amsterdam costs around US$930, low season US$400.

From Canada, KLM/Northwest flies direct to Amsterdam from Vancouver with a round-trip fare of roughly CDN$1650 in the high season, CDN$940 in the low, Toronto CDN$1300/1000.

Airlines and routings

Air Canada ☎1-888/247-2262, ⓦwww .aircanada.com. Toronto to Amsterdam. Also Vancouver, Calgary, Montréal and St Johns, Newfoundland to London.

Air France US ☎1-800/237-2747, ⓦwww .airfrance.com; Canada ☎1-800/667-2747; ⓦwww.airfrance.ca. Range of transatlantic flights from USA hub cities to Paris, including New York and Los Angeles to Amsterdam via Paris.

American Airlines ☎1-800/433-7300, ⓦwww .aa.com. Wide range of Transatlantic flights routed from USA hub cities to UK airports and Brussels.

Continental Airlines Domestic ☎1-800/523-FARE, International ☎1-800/231-0856, ⓦwww .continental.com. Non-stop flights from Newark, New Jersey, and Houston to Amsterdam.

Delta Domestic ☎1-800/221-1212, International ☎1-800/241-4141, ⓦwww.delta.com. Three non-stop services to Amsterdam from the USA – from New York (JFK), Atlanta and Cincinnati.

KLM (Royal Dutch Airlines) See Northwest/KLM.

Martinair ☎1-800/627-8462, ⓦwww.martinair .com. From May to September, Martinair have non-stop flights from Canada's Calgary, Edmonton and Vancouver to Amsterdam; they also operate a Toronto to Amsterdam non-stop flight from April to October. In

the USA, they fly from Miami and Orlando non-stop to Amsterdam from May to September

KLM/Northwest Domestic ☎1-800/225-2525, International ☎1-800/447-4747, ⓦwww.nwa .com, ⓦwww.klm.com. Direct or one-stop flights to Amsterdam from around a dozen US cities, and connections from plenty more.

United Airlines Domestic ☎1-800/241-6522, International ☎1-800/538-2929, ⓦwww.united .com. Two direct services to Amsterdam, from Chicago and Washington DC.

Specialist flight and travel agents

Air Brokers International ☎1-800/883-3273, ⓦwww.airbrokers.com. Consolidator and specialist in Round-the-World tickets.

Airtreks ☎1-877/AIRTREKS, ⓦwww.airtreks .com. Round-the-world tickets. The website features an interactive database that lets you build and price your own itinerary.

Flightcentre US ☎1-866/WORLD-51, ⓦwww .flightcentre.us, Canada ☎1-888/WORLD-55, ⓦwww.flightcentre.ca. Rock-bottom fares worldwide.

New Frontiers US ☎1-800/677-0720, ⓦwww .newfrontiers.com. Discount firm, specializing in travel from the US to Europe, with hotels and package deals.

Student Flights ☎1-800/255-8000 or 480/951-1177, ⓦwww.isecard.com/ studentflights . Student/youth fares, plus student IDs and European rail and bus passes.

TFI Tours ☎1-800/745-8000 or 212/736-1140, ⓦwww.lowestairprice.com. Well-established consolidator with a wide variety of global fares.

Tour operators

Abercrombie & Kent ☎1-800/323-7308, ⓦwww.abercrombiekent.com. Guided canal and river cruises in the Netherlands and Belgium that tie in with the prime tulip time (April & May).

CBT Tours ☎1-800/736-2453, ⓦwww.cbttours .com. Escorted bicycle tours from Amsterdam to Brussels following the North Sea coast.

Venture Out ☎1-888/431-6789, ⓦwww .venture-out.com. Offers week-long cycling and cultural small-group tour of Holland, beginning and ending in Amsterdam. The tour is popular with gay travellers and there's an optional pre-tour add-on for Amsterdam's Gay Pride.

From Australia and New Zealand

There's no shortage of flights to **Amsterdam** from Australia and New Zealand, though all of them involve **at least one stop**. Singapore Airlines and Malaysian offer two of the most direct routes out of Sydney (stopping in Singapore and Kuala Lumpur respectively). One further option is to pick up a cheap ticket to London, and then continue your journey onto Amsterdam with one of the UK's no-frills budget airlines (see p.20).

Tickets purchased direct from the airlines tend to be expensive, with published fares ranging from A$2000/NZ$2200 in low season to A$3500/NZ$3800 in high season. **Travel agents** can offer better deals, and have the latest information on special promotions. For extended trips, a **round-the-world** (RTW) ticket, valid for up to a year, can be good value. The lowest-priced tickets usually involve three to four stopovers, with prices rising the further you travel or the more stops you add.

Airlines

Air Canada Australia ☎ 1300/655 747 or 02/8248 5757, New Zealand ☎ 09/379 3371, Ⓦ www.aircanada.com.

Air New Zealand Australia ☎ 13 24 76, Ⓦ www.airnz.com.au, New Zealand ☎ 0800/737 000, Ⓦ www.airnz.co.nz.

American Airlines Australia ☎ 1300/130 757, New Zealand ☎ 0800/887 997, Ⓦ www.aa.com.

British Airways Australia ☎ 1300/767 177, New Zealand ☎ 0800/274 847 or 09/356 8690, Ⓦ www.britishairways.com

Cathay Pacific Australia ☎ 13 17 47, New Zealand ☎ 0508/800 454 or 09/379 0861, Ⓦ www.cathaypacific.com.

Continental Airlines Australia ☎ 1300/361 400, New Zealand ☎ 09/308 3350, Ⓦ www.continental.com.

Delta Australia ☎ 02/9251 3211, New Zealand ☎ 09/379 3370, Ⓦ www.delta.com.

Emirates Australia ☎ 1300/303 777 or 02/9290 9700, New Zealand ☎ 09/377 6004, Ⓦ www.emirates.com.

KLM Australia ☎ 1300/303 747, New Zealand ☎ 09/309 1782, Ⓦ www.klm.com.

Malaysia Airlines Australia ☎ 13 26 27, New Zealand ☎ 0800/777 747, Ⓦ www.malaysia-airlines.com.

Qantas Australia ☎ 13 13 13, New Zealand ☎ 0800/808 767 or 09/357 8900, Ⓦ www.qantas.com.

SAS Scandinavian Airlines Australia ☎ 1300/727 707, Ⓦ www.scandinavian.net.

Singapore Airlines Australia ☎ 13 10 11, New Zealand ☎ 0800/808 909, Ⓦ www.singaporeair.com.

Thai Airways Australia ☎ 1300/651 960, New Zealand ☎ 09/377 3886, Ⓦ www.thaiair.com.

United Airlines Australia ☎ 13 17 77, Ⓦ www.united.com.

Specialist flight and travel agents

Flight Centre Australia ☎ 13 31 33, Ⓦ www.flightcentre.com.au, New Zealand ☎ 0800 243 544, Ⓦ www.flightcentre.co.nz. Rock-bottom fares worldwide.

Holiday Shoppe New Zealand ☎ 0800/808 480, Ⓦ www.holidayshoppe.co.nz. Great deals on flights, hotels and holidays.

OTC Australia ☎ 1300/855 118, Ⓦ www.otctravel.com.au. Deals on flights, hotels and holidays.

Student Uni Travel Australia ☎ 02/9232 8444, Ⓦ www.sut.com.au, New Zealand ☎ 09/379 4224, Ⓦ www.sut.co.nz. Great deals for students.

Trailfinders Australia ☎ 02/9247 7666, Ⓦ www.trailfinders.com.au. One of the best-informed and most efficient agents for independent travellers.

travel.com.au and **travel.co.nz** Australia ☎ 1300/130 482 or 02/9249 5444, Ⓦ www.travel.com.au, New Zealand ☎ 0800/468 332, Ⓦ www.travel.co.nz. Comprehensive online travel company, with discounted fares.

Tour operators

Abercrombie & Kent Australia ☎ 1300/851 800, New Zealand ☎ 0800/441 638, Ⓦ www.abercrombiekent.com.au. Upmarket canal and river cruises in the Netherlands and Belgium that link with the prime tulip time (April & May). Tours start in Amsterdam.

Kumuka Expeditions Australia ☎ 1300/667 277 or 02/9279 0491, Ⓦ www.kumuka.com.au. Independent tour operator, which covers the Netherlands as part of a western and central European overland trip.

Martin Randall Travel Australia ☎ 1300/559 595, Ⓦ www.martinrandall.com. Organizes small-group, architectural, musical and historical tours of Amsterdam and the Netherlands, led by an appropriate expert.

Viator Australia ☎ 02/8219 5400, Ⓦ www.viator.com. Mainstream fly-drive packages in the Netherlands, plus city tours and canal cruises in Amsterdam; bookable on line.

From Europe

A veritable raft of **rail lines** run into the Netherlands from France and Germany with many services calling in on, or terminating at, Amsterdam's Centraal Station. Apart from the regular trains, there are also the express trains of **Thalys**, a combined project of the Belgian, Dutch, French and German railways. The hub of the Thalys network is Brussels, from where there are regular trains to Amsterdam. For rail contacts and websites, see p.21.

Red tape and visas

Citizens of the UK and Ireland as well as other EU/EEA countries, Canada, the USA, Australia and New Zealand, need only a valid passport to stay up to ninety days in the Netherlands.

For stays of **over ninety days**, both EU and non-EU nationals enter the realm of **residence permits**, whose complex rules and regulations relate to the length of the proposed stay and the reasons for it, with the applicant's nationality being a further consideration. Technically, some nationals – including those of some EU countries – do not need a residence permit, but things can get mightily confused if an application is not made. As you might expect, if you want to work during your stay, then you will need a **work permit** too. Work permit applications from EU/EEA citizens are far more likely to succeed than those of non-EU/EEA nationals. For further information, visit either the Dutch Ministry of Foreign Affairs website at ⓦ www.minbuza.nl or the Immigration and Naturalisation board website at ⓦ www.immigratiedienst.nl. The Ministry's website also carries comprehensive details of Dutch embassies and consulates worldwide.

Netherlands embassies abroad

Australia 120 Empire Circuit, Yarralumla, ACT 2600 ☎ 02/6220 9400, ⓦ www.netherlands.org.au.

Canada 350 Albert St #2020, Ottawa, ONT, K1R 1A4 ☎ 613/237 5030, ⓦ www.netherlandsembassy.ca.
Ireland 160 Merrion Rd, Dublin 4 ☎ 01/269 3444, ⓦ www.netherlandsembassy.ie.
New Zealand Investment House, Ballance/Featherston St, Wellington ☎ 04/471 6390, ⓦ www.netherlandsembassy.co.nz.
UK 38 Hyde Park Gate, London, SW7 5DP ☎ 020/7590 3200, ⓦ www.netherlands-embassy.org.uk.
USA 4200 Linnean Ave NW, Washington, DC 20008 ☎ 202/244 5300, ⓦ www.netherlands-embassy.org.

Embassies in the Netherlands

Australia Carniegielaan 4, 2517 KH Den Haag ☎ 070/310 8200, ⓦ www.australian-embassy.nl.
Canada Sophialaan 7, 2514 JP Den Haag ☎ 070/311 1600, ⓦ www.canada.nl.
Ireland Dr Kuyperstraat 9, 2514 BA Den Haag ☎ 070/363 0993, ⓦ www.irishembassy.nl.
New Zealand Carnegielaan 10, 2517 KH Den Haag ☎ 070/346 9324, ⓦ www.nzembassy.com.
UK Lange Voorhout 10, 2514 EG Den Haag ☎ 070/427 0427, ⓦ www.britain.nl.
USA Lange Voorhout 102, 2514 EJ Den Haag ☎ 070/310 9209, ⓦ www.usemb.nl.

Insurance and health

Even though EU health care privileges apply in the Netherlands, any traveller – no matter what their nationality – would do well to take out an insurance policy before travelling to cover against theft, loss and illness or injury. Before paying for a new policy, however, it's worth checking whether you are already covered: some all-risks home insurance policies may cover your possessions when overseas, and many private medical schemes include cover when abroad.

If you're not already covered, you might want to contact a specialist travel insurance company, or consider the travel insurance deal we offer (see box below). A typical travel insurance policy usually provides cover for the loss of baggage, tickets and – up to a certain limit – cash or cheques, as well as cancellation or curtailment of your journey. Most of them exclude so-called **dangerous sports** unless an extra premium is paid. Many policies can be chopped and changed to exclude coverage you don't need – for example, sickness and accident benefits can often be excluded or included at will. If you do take medical coverage, ascertain whether benefits will be paid as treatment proceeds or only after you return home, and if there is a 24-hour medical emergency number. When securing baggage cover, make sure that the per-article limit – typically under £500/$750 and sometimes as little as £250/$400 – will cover your most valuable possession. If you need to make a claim, you should keep receipts for medicines and medical treatment, and in the event you have anything stolen, you must obtain a crime report statement from the police.

Health

EU citizens can take advantage of Dutch health services under the same terms as Amsterdam's residents, but you'll need a completed E111 form, available from any main post office. The Australian Medicare system also has a reciprocal health-care arrangement with the Netherlands. We've listed pharmacies and English-speaking dentists and doctors in the Directory chapter (emergency numbers are listed on p.39).

Rough Guides Travel Insurance

Rough Guides has teamed up with Columbus Direct to offer you travel insurance that can be tailored to suit your needs. Readers can choose from many different travel-insurance products, including a **low-cost backpacker** option for long stays; a **short break** option for city getaways; a typical **holiday package** option, and many others. There are also **annual multi-trip** policies for those who travel regularly, with variable levels of cover available. Different sports and activities (trekking, skiing, etc) can be covered if required on most policies.

Rough Guides travel insurance is available to the residents of 36 different countries with different language options to choose from via our website – ⓦwww.roughguidesinsurance.com – where you can also purchase the insurance.

Alternatively call direct: UK residents ☏0800 083 9507; US citizens ☏1-800 749-4922; Australians ☏1 300 669 999; all other nationalities ☏+44 870 890 2843.

Information, websites and maps

Information on Amsterdam is easy to get hold of, either from the Netherlands Board of Tourism, via the Internet, or, after arrival, from any of the city's tourist offices, the VVVs.

The Netherlands Board of Tourism

Before you leave for Amsterdam, you might consider contacting the **Netherlands Board of Tourism** (NBT; ⓦ www.holland.com) for information. One of their most useful publications is their country-wide *Accommodation* guide, complete with hotel prices, addresses, phone numbers, email addresses and Internet sites, as well as photographs of the hotels and brief (if sometimes rather flattering) descriptions. Amsterdam's three VVVs (see below) sell this booklet too.

Netherlands Board of Tourism offices

Canada 601 Dundas Street West, Box 24010 1078, Whitby, Ontario L1N 8X8 ☎ 905 666 5960, ⓔ info@holland.com.

UK 15-19 Kingsway, 7th Floor, Imperial House, London WC2B 6UN ☎ 020/7539 7950, brochures ☎ 0906/871 7777 (premium line), ⓔ info-uk@holland.com.

USA 355 Lexington Ave, New York, NY 10017 ☎ 1-888-GO-HOLLAND, ⓔ info@goholland.com. There are no offices in Australia or New Zealand.

Amsterdam Tourist Board

The Amsterdam Tourist Board (ⓦ www .visitamsterdam.nl) runs three **tourist offices** in the city centre: on platform 2, Centraal Station (Mon–Sat 8am-8pm, Sun 9am-5pm); on Stationsplein, across from the entrance to Centraal Station (Mon–Wed & Sun 9am–5pm, Thurs-Sat 9am–8pm); on Leidsestraat, just off the Leidseplein (daily 9.15am–5pm). They share one premium-rate **information line** on ☎ 0900/400 4040 (Mon-Fri 9am-5pm); calls currently cost €0.55 per minute.

These offices, known here as elsewhere in the Netherlands as the **VVV** (pronounced "fay-fay-fay"), offer a wide range of services and sell a competent range of maps and guidebooks as well as tickets and passes for public transport. They are extremely popular, so come early if you want to beat the queues, especially in the summer; note also that the VVV office on Leidseplein is often not as busy as its counterparts. In addition, the VVV takes in-person bookings for canal cruises and other organized excursions (see box, p.29) and operates an extremely efficient accommodation reservation service. The latter is especially useful in the height of the season, when accommodation gets mighty tight; the service costs just e3.50 plus a refundable deposit which is subtracted from your final hotel bill. For further details on booking accommodation, see p.163.

As for cultural events, the VVV sells a comprehensive, but largely uncritical monthly listings magazine, *Day by Day* (€1.75), which details everything from theatre and ballet through to rock concerts. They also sell tickets for most upcoming performances, as does the Amsterdam Uitburo, or AUB, operated by the city council. The latter has a walk-in booking centre tucked away in a corner of the Stadsschouwburg theatre on Leidseplein (Mon-Sat 10am-6pm, Thurs until 9pm, Sun noon-6pm; ☎0900/0191). For more details on entertainment, see Chapter Ten.

There's also a Holland Tourist Office (daily 7am–10pm) at Schiphol airport though this has surprisingly little printed English-language information; the compensation is that they will book accommodation anywhere in the country on your behalf for a modest fee.

Useful websites

ⓦ **www.ajax.nl** Virtual home of the world-famous Ajax Amsterdam football team (but doesn't sell match tickets).

ⓦ **www.amsterdam.nl** Excellent site maintained by the Amsterdam Tourist Board, with a useful facility

Tourist passes

The VVV's much touted **Amsterdam Pass** provides free and unlimited use of the city's public transport network, a complimentary canal cruise and free admission to the bulk of the city's museums and attractions. It costs €31 for one day, €41 for two consecutive days and €51 for three, again consecutive days. Altogether it's not a bad deal, but you have to work fairly hard to make it worthwhile. A much more tempting proposition, especially if you're staying for more than a couple of days, is the **Museumkaart** (museum card). This pass gives free entry to most museums in the whole of the Netherlands for a year; it costs €25 for anyone over 25 years old, €12.50 for those 24 years old and under; all the major museums in the scheme issue the pass; all you need is ID, preferably a passport. For details of public transport passes, see p.31.

enabling you to print a map for any address in the city. Also provides an accommodation database, as well as information about working in Amsterdam.

ⓦ **www.amsterdamhotspots.nl** City guide emphasizing music and club listings. Also good for the gay scene, coffee shops and the Red Light District.

ⓦ **www.coffeeshop.freeuk.com** Comprehensive site detailing over 1000 coffeeshops and smartshops in the Netherlands. Links to coffeeshop websites and a printable map.

ⓦ **www.concertgebouworkest.nl** Royal Concertgebouw Orchestra website, providing a listing of the world-renowned orchestra's concerts, and enabling online ticket reservation.

ⓦ **www.holland.com** Excellent, all-embracing official site of the Netherlands Board of Tourism.

ⓦ **www.koninklijkhuis.nl** The Dutch royal family.

ⓦ **www.learndutch.org** Good resource for getting to grips with the Dutch language.

ⓦ **www.museumserver.nl** Provides links to over 400 museums in the Netherlands.

ⓦ **www.rnw.nl** Radio Netherlands online, broadcasting Dutch news in English, with articles on current affairs, lifestyle issues, science, health and social issues.

ⓦ **www.thehollandring.com** Over 300 pages of information on all things Dutch, aimed mainly at the Dutch expat community; provides a good overview on Dutch culture, history and folklore.

ⓦ **www.woodenshoes.nl** Traditional workshop and museum situated at Zaanse Schans, northwest of Amsterdam. Provides history as well as online shopping for the famous wooden shoes.

Maps

Our **maps** are more than adequate for most purposes, but if you need one on a larger scale, or with a street index, then pick up *Amsterdam: The Rough Guide Map*, which has the added advantage of being rip-proof and waterproof and marks all the key sights

as well as most restaurants, bars and hotels. If you want a map covering the outer suburbs as well, the best bet is the Falk map of *Amsterdam* (1:15,000).

Other options include the city maps sold by the VVV, which come complete with a street index, and the handily compact, spiral-bound street atlases produced by Falk (Suburbs: 1:12,500; centre 1:7500). The Rough Guide Map is available at most good bookshops in the UK, but is harder to get elsewhere, especially in Amsterdam, but the reverse is true of the Falk maps. For information on bookshops in Amsterdam, see p.218.

Map outlets

UK and Ireland

Blackwell's UK ☏01865/333 623, ⓦwww.blackwell.co.uk.

Easons Dublin ☏01/858 3881, ⓦwww.eason.ie.

Hodges Figgis Dublin ☏01/677 4754, ⓦwww.hodgesfiggis.com.

Map Shop UK ☏0116/247 1400, ⓦwww.mapshopleicester.co.uk.

Stanfords UK ☏020/7836 1321, ⓦwww.stanfords.co.uk.

US and Canada

Adventurous Traveler US ☏1-800/282-3963, ⓦwww.adventuroustraveler.com.

Elliot Bay Book Co. US ☏1-800/962-5311, ⓦwww.elliotbaybook.com.

Globe Corner US ☏1-800/358-6013, ⓦwww.globecorner.com.

Rand McNally US ☏1-800/333-0136, ⓦwww.randmcnally.com.

World of Maps Canada ☏1-800/214-8524, ⓦwww.worldofmaps.com.

Australia and New Zealand

Map Shop Australia ☎ 08/8231 2033, ☻ www
.mapshop.net.au.

Mapland Australia ☎ 03/9670 4383, ☻ www
.mapland.com.au.
Map World NZ ☎ 0800/627 967, ☻ www
.mapworld.co.nz.

Arrival

Arriving in Amsterdam by train and plane could hardly be easier. Schiphol, Amsterdam's international airport, is a quick and convenient train ride away from Centraal Station, the city's international train station, which is itself a ten-minute metro ride from Amstel Station, the terminus for long-distance and most international buses Centraal Station is also the focal point of an excellent public transport network, whose trams, buses and metro combine to delve into every corner of the city and its suburbs.

By air

Amsterdam's international airport, **Schiphol** (☎ 0900/7244 7465, ☻ www.schiphol.nl), is located about 18km southwest of the city centre. Regularly voted "best airport in Europe" it is also one of the busiest, with connections to major international transport hubs, including an efficient transfer system to the city and the surrounding provinces. Arriving passengers are funnelled via walk-ways into a large, well-signposted plaza, which has all the standard facilities, including bureaux de change, car rental outlets, left luggage lockers and ATMs. In addition, there's a Netherlands Railways (NS) ticket office and a **Holland Tourist Office** (see p.28).

From the airport, trains run to Amsterdam Centraal Station (Amsterdam C.S.) – a fast service leaving every ten minutes during the day, and every hour at night (12.30pm–6am). The journey takes between fifteen and twenty minutes and costs €3.40. There are also trains from Schiphol to most of the suburban stations around Amsterdam as well as direct express services to many other Dutch cities. The main alternative to the train is the Airport Hotel Shuttle bus (☎ 020/653 4975), which departs from the designated bus stop outside the Arrivals hall, though note that the buses themselves bear several different liveries; the main company is Connexxion, which follows three routes to over fifty hotels

on the shuttle list. Buses depart every fifteen minutes or so between 7am-9pm from bus stop A7 in front of the Arrivals hall; a single fare costs €11, return €18. Passengers do not have to be hotel guests to use it. It takes about thirty minutes for the bus to get from the airport to the Old Centre. The bus follows a similar route on the return journey and pick-up can be arranged from most of the larger hotels and is available to non-guests. Finally, the taxi fare from Schiphol to the Old Centre is €35–40.

By train

Amsterdam's **Centraal Station** (CS) has regular connections with key cities in Germany, Belgium and France, as well as all the larger towns and cities of the Netherlands. Amsterdam also has several suburban train stations, but these are principally for the convenience of commuters. For all rail enquiries contact NS (Netherlands Railways; international enquiries ☎ 0900/9296; domestic enquiries ☎ 0900/1475; ☻ www.ns.nl).

As you would expect, Centraal Station has a good spread of facilities, including ATMs, a bureau de change and both coin-operated luggage lockers (daily 7am–11pm) and a staffed left-luggage office (daily 7am–11pm). Small coin-operated lockers cost €3.50, the larger ones €5.50 per 24 hours; left luggage costs €8 per item. In addition, there's a VVV tourist office on platform 2 and a second directly across from the main station entrance on Stationsplein. If you arrive late at night it's best to take a taxi to your hotel – there are too many shifty characters to make wandering aimlessly around advisable.

By bus

Anglia Lines buses from London Victoria pull up just across from Centraal Station, while Eurolines and other international buses arrive at **Amstel Station**, about 3.5km to the southeast of Centraal Station. The metro journey to Centraal Station takes about ten minutes.

By car

Arriving **by car** on either the A4 (E19) from The Hague or the A2 (E35) from Utrecht, you should experience few traffic problems. The city centre is clearly signposted as soon as you approach Amsterdam's southern reaches. Both the A4 and the A2 lead to the A10 (E22) ring road; on its west side, leave the A10 at either the Osdorp or Geuzenveld exits for the centre. However, be warned that driving in central Amsterdam – never mind parking – is extremely difficult; see p.33 for further details.

City transport

Almost all of Amsterdam's leading attractions are clustered in or near the city centre, within easy walking- and even easier cycling distance of each other. For longer jaunts, the city has a first-rate public transport system, run by the GVB, comprising trams, buses, a smallish metro and four passenger ferries across the river IJ to the northern suburbs. Centraal Station is the hub of the system with a multitude of trams and buses departing from outside on Stationsplein, which is also the location of a metro station and a GVB public transport information office. There's a taxi rank on Stationsplein too.

Trams, buses and the metro

The city centre is crisscrossed by **trams**. Two of the more useful are trams #2 and #5, which link Centraal Station with Leidsestraat and the Rijksmuseum every ten minutes or so during the day. **Buses** are mainly useful for going to the outskirts, and the same applies to the **metro**, which has just two downtown stations, Nieuwmarkt and Waterlooplein. Trams, buses and the metro operate daily between 6am and midnight, supplemented by a limited number of nightbuses (*nachtbussen*). All tram and bus stops display a detailed map of the network. For further details on all services, head for the main GVB information office (Mon–Fri 7am–9pm, Sat & Sun 8am–9pm; ☏0900/8011, ⊛www.gvb.nl) on Stationsplein. Their free, English-language *Tourist Guide to Public Transport* is very helpful.

Tickets and passes

The most common type of **ticket**, usable on all forms of GVB transport, is the **strippenkaart**, a card divided into strips: fold your *strippenkaart* over to expose the number of strips required for your journey and then insert it into the on-board franking machine. Amsterdam's public transport system is divided into zones and one person making a journey within one zone costs two strips. The "Centre" zone covers the city centre and its immediate surroundings (well beyond Singelgracht), and thus two strips will cover more or less every journey you're likely to make. If you travel into an additional zone, it costs three strips, and so on. More than one person can use a *strippenkaart*, as long as the requisite number of strips is stamped. After franking, you can use any GVB tram, bus and the metro for up to one hour. Currently, a two-strip *strippenkaart* costs €1.60, three-strip €2.40, fifteen-strip €6.40 and a 45-strip €18.90.

You can opt instead for a dagkaart (day ticket), which gives unlimited access to the GVB system for up to a maximum of three days. Prices are €6.30 for one day, €10 for two, and €13 for three. Tickets and passes are available from tobacconists, the GVB, the VVV and metro stations; the smaller strippenkaart are also available from bus and tram drivers. Finally, note that GVB tries hard to keep fare dodging down to a minimum and wherever you're travelling, and at whatever time of day, there's a reasonable chance you'll have your ticket checked. If you are caught without a valid ticket, you risk an on-the-spot fine of €29.40.

The Canal Bus

One good way to get around Amsterdam's waterways is to take the **Canal Bus** (℡020/623 9886, Ⓦwww.canal.nl). This operates on three circular routes, which meet once, at the jetty opposite Centraal Station beside Prins Hendrikkade. Two of the three routes also meet at three other locations – on the Singelgracht (opposite the Rijksmuseum), behind the Leidseplein and beside City Hall on Waterlooplein. There are eleven stops in all and together they give easy access to all the major sights. Boats leave from opposite Centraal Station (every 10–20min; 10am–5.30pm) and at least every half-hour from any other jetty. A day ticket for all three routes, allowing you to hop on and off as many times as you like, costs €16 per adult, €11 for children (4–12 years old); it's valid until noon the following day and entitles the bearer to minor discounts at several museums.

The Museumboot

A similar boat service, the **Museumboot** (℡020/530 1090, Ⓦwww.lovers.nl), calls at seven jetties located at or near many of the city's major attractions. It departs from opposite Centraal Station (every 30min; 9.30am–5pm) and a come-and-go-as-you-please day ticket costs €14.25, children €9.50 (4–12 years old).

Canal Bikes

Canal Bikes (℡020/626 5574, Ⓦwww .canal.nl) are four-seater **pedaloes** which take a lifetime to get anywhere but are nevertheless good fun unless – of course – it's raining. You can rent them at four central locations: on the Singelgracht opposite the Rijksmuseum; the Prinsengracht outside the Anne Frank House; on Keizersgracht at Leidsestraat; and behind Leidseplein. Rental prices per person per hour are €7 (3–4 people) or €8 (1–2 people), plus a refundable deposit of €50. They can be picked up at one location and left at any of the others; opening times are daily 10am–6pm, till 9.30pm in July and August.

Bicycles

One of the most agreeable ways to explore Amsterdam is by **bicycle**. The city has an excellent network of designated bicycle lanes (*fietspaden*) and for once cycling isn't a fringe activity – there are cyclists everywhere. Indeed, much to the chagrin of the city's taxi drivers, the needs of the cyclist often take precedence over those of the motorist and by law if there's a collision it's always the driver's fault. Bike rental is straightforward. There are lots of **rental companies** (*fietsenverhuur*) but MacBike (℡020/620 0985, Ⓦwww.macbike.nl) sets the benchmark, charging €4 for two hours, €6.50 per day, €16.50 for three days and €30 for a week for a standard bicycle; 21-speed cycles cost twice as much. MacBike have three rental outlets in central Amsterdam, one at the east end of Centraal Station, a second beside Waterlooplein at Mr Visserplein 2, and a third near Leidseplein at Weteringschans 2. All companies, including *MacBike*, ask for some type of security, usually in the form of a cash deposit (some will take credit card imprints) and/or passport.

If you want to buy a bike a well-worn bone-shaker will set you back about €100, while €170 should get you quite a decent machine – see p.218 for a list of bike shops. Never accept a bike from someone off the street as it will almost certainly have been stolen. Also, bike theft is a real problem so always use a decent lock – they are sold at all the city's flea markets. For useful cycling terms in Dutch, see p.293.

Driving

The centre of Amsterdam is geared up for trams and bicycles rather than **cars** as a matter of municipal policy. Pedestrianized zones as such are not extensive, but motorists still have to negotiate a convoluted one-way system, avoid getting boxed onto tram lines and steer around herds of cyclists. **On-street parking** is also very limited – with far too many cars chasing too few spaces – and quite expensive. Every city-centre street where parking is permitted is metered with a standard cost of €3.20 for one hour (Mon-Sat 9am-midnight, Sun noon-midnight), €19.20 for the day (9am-7pm) and €12.80 for the evening (7pm-midnight). A day's parking (9am-midnight) costs €28.80, Sunday (noon-midnight) €23. If you overrun your ticket, you can expect to be clamped by eager-beaver traffic wardens, and thereafter, if you don't follow the instructions posted on your windscreen promptly, your vehicle will soon be heading off to the municipal pound. The good news is that signs on all the main approach roads to Amsterdam indicate which of the city's **car parks** have spaces. Car parks in the centre (see p.253 for a list) charge comparable rates to the metered street spaces, but those on the outskirts are a good deal less expensive and are invariably but a short journey from the centre by public transport. One of the cheapest is Q-Park Europarking, at Marnixstraat 250, which charges €2.50 an hour and €27.50 for day. Finally, note that some of the better hotels either have their own parking spaces or offer special deals with nearby car parks.

Taxis

Taxis are plentiful in Amsterdam and taxi ranks are liberally distributed across the city centre and they can also be hailed on the street. If all else fails, call the city's central, 24-hour taxi number on ☎020/677 7777. **Fares** are metered and pricey, but distances are small: the trip from Centraal Station to the Leidseplein, for example, costs just €11, €2 more to Museumplein – and about fifteen percent more late at night.

Organized tours

No one could say the Amsterdam tourist industry doesn't make the most of its canals with a veritable armada of glass-topped **cruise boats** shuttling along the city's inner waterways, offering everything from a quick hour-long excursion to a fully-fledged dinner cruise. There are several major operators and they occupy the prime pitches – the jetties near Centraal Station on Stationsplein, beside the Damrak, and on Prins Hendrikkade. Despite the competition, **prices** are fairly uniform with a one-hour tour costing around €8.50 per adult, €5.75 per child (4–12 years old), and €24 (€15.75) for a two-hour candlelit cruise. The big companies also offer more specialized boat trips, including the weekly Architecture Cruise (€19.50/€14.50) run by Lovers (☎020/530 1090; ◉www.lovers.nl) through to the Red Light District Cruises operated by just about everyone. All these cruises – and especially the shorter and less expensive ones – are extremely popular and long **queues** are commonplace throughout the summer. One way of avoiding much of the crush is to walk down the Damrak from Centraal Station to the jetty at the near end of the Rokin, where the first-rate Reederij P. Kooij (see below) offers all the basic cruises at very competitive prices. Finally, although for many visitors a canal trip is delightful, for others the running commentary is purgatorial and the views disappointing, though it's certainly true that Amsterdam can look especially enchanting at night when the bridges are illuminated.

There are also plenty of tours on dry land from guided cycle rides to a meander around the city on foot. A selection is given below, but if you have a specific interest – Dutch art, for example – it's well worth asking at the VVV to see what's on offer.

Tour companies

Mee in Mokum Hartenstraat 18 ☎020/625 1390 between 1-4pm Mon-Fri, ◉www.gildeamsterdam .nl. Three-hour guided walking tours of the older parts of the city provided by long-time – and older (50+) – Amsterdam residents. Tours Tues-Sun 11am only; e3 per person. Advance reservations required.
Reederij P.Kooij on the Rokin, beside the Queen Wilhelmina statue ☎020/623 3810 ◉www .rederijkooij.nl. Perhaps the best of the waterway cruise operators, with a standard range of cruises by day and by night. Also has a (more crowded) jetty opposite Centraal Station on Stationsplein.

Urban Home & Garden Tours ☎ 020/688 1243, ⊛ www.uhgt.nl. Three-hour tour (26 April-Oct) exploring a number of the city's houses and gardens, and guided by landscape gardeners and art historians. Tours cost €25 (10.15am Mon-Fri, Sat 11.15am) and includes refreshments. Special concert tours available for €37.50.

Yellow Bike Tours Nieuwezijds Kolk 29, off Nieuwezijds Voorburgwal ☎ 020/620 6940, ⊛ www.yellowbike.nl. This efficient company organizes a lively programme of three-hour guided cycling tours around the city and its environs (April to mid-Oct 1 or 2 daily). Tours cost €17 per person, including the bike. Advance reservations are required.

Costs, money and banks

By west European standards, Amsterdam is fairly expensive when it comes to accommodation, with rooms regularly thirty percent more than in the rest of the country. Food is moderately expensive, but not noticeably so. These costs are partly offset by the low cost of public transport. More precise costs for places to stay and eat are given in the Guide, and you should consult p.163 for general guidelines on accommodation prices. ATMs are routine across the city and are the easiest way to get cash, but currency exchange facilities are widespread too.

Average costs

If you're prepared to stay in hostels, and stick to the least expensive bars and restaurants, you could get by on around €35 a day. Staying in two-star hotels, eating out in medium-range restaurants most nights and drinking in bars, you'll get through at least €90 day with the main variable being the cost of your room. On €150 a day and upwards, you'll be limited only by your energy reserves – though if you're planning to stay in a five-star hotel and to have a big night out, this still won't be enough. As always, if you're travelling alone you'll spend much more on accommodation than you would in a group of two or more: most hotels do have single rooms, but they're fixed at about 75 percent of the price of a double.

Currency and exchange rates

The **currency** of the Netherlands is the **euro** (€), divided into 100 cents. There are seven euro **notes** – in denominations of €500, €200, €100, €50, €20, €10 and €5, each a different colour and size – and eight different **coins**, €2 and €1, then 50, 20, 10, 5, 2

and 1 cents. Euro coins feature a common EU design on one face, but different country-specific designs on the other. All euro notes and coins can be used in any of the twelve "euro-zone" states.

At the time of writing, €1 is worth £0.70, US$1.32, CDN$1.55, AU$1.67 and NZ$1.85. For the latest rates, check the currency converter website ⊛ www.oanda .com.

Traveller's cheques

The main advantage of buying **traveller's cheques** is that they are a safe way of carrying funds. All well-known brands of traveller's cheque in all major currencies are widely accepted in Amsterdam, with euro and US dollar cheques being the most common. The usual fee for their purchase is one or two percent of face value, though this fee is often waived if you buy the cheques through a bank where you have an account. You'll find it useful to purchase a selection of denominations. When you **cash your cheques**, almost all banks make a percentage charge per transaction on top of a basic minimum charge.

In the event that your cheques are **lost**

or stolen, the issuing company will expect you to report it immediately. Make sure you keep the purchase agreement, a record of cheque serial numbers, and the details of the company's emergency contact numbers or the addresses of their local offices, safe and separate from the cheques themselves. Most companies claim to replace lost or stolen cheques within 24 hours.

ATMs, debit and credit cards

Amsterdam has plenty of **ATMs** with a particular concentration in the city centre. Most ATMs give instructions in a variety of languages, and accept a host of **debit cards**, including all those carrying the Visa and Maestro logos. If in doubt, check with your bank to find out whether the card you wish to use will be accepted – and if you need a new (international) PIN. It's also worth finding out how much you will be charged each time you use the card abroad; this can add up with some banks applying "cash handling fees" in addition to offering poor exchange rates. **Credit cards** can be used in ATMs too, but in this case transactions are treated as loans, with interest accruing daily from the date of withdrawal. All major credit cards, including American Express, Visa and Mastercard, are widely accepted in Amsterdam.

Lost and stolen cards

American Express ☎ 020/504 86 86.
Diners Club ☎ 020/654 55 11.
Mastercard ☎ 030/283 55 55
Visa ☎ 0800/022 41 76

Banks and exchange

If you need to change money, Amsterdam's **banks and post offices** usually offer the best deals. Bank opening hours are Monday to Friday 9am to 4pm, with a few also open Thursday until 9pm or on Saturday morning; all are closed on public holidays (see p.38). For post office opening hours, see below. Outside these times, you'll need to go to one of the many **bureaux de change** scattered around town. **GWK**, whose main 24-hour branches are at Centraal Station and Schiphol airport, offers competitive rates and is very efficient. Incidentally, beware of less well-known agencies as some offer great rates but then slap on an extortionate commission, or, conversely, charge no commission but give bad rates.

Communications

As you might expect, the Netherlands in general and Amsterdam in particular has an efficient postal system and a first-rate telephone network, including excellent mobile phone coverage. Telephone booths, mail boxes and internet cafés are liberally distributed across the city – and charges are reasonable.

Post

In Amsterdam, **post offices** are plentiful and mostly open Monday to Friday 9am to 5pm, with the larger ones also open on Saturday mornings from 9am to noon. The main post office (Mon–Fri 9am–6pm, Thurs till 8pm, Sat 10am–1.30pm) is at Singel 250, on the corner with Raadhuisstraat. They have a Poste Restante service; to collect items, you need your passport. **Stamps** are sold at a wide range of outlets including many shops and hotels. **Post boxes** are everywhere, but be sure to use the correct slot – the one labelled *overige* is for post going outside the immediate locality.

Public phones

Phone booths are common, though the irresistible rise of the mobile means that their numbers will not increase and may well

Useful phone numbers

Operator (domestic and international) ☎ 0800 0410.
Directory enquiries
- domestic ☎ 0900 8008 (premium line).
- international ☎ 0900 8418 (premium line).
Phoning abroad from Amsterdam
To the UK: ☎ 0044 + area code minus zero + number.
To the Republic of Ireland: ☎ 00353 + area code minus zero + number.
To the US or Canada: ☎ 001 + area code + number.
To Australia: ☎ 0061 + area code minus zero + number.
To New Zealand: ☎ 0064 + area code minus zero + number.
Phoning Amsterdam from abroad
From the UK, Ireland and New Zealand: ☎ 00 + 31 (Netherlands) + 20 (Amsterdam) + number.
From the US and Canada: ☎ 011 + 31 (Netherlands) + 20 (Amsterdam) + number.
From Australia: ☎ 0011 + 31 (Netherlands) + 20 (Amsterdam) + number.

diminish. The vast majority take phone cards or credit cards, but not cash; where this is not the case, they are of the usual European kind, where you deposit the money before you make your call. Most phone booths have English instructions displayed inside. **Phone cards** can be bought at many outlets, including post offices, tobacconists and VVV offices, and in several specified denominations, beginning at €5. It is worth bearing in mind, however, that phone boxes are provided by different companies and their respective phone cards are not always mutually compatible. KPN phones (and cards) are the most common. The cheap-rate period for international calls is between 8pm and 8am during the week and all day at weekends. Numbers prefixed ☎ 0800 are free, while those prefixed ☎ 0900 are premium-rated; a (Dutch) message before you're connected tells you how much you will be paying for the call. Finally, remember that although most hotel rooms have phones, there is almost always an exorbitant surcharge for their use.

International charge cards

One of the most convenient ways of phoning home from abroad is via a **telephone charge card** issued by your domestic telephone company. Using a PIN number, you can make calls from most hotels, public and private phones that will be charged to your home account. Since most major charge cards are free to obtain, it's certainly worth getting one at least for emergencies (contact your home provider); bear in mind, however, that rates aren't necessarily cheaper than calling from an Amsterdam public phone.

Mobile phones

If you want to use your **mobile phone** in Amsterdam, you may need set up international roaming with your phone provider before you set out. Also check out their **call charges** as these can be exorbitant, especially as you are likely to be charged higher rates for incoming calls that originate from back home as the people calling you will be paying the usual (national) rate. The same sometimes applies to **text messages**, though in most cases these can now be received with the greatest of ease – no fiddly codes and so forth – and at ordinary rates. In Amsterdam, the mobile network covers almost every corner of the city and works on GSM 900/1800. Note that mobiles bought in **North America** need to be **triband** to access the cellular system in Europe.

Email and Internet

One of the best ways to keep in touch while travelling is to sign up for a free Internet email address that can be accessed from anywhere – for example, YahooMail (🌐 www.yahoo.com) or Hotmail (🌐 www.hotmail.com). You can then check your email at one of Amsterdam's many **Internet cafés** – see below for a selection; a good number of them are in so-called "smart shops" (see box on p.227). In addition, most of the better hotels provide online access for their guests at free or minimal charge.

Recommended Internet cafés

Conscious Dreams Kokopelli Warmoestraat 12 ⓣ 020/421 7000, ⓦ www.consciousdreams.nl. A smart shop offering Internet access and even DJs at the weekend. Located in the Red Light District. Daily 11am-10pm; e4.70 per hour.

Dreamlounge Kerkstraat 93 ⓣ 020/626 6907, ⓦ www.consciousdreams.nl. A small Grachtengordel smart shop with internet facilities. Tues-Sat 11am-9pm, Sun & Mon noon-6pm; e4.70 per hour.

easyInternetcafé ⓦ www.easyeverything.com. International chain with three outlets in Amsterdam: Centraal Station at Damrak 33 (daily 9am–10pm), Reguliersbreestraat 22, near Rembrandtplein (daily 9am–10pm), and Leidsestraat 24 (Mon 11am–7pm, Tues–Sat 9.30am–7pm & Sun 11am–6pm), on the corner with Keizersgracht. You can get online for €0.50.

Het Internetcafe Martelaarsgracht 11 ⓣ 020/627 1052, ⓦ www.internetcafe.nl. Straightforward Internet café just 200m from Centraal Station. Open daily from 7am until late. €1 for half an hour.

The media

Media-addicted English speakers will feel at home in Amsterdam: Dutch TV broadcasts a wide range of British and American programmes, and English-language newspapers are readily available.

The press

There's no difficulty in finding **British newspapers** – they're on sale at almost every newsagent on the day of publication, for around €3. Current issues of UK and US magazines are widely available too, as is the *International Herald Tribune*. Centraal Station has several newsagents and you'll always find a good selection of titles there.

Of the **Dutch newspapers**, *NRC Handelsblad* is a right-of-centre paper that has perhaps the best news coverage and a liberal stance on the arts, whilst *De Volkskrant* is a progressive, leftish daily. There's also the popular right-wing *De Telegraaf*, which boasts the largest circulation and has a well-regarded financial section, and *Algemeen Dagblad*, a right-wing broadsheet. Both the middle-of-the-road *Het Parool* ("The Password") and the news magazine *Vrij Nederland* ("Free Netherlands") are the successors of underground Resistance newspapers printed during wartime occupation; *Het Parool* is good for entertainments listings on Saturdays. The Protestant *Trouw* ("Trust"), another former underground paper, has a centre-left orientation with a religious bent.

TV and radio

Dutch TV isn't too exciting, but English-language programmes and films fill up a fair amount of the schedule – and they are always subtitled, never dubbed. Many bars and most hotels have at least two of the big pan-European **cable and satellite** channels – including MTV, CNN and Eurosport – and most cable companies also give access to a veritable raft of foreign television channels, including the BBC.

As for **Dutch radio**, the one-time stalwart of the squatter movement (see p.268), Radio Honderd, which is only available in and around Amsterdam, at 99.3FM, offers a wide-ranging playlist from world dance to electronica. Jazz Radio, at 99.8FM, speaks for itself. The Dutch Classic FM, at 101.2FM, plays mainstream classical music, with jazz after 10pm. There's next to no English-language radio programming, but frequencies and schedules for the BBC World Service (ⓦ www.bbc.co.uk/worldservice), Voice of America (ⓦ www.voa.gov) and Radio Canada International (ⓦ www.rcinet.ca) are listed on their respective websites.

Opening hours and public holidays

Although there's recently been some movement towards greater flexibility, opening hours for shops, businesses and tourist attractions – including museums – remain a little restrictive. In addition, travel plans can be disrupted on public holidays, when most things close down, apart from restaurants, bars and hotels, and public transport is reduced to a Sunday timetable.

Opening hours

The Amsterdam weekend fades painlessly into the working week with many smaller **shops and businesses**, even in the centre, staying closed on Monday mornings until noon. Normal **opening hours** are, however, Monday to Friday 9/10am to 5.30/6pm and – for shops not businesses – Saturday 9/10am to 5pm, though some, especially along the main shopping streets, are staying open to 6pm, with a late night on Thursday and Friday, and many are open on Sunday. A handful of night shops – *avondwinkels* – stay open round the clock; see p.226 for a list. **Banks** are open Monday to Friday 9am to 4pm.

Museums, especially those that are state-run – and these are the majority – tend to stick to a pattern: closed on Monday, and open Tuesday to Sunday from 10am to 5pm. The exceptions are the major museums such as the Van Gogh and Rijksmuseum which open daily from 9am or 10am to 5pm or 6pm. Precise opening hours are given in the Guide.

Most restaurants are open for dinner from about 6 or 7pm, and though many close as early as 9.30pm, a few stay open past 11pm. Bars, cafés and coffeeshops are either open all day from around 10am or don't open until about 5pm; both varieties close around 1am during the week and 2am at weekends. Nightclubs generally function from 11pm to 4am during the week, though few open every night, and stay open until 5am on the weekend.

Public holidays

Public holidays (*Nationale feestdagen*) provide the perfect excuse to take to the streets. The most celebrated of them all is **Queen's Day on April 30**, when the Dutch indulge in the equivalent of a national flea market: tradition dictates that each household sells all the junk it has accumulated over the past year on the streets. April 30 is also celebrated in style by the city's gay community (see chapter 12 for more details).

January 1 New Year's Day
Good Friday (although many shops open)
Easter Sunday
Easter Monday
April 30 Queen's Day
May 5 Liberation Day
Ascension Day
Whit Sunday and Monday
December 25 and 26 Christmas

Crime, personal safety and drugs

Amsterdam is one of the safer cities in Europe and, despite its much-touted associations with cannabis smoking and prostitution, visitors can expect very few hassles. However, common-sense precautions are needed here as in any large city.

Petty crime

Almost all the problems tourists encounter in Amsterdam are to do with **petty crime** – pickpocketing and bag-snatching – rather than more serious physical confrontations, so it's as well to be on your guard and know where your possessions are at all times. Thieves often work in pairs and, although **theft** is far from rife, you should be aware of certain distraction ploys, such as someone asking for directions while an accomplice puts their hand in your bag, and if you're in a crowd, watch out for people moving in unusually close. Like any city, Amsterdam is not without its **card crime** and you should always be cautious when using ATMs, especially late at night. Be aware of who is around you or of any suspicious-looking devices fitted around the card slot, and if in doubt don't use it.

Sensible precautions against petty crime include: carrying bags slung across your neck and not over your shoulder; not carrying anything in pockets that are easy to dip into; and having photocopies of your passport, airline ticket and driving licence, while leaving the originals in your hotel safe. When you're looking for a hotel room, never leave your bags unattended, and similarly if you have a car, don't leave anything in view when you park; vehicle theft is still fairly uncommon, but luggage and valuables do make a tempting target. Again, if you're using a bicycle, make sure it is well locked up – bike theft and resale is a big deal here. Mobile phone theft can also be a costly experience with many thieves managing to run up huge bills in next to no time. Keep your network provider number handy just in case you need to bar your phone.

If you are robbed, you'll need to go to the police as your insurance company will require a police report; remember to make a note of the report number and a copy of the statement itself. Don't expect a great deal of concern if your loss is relatively small – and don't be surprised if the process of completing forms and formalities takes ages.

Personal safety

Although it's generally possible to walk around the city without fear of harassment or assault, certain parts of Amsterdam are decidedly shady, and wherever you go at night it's always better to err on the side of caution. Particularly, in and around **Centraal Station**, the **De Pijp** area, south of the Sarphatipark, and in the **Red Light District**, where despite a major police crackdown on drug-related crime over recent years, there's still an unpleasant, sometimes menacing undertow amongst the narrow streets between the Oude Kerk and Zeedijk; play safe and avoid these streets if you can or, in the case of Centraal Station, don't wander around looking lost. As a general **precaution**, avoid unlit or empty streets and don't go out brimming with valuables. Using public transport isn't usually a problem, but lone travellers late at night might be wise to take a taxi.

In the unlikely event that you are mugged, or otherwise threatened, never resist, and try to reduce your contact with the robber to a minimum; either just hand over what's wanted, or throw money in one direction and take off in the other. Afterwards go straight to the police, who will be much more sympathetic and helpful on these occasions. Most police officers speak at least some English.

Police

There's little reason why you should ever come into contact with Amsterdam's **police force** (*politie*), a laid-back bunch in dodgem-sized patrol cars or on bicycles. However, if you do need to report a crime there is usually a police station located in or around one of the centre's districts. We've listed the main stations below.

HQ Elandsgracht 117 ☎020/5599 111.
De Pijp Ferdinand Bolstraat 190.
Jordaan Lijnbaansgracht 219.
Red Light District Warmoesstraat 44.

Drugs

Thousands of visitors come to Amsterdam just to get stoned; in fact what most people don't realize is that all **soft drugs** – as well as hard – are technically illegal, its just that possession and consumption have been partly decriminalized. Since 1976, the possession of small amounts of **cannabis** (up to 30g/1oz) has been ignored by the police, and sales have been tolerated to a selection of coffeeshops, where over-the-counter sales of cannabis are technically limited to 5g (under one-fifth of an ounce) per purchase. Outside of the coffeeshops, it's acceptable to smoke in some bars, but many are strongly against it so don't make any automatic assumptions. "Space cakes" (cakes baked with hashish and sold by the slice), although widely available, count as hard drugs and are illegal. And a word of warning: since all kinds of cannabis are so widely available in coffeeshops, there's no need to buy any on the street – if you do, you'll likely to become a magnet to some rather unsavoury characters, as well attract the attention of the police. Needless to say, the one thing you shouldn't attempt to do is take cannabis out of the country – a surprising number of people think (or claim to think) that if it's bought in Amsterdam it can be taken back home legally.

As far as **other drugs** go, the Dutch law surrounding magic mushrooms is that you can legally buy and possess any amount so long as they are fresh, but as soon as you tamper with them in any way (dry or process them, boil or cook them) they become illegal. Conscious Dreams, at Kerkstraat 117 (among other shops), has sold mushrooms openly for years, and continues to do so – see p.227. Cocaine, heroin, ecstasy, acid and speed are all as illegal in the Netherlands as they are anywhere else.

Travellers with disabilities

Despite its general social progressiveness, the Netherlands is only just getting to grips with the particular requirements of people with mobility problems.

In Amsterdam, the most obvious difficulty is in negotiating the cobbled streets and narrow, often broken pavements of the older districts, where the key sights are mostly located. Similarly, provision for people with disabilities on the country's urban public transport is only average, although improving – many new buses, for instance, are now wheelchair-accessible. And yet, while it can be difficult simply to get around, practically all public buildings, including museums, theatres, cinemas, concert halls and hotels, are obliged to provide access, and do. Places that have been certified wheelchair-accessible now bear an International Accessibility Symbol (IAS). Bear in mind, however, that a lot of the older, narrower hotels are not allowed to install lifts, so check first. The national tourist office website ⓦwww.visitholland.com has an online search facility within its Services menu, where you can find attractions and accommodation that have a wheelchair available and/or bear an IAS symbol. In addition, the Amsterdam Forum for the Disabled (SGOA) publishes a free guide, which details the accessibility of 130 hotels, attractions and restaurants, and has useful information on wheelchair taxi rental and disabled parking, and is available from the Uitburo on Leidseplein (see p.202). The tourist board also provides access information and local contact numbers.

If you're planning to use the Dutch train network during your stay and would appreciate assistance on the platform, phone the Bureau Assistentieverlening Gehandicapten (Disabled Assistance Office) on ☎030/235 7822 at least three hours before your train departs, and there will be someone to meet and help you at the station. NS publishes information about train travel for people with disabilities in various leaflets, stocked at main stations.

Contacts for travellers with disabilities

UK and Ireland

Access Travel ☎01942/888 844, ⓦwww .access-travel.co.uk. Small, personal-service tour operator that can arrange flights, transfers and accommodation for Amsterdam city breaks.
Holiday Care ☎0845/124 9971, Minicom ☎0845/124 9976, ⓦwww.holidaycare.org.uk. Provides an information pack for £2.50 which details transport options, accommodation, special services, tour operators and useful contacts for travelling around the Netherlands, Belgium and Luxembourg.
Irish Wheelchair Association ☎01/818 6455, ⓦwww.iwa.ie. Useful information about travel abroad.
RADAR (Royal Association for Disability and Rehabilitation) ☎020/7250 3222, Minicom ☎020/7250 4119, ⓦwww.radar.org.uk. A good source of advice, with a useful website.

US and Canada

Access-Able ⓦwww.access-able.com. Online resource for travellers with disabilities.
Directions Unlimited ☎1-800/533-5343 or 914/241-1700, ⓔcruisesusa@aol.com. Tour operator.
Mobility International USA ☎541/343-1284, ⓦwww.miusa.org. Information and referral services, access guides, tours and exchange programmes.
Society for the Advancement of Travelers with Handicaps (SATH) ☎212/447-7284, ⓦwww.sath.org. Non-profit educational organization with tips on travelling and links to airlines.
Wheels Up! ☎1-888/389-4335, ⓦwww .wheelsup.com. Provides discounted airfare and tour prices and a free monthly newsletter. Comprehensive website.

Australia and New Zealand

ACROD (Australian Council for Rehabilitation of the Disabled) ☎02/6282 4333, ⓦwww.acrod .org.au. Provides lists of travel agencies and tour operators.
Disabled Persons Assembly (NZ) ☎04/801 9100, ⓦwww.dpa.org.nz. Resource centre with lists of travel agencies and tour operators.

The Netherlands

Landelijk Bureau Toegankelijkheid National Bureau for Accessibility, Maarssen ☎034/659 0115, ⓦwww.lbt.nl. Part of the Stichting Dienstverleners Gehandicapten (Foundation for Rehabilitation), which promotes accessibility, mobility and technology.
Mobility International Nederland Heidestein 7, 3971 ND Driebergen ☎034/352 1795, ⓔbijning@worldonline.nl. Largest Dutch information and advice service for people with disabilities.
Stadsmobiel Postbus 2131, 1000 CC Amsterdam ☎ & ⓕ020/460 5460, ⓦwww.gvb.nl/stadsmobiel. Provides an accessible shuttle service in and around Amsterdam (including the airport) for members.
Stichting Recreatie Gehandicapten Postbus 4140, 2003 EC Haarlem ☎023/536 8409, ⓦwww .srg-vakanties.nl. Organizes tours around Amsterdam and Europe.

Gay and lesbian travellers

Amsterdam ranks as one of the top gay-friendly holiday destinations in Europe. Attitudes in the city are tolerant, gay bars are plentiful, and support groups and facilities unequalled – see Chapter Twelve.

Contacts for gay and lesbian travellers

UK

www.gaytravel.co.uk. Online travel agent, offering good deals on all types of holiday. Also lists gay- and lesbian-friendly hotels around the world.
Dreamwaves Holidays ☎0870/042 2475, **www.gayholidaysdirect.com**. Specializes in exclusively gay package holidays.
Madison Travel ☎01273/202 532, **www.madisontravel.co.uk**. Specializing in packages to gay- and lesbian-friendly mainstream destinations, and also to gay/lesbian destinations.
Respect Holidays ☎0870/770 0169, **www.respect-holidays.co.uk**. Offers exclusively gay packages to popular European resorts and cities.

US and Canada

Damron ☎1-800/462-6654 or 415/255-0404, **www.damron.com**. Publishes five annual travel guidebooks for gay men and women. Itss Amsterdam guide covers hotels, bars, clubs and resources.

gaytravel.com ☎1-800/GAY-TRAVEL, **www.gaytravel.com**. The premier site for trip planning, bookings and general information about international gay and lesbian travel.
International Gay & Lesbian Travel Association ☎1-800/448-8550 or 954/776-2626, **www.iglta.org**. Trade group that can provide a list of gay- and lesbian-owned or -friendly travel agents, accommodation and other travel businesses.

Australia and New Zealand

Gay and Lesbian Tourism Australia **www.galta.com.au**. Directory and links for gay and lesbian travel worldwide.
Parkside Travel ☎08/8274 1222, **@parkside@harveyworld.com.au**. Gay travel agent specializing in all aspects of gay and lesbian travel worldwide.
Tearaway Travel ☎03/9827 4232, **www.tearaway.com**. Gay-specific business dealing with international and domestic travel.

The City

The City

The Old Centre

A
msterdam's most vivacious district, the **Old Centre** is an oval-shaped affair whose tangle of antique streets and narrow canals are confined in the north by the River IJ and to the west and south by the Singel, which once girdled the entire city. Given the dominance of **Centraal Station** on most transport routes, this is where you'll probably arrive. Immediately outside, **Stationsplein** is home to the main tourist and transport information offices – a busy maelstrom of buskers and bicycles, trams and tourists. From here, a stroll across the bridge will take you onto **Damrak**, which divided the **Oude Zijde** (Old Side) of the medieval city to the east from the smaller **Nieuwe Zijde** (New Side) to the west. It also led – and leads – to the heart of the Old Centre, **Dam Square**, which is overseen by two of the city's most impressive buildings, the **Koninklijk Paleis** (Royal Palace) and the **Nieuwe Kerk** (New Church). Nowadays, much of the Oude Zijde is taken up by the world-famous **Red Light District**, which stretches across Warmoesstraat and the two canals – Oudezijds Voorburgwal and Oudezijds Achterburgwal – that formed the heart of medieval Amsterdam. There's a prevailing seediness in the Red Light District that inevitably dulls many architectural charms, but there are still one or two signs that you are in what the city's most historic quarter: the delightful **Amstelkring**, a clandestine Catholic church dating from the seventeenth century, and the charming Gothic architecture of the **Oude Kerk**, not to mention the relatively unpretentious beauty of the **canals** themselves (if you can block out the prevailing neon). The sleazy atmosphere decreases the further east you go, towards **Nieuwmarkt**, a large and unassuming square that marks the start of **Kloveniersburgwal**, a large and stately canal that effectively marks the border of the Red Light District. Another canal, **Groenburgwal** beyond here, is one the most beguiling parts of the Old Centre, with a medley of handsome old houses lining what is one of its prettiest stretches of water. From here, you're a short walk from the **Muntplein**, a busy traffic intersection that boasts a floating **flower market** on the curve of the Singel and the distinctive **Munttoren** (Mint Tower). Muntplein lies at the end of the **Rokin**, which runs south from Dam Square, parallel to pedestrianised **Kalverstraat**, which is the city's prime mainstream shopping street. Sights-wise, the main targets in this area are the secluded **Begijnhof**, a circle of dignified old houses originally built to house a semi-religious community in the 1340s, and the **Amsterdam Historical Museum**.

Some history

Amsterdam's **Old Centre** follows the core of the original city, its narrow streets and canals confined to the north by the River IJ and the harbour, and to the west and south by the Singel, which used to form the boundary of the old port. This was where Amsterdam began, starting out as a humble fishing

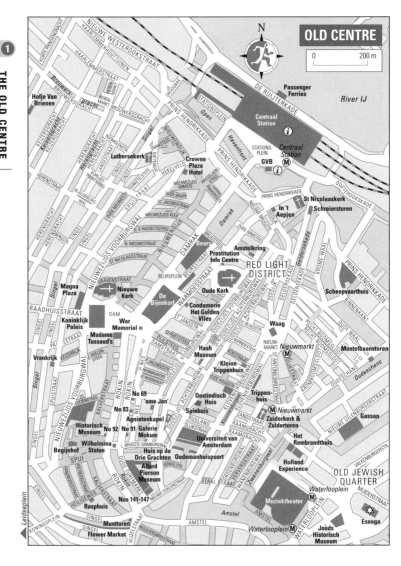

OLD CENTRE

N

0   200 m

Passenger Ferries

River IJ

Hofje Van Brienen

Centraal Station

Luthersekerk

Crowne Plaza Hotel

GVB

St Nicolaaskerk

In 't Aepjen

Schreierstoren

Beurs

Amstelkring

Prostitution Info Centre

RED LIGHT DISTRICT

Magna Plaza

Nieuwe Kerk

De Bijenkorf

Oude Kerk

Condomerie Het Gulden Vlies

Scheepvaarthuis

Koninklijk Paleis

DAM

War Memorial

Waag

Montelbaanstoren

Madame Tussaud's

Hash Museum

Nieuwmarkt

Vrankrijk

Kleine Trippenhuis

Trippen-huis

Oostindisch Huis

Zuiderkerk & Zuidertoren

Gassan

No 69

'ome Jan'

No 83

Spinhuis

No 92   No 91 Galerie Mokum

Het Rembrandthuis

Agnietenkapel

Historisch Museum

Universiteit van Amsterdam

Wilhelmina Statue

Begijnhof

Huis op de Drie Grachten

Oudemanhuispoort

Holland Experience

Allard Pierson Museum

OLD JEWISH QUARTER

Nos 141-147

Waterlooplein

Rasphuis

Muziektheater

Esnoga

Munttoren

Flower Market

Amstel

Waterlooplein

Joods Historisch Museum

village at the marshy mouth of the River Amstel before the local lord gave it some significance by building a castle here in 1204. Sixty years later, the Amstel was dammed – leading to the name "Amstelredam" – and the village began to flourish as a trading centre, receiving its municipal charter from a new feudal overlord, the Count of Holland, in about 1300. Thereafter, the city developed in stages, each of which was marked by the digging of new canals to either side of the main canal linking the River IJ with Dam square, along today's Damrak. The city developed at first around the canals of today's Red Light District and after that on the other side of Damrak. Time and again the wooden canalside buildings of medieval Amsterdam went up in smoke, until finally, after a particularly severe fire in 1452, timber was banned in favour of brick and stone – and it's these handsome buildings of the seventeenth and eighteenth centuries which provide the Old Centre with most of its architectural highpoints.

Damrak and the Nieuwe Zijde

Running from Centraal Station to Dam Square, the **Damrak** was a canal until 1672, when it was filled in, but up until then it had been the medieval city's main nautical artery, with boats sailing up it to discharge their goods right in the centre of town on the main square. Thereafter, with the docks moved elsewhere, the Damrak became a busy commercial drag, as it remains today, and the Dam became the centre of municipal power. To the west of the Damrak lies the Old Centre's **Nieuwe Zijde**, whose outer boundary was marked in the 1500s by a defensive wall, hence the name of its principal avenue, **Nieuwezijds Voorburgwal** ("In Front of the Town Wall on the New Side"). The wall disappeared as the city grew, and in the nineteenth century the canal that ran through the middle of the street was earthed in, leaving the unusually wide swathe that you see today. This area was, however, badly mauled by the developers in the 1970s and – give or take a scattering of old canal houses on Nieuwezijds Voorburgwal – there's no great reason to linger.

Centraal Station and around

With its high gables and cheerful brickwork, the neo-Renaissance **Centraal Station** is an imposing prelude to the city. At the time of its construction in the 1880s, it aroused much controversy because it effectively separated the centre from the River IJ, source of the city's wealth, for the first time in Amsterdam's long history. There was controversy about the choice of architect too. The man chosen, Petrus J.H. Cuypers, was Catholic, and in powerful Protestant circles there were mutterings about the vanity of his designs (he had recently completed the Rijksmuseum) and their unsuitability for Amsterdam. In the event, the station was built to Cuypers' design, but it was to be his last major commission; thereafter he spent most of his time building parish churches.

Outside the station, **Stationsplein** is a messy open space, edged by ovals of water, packed with trams and dotted with barrel organs and chip stands, with street performers completing the picture in the summer. Across the water, to the southeast on Prins Hendrikkade, rise the twin towers and dome of **St Nicolaaskerk**, dedicated to the patron saint of sailors (and of Amsterdam) (Tues–Fri 11am–4pm, Sat noon–3pm; free), the city's foremost Catholic Church. Like the station, dating back to the 1880s, the cavernous interior holds some pretty dire

---

Wal

As befits a country that has spent so much of its time keeping the sea at bay, the Dutch word **wal** (wall or embankment) is used in all sorts of colloquialisms, including *tussen wal en schip raken*, literally ending up between wall and ship – that is, not knowing what to do – and *aan lager wal raken* – to end up at a lower wall, meaning someone's bad fortune was beyond their control. Or you might try *van de wal in de sloot* – from the frying pan to the fire.

△ Centraal Station

religious murals, mawkish concoctions only partly relieved by swathes of coloured brickwork. Above the high altar is the crown of the Habsburg Emperor
Maximilian, very much a symbol of the city and one you'll see again and again.
Amsterdam had close ties with Maximilian: in the late fifteenth century he
came here as a pilgrim and stayed on to recover from an illness. The burghers
funded many of his military expeditions and, in return, he let the city use his
crown in its coat of arms – a practice which, rather surprisingly, survived the
seventeenth-century revolt against Spain.

Just along from St Nicolaaskerk, at the top of the Geldersekade canal, is the squat **Schreierstoren** (Weepers' Tower), a rare surviving chunk of the city's medieval wall. Originally, the tower overlooked the River IJ and it was here that women gathered to watch their menfolk sail away, though like many good stories this is apparently apocryphal: "Schreierstoren" refers to the sharp angle – the "schreye" – at which it was built rather than the weeping women. Nonetheless an old and badly weathered stone plaque inserted in the wall is a reminder of all those supposed sad goodbyes and, another, much more recent, plaque recalls the departure of Henry Hudson from here in 1609. On this particular voyage Hudson stumbled across the "Hudson" river and an island the locals called Manhattan. The colony that grew up there became known as New Amsterdam, a colonial possession that was only re-named New York after the English seized it in 1664. These days the Schreierstoren houses a small café with a terrace overlooking the canal.

In the opposite direction from the St Nicolaaskerk, it's a few metres to the end of **Zeedijk**, which was originally just that – a dike to hold back the sea – and it now girdles around the north end of the Red Light District. Not so long ago this narrow thoroughfare was the haunt of junkies, and very much a no-go area at night. But it's been spruced up and now forms a lively route through to Nieuwmarkt, on the eastern edge of the Red Light District, as well as being the main hub of Amsterdam's small but growing Chinatown. Its seaward end is home to a couple of the oldest bars in the city and there are any number of Chinese, Thai and Vietnamese foodie treats as you make your way further down.

Damrak

From Stationsplein, **Damrak**, a wide but unenticing avenue lined with tacky restaurants, bars and bureaux de change, slices south into the heart of the city, first passing an inner harbour crammed with the bobbing canal cruise boats of Amsterdam's considerable tourist industry. Just beyond the harbour is the imposing bulk of the **Beurs**, the old Stock Exchange (Times and admission depends on exhibition; guided tours on ☎020 620.8112; ⓦwww.beursvanberlage .nl) – known as the "Beurs van Berlage" – a seminal work designed at the turn of the twentieth century by the leading light of the Dutch Modern movement, Hendrik Petrus Berlage (1856–1934). Berlage re-routed Dutch architecture with this building, forsaking the historicism that had dominated the nineteenth century, and whose prime practitioner had been Cuypers (see p.47). Instead he opted for a style with cleaner, heavier lines, inspired by the Romanesque and the Renaissance, but with a minimum of ornamentation – and in so doing anticipated the Expressionism that swept northern Europe from 1905 to 1925. The Beurs has long since lost its commercial function and nowadays holds exhibitions on modern art and design, but the building is the main event, from the graceful exposed ironwork and shallow-arched arcades of the main hall through to a fanciful frieze celebrating the stockbroker's trade. They have also recently restored the safe deposit boxes in the basement. If you have time for nothing else, have a coffee at the café that fronts onto Beursplein.

Just up from the Beurs, the enormous **De Bijenkorf** – literally "beehive" – department store extends south along the Damrak. Amsterdam's answer to Harrods, De Bijenkorf posed all sorts of problems for the Germans when they first occupied the city in World War II. It was a Jewish concern, so the Nazis didn't really want their troops shopping here, but it was just too popular to

△ Damrak

implement a total ban. The bizarre solution was to prohibit German soldiers from shopping on the ground floor, where the store's Jewish employees were concentrated, as they always had been, in the luxury goods section.

The Nieuwe Zijde

Running parallel to, and west of, the Damrak, **Nieuwezijds Voorburgwal** kicks off with the **Crowne Plaza Hotel**, at no. 5, formerly the Holiday Inn, built on the site of an old tenement building called **Wyers**. The 1985 clearance of squatters from Wyers ranks among the more infamous of that decade's anti-squatting campaigns, involving a great deal of protest (and some violence) throughout the city. The squatters had occupied the building in an attempt to prevent yet another slice of the city being converted from residential to business use. They were widely supported by the people of Amsterdam, but they could not match the clout of the American hotel company and riot police were sent in; construction of the hotel followed soon after.

From the hotel, it's a short walk along Hekelveld and a right turn down Kattengat to the **Lutherse Kerk**, a round seventeenth-century edifice whose copper dome gives this area its nickname, **Koepelkwartier** ("Copper quarter"). It's a grand, self-confident building, seen to best advantage from the Singel canal, but it has been dogged by bad luck: in 1882 the interior was gutted by fire and, although it was repaired, the cost of maintenance proved too high for the congregation, who decamped in 1935. After many years of neglect, the adjacent

Renaissance Hotel bought the church, turning it into a conference centre. Church domes are a rarity in Amsterdam, but this one was no stylistic peccadillo; until the late eighteenth century, only Dutch Reformed churches were permitted the (much more fashionable) bell towers, so the Lutherans got stuck with a dome.

Doubling back to Nieuwezijds Voorburgwal, you soon reach **Nieuwezijds Kolk**, where the angular, glassy and ultramodern building on the corner is testament to the recent large-scale construction work that has transformed the area. When the underground car park was being dug here, workers discovered archeological remains dating back to the thirteenth century; this turned out to be the castle of the "Lords of Amstel", which, it is thought, had occupied the site when it was open marshland, even before the Amstel was dammed. The series of pedestrianized **alleys** that link Nieuwezijds Voorburgwal to the Damrak to the south of Nieuwezijds Kolk are without much charm. Consequently, it's better to stay on Nieuwezijds Voorburgwal as it heads south, its trees partly concealing a series of impressive canal houses, though these fizzle out as you approach Dam Square.

Dam Square

Situated at the heart of the city, **Dam Square** gave Amsterdam its name – it was here, in the thirteenth century, that the River Amstel was dammed. Boats could sail into the square down the Damrak and unload right in the middle of the settlement, which soon prospered by trading herrings for Baltic grain. In the early fifteenth century, the building of Amsterdam's principal church, the Nieuwe Kerk, and thereafter the town hall (now the Royal Palace), formally marked the Dam as Amsterdam's centre. Today it's open and airy but somehow rather desultory, despite – or perhaps partly because of – the presence of the main municipal **war memorial**, a prominent stone tusk adorned by bleak, suffering figures and decorated with the coats of arms of each of the Netherlands' provinces (plus the ex-colony of Indonesia). The memorial was designed by Jacobus Johannes Pieter Oud (1890–1963), a De Stijl stalwart who thought the Expressionism of Berlage much too flippant. The Amsterdam branch of **Madame Tussaud's** waxworks is on the Dam too, at no. 20 (daily 10am–6.30pm; €23, children 5–15 €17.50), and although it has a few Dutch celebs you won't necessarily know, most of its models are either international stars, royalty, or Dutch footballers like Johann Cruyff.

The Koninklijk Paleis

Dominating the Dam is the **Koninklijk Paleis** (Royal Palace; daily 12.30–5pm when not being used for offical occasions – call or check the website for details of these; ☏020/620 4060; €4.50, €6.50 with audio tour; ⊕www .koninklijkhuis.nl)), although the title is deceptive, given that this vast sandstone structure was built as the city's Stadhuis (town hall), and only had its first royal occupant when Louis Bonaparte moved in during the French occupation (1795–1813).

From Town Hall to Royal Palace

At the time of the building's construction in the mid-seventeenth century, Amsterdam was at the height of its powers. The city was pre-eminent amongst

Dutch towns, and had just resisted William of Orange's attempts to bring it to heel; predictably, the council craved a residence that was a declaration of the city's municipal power and opted for a startlingly progressive design by Jacob van Campen, who proposed a Dutch rendering of the classical principles revived in Renaissance Italy. Initially, there was opposition to the plan from the council's Calvinist minority, who pointed out that the proposed **Stadhuis** would dwarf the neighbouring Nieuwe Kerk (see opposite), an entirely inappropriate ordering, so they suggested, of earthly and spiritual values. However, when the Calvinists were promised a new church spire (it was never built) they promptly fell in line and in 1648 work started on what was then the largest town hall in Europe, supported by no less than 13,659 wooden piles driven into the Dam's sandy soil – a number every Dutch schoolchild remembers by adding a "1" and a "9" to the number of days in the year. The poet Constantijn Huygens called the new building "The world's Eighth Wonder / With so much stone raised high and so much timber under".

The Stadhuis received its **royal designation** in 1808, when Napoleon's brother Louis, who had recently been installed as king, commandeered it as his residence. Lonely and isolated, Louis abdicated in 1810 and hightailed it out of the country. Afterwards, possession of the palace became something of a sore point between the Royal family and the city; the initial compromise kept the building as royal property on condition that the royals stayed here for part of the year, but the Oranges almost universally failed to make much of an appearance. This irritated many Amsterdammers and in the 1930s the Oranges offered the city 15 million guilders to build a new city hall in return for a new agreement, which allowed them to use the Palace whenever they wanted with ownership passing to the state (as distinct from the city); the new town hall, on Waterlooplein (see p.101), was finally completed in the 1980s. Nowadays the Dutch royals live down in the Huis ten Bosch, near the Hague, and only use the Royal Palace for state occasions.

The building

The **exterior** of the palace is very much to the allegorical point: twin tympani depict Amsterdam as a port and trading centre, the one at the front presided over by Neptune and a veritable herd of unicorns. Above these panels are representations of the values the city council espoused – at the front, Prudence, Justice and Peace, to the rear Temperance and Vigilance to either side of a muscular, globe-carrying Atlas. One deliberate precaution, however, was the omission of a central doorway – just in case the mob turned nasty (as they were wont to do) and stormed the place.

The **interior** also proclaims the pride and confidence of the Golden Age, principally in the lavish **Citizen's Hall**, an extraordinarily handsome arcaded marble chamber where the enthroned figure of Amsterdam looks down on the earth and the heavens, which are laid out at her feet in three circular, inlaid marble maps, one each of the eastern and western hemispheres, the other of the northern sky. Other allegorical figures ram home the municipal point: flanking "Amsterdam" to left and right are Wisdom and Strength and the reliefs to either side of the central group represent good governance: on the left is the god Amphion, who plays his lyre to persuade the stones to pile themselves up into a wall, and to the right Mercury attempts to lull Argos to sleep – stressing the need to be vigilant. All this is part of a good-natured and witty symbolism that pervades almost all of the building: cocks fight above the entrance to the Commissioner of Petty Affairs; Ferdinand Bol's painting in the Burgomasters' Council room depicts an unsuccessful attempt to bribe and then frighten (with the elephant trumpeting behind the curtain) a Roman consul – one Gaius Luscinus; and a plaque above the door of the Bankruptcy Chamber shows the *Fall of Icarus*, surrounded by marble carvings depicting hungry rats scurrying around an empty money chest and nibbling at unpaid bills. In the Magistrates' Court is a second Bol **painting**, *Moses the Lawgiver*, depicting Moses descending from Mount Sinai with the Ten Commandments, but most of the paintings displayed in the palace are of little distinction.

The decorative whimsy fizzles out in the **High Court of Justice** at the front of the building, close to the entrance. A consciously intimidating chamber, the judges sat on the marble benches flanked by heavyweight representations of Righteousness, Wisdom, Mercy and so forth as they passed judgment on the hapless "criminal' in front of them; possibly even worse, the crowd on the Dam could view the proceedings through the barred windows, almost always baying for blood. They usually went home contented: as soon as the judges had passed the death sentence, the condemned were whisked up to the wooden scaffold attached to the front of the building and promptly dispatched.

Magna Plaza

Behind the Royal Palace, on Nieuwezijds Voorburgwal, you can't miss the old neo-Gothic post office of 1899, now converted into the **Magna Plaza** shopping mall. It was a great place to buy stamps, but the post office was never very popular despite its whimsical embellishments, which continued the town's tradition of plonking towers on every major building partly as a matter of civic pride, and partly to contribute to the city's spikey skyline. The architect responsible, a certain C.G. Peters, took a surprising amount of flack for his creation, which was mocked as "postal Gothic".

The Nieuwe Kerk

Vying for importance with the Royal Palace is the adjacent **Nieuwe Kerk** (opening hours & admission vary with exhibitions, but usually daily 10am–6pm; ☎020/638 6909, ⊛www.nieuwekerk.nl). Despite its name (literally "new church"), it's an early fifteenth-century structure built in a late flourish of the Gothic style, with a forest of pinnacles and high, slender gables. Badly damaged by fire on several occasions and unceremoniously stripped of most of its fittings by the Calvinists, the **interior** is a hangar-like affair of sombre demeanour, whose sturdy compound pillars soar up to support the wooden vaulting of the ceiling. Amongst a scattering of decorative highlights, look out for an extravagant, finely carved mahogany pulpit that was fifteen years in the making, a cleverly worked copper chancel screen and a flashily Baroque organ case. There's also the spectacularly vulgar tomb of Admiral Michiel de Ruyter (1607–1676), complete with trumpeting angels, conch-blowing Neptunes and cherubs all in a tizzy. In a long and illustrious naval career Ruyter trounced in succession the Spaniards, the Swedes, the English and the French, and his rise from deck hand to Admiral-in-Chief is the stuff of national legend. His most famous exploit was a raid up the River Thames to Medway in 1667 and the seizure of the Royal Navy's flagship, The Royal Charles; the subsequent Dutch crowing almost drove Charles II to distraction. Ruyter was buried here with full military honours and the church is still used for state occasions: the coronations of queens Wilhelmina, Juliana and, in 1980, Beatrix, were all held here. After the church, pop into the adjoining *'t Nieuwe Kafé*, which occupies one of the old ecclesiastical lean-tos and serves excellent coffee and delicious lunches and snacks.

The Red Light District

The whole area to the east of Damrak, between Warmoesstraat, Nieuwmarkt and Damstraat, is the **Red Light District**, known locally as the "De Walletjes" ('Small Walls') on account of the series of low brick walls that contain its canals. The district stretches across the two narrow canals that marked the eastern edge of medieval Amsterdam, **Oudezijds Voorburgwal** and **Oudezijds Achterburgwal**, both of which are now fairly sleazy, though the legalized prostitution here is world renowned and has long been one of the city's most distinctive and popular draws. The two canals, with their narrow connecting passages, are thronged with "**window brothels**" and at busy times the crass, on-street haggling over the price of various sex acts is drowned out by a surprisingly festive atmosphere – entire families grinning more or less amiably at the women in the windows or discussing the specifications (and feasibility) of the sex toys in the shops. There's also the hawkers who line the streets touting the peep shows and "live sex" within (and, unlike in London or New York, there actually is live sex within). All in all, though, there's an undertow to the district that's not particularly pleasant, and, with the added delights of the junkies that hang around during the day, especially down towards the Zeedijk end of the two main canals, you might not want to spend any longer here than is necessary. And don't even think about taking a picture of a "window brothel" unless you're prepared for some major grief from the camera-shy prostitutes. Dodging the dealers, the district also contains two prime attractions, the medieval **Oude Kerk** and the clandestine **Amstelkring** Catholic church.

Warmoesstraat

Soliciting hasn't always been the principal activity on sleazy **Warmoesstraat**. It was once one of the city's most fashionable streets, home to Holland's foremost poet, **Joost van den Vondel** (1587–1679), who ran his hosiery business from no. 110, in between writing and hobnobbing with the Amsterdam elite. Vondel was a kind of Dutch Shakespeare: his *Gijsbrecht van Amstel*, a celebration of

---

Commercial sex in Amsterdam

Developed in the 1960s, The Netherlands' – and specially Amsterdam's – liberal approach to social policy has had several unforeseen consequences, the most dramatic being its international reputation as a centre for both drugs and **prostitution**. However, the tackiness of the Red Light District is just the surface sheen on what is a serious attempt to address the reality of sex for sale, and to integrate this within a normal, ordered society. In Dutch law, prostituting oneself has long been legal, but the state has always drawn the line at brothels and soliciting in public. The difficulties this created for the police were legion, so finally, in 1996, a special soliciting zone was established and a couple of years later brothels were legalized in the hope that together these changes would bring a degree of stability to the sex industry. The authorities were particularly keen to get a grip on the use of illegal immigrants as prostitutes and also to alleviate the problem of numbers; the number of "window brothels" is limited, so a significant group of women ply their trade illicitly in bars and hotels. This new legislation is partly the result of a long and determined campaign by the prostitutes' trade union, *De Rode Draad* ("The Red Thread"), which has improved the lot of its members by setting up nascent health insurance and pension schemes – and generally fighting for regular employment rights for prostitutes.

△ Condomerie Het Gulden Vlies

Amsterdam during its Golden Age, is one of the classics of Dutch literature, and he wrote regular, if ponderous, official verses, including well over a thousand lines on the inauguration of the new town hall. He had more than his share of hard luck too. His son frittered away the modest family fortune and Vondel lived out his last few years as doorkeeper of the pawn shop on Oudezijds Voorburgwal, dying of hypothermia at what was then the remarkable age of 92. Witty to the end, his own suggested epitaph ran "Here lies Vondel, your grief withhold, for he hath suffered death from cold."

Vondel's Warmoesstraat house was knocked down decades ago, but the street does have two minor attractions – the **Condomerie Het Gulden Vlies**, at no. 141, which specializes in every imaginable design and make of condom, in sizes ranging from the small to the remarkable, and the **Prostitution Information Centre**, at Enge Kerksteeg 3, right by the Oude Kerk (Tues, Wed, Fri & Sat noon–7pm; ☏020/420 7328 ⊛www.pic-amsterdam. com), a legally recognized *stichting* or charitable foundation that was set up a decade ago (by an ex-prostitute, Mariska Majoor) to provide prostitutes, their clients and visitors with clear, dispassionate information about prostitution. It sells books and pamphlets, souvenirs of the Red Light District – postcards, fridge magnets, t-shirts – publishes the *Pleasure Guide* in Dutch and English, which bills itself as "an informative magazine about having a paid love-life", and even exhibits art by Mariska's artist father. All in all it does a great job of ridding prositution of its seedy mystique, as well as subverting the old exploitative dominance of underworld pimps.

The Oude Kerk

Just to the east of Warmoesstraat, bang in the middle of the Red Light District, is Amsterdam's most appealing church, the **Oude Kerk** (Mon–Sat 11am–5pm, Sun 1–5pm; €6; ⊛www.oudekerk.nl), an attractive Gothic structure with high-pitched gables and finely worked lancet windows. There's been a church on this site since the middle of the thirteenth century, but most of the present building dates from a century later, funded by the pilgrims who came here in their hundreds following a widely publicized miracle. The story goes that, in 1345, a dying man regurgitated the Host he had received here at Communion and when it was thrown on the fire afterwards, it did not burn. The unburnable Host was placed in a chest and installed in a long-lost chapel somewhere off Nieuwezijds Voorburgwal, before finally being transferred to the Oude Kerk a few years later. It disappeared during the Reformation, but to this day thousands of the faithful still come to take part in the annual Stille Omgang, a silent nocturnal procession terminating at the Oude Kerk and held in mid-March. The church is also regularly used for art displays and concerts.

The Protestants cleared the church of almost all of its ecclesiastical tackle during the Reformation, but its largely bare **interior** does hold several interesting features. These include some folksy misericords, a few faded vault paintings recovered from beneath layers of whitewash in the 1950s and the unadorned memorial tablet of Rembrandt's first wife, Saskia van Uylenburg – a meter or so from the smaller of the two organs. Much more diverting, however, are the three beautifully coloured **stained-glass windows** beside the ambulatory in what was once the Chapel of Our Lady. Dating from the 1550s, all three depict religious scenes, from left to right the *Annunciation*, the *Adoration of the Shepherds* and the *Dormition of the Virgin*, and each is set above its respective donors. The characters are shown in classical gear with togas and sandals and the buildings in the background are firmly classical too, reflecting both artistic fashion and a belief that Greco-Roman detail was historically accurate. A fourth, contrasting stained-glass window is located on the other side of the ambulatory. A secular piece of 1655, it features the Spanish king Philip IV ceding independence to a representative of the United Provinces (the Netherlands) under the terms of the Treaty of Munster of 1648, which wrapped up the Thirty Years' War. Like the earlier windows, the architectural backdrop is classical, but here it's to emphasize the dignity of the proceedings – and the king and the Dutch emissaries wear contemporary clothes.

OZ Voorburgwal and the Amstelkring

The front of the Oude Kerk overlooks the northern reaches of **Oudezijds Voorburgwal**, whose handsome facades recall ritzier days when this was one of the wealthiest parts of the city, richly earning its nickname the "Velvet Canal". A few metres north of the church, at Oudezijds Voorburgwal 40, is the clandestine **Amstelkring** (Mon–Sat 10am–5pm, Sun 1–5pm; €7, ⊛www.museumamstelkring.nl), which was momentarily the city's principal Catholic place of worship and is now one of Amsterdam's most enjoyable museums. Despite the reformation of 1578, the new regime treated its Catholics well, broadly speaking – commercial pragmatism has always outweighed religious zeal here – but there was a degree of discrimination: Catholic churches were recycled for Protestant use and their members no longer allowed to practise openly. The result was an eccentric compromise: Catholics were allowed to hold services in any private building providing that the exterior revealed no sign of their activities – hence the development of the city's clandestine churches (*schuilkerken*), amongst which the Amstelkring is the only one to have survived intact.

The Amstelkring, more properly Ons Lieve Heer Op Solder ("Our Dear Lord in the Attic"), occupies the loft of a wealthy merchant's house and is perfectly delightful, with a narrow nave skilfully shoehorned into the available

> ## Junkies in the Red Light District
>
> The police estimate that there are around a thousand hard-drug users in Amsterdam, who, as they put it, "cause nuisance", and there remain a few groups of hang-around **junkies** on the northern edge of the Red Light District. They are unlikely to molest strangers, but can still be a threatening presence. In fairness, though, the police have done their best to clean things up, and have dramatically improved the situation on the Zeedijk and Nieuwmarkt, which were once notorious for hard drugs, and at the canal bridge on Oude Hoogstraat, formerly nicknamed the "Pillenbrug" ("Pill Bridge").

space. Flanked by elegant balconies, the nave has an ornately carved organ at one end and a mock-marble high altar, decorated with Jacob de Wit's mawkish *Baptism of Christ*, at the other. Even the patron of the church, one Jan Hartman, clearly had doubts about de Wit's efforts – the two spares he procured just in case are now displayed behind the altar. The rest of the house has been left untouched, its original furnishings reminiscent of interiors by Vermeer or De Hooch. Amstelkring, meaning "Amstel Circle", is the name of the group of nineteenth-century historians who saved the building from demolition.

Nieuwmarkt and around

The Red Light District peters out at the cobbled **Nieuwmarkt**, a wide open, sometimes druggy square that centres on the turreted Waag. It is within easy walking distance of a pleasant residential district situated between two canals – **Geldersekade** and **Oude Schans**, and lies at the bottom of the outermost of the three eastern canals of fifteenth-century Amsterdam, **Kloveniersburgwal** – a long, dead-straight waterway framed by a string of old and dignified facades. Together these canals make for one of the most engaging parts of the city, especially at the southern end, where a small pocket of placid waterways and handsome antique canal houses spreads over to neighbouring **Groenburgwal** – a narrow and almost impossibly pretty waterway – and in the opposite direction to OZ Achterburgwal, where the buildings of Amsterdam's university define the district.

Nieuwmarkt and Oude Schans

Nieuwmarkt was long one of the city's most important markets and the place where Gentiles and Jews from the nearby Jewish Quarter – just southeast along St Antoniebreestraat (see chapter 4) – traded. All that came to a traumatic end during World War II, when the Germans cordoned off the Nieuwmarkt with barbed wire and turned it into a holding pen. After the war, the square's old exuberance never returned and these days the market has all but vanished, though there is a small market for organic food on Saturdays (9am–5pm).

The focus of the square, the sprawling multi-turreted **Waag**, dating from the 1480s, has had a chequered history. Built as one of the city's fortified gates, Sint Antoniespoort, Amsterdam's expansion soon made it obsolete and the ground floor was turned into a municipal weighing-house (*waag*), with the rooms upstairs taken over by the surgeons' guild. It was here that the surgeons held lectures on anatomy and public dissections, the inspiration for Rembrandt's *Anatomy Lesson of Dr Tulp*, displayed in the Mauritshuis Collection in The Hague. Abandoned by the surgeons and the weigh-masters in the nineteenth century, the building served as a furniture store and fire station before falling into disuse, though it has recently been renovated to house a good café-bar and restaurant, *In de Waag* (see p.192).

△ The Kleine Trippenhuis

Strolling along Recht Boomssloot from the northeast corner of Nieuwmarkt, it only takes a couple of minutes to reach the **Montelbaanstoren**, a sturdy tower dating from 1512 that overlooks the **Oude Schans**, a canal dug around the same time to improve the city's shipping facilities. The tower was built to protect the city's eastern flank but its decorative spire was added later, when the city felt more secure, by Hendrik de Keyser (1565–1621), the architect who did much to create Amsterdam's prickly skyline.

At the top of Oude Schans, turn left along busy Prins Hendrikkade for the 300-metre amble to the **Scheepvaarthuis** (Shipping Building), an unusual edifice at no. 108 – on the corner of Binnenkant. Completed in 1917, this is one of the flashiest of the buildings designed by the Amsterdam School of architecture, the work of a certain Johann Melchior van der Mey (1878–1949). An almost neurotically decorated edifice covered with a welter of detail celebrating the city's marine connections, the entrance is shaped like a prow and surmounted by statues of Poseidon and Amphitrite, his wife. Up above them are female representations of the four points of the compass, whilst slender turrets and Expressionistic carvings playfully decorate the walls.

Kloveniersburgwal

Heading south along Kloveniersburgwal from Nieuwmarkt, it's a short hoof to the **Trippenhuis**, at no. 29, an overblown mansion complete with Corinthian pilasters and a grand frieze built for the Trip family in 1662. One of the richest families in Amsterdam, the Trips were a powerful force among the **Magnificat**, the clique of families (Six, Trip, Hooft and Pauw) who shared power during the Golden Age. One part of the Trip family dealt with the Baltic trade, another with the manufacture of munitions (in which they had the municipal monopoly), but in addition they also had trade interests in Russia and the Middle East, much like the multinationals of today. In the nineteenth century the Rijksmuseum collection was displayed here, but the house now contains the Dutch Academy of Sciences.

Almost directly opposite, on the west bank of the canal, the **Kleine Trippenhuis**, at no. 26 (now a lingerie shop), is by contrast one of the narrowest houses in Amsterdam, albeit with a warmly carved facade with a balustrade featuring centaurs and sphinxes. Legend asserts that Mr Trip's coachman was so taken aback by the size of the new family mansion that he exclaimed he would be happy with a home no wider than the Trips' front door – which is exactly what he got; his reaction to his new lodgings is not recorded.

A few metres away, on the corner of Oude Hoogstraat, is the former headquarters of the Dutch East India Company, the **Oostindisch Huis**, a monumental red-brick structure with high-pitched gables and perky dormer windows built in 1605 shortly after the founding of the company. It was from here that the Company organized and regulated its immensely lucrative trading interests in the Far East, importing shiploads of spices, perfumes and exotic woods (see box, p.108). This trade underpinned Amsterdam's Golden Age, but predictably the people of what is now Indonesia, the source of most of the raw materials, received little in return. Nevertheless, despite the building's historic significance, the interior is of no interest today, being occupied by university classrooms and offices.

Continuing on up Kloveniersburgwal takes you into the student district, where the buildings here and across the top of the adjoining canals house the various departments of the **University of Amsterdam**. At the heart of this is the **Oudemanhuispoort**, a covered passageway that leads between Kloveniersburgwal and OZ Achterburgwal. Now lined by secondhand bookstalls, it was formerly part of an almshouse complex for elderly men – hence the unusual name ('Oudemanhuis' is basically an almshouse for men). The buildings off the passageway now house various university faculties and their gardens provide a quiet place to rest between sights. Still on the Kloveniersburgwal, take a look at its southern reaches, which are flanked by a comely collection of old canal houses interrupted by the occasional nineteenth-century extravagance. In particular, cross the canal along **Staalstraat** and stop at the second of the two dinky little swing bridges for one of the finest views in the city, down the slender **Groenburgwal** with the Zuiderkerk (see p.98) looming beyond.

OZ Achterburgwal

A block across from Kloveniersburgwal, next door to Oudezijds Achterburgwal 185, at Spinhuissteeg 1, the **Spinhuis** was once a house of correction for "fallen women", who were put to work here on the looms and spinning wheels. Curiously, workhouses like this used to figure on tourist itineraries: for a small fee the public was allowed to watch the women at work, and at carnival times admission was free and large crowds came to jeer and mock. The justification for this was that shame was supposed to be part of the reforming process, but in fact the municipality unofficially tolerated brothels and the incarcerated women had simply been singled out for exemplary punishment. As the eighteenth-century commentator Bernard de Mandeville observed, "The wary magistrates preserve themselves in the good opinion of the weaker sort of people, who imagine the government is always trying to suppress those [brothels] it really tolerates." The Spinhuis has been turned into offices, but the old front door has survived intact, with an inscription by the seventeenth-century Dutch poet Pieter Cornelisz Hooft: "Cry not, for I exact no vengeance for wrong but to force you to be good. My hand is stern but my heart is kind."

Across the canal from the Spinhuis, the **Hash Marihuana Hemp Museum**, Oudezijds Achterburgwal 148 (daily 11am–11pm; €5.70, @www .hashmuseum.com), which is still going strong despite intermittent battles with the police. As well as featuring displays on the various types of dope and numerous ways to smoke it, the museum has a live indoor marijuana garden, samples of textiles and paper made with hemp, and pamphlets explaining the medicinal properties of cannabis. There's also a shop selling pipes, books, videos and plenty of souvenirs. Amsterdam's reliance on imported dope ended in the late 1980s when the growth of hydroponic growing techniques, whereby marijuana – and in particular a reddish variety bred in America, called "skunk" – was able to flourish under artificial lights without water. Nowadays over half the dope sold in the coffeeshops is grown in the Netherlands, and this place is positively evangelical about how to join in.

The triangular parcel of land at the southern end of **Oudezijds Achterburgwal** is packed with university buildings, mostly modern or nineteenth-century structures built in a vernacular Dutch style. Together they form a pleasant urban ensemble, but the red-shuttered, mullion-windowed early seventeenth-century step-gabled **Huis op de Drie Grachten** ('House on the Three Canals') stands out, sitting prettily on the corner of Oudezijds Achterburgwal and Oudezijds Voorburgwal. Nearby, through an ornate gateway at Oudezijds Voorburgwal 231, is the **Agnietenkapel** (currently under restoration), originally part of a Catholic convent, but now owned by the university. Upstairs the chapel has a good-looking, first-floor auditorium dating from the fifteenth century; it's used for temporary exhibitions mainly devoted to the university's history. Roughly opposite, just over the footbridge, the large brick and stone-trimmed building at

Oudezijds Voorburgwal 302 has long been known as **ome Jan** ("Uncle John's") for its former function as central Amsterdam's pawn shop. The poet Vondel (see p.54) ended his days working here, and a short verse above the fancy stone entranceway, which comes complete with the city's coat of arms, extols the virtues of the pawn shop and the evils of usury. From ome Jan, it's a couple of hundred metres to the southern end of Oudezijds Voorburgwal, where the **Galerie Mokum** art shop uses the old Jewish nickname for the city; the trams and traffic of Rokin are close by.

Rokin, Kalverstraat and Spui

Sandwiched between the Singel and the **Rokin**, the southern part of the Old Centre is one of Amsterdam's busiest districts, mostly on account of pedestrianized **Kalverstraat**, a hectic shopping street. Taken as a whole, it's not a particularly engaging area, but it does have its moments, most enjoyably in the cloistered tranquillity of the **Begijnhof**, at the floating **flower market** near Muntplein and amongst the bars and cafés of the **Spui**. Here also is a brace of moderately diverting museums – the **Amsterdams Historisch Museum** and the archeological **Allard Pierson Museum**.

Rokin to Muntplein

The **Rokin** picks up where the Damrak leaves off, cutting south in a wide sweep that follows the former course of the River Amstel. The Rokin was the business centre of the nineteenth-century city and although it has lost much of its prestige, it is still flanked by an attractive medley of architectural styles incorporating everything from grandiose nineteenth-century mansions to more utilitarian modern stuff. One initial highlight as you stroll south is the handsome Art Nouveau-meets-Art Deco Marine Insurance building at **no. 69**; others are the much earlier canal house at **no. 83** and the attractive stone mansion at **no. 91**. Across the street, at **no. 92**, is the Hajenius cigar shop with its flashy gilt interior, while a prominent equestrian **statue** of Queen Wilhelmina marks the spot where the Rokin hits the canal system. Born in The Hague, **Wilhelmina** (1880–1962) came to the throne in 1890 and abdicated in favour of her daughter, Juliana, 58 years later – a mammoth royal stint by any standard. After her retirement, she wrote *Lonely but not Alone*, which explored her strong religious beliefs, but her popularity was based on her determined resistance to the Germans in World War II, when she was the figurehead of the government-in-exile in London.

Close by, overlooking the canal at Oude Turfmarkt 127, the **Allard Pierson Museum** (Tues–Fri 10am–5pm, Sat & Sun 1–5pm; €5) is a good old-fashioned archeological museum in a solid Neoclassical building dating from the 1860s. Spread over two floors – and labelled in English and Dutch – it has a wide-ranging, albeit fairly small, collection of finds retrieved from the Middle East, especially Egypt, Greece and Italy. The particular highlight is the museum's Greek pottery with fine examples of both the black- and red-figured wares produced in the sixth and fifth centuries BC. Look out also for the Roman sarcophagi, especially a marble whopper decorated with Dionysian scenes, a very unusual wooden coffin from c.150 AD which is partly carved in the shape of the man held within and Etruscan funerary urns and carvings, including an amazing statue of a baby in swaddling clothes. Of the Egyptian artefacts, a model of a ship and its crew from the Middle Kingdom stands out – another funerary object, used to transport the soul of the dead to the afterlife.

Pushing on down past the museum, **nos. 141–147 Oude Turfmarkt** are classic seventeenth-century canal houses, graced by bottle- and spout-shaped gables. Just beyond, at the end of Rokin, is the **Muntplein**, a dishevelled square where the **Munttoren** of 1480 was originally part of the old city wall. Later, it was adopted as the municipal mint – hence its name – a plain brick structure to which Hendrik de Keyser, in one of his last commissions, added a flashy spire in 1620, and nowadays it sports a carillon which is used for summer evening concerts every Saturday at 8pm. A few metres away, the floating **Bloemenmarkt**, or flower market (daily 9am–5pm, though some stalls close on Sun), extends along the southern bank of the Singel. Popular with locals and tourists alike, the market is one of the main suppliers of flowers to central Amsterdam, but its blooms and bulbs now share stall space with souvenir clogs, garden gnomes and delftware.

Kalverstraat, the Spui and the Begijnhof

The Munttoren sits at the top of **Kalverstraat**, a pedestrianized shopping strip that runs north to Dam square. The street has been a commercial centre since medieval times, when it was used as a calf market, and it was also here, in 1345, that the city witnessed the miracle of the host (see above the "Oude Kerk") and became a route for pilgrims. There's not much to say about Kalverstraat – it really could be any European shopping street – but if you want to do any kind of clothes shopping, and you're not looking for designer labels, this is the place to come.

A little way down Kalverstraat, workaday **Heiligeweg**, or "Holy Way", was once part of a much longer route used by pilgrims heading into Amsterdam and is still used for part of the Stille Omgang (Silent Procession, see p.249). Every other religious reference disappeared centuries ago, but there is one interesting edifice here, the fanciful gateway of the old **Rasphuis** (House of Correction) that now fronts a shopping mall at the foot of Voetboogstraat. The gateway is surmounted by a sculpture of a woman punishing two criminals chained at her sides above the single word "Castigatio" (punishment). Beneath is a carving by Hendrik de Keyser showing wolves and lions cringing before the whip; the inscription reads "It is a virtue to subdue those before whom all go in dread."

Cut up Voetboogstraat and you soon reach the **Spui**, whose west end opens out into a wide, tram-clanking square flanked by the Athaeneum bookshop and a number of café-bars. In the middle is a cloying statue of a young boy, known as **'t Lieverdje** ("Little Darling" or "Loveable Scamp"), a gift to the city from a cigarette company in 1960. It was here in the mid-1960s, with the statue seen as a symbol of the addicted consumer, that the playful **Provos** organized some of their most successful *ludiek* (pranks).

From the Spui, you can either follow **Spuistraat** north towards the station, a happening street, liberally sprinkled with bars and restaurants and the possessor of Amsterdam's last remaining **squat**, *Vrankrijk*. Or, by way of the fancy little gateway on the north side of the Spui, you can sneak into the **Begijnhof** (daily 8am–1pm; free), where a huddle of immaculately maintained old houses looks onto a central green, their backs to the outside world; if this door is locked, try the main entrance, just a couple of hundred metres north of the Spui on Gedempte Begijnensloot. The Begijnhof was founded in the fourteenth century as a home for the *Beguines* – members of a Catholic sisterhood living as nuns,

The beguinages

One result of the urbanization of the Low Countries from the twelfth century onwards was the establishment of **beguinages** (*begijnhoven* in Dutch, *béguinages* in French) in almost every city and town. These were semi-secluded communities, where widows and unmarried women – the **Beguines** (*Begijns*) – lived together, the better to do pious acts, especially caring for the sick. In **construction**, beguinages follow the same general plan with several streets of whitewashed, brick terraced cottages hidden away behind walls and gates and surrounding a central garden and chapel.

The **origins** of the Beguine movement are somewhat obscure, but it would seem that the initial impetus came from a twelfth-century Liège priest, a certain Lambert le Bègue (the Stammerer). The main period of growth came later with the establishment of dozens of new beguinages, like the ones in Ghent and Bruges in Belgium and Breda and Amsterdam in the Netherlands. All were sponsored by the nobility and the later foundations – like the one here in Amsterdam – were established despite the opposition of the Papacy, which had declared against them as a potential source of heresy at the Council of Vienna in 1311.

Beguine communities were different from convents in so far as the inhabitants did not have to take vows and had the right to return to the secular world if they chose. At a time when hundreds of women were forcibly shut away in convents for all sorts of reasons (primarily financial), this element of choice made them an attractive proposition. In the Netherlands. the beguine movement was pretty much polished off by the Reformation – and the Calvinist assertion of the individual's need to have a direct relationship with God without the Church acting as intermediary; the convents closed down too. Almshouses, arguably the predecessors of state subsidized housing, did something to fill the gap.

but without vows and with the right of return to the secular world (see box). The original medieval complex comprised a series of humble brick cottages, but these were mostly replaced by the larger, grander houses of today shortly after the Reformation, though the secretive, enclosed design survived. However, a couple of pre-Reformation buildings do remain, including the **Houten Huys**, at no. 34, whose wooden facade dates from 1477, the oldest in Amsterdam and erected before the city forbade the construction of timber houses as an essential precaution against fire. The **Engelse Kerk** (English Reformed Church), which takes up one side of the Begijnhof, is of medieval construction too, but it was taken from the *beguines* and given to Amsterdam's English community during the Reformation. Plain and unadorned, the church is of interest for its carefully worked pulpit panels, several of which were designed by a youthful **Piet Mondriaan** (1872–1944), the leading De Stijl artist – although to see them you'll have to attend one of its services on Sundays at 10.30am. After they had lost their church, and in keeping with the terms of the Alteratie (see p.262), the *beguines* were allowed to celebrate Mass inconspicuously in the clandestine Catholic **kapel** (Mon 1–6.30pm, Tues–Fri 9am–6.30pm; free), which they established in the house opposite their old church. It's still used today, a homely little place with some terribly sentimental religious paintings, one of which – to the left of the high altar – depicts the miracle of the unburnable Host.

The Amsterdams Historisch Museum

Emerging from the east side of the Begijnhof, turn left onto narrow **Gedempte Begijnensloot** and it's 100m or so to the **Schuttersgalerij** – the Civic Guard Gallery. Here, an assortment of huge group portraits of the Amsterdam militia,

△ Amsterdams Historisch Museum

ranging from serious-minded paintings of the 1540s through to lighter affairs from the seventeenth century, is displayed for free in a glassed-in passageway. They are interesting paintings, no doubt, and the pick are those by **Nicolaes Pickenoy** (1588–1650), but the finest militia painting by a long chalk – Rembrandt's *The Night Watch* – is exhibited in the Rijksmuseum.

The Schuttersgalerij is part of the **Amsterdams Historisch Museum** (Mon–Fri 10am–5pm, Sat & Sun 11am–5pm; €6; ⊛www.ahm.nl), which occupies the smartly restored but rambling seventeenth-century buildings of the municipal orphanage. The museum surveys the city's development with a scattering of artefacts and lots of paintings from the thirteenth century onwards, but it's a slightly difficult collection to find your way around, and you need to pay close attention to the colour-coded signs that attempt to guide you through chronologically. The labelling at least is in English as well as Dutch which makes it all much easier. Maps and paintings punctuate the galleries and record the growth of the city, starting with a lot of **old views of Amsterdam** back before the Golden Age, of which Cornelisz Anthonisz's 1538 *Bird's Eye View of Amsterdam,* in effect the oldest surviving plan of the city, stands out. There are paintings illustrating the country's former maritime prowess in Room 5, titled "Rulers of the Seas", and in Room 6 there is a view of Dam Square in the early seventeenth century that show both the old and new town hall painter's name, while Room 7 has a rare cityscape by Jacob van Ruisdael that shows Dam Square and the harbour along Damrak. Room 10, "Social Care & Stern Discipline", examines the harsh paternalism of the city's merchant oligarchy, with paintings depicting the regents of several orphanages, self-contented bourgeoisie in the company of the grateful poor, while nearby Room 11, "**The Art of the Golden Age**", is distinguished by two paintings of the surgeons' guild at work – look out for Rembrandt's wonderful if gruesome *Anatomy Lesson of Dr Jan Deijman* – as well as Bartholomew van der Helst's *Governors and Govern-*

esses of the Spinhuis, which captures both the sternness of the institution and the action going on behind them. The museum doesn't just focus on the Golden Age, but dutifully and effectively records the **modern era** as well, starting with Breitner's *Dam Square* of 1898 and Jacob Maris's view of the *Schreierstoren*, and moving upstairs for the twentieth century, where there is an inevitable focus on the war years and Nazi occupation, including film footage of the city's liberation. Post-war material includes a display on the postwar CoBrA art movement (see p.282) and Karel Appel's murals for the town hall (now decorating the city's Grand Hotel restaurant), the development of Schipol airport, the liberalisation of dope and rise of coffeeshops, even a mock-up of an old brown café.

The Grachtengordel

The western reaches of medieval Amsterdam were once enclosed by the **Singel**, part of the city's protective moat, but this is now just the first of five canals that stretch right around the city centre, extending anticlockwise from Brouwersgracht to the River Amstel in a "girdle of canals" or **Grachtengordel**. This is without doubt the most charming part of Amsterdam, a lattice of olive-green waterways and dinky humpback bridges overlooked by street upon street of handsome seventeenth-century canal houses, almost invariably undisturbed by later development. Of the three main canals, **Herengracht** (Gentlemen's Canal) was the first to be dug, followed by the **Keizersgracht**, the Emperor's Canal, named after the Holy Roman Emperor and fifteenth-century patron of the city, Maximilian. Further out still lies the **Prinsengracht**, the Princes' Canal, named in honour of the princes of the House of Orange. It's a subtle cityscape – full of surprises, with a bizarre carving here, an unusual facade stone (used to denote name and occupation) there – and one where the **gables** overlooking the canals gradually evolved. The earliest, dating from the early seventeenth-century, are **crow-stepped gables** but these were largely superseded from the 1650s onwards by **neck gables** and **bell gables**. Some are embellished, many have decorative cornices, and the fanciest, which almost invariably date from the eighteenth century, sport full-scale **balustrades**. The plainest gables are those of former **warehouses**, where the deep-arched and shuttered windows line up to either side of loft doors, which were once used for loading and unloading goods, winched by pulley from the street down below. Indeed, outside **pulleys** remain a common feature of houses and warehouses alike, and are often still in use as the easiest way of moving furniture into the city's myriad apartments.

The grandest Grachtengordel houses are concentrated along the so-called **De Gouden Bocht** – the Golden Bend – on Herengracht between Leidsestraat and the Amstel. Here, the architectural decorum – and arguably the aesthetic vigour – of the seventeenth century are left behind for the over-blown, French-influenced mansions that became popular with the city's richest merchants in the 1700s. Nevertheless, it is perhaps the district's overall atmosphere that

---

This chapter covers the first four canals of the Grachtengordel – the Singel, Herengracht, Keizersgracht and Prinsengracht – as they sweep down from Brouwersgracht to the Amstel. We've split it into two areas – **Grachtengordel west** and **Grachtengordel south** – divided at roughly the halfway point, Leidsegracht. There's no obvious **walking route** around the area – indeed you may prefer to wander around as the mood takes you – but the description we've given below goes from north to south, taking in all the highlights on the way. On all three of the main canals, **street numbers** begin at Brouwersgracht and increase as you go south.

appeals rather than any specific sight, with one remarkable exception: the **Anne Frankhuis**, where the young – and now internationally famous – Jewish diarist hid from the Nazis in World War II.

Expanding the city

Three of the **Grachtengordel canals** were dug in the seventeenth century as part of a comprehensive plan to extend the boundaries of a city no longer able to accommodate its burgeoning population. The idea was that the council would buy up the land around the city, dig the canals, and lease plots back to developers, thus increasing the size of the city from two to seven square kilometres. The plan was passed in 1607 and work began six years later, against a backdrop of corruption – Amsterdammers in the know buying up the land they thought the city would soon have to purchase.

It was a monumental task, and the conditions imposed by the council were strict. The three **main waterways** – Herengracht, Keizersgracht and Prinsengracht – were set aside for the residences and businesses of the richer and more influential Amsterdam merchants, while the **radial cross-streets** were reserved for more modest artisans' homes; meanwhile, immigrants, newly arrived to cash in on Amsterdam's booming economy, were assigned, albeit informally, the Jodenhoek (see Chapter Four) and the Jordaan (see Chapter Three). In the Grachtengordel, everyone, even the wealthiest merchant, had to comply with a set of strict and detailed **planning regulations**. In particular, the council prescribed the size of each building plot – the frontage was set at thirty feet, the depth two hundred – and although there was a degree of tinkering, the end result was the loose conformity you can see today: tall, narrow residences, whose individualism is mainly restricted to the stylistic permutations amongst the gables. Even the colour of the front doors was once regulated, with choice restricted to a shade that has since become known as "Amsterdam Green" – still something of a rarity outside Holland. It took decades to complete the project, but by the 1690s it was all pretty much finished off – at a time, ironically, when Amsterdam was in economic decline. In essence, therefore, the Grachtengordel is a tribute to the architectural tastes of the city's middle class, an amalgam of personal wealth and aesthetic uniformity – individuality and order – that epitomized Amsterdam's Protestant bourgeoisie in its pomp.

Grachtengordel west

Stretching south from the Brouwersgracht to the Leidsegracht, **Grachtengordel west** contains a fine selection of seventeenth-century canal houses. These are at their prettiest along **Herengracht** between Huidenstraat and Leidsegracht, and this is where you'll also find the **Bijbels Museum** (Biblical Museum), home to an odd assortment of models of ancient Jewish temples. However, easily the most popular attraction is the **Anne Frankhuis**, on Prinsengracht; close by is the soaring architecture of the **Westerkerk** and the mildly enjoyable **Theatermuseum**.

South from Brouwersgracht to Prinsenstraat

Running east to west along the northern edge of the three main canals is **Brouwersgracht**, one of the most picturesque waterways in the city. Look down

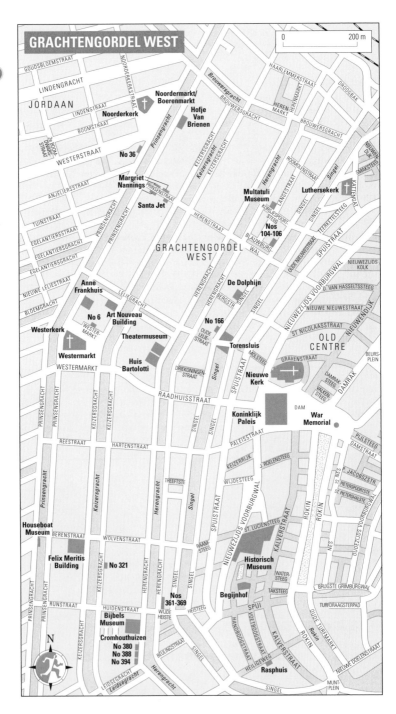

GRACHTENGORDEL WEST

0   200 m

GOUDSBLOEMSTRAAT

LINDENGRACHT

JORDAAN

LINDENSTRAAT

BOOMSTRAAT

WESTERSTRAAT

NOORDERKERKSTRAAT

Brouwersgracht

HAARLEMMERSTRAAT

HERENMARKT

DROOGBAK

BROUWERSGRACHT

HERENMARKT

BROUWERSGRACHT

Noordermarkt/
Boerenmarkt

Noorderkerk

Hofje
Van
Brienen

No 36

Prinsengracht

KEIZERSGRACHT

KEIZERSGRACHT

Herengracht

ROOMOLENSTRAAT

Singel

NIEUWE
DIJK

SMAKSTEEG

Margriet
Nannings

ANJELIERSSTRAAT

PRINSENSTRAAT

Multatuli
Museum

LANGESTEEG

KORSJESPOORT
STEEG

Luthersekerk

SINGEL

KATTENGAT

TEERKETELSTEEG

Santa Jet

HERENSTRAAT

Nos
104-106

BLAUWBURG-
WAL

SINGEL

SPUISTRAAT

TUINSTRAAT

PRINSENGRACHT

EGELANTIERSSTRAAT

EGELANTIERSGRACHT

EGELANTIERSGRACHT

GRACHTENGORDEL
WEST

OUDE NIEUWEZIJDS

NIEUWEZIJDS
KOLK

NIEUWE LELIESTRAAT

Anne
Frankhuis

LELIEGRACHT

De Dolphijn

HERENGRACHT

BERGSTR.

SINGEL

NIEUWEZIJDS VOORBURGWAL

D. VAN HASSELTSSTEEG

BLOEMGRACHT

No 6

Art Nouveau
Building

WESTER-
MARKT.

No 166

OUDE
LELIE-
STRAAT

NIEUWE NIEUWESTRAAT

ST. NICOLAASSTRAAT

NIEUWENDIJK

Westerkerk

Theatermuseum

Torensluis

MOLSTEEG

OLD
CENTRE

Westermarkt

Huis
Bartolotti

DRIEKONINGEN-
STRAAT

Singel

SPUISTRAAT

Nieuwe
Kerk

GRAVENSTRAAT

DAMRAK
STEEG

BEURS-
PLEIN

DAMRAK

WESTERMARKT

RAADHUISSTRAAT

VALKEN-
STEEG

DAMRAK

PRINSENGRACHT

PRINSENGRACHT

KEIZERSGRACHT

KEIZERSGRACHT

SINGEL

SINGEL

Koninklijk
Paleis

DAM

War
Memorial

PIJLSTEEG

REESTRAAT

HARTENSTRAAT

PALEISSTRAAT

DAMSTRAAT

Prinsengracht

Keizersgracht

TREEFTSTE

Herengracht

Singel

KEIZERRIJK

J. ROELENSTEEG

WIJDESTEEG

NES

P. JACOBSZSTR.

ST. PETERSPOORTSTE

ST. PETERSHALSTEEG

NIEUWEZIJDS VOORBURGWAL

OUDEZIJDS VOORBURGWAL

Houseboat
Museum

BERENSTRAAT

WOLVENSTRAAT

RAAM-
STEEG

ST. LUCIENSTEEG

KALVERSTRAAT

ROKIN

ROKIN

NES

Felix Meritis
Building

No 321

KEIZERSGRACHT

HERENGRACHT

HERENGRACHT

SINGEL

SINGEL

Historisch
Museum

WATER-
STEEG

L. BRUGSTE GRIMBURGWAL

RUNSTRAAT

HUIDENSTRAAT

Nos
361-369

HEISTEEG

Begijnhof

TAKSTEEG

SPUI

TURFDRAAGSTERPAD

PRINSENGRACHT

KEIZERSGRACHT

Bijbels
Museum

WIJDE
HEISTE

HANDBOOGSTRAAT

VOETBOOGSTRAAT

OUDE TURFMARKT

ROKIN

Cromhouthuizen

No 380
No 388
No 394

BEULINGSTRAAT

HEILIGEWEG

KALVERSTRAAT

N

KEIZERSGRACHT

LEIDSEGRACHT

Herengracht

Leidsegracht

SINGEL

Rasphuis

NIEUWE DOELENSTRAAT

MUNT-
PLEIN

any of the major canals from here and you'll see the gentle interplay of water, brick and stone that gives the city its distinctive draw. Strolling south along the west side of **Prinsengracht** from Brouwersgracht, past a huddle of houseboats, you soon reach the **Noorderkerk** (see p.89), a lugubrious pile on the edge of the Jordaan that oversees the **Noordermarkt**, the site of several markets, including a flea market (Mon 9am–1pm & Sat 8am–3pm) and a farmers' produce market (Sat 9am–3pm). Just along the canal from the Noordermarkt, **Prinsengracht 36** has an especially well-proportioned facade, its neck gable, pilasters and pediment dating from the 1650s.

Cross the canal at the next bridge down and turn left for the **Hofje Van Brienen** (daily 6am–6pm & Sat 6am–2pm; free), a brisk, brown-brick courtyard complex at Prinsengracht 85–133. Originally the site of a brewery, the *hofje* (see box, p.86) was built in 1804 to the order of a certain Arnout van Brienen, who added a matching brick church (no entry) for good measure. A well-to-do merchant, Brienen had locked himself in his own strong room by accident and, in a panic, he vowed to build a *hofje* if he was rescued – he was and he did.

From the Hofje Van Brienen, it's the briefest of walks to the first of the Grachtengordel's cross-streets, **Prinsenstraat/Herenstraat**, where the modest old tradesmen's houses now accommodate a string of knick-knack and clothes shops. It's here you'll find a potpourri of hand-made Latin American items at *Santa Jet*, Prinsenstraat 7, and designer clothes at *Margriet Nannings*, Prinsenstraat 8, 15 & 24.

The Multatuli Museum

Herenstraat opens out into the **Blauwburgwal**, a short and inordinately pretty slip of a canal, which had the misfortune to be hit by a bomb during the German invasion of 1940. The speed of the German victory meant that central Amsterdam was hardly bombed at all, but this incident alone cost 51 lives. From here, it's a quick gambol to Amsterdam's tiniest museum, the **Multatuli Museum**, just off the Herengracht at Korsjespoortsteeg 20 (Tues 10am–5pm, Sat & Sun noon–5pm; free; ⑩www .multatuli-museum.nl). This was the birthplace of **Eduard Douwes Dekker** (1820–1887), Holland's most celebrated nineteenth-century writer and a champion of free thinking, who wrote under the pen name Multatuli. Dekker worked as a colonial official in the Dutch East Indies for eighteen years, becoming increasingly disgusted by the graft and corruption. He returned to Amsterdam in 1856 and spent the next four years encapsulating his East Indies experiences in an elegantly written satirical novel *Max Havelaar*, which enraged the Dutch merchant class, but is now something of a Dutch literary classic (see p.288). The museum's one room is filled with letters, first editions and a small selection of his furnishings, including the **chaise longue** on which he breathed his last.

The Singel – from Korsjespoortsteeg to Leliegracht

Slipping through to the Singel, turn right along the canal to reach **nos. 104–106**, twin mansions dating to the 1740s and equipped with the largest bell gables in the city – big but not especially pretty. Pushing on, it's a few metres more to the red-brick and stone-trimmed **De Dolphijn** (The Dolphin), at nos. 140–142. This was once home of Captain Banningh Cocq, one of the militiamen depicted in Rembrandt's *The Night Watch* (see p.120), but it takes its name from a late-sixteenth-century Dutch grammar book written by the first owner, one Hendrick Spieghel. Nearby, Singel **no. 166** has the narrowest facade in the city – just 1.8m wide – and it overlooks the **Torensluis**, easily the widest bridge in the Grachten-gordel and decorated with a whopping bust of Multatuli**.**

Cut back along Oude Leliestraat and you soon reach **Leliegracht**, one of the tiny radial canals that cut across the Grachtengordel. It's a charming street, an attractive home to a number of bookshops and bars, and it also holds one of the city's finest examples of Art Nouveau architecture – the tall and striking build-ing at the Leliegracht-Keizersgracht junction designed by Gerrit van Arkel in 1905. It was originally the headquarters of a life insurance company, hence the two mosaics with angels recommending policies to bemused earthlings.

The Anne Frankhuis

In 1957 the Anne Frank Foundation set up the **Anne Frankhuis** (daily: April–Aug 9am–9pm; Sept–March 9am–7pm; closed Yom Kippur; €7.50, 10- to 17-year-olds €3.50, under-10s free; ⓦwww.annefrank.nl) in the house

The story of Anne Frank

The story of **Anne**, her family and friends, is well known. Anne's father, **Otto Frank**, was a well-to-do Jewish businessman who fled Germany in December 1933 after Hitler came to power, moving to Amsterdam, where he established a spice-trading business on the Prinsengracht. After the German occupation of the Netherlands, Otto felt – along with many other Jews – that he could avoid trouble by keeping his head down. However, by 1942 it was clear that this would not be possible: Amsterdam's Jews were isolated and conspicuous, being confined to certain parts of the city and forced to wear a yellow star, and roundups were becoming increasingly common. In desperation, Otto Frank decided to move the family into the unused back of their Prinsengracht premises, first asking some of his Dutch office staff if they would help him with the subterfuge – and they bravely agreed. The Franks went into hid-ing in July 1942, along with a Jewish business partner and his family, the Van Pels (renamed the Van Daans in the *Diary*). Their new "home" was separated from the rest of the building by a **bookcase** that doubled as a door. As far as everyone else was concerned, they had fled to Switzerland.

So began the two-year incarceration in the **achterhuis**, or back annexe. The two families were joined in November 1942 by a dentist friend, Fritz Pfeffer (the *Diary's* Albert Dussel). Otto's trusted office staff continued working in the front part of the building, regularly bringing supplies and news of the outside world. In her diary Anne Frank describes the day-to-day lives of the inhabitants of the annexe: the quarrels, frequent in such a claustrophobic environment; celebrations of birthdays, or of a piece of good news from the Allied Front; and of her own, slightly unreal, growing up (much of which, it's been claimed, was deleted by her father).

Two years later, the atmosphere was optimistic: the Allies were clearly winning the war and liberation seemed within reach. It wasn't to be. One day in the summer of 1944 the Franks were **betrayed** by a Dutch collaborator and the Gestapo arrived and forced open the bookcase. Thereafter, the occupants of the annexe were arrested and dispatched to Westerbork – the transit camp in the north of the country where all Dutch Jews were processed before being moved to Belsen or Auschwitz. Of the eight from the annexe, only Otto Frank survived; Anne and her sister died of typhus within a short time of each other in Belsen, just one week before the German surrender.

Anne Frank's **diary** was among the few things left behind in the annexe. It was retrieved by one of the family's Dutch helpers and handed to Otto on his return from Auschwitz. In 1947, Otto decided to publish his daughter's diary and since then it has been translated into over sixty languages and sold millions of copies. The identity of the collaborator has never been confirmed.

at Prinsengracht 263 where the young diarist and her family hid from the Germans during World War II. Since the posthumous publication of her diaries, Anne Frank has become extraordinarily famous, in the first instance for recording the iniquities of the Holocaust, and latterly as a symbol of the fight against oppression and especially racism, as explored in a challenging exhibition seen at the end of a visit.

The **rooms** the Franks occupied for two years have been left much the same as they were during the war – even down to the movie star pin-ups in Anne's bedroom and the marks on the wall recording the children's heights. Remarkably, despite the number of visitors – try to come early or late to avoid the crush – there is a real sense of the personal here see and only the coldest of hearts could fail to be moved. Apposite video clips on the family in particular and the Holocaust in general give the background. Anne Frank was only one of about 100,000 Dutch Jews who died during World War II, but this, her final home, provides one of the most enduring testaments to its horrors. Her diary has been a source of inspiration to many, including Nelson Mandela and Primo Levi.

Westerkerk

Trapped in the achterhuis, Anne Frank liked to listen to the bells of the **Westerkerk** (April–Sept Mon–Fri 11am–3pm, plus July & Aug Sat 11am–3pm; free), just along Prinsengracht, until they were taken away to be melted down for the German war effort. The church still dominates the district, its 85-metre **tower** (April–Sept Mon–Sat 10am–4/5pm; €5; ⓦwww.westerkerk.nl) – without question Amsterdam's finest – soaring graciously above its surroundings and offering panoramic views of the city centre from its balconies. On its top perches the crown of the Emperor Maximilian, a constantly recurring symbol of Amsterdam (see p.48) and the finishing touch to what was then only the second city church to be built expressly for the Protestants. The church was designed by **Hendrick de Keyser** (see box, p.73), and completed in 1631 as part of the general enlargement of the city, but whereas the exterior is all studied elegance, the interior – as required by the Calvinist congregation – is bare and plain. Apart from the soaring stone columns and long windows, which allow the light to pour in, the only feature of note is the fancy wooden pulpit, where Protestant ministers once thundered away for hours on end.

The church was also the last resting place of **Rembrandt**, though the location of his paupers' tomb is not known. Instead, a small memorial in the north aisle commemorates the artist, close to the spot where his son Titus was buried. Rembrandt adored his son – as evidenced by numerous portraits – and the boy's death dealt a final crushing blow to the ageing and embittered artist, who died just over a year later. During renovation of the church in the early 1990s, bones were unearthed that could have been those of Rembrandt – a possibility whose tourist potential excited the church authorities no end. Admittedly it was a long shot – paupers' tombs were usually cleared of their accumulated bodies every twenty years or so – but the obvious way to prove it was through a chemical analysis of the bones' lead content, expected to be unusually high if they were his, as lead was a major ingredient of paint. The bones were duly taken to the University of Groningen for analysis, but the tests proved inconclusive.

Westermarkt

Westermarkt, an open square in the shadow of the Westerkerk, possesses two evocative statues. Just to the south of the church entrance, by Prinsengracht, is a

△ Anne Frank statue

small but expressive **statue of Anne Frank** by the gifted Dutch sculptor Mari Andriessen (1897–1979), who was also the creator of the dockworker statue outside Amsterdam's Portuguese Synagogue (see p.102). The second piece, at the the back of the church, beside Keizersgracht, is the three pinkish granite triangles (one each for the past, present and future) of the **Homo Monument**. The world's first memorial to persecuted gays and lesbians, commemorating all those who died at the hands of the Nazis, it was designed by Karin Daan and recalls the pink triangles the Germans made homosexuals sew onto their clothes during World War II. The monument has become a focus for the city's gay community and the site of ceremonies and wreath-laying throughout the year, most notably on Queen's Day (April 30), Coming-Out Day (Sept 5) and World AIDS Day (Dec 1). The monument's inscription, by the Dutch writer Jacob Israel de Haan, translates as "Such an infinite desire for friendship".

Incidentally, the French philosopher **René Descartes** (1596–1650) once lodged at **Westermarkt 6**, a good-looking house with an attractive neck gable and fancy fanlight. Happy that the Dutch were indifferent to his musings – and that therefore he wasn't going to be persecuted – he wrote "Everybody except me is in business and so absorbed by profit-making I could spend my entire life here without being noticed by a soul". Descartes spent twenty years in the

Netherlands before accepting an invitation from Queen Christina to go to Stockholm in 1649. In the event, it was a poor choice: no sooner had he got there, than he caught pneumonia and died.

The Theatermuseum and Huis Bartolotti

A brief walk from the Westermarkt, past the curving neo–Gothic terraces of **Raadhuisstraat**, is the enjoyable **Theatermuseum**, at Herengracht 168 (Theatre Museum; Mon–Fri 11am–5pm, Sat & Sun 1–5pm; €4.50; ⊛www.tin.nl). The museum spreads over two floors with the upper level devoted to temporary exhibitions and the ground floor holding the permanent collection. The latter is divided into a sequence of very different displays: there is a small exhibition on the history of Dutch theatre, a larger and rather more inventive display on modern Dutch theatre featuring seminal stage sets and productions, and, most unusual of all, a so–called **Chamber Theatre** of 1781. Built for the domestic delight of one of the city's richest merchants, a certain Baron van Slingelandt, this miniature theatre – apparently the only one of its type to have survived in the whole of Europe – is equipped with a network of wooden handles hidden under the stage floor. By means of these handles, the scenery can be changed and simple special effects introduced – cloudy skies, rolling seas and so forth. Currently, visitors can't venture under the stage floor to have a go themselves, but there is a toy–town replica nearby and you can twiddle away here to your heart's content.

Just as interesting as the collection is the building itself, a Dutch Renaissance classic designed by **Philip Vingboons** (1607–1678), arguably the most talented architect involved in the creation of the Grachtengordel. The house was built for Michael de Pauw, a leading light in the East India Company in the 1630s, its fetching sandstone facade a suitably grand preamble to the foyer, which sports an extravagant painted ceiling of the *Four Seasons* by Jacob de Wit (1696–1754) as well as romantic wall paintings of rural Italy. There are fancily carved wooden doors too, a riot of flamboyant stucco work and a splendid spiral staircase.

Next door, **Huis Bartolotti**, at nos. 170–172, is a tad earlier and a good deal flashier, its imposing facade of red-brick and stone dotted with urns and columns, faces and shells. The house is an excellent illustration of the Dutch Renaissance style, and as such is much more ornate than the typical Amsterdam canal house. The architect was **Hendrick de Keyser** (see box below) with Willem van den Heuvel, a director of the West India Company, footing the bill. Heuvel inherited a fortune from his Italian uncle and changed his name in his honour to Bartolotti – hence the name of the house.

Hendrick de Keyser

Born in Utrecht, the son of a carpenter, **Hendrick de Keyser** (1565–1621) moved to Amsterdam in 1591. Initially employed as an apprentice sculptor, de Keyser soon ventured out on his own, speedily establishing himself as one of the city's most sought-after sculptor/architects. In 1595 he was appointed the city's official stone mason, becoming city architect too in 1612. His municipal commissions included three churches – the Zuiderkerk (see p.98), the Noorderkerk (see p.89) and the Westerkerk (see p.71) – and the upper storeys of the Munttoren (see p.62). His domestic designs were, however, more playful – or at least ornate – and it was here that he pioneered what is often called **Amsterdam Renaissance style**, in which Italianate decorative details – tympani, octagonal turrets, pilasters, pinnacles and arcading – were imposed on traditional Dutch design. The usual media were red brick and sandstone trimmings – as in the Huis Bartolotti.

South to the Houseboat Museum and the Felix Meritis building

Between Westermarkt and Leidsegracht, the main canals are intercepted by a trio of **cross streets**, which are themselves divided into shorter streets, mostly named after animals whose pelts were once used in the local tanning industry. There's Reestraat (Deer Street), Hartenstraat (Hart), Berenstraat (Bear) and Wolvenstraat (Wolf), not to mention Huidenstraat (Street of Hides) and Runstraat – a "run" being a bark used in tanning. The tanners are long gone and today the three are eminently appealing **shopping streets**, where you can buy everything from carpets to handmade chocolates, designer toothbrushes to beeswax candles.

△ Felix Meritis building

As for the main canals, the **Houseboat Museum** (March–Oct Tues–Sun 11am–5pm; Nov–Feb Fri–Sun 11am–5pm; €3; ⓦwww.houseboatmuseum.nl), opposite Prinsengracht 296, is an old Dutch houseboat of 1914 that doubles as a tourist attraction with a handful of explanatory plaques about life on the water. Some 3000 barges and houseboats are connected to the city's gas and electricity networks. They are regularly inspected and there are strict controls to ensure their numbers don't proliferate.

From the boat, it's one block east along Berenstraat to the **Felix Meritis building**, at Keizersgracht 324. A Neoclassical monolith of 1787, the mansion was built to house a science and arts society, which was the cultural focus of the city's upper crust for nearly one hundred years. Dutch cultural aspirations did not, however, impress everyone. It's said that when Napoleon visited the city the entire building was redecorated for his reception, only to have him stalk out in disgust, claiming that the place stank of tobacco. Oddly enough, it later became the headquarters of the Dutch Communist Party, but they sold it to the council who now lease it to the Felix Meritis Foundation (ⓦwww.felix.meritis .nl), which concentrates on the experimental and avant-garde arts.

Keizersgracht 321 and Hans Van Meegeren

On the other side of the canal, **Keizersgracht 321** is in itself fairly innocuous, but this was once the home of the Dutch art forger **Hans Van Meegeren** (1889–1947). During the German occupation of World War II, Meegeren sold a "previously unknown" Vermeer to a German art dealer working for Herman Goering. What neither the agent nor Goering realized was that Meegeren had painted it himself. A forger par excellence, Meegeren had developed a sophisticated ageing technique in the early 1930s. He mixed his paints with phenol formaldehyde resin dissolved in benzene and then baked the finished painting in an oven for several hours; the end result fooled everyone, including the curators of the Rijksmuseum, who had bought another "Vermeer" from him in 1941. Indeed, the forgeries may well have never been discovered but for a strange sequence of events. In May 1945 a British captain by the name of Harry Anderson discovered Meegeren's Vermeer in Goering's art collection. Meegeren was promptly arrested as a collaborator and, to get himself out of a pickle, Meegeren soon confessed to this and other forgeries. His reward was a short prison sentence, but he died before he was imprisoned.

Herengracht 361–369 and the Cromhouthuizen

Moving on, double back to cut across Wolvenstraat and turn right for **Herengracht 361–369**, a row of five houses, where you can compare and contrast the main types of **gable**: stepped at no. 361, bell at nos. 365 and 367 and finally neck at no. 369. Across the canal, at Herengracht 364–370, the graceful and commanding **Cromhouthuizen** consist of four matching stone mansions, frilled with tendrils, carved fruit and scrollwork, graced by dinky little bull's-eye windows and capped by elegant neck gables. Built in the 1660s for one of Amsterdam's wealthy merchant families, the Cromhouts, the houses were designed by **Philip Vingboons** (1607–1678), the most inventive of the architects who worked on the Grachtengordel during the city's expansion. As a Catholic, Vingboons was confined to private commissions, inconvenient no doubt, but at a time when Protestants and Catholics were at each other's

△ Herengracht houses

throats right across Europe, hardly insufferable. Two of the houses have been adapted to hold the Bijbels Museum.

The Bijbels Museum

The plush interiors of the Cromhouthuizen disappeared years ago, but the two that now hold the **Bijbels Museum** ("Bible Museum", Mon–Sat 10am–5pm, Sun 11am–5pm; €6; ⓦwww.bijbelsmuseum.nl), at Herengracht 366-368, do exhibit several decorative flourishes from their original function as homes for the wealthy. The pick are on the ground floor behind the entrance, and comprise a handsome spiral staircase and two painted ceilings of classical gods and goddesses by Jacob de Wit. You'll spot these at the end of a visit to the museum, which begins on Floor 3 (the top floor), reached via the lift at reception and featuring a large and detailed nineteenth-century model of the **Tabernacle**, the portable sanctuary in which the Israelites carried their holy of holies, the Ark of the Covenant. Attempts to reconstruct Biblical scenes were something of a cottage industry in the Netherlands in late 1800s, with scores of Dutch antiquarians beavering away, bible in one hand and modelling equipment in the other, but the creator of this particular model, a Protestant vicar by the name of **Leendert Schouten** (1828–1905), went one step further, making it his lifetime's work. It was a good move: Schouten became a well-known figure and his model proved a popular attraction, drawing hundreds of visitors to his home. Schouten also assembled a small but interesting collection of Middle Eastern archeological finds dating from the period when the Israelites were in exile in Egypt, and this is displayed on the third floor too.

Floor 2 warms to a similar theme, with the main exhibit being a large and detailed model of Jerusalem's Temple Mount made at the end of the nineteenth century when Palestine was part of the Ottoman Empire. There are yet more models on Floor 1, this time of the temples of David, Solomon and Herod, and finally there's an outstanding collection of **antique bibles** in the cellar. Although the exhibits are regularly rotated, there is a good chance you'll see the first Dutch-language bible ever printed, dating from 1477, plus a copy of the Statenvertaling, a seminal text in the development of Dutch Protestantism. Published in 1637, the Statenvertaling was the result of years of study by the country's leading scholars, who returned to the original Greek and Hebrew texts for this translation, which proved immensely popular.

Herengracht 380–394

The gracious symmetry of the Cromhouthuizen contrasts with the grandiose pretension of **Herengracht 380**, built in the style of a French château for a tobacco planter in 1889. Ornately dressed, the mansion's main gable is embellished with reclining figures and the bay window by cherubs, mythical characters and an abundance of acanthus leaves; it was the first house in the city to be supplied with electricity. Roughly opposite, across the canal, is the only spot in Amsterdam where the houses come straight out of the water, Venice-like, without the intervention of a pavement.

Keeping to the west side of the canal, **Herengracht 388** is another handsome Philip Vingboons building, whilst **Herengracht 394**, the narrow house with the bell gable at the corner of Leidsegracht, bears a distinctive **facade stone** that illustrates the legend of the four Aymon brothers, who are depicted astride their steed. The subject of a popular medieval *chanson*, the legend is all about honour, loyalty and friendship, dynastic quarrels and disputes. Picaresque in form, it doesn't really make much sense, but it revolves around the trials and tribulations of the horse. The clearest part of the tale is the end, where the redoubtable beast repeatedly breaks free from the millstones tied around its neck and refuses to drown. The third time it comes to the surface, the brothers walks away, no longer able to watch the agonies of their animal; assuming he's been abandoned, the horse cries out and promptly expires.

Leidsegracht

Herengracht 394 abuts the **Leidsegracht**, a mostly residential canal, lined with chic town houses and a medley of handsome gables. It's a tranquil scene – or at least it would be were it not for the flat-topped tour boats, who use the canal as a short cut, billowing out diesel fumes as they shunt into Prinsengracht. An eighteenth-century wine merchant by the name of Paling would have welcomed the sight of a boat, when he slipped into the Leidsegracht on a dark November evening. Well known as one of the greediest men in Amsterdam, he could apparently shovel down seven pounds of beef, a leg of lamb and thirty herrings in one sitting. He also liked his wine, a weakness that prompted his early demise when he fell – or staggered – into the canal.

Turn left off Leidsegracht for **Prinsengracht 681–693**, where an exquisite set of seven neck gables – one each for the provinces that broke away from the Habsburgs – comprises an especially harmonious ensemble that dates back to 1715. From here, it's the briefest of walks to Leidseplein and Leidsestraat (see pp.79–80).

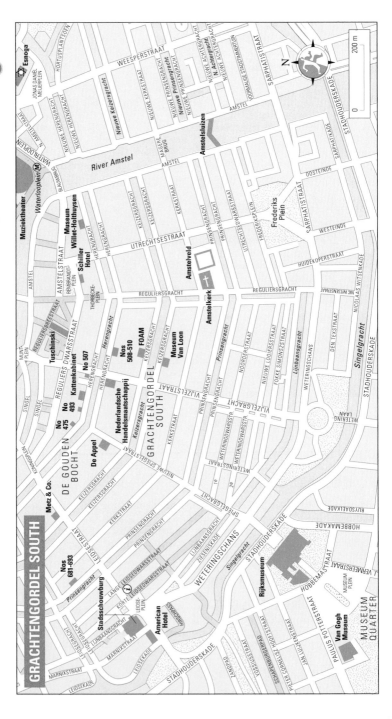

Grachtengordel south

The southern reaches of the Grachtengordel, **Grachtengordel south**, contain many of the city's proudest and most touted mansions, clustered along **De Gouden Bocht** – the Golden Bend – the curve of Herengracht between Leidsestraat and the River Amstel. It's on this stretch that the merchant elite abandoned the material modesty of their Calvinist forebears, indulging themselves with lavish mansions, whose fancy facades more than hinted at the wealth within. In the late seventeenth and eighteenth centuries, this elite forsook brick for stone and the restrained details of traditional Dutch architecture for an overblown Neoclassicism, their defeat of the Spanish Habsburgs, allied with their commercial success, prompting them to compare themselves with the Greeks and Romans. In the event, it was all an illusion – the bubble burst when Napoleon's army arrived in 1793 – and, although the opulent interiors of two old mansions, the **Museum Willet-Holthuysen** and the **Van Loon Museum**, still give the flavour of those heady days, for the most part all that's left – albeit a substantial legacy – are the wonderful facades.

Grachtengordel south also contains some rather less savoury areas, where ill-considered twentieth-century development has blemished the city – from the seediness of the **Rembrandtplein** to the mediocrity of Vijzelstraat and **Leidseplein**.

Leidseplein

Lying on the edge of the Grachtengordel, **Leidseplein** is the bustling hub of Amsterdam's nightlife, a rather cluttered and disorderly open space that has never had much character. The square once marked the end of the road in from Leiden and, as horse-drawn traffic was banned from the centre long ago, it was here that the Dutch left their horses and carts – a sort of equine car park. Today, it's quite the opposite: continual traffic made up of trams, bikes, cars and pedestrians gives the place a frenetic feel, and the surrounding side streets are jammed with bars, restaurants and clubs in a bright jumble of jutting signs and neon lights. It's not surprising, therefore, that on a good night Leidseplein can be Amsterdam at its carefree, exuberant best.

Leidseplein also contains two buildings of some architectural note. The first is the grandiose **Stadsschouwburg**, a neo-Renaissance edifice dating from 1894 which was so widely criticized for its clumsy vulgarity that the city council of the day temporarily withheld the money for decorating the exterior. Home to the National Ballet and Opera until the Muziektheater was completed on Waterlooplein in 1986, it is now used for theatre, dance and music performances. However, its most popular function is as the place where the Ajax football team gather on the balcony to wave to the crowds whenever they win anything – as they often do.

Close by, just off the square at Leidsekade 97, is the five-star **American Hotel**, or more properly the Crowne Plaza Amsterdam–American Hotel (see p.168). One of the city's oddest buildings, it's a monumental and slightly disconcerting rendering of Art Nouveau, with angular turrets, chunky dormer windows and fancy brickwork. Completed in 1902, the present structure takes its name from its demolished predecessor, which was – as the stylistic peccadillo of its architect, one W. Steinigeweg – decorated with statues and murals of North American scenes. Inside the present hotel is the *Café Americain*, once the fashionable haunt of Amsterdam's literati, but now a mainstream location for coffee and lunch. The

△ American Hotel

Art Nouveau decor is well worth a peek – an artful combination of stained glass, shallow arches and geometric patterned brickwork.

Leidsestraat and the Spiegelkwartier

Heading northeast from Leidseplein is **Leidsestraat**, one of Amsterdam's principal shopping streets – a long, slender gauntlet of fast food, fashion and shoe shops of little distinction. That said, **Metz & Co**, the department store (see "Shopping" p.223) at the junction with Keizersgracht, does occupy a good-looking stone building of 1891, complete with caryatids and fancy corner dome. At the time of its construction, it was the tallest commercial building in the city – one reason why the owners were able to entice **Gerrit Rietveld** (1888–1964), the leading architectural light of De Stijl, to add a rooftop glass and metal showroom in 1933. The showroom has survived and is now a café offering an attractive view over the city centre; perhaps surprisingly, Rietveld designed just one other building in Amsterdam – the Van Gogh Museum.

One block east of Metz & Co is Nieuwe Spiegelstraat, an appealing mixture of bookshops and corner cafés that extends south into Spiegelgracht to form the **Spiegelkwartier**. The district is home to the pricey end of Amsterdam's antiques trade and **De Appel**, a lively centre for contemporary art at Nieuwe Spiegelstraat 10 (Tues–Sun 11am–6pm; €2.50, ⓦwww.deappel.nl).

The Gouden Bocht

Nieuwe Spiegelstraat meets the elegant sweep of **Herengracht** near the west end of the so-called **De Gouden Bocht** (Golden Bend), where the canal is overlooked by a long sequence of double-fronted mansions, some of the most opulent dwellings in the city. Most of the houses here were extensively remodelled in the late seventeenth and eighteenth centuries. Characteristically, they have double stairways leading to the entrance, underneath which the small door was for the servants, whilst up above the majority are topped off by the ornamental cornices that were fashionable at the time. Classical references are common, both in form – pediments, columns and pilasters – and decoration, from scrolls and vases through to geometric patterns inspired by ancient Greece.

One of the first buildings to look out for on the north side of the canal – just across from (and to the west of) Nieuwe Spiegelstraat – is **Herengracht 475**, an extravagant stone mansion decorated with allegorical figures and surmounted by a slender balustrade. Typically, the original building was a much more modest affair, dating to the 1660s, but eighty years later the new owner took matters in hand to create the ornate facade of today. Just along the canal, **no. 493** is similarly grand, though here the building is polished off with an extravagantly carved pediment. Close by, **no. 497** is, by comparison, rather restrained, but the interior has been turned into the peculiar **Kattenkabinet** (Cats' Cabinet; Mon–Fri 10am–2pm, Sat & Sun 1–5pm; €4.50; ⓦwww.kattenkabinet.nl), an enormous collection of art and artefacts relating to cats. They were installed by a Dutch financier, whose cherished moggy, John Pierpont Morgan (named after the American financier), died in 1984; feline fanatics will be delighted. A hop, skip and a jump away, **Herengracht 507** is an especially handsome house, not too grand, its Neoclassical pilasters, pediment, mini-balcony and double-stairway nicely balanced by its slender windows. It was once the home of Jacob Boreel, the one-time mayor whose attempt to impose a burial tax prompted a riot during which the mob ransacked his house. Opposite, at the corner of Vijzelstraat, is the monumentally inappropriate **Nederlandsche Handelsmaatschappij**, a heavyweight structure with Expressionistic flourishes that dates back to 1923.

On the far side of Vijzelstraat, the facades of **Herengracht 508–510** are well worth a second look too, their neck gables, dating from the 1690s, sporting sea gods straddling dolphins and tritons – half-men, half-fish – trumpeting conch shells to pacify the oceans.

The Museum Willet-Holthuysen

The **Museum Willet-Holthuysen** (Mon–Fri 10am–5pm, Sat & Sun 11am–5pm; €4; ⓦwww.museumwilletholthuysen.nl), beyond Thorbeckeplein (see p.83) and near the Amstel at Herengracht 605, is billed as "a peep behind the curtains into an historic Amsterdam canal house", which just about sums it up. The house itself dates from 1685, but the interior was remodelled by successive members of the coal-trading Holthuysen family until the last of the line, Sandra Willet-Holthuysen, gifted her home and its contents to the city in 1895. Renovated a number of years ago, most of the public rooms, notably the **Blue Room** and the **Dining Room**, have been returned to their original eighteenth-century Rococo appearance – a flashy and ornate style copied from France, which the Dutch merchants held to be the epitome of refinement and good taste. The chandeliers are mostly gilded, heavy affairs, the plasterwork neat and fancy, and graceful drapes hang to either side of long and slender windows. The museum **entrance** is through the old servants' door, which leads into the basement – with the public rooms on the floor above. The basement holds the small collection of fine and applied arts that was assembled by Sandra's husband, Abraham Willet; its forte is glass, silver, majolica and ceramics, but there are also four finely carved ivory pieces depicting the elements. The basement gives access to the formal **gardens**, a neat pattern of miniature hedges graced by the occasional stone statue that lies at the back of the house.

The Amstel and the Magere Brug

Just beyond Willet-Holthuysen, Herengracht comes to an abrupt halt beside the wide and windy **River Amstel**, which was long the main trade route into the Dutch interior – goods arriving by barge and boat were traded for the imported materials held in Amsterdam's many warehouses. Turning left here takes you to the Blauwbrug (Blue Bridge) and the Old Jewish Quarter, whilst in the opposite direction is the **Magere Brug** (Skinny Bridge), the most famous and arguably the cutest of the city's many swing bridges. Legend has it that the current bridge, which dates back to about 1670, replaced an even older and skinnier version, originally built by two sisters who lived on either side of the river and were fed up with having to walk so far to see each other. From this bridge, it's a few metres further south along the Amstel to the **Amstel sluizen**, the Amstel locks. Every night, the municipal water department closes these locks to begin the process of sluicing out the canals. A huge pumping station on an island out to the east of the city then starts to pump fresh water from the IJsselmeer into the canal system; similar locks on the west side of the city are left open for the surplus to flow into the IJ and, from there, out to sea via the North Sea Canal. The city's canal water is thus refreshed every three nights – though, what with three centuries of prams, shopping trolleys and a few hundred rusty bikes, the water is only appealing as long as you're not actually in it.

To Reguliersgracht, the Museum Van Loon and FOAM

From the Amstel sluizen, head west along the north side of Prinsengracht and you soon reach the small open space of the **Amstelveld**, where youngsters gather to play football, with the plain seventeenth-century white wooden **Amstelkerk** occupying one of its corners. It's here also that Prinsengracht intersects with **Reguliersgracht**, perhaps the prettiest of the three surviving radial canals that cut across the Grachtengordel – its dainty humpback bridges and greening waters overlooked by charming seventeenth- and eighteenth-century canal houses.

Proceeding north up Reguliersgracht, turn left along Keizersgracht for the **Museum Van Loon**, at no. 672 (Fri–Mon 11am–5pm; e5; @www.musvloon .box.nl), which possesses the grandest accessible canal house interior in Amsterdam. Built in 1672, the first tenant of the property was the artist Ferdinand Bol, who married an exceedingly wealthy widow and promptly hung up his easel for the rest of his days. The last owners were the Van Loons, co-founders of the East India Company and long one of the city's leading families, who came something of a cropper at the end of World War II. In 1884, one of the family, Hendrik, purchased this house for his son, Willem (1855-1935), on the occasion of his marriage to Thora Egidius (1865–1945). Thora had friends and relatives in Germany and during the occupation she entertained them, unwisely considering that several of her guests were high-ranking Nazi officials. After the war, allegations of collaboration besmirched Thora's reputation and an embarrassed Queen Wilhelmina fired Thora as her *dame du palais*, a position she had held since 1898; Thora died two months later.

The **interior** of the house has been returned to its eighteenth-century appearance, though the fancy stucco work, wood panelling and colourful wallpaper of that period are overlaid by some later, gloomier decoration. Highlights include the ornate copper **balustrade** on the staircase, into which is worked the name "Van Hagen-Trip" (former owners of the house); the Van Loons later filled the spaces with the letters with fresh iron curlicues to prevent their children falling through. The top-floor landing has several pleasant Grisaille **paintings** sporting Roman figures and one of the bedrooms – the "painted room" – is decorated with a Romantic painting of Italy, depicting a coastal scene with overgrown classical ruins and diligent peasants – a favourite motif in Amsterdam from around 1750 to 1820. The oddest items are the **fake bedroom doors**: the eighteenth-century owners were so keen to avoid any lack of symmetry that they camouflaged the real bedroom doors and created imitation, decorative doors in the "correct" position instead. The other oddity is at the bottom of the garden, where the old **coach house** has *trompe l'oeil* windows: again, symmetry dictated that the building must have windows, but no self-respecting aristocrat wanted to be watched by his servants – hence the illusion.

Across the canal from the Van Loon Museum, at Keizersgracht 609, is **FOAM**, (Fotografiemuseum; Sat–Wed 10-5, Thurs & Fri 10am-9pm; €5; ⓦwww.foam .nl), which offers a lively programme of photographic exhibitions, many of which have a local (and modish) theme.

Thorbeckeplein, Rembrandtplein and Reguliersbreestraat

Returning to Reguliersgracht, it's a couple of minutes north to short and stumpy **Thorbeckeplein**, where a routine assortment of bars and restaurants flanks a statue of **Rudolf Thorbecke** (1798–1872), a far-sighted liberal politician and three times Dutch premier whose reforms served to democratize the country in the aftermath of the European-wide turmoil of 1848. Thorbeckeplein leads into **Rembrandtplein**, where the centre piece is a **statue** of Rembrandt, which lords it over a dishevelled bit of greenery. Previously the city's butter market, the square took its present name in 1876 and is now one of Amsterdam's nightlife centres, though its crowded restaurants and bars see many more tourists than Amsterdammers. Of the prodigious number of cafés and bars here, only the café of the *Schiller Hotel* at no. 26 stands out, with an original Art Deco interior somewhat reminiscent of an ocean liner.

Neither are the narrow streets edging Rembrandtplein exactly peaceful. The crumbling alleys to the north contain several of the city's raunchier gay bars, whilst **Reguliersbreestraat** is just supremely tacky. Nevertheless, tucked in among the slot-machine arcades, fast-food joints and sex shops, is the city's most extraordinary cinema – the **Tuschinski** at nos. 26–28 (see also p.215. Opened in 1921 by a Polish Jew, Abram Tuschinski, the cinema boasts a marvellously well-preserved Art Deco façade and interior, Expressionist paintings, coloured marbles and a wonderful carpet, handwoven in Marrakesh to an original design. Tuschinski himself died in Auschwitz in 1942. The network of alleys behind the Tuschinski was once known as **Duivelshoek** (Devil's Corner), and, although it's been tidied up and sanitized, enough backstreet seediness remains to make it a spot to be avoided late at night.

Reguliersbreestraat leads west to Muntplein, for more on which see p.62.

The Jordaan and the Westerdok

Lying to the west of the city centre, the **Jordaan** (pronounced "yoardarn") is a likeable and easily explored area of slender canals and narrow streets flanked by an agreeable mix of architectural styles, from modest, modern terraces to handsome seventeenth-century canal houses. Traditionally the home of Amsterdam's working class, with its boundaries clearly defined by the Prinsengracht to the east and the Lijnbaansgracht in the west, the Jordaan's character has been transformed in recent years by a middle-class influx, with the district now one of the city's most sought-after residential neighbourhoods. Before then, and indeed until the late 1970s, the Jordaan's inhabitants were primarily stevedores and factory workers, earning a crust amongst the docks, warehouses, factories and boat yards that extended north beyond **Brouwersgracht**, the Jordaan's northern boundary and nowadays one of Amsterdam's prettiest canals. Specific sights are, however, few and far between – the best you'll do is probably the **Noorderkerk** – but nonetheless it's still a pleasant area to wander in.

The pint-sized **Scheepvaartsbuurt** (Shipping Quarter), part of the city's old industrial belt and now a mixed shopping and residential quarter, edges the Jordaan to the north, falling to either side of Haarlemmerstraat and its continuation the Haarlemmerdijk. Just to the north lies the **Westerdok**, the oldest part of the sprawling complex of artificial islands that today sweeps along the south side of the River IJ, containing many of the city's maritime facilities. The Westerdok itself was dredged out of the river to provide extra warehousing and dock space in the seventeenth century. The maritime bustle has pretty much disappeared here, but, after a long period of neglect, the area is rapidly finding new life as a chichi residential quarter with smart apartments installed in its warehouses and its clutch of handsome canal houses revamped and reinvigorated, especially on **Zandhoek**. Finally, the working-class neighbourhood to the west of the Westerkanaal, which marks the limit of the Westerdok, is of interest for **Het Schip**, a wonderful example of the Amsterdam School of architecture and perhaps more importantly an example of social housing at its most optimistic.

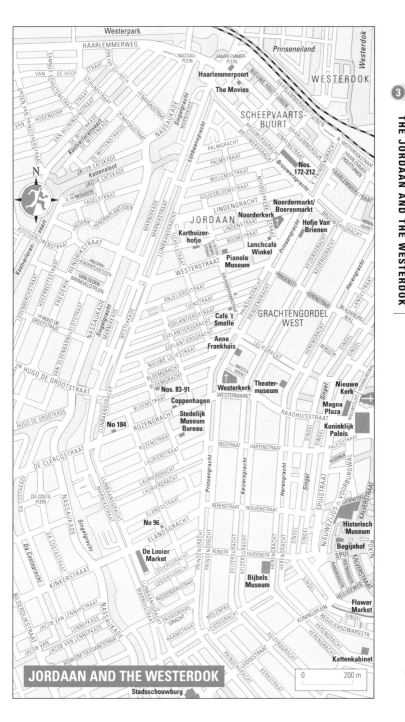

JORDAAN AND THE WESTERDOK

0   200 m

The Jordaan

In all probability the **Jordaan** takes its name from the French word *jardin* ("garden"), since the area's earliest settlers were Protestant Huguenots, who fled here to escape persecution in the sixteenth and seventeenth centuries. Another possibility is that it's a corruption of the Dutch word for Jews, *joden*. Whatever the truth, the Jordaan developed from open country – hence the number of streets and canals named after flowers and plants – into a refugee enclave, a teeming, cosmopolitan quarter beyond the pale of bourgeois respectability. Indeed, when the city fathers planned the expansion of the city in 1610, they made sure the Jordaan was kept outside the city boundaries. Consequently, the area was not subject to the rigorous planning restrictions of the main *grachten* – Herengracht, Keizersgracht and Prinsengracht – and its lattice of narrow streets followed the lines of the original polder drainage ditches rather than any municipal outline. This gives the district its distinctive, mazy layout, and much of its present appeal.

By the late nineteenth century, the Jordaan had become one of Amsterdam's toughest neighbourhoods, a stronghold of the city's industrial **working class**, mostly crowded together in cramped and unsanitary housing. Unsurprisingly, it was a highly politicized area, where protests against poor conditions were frequent, often coordinated by an influential and well-organized Communist Party. In the postwar period the slums were cleared or renovated, but rocketing property prices in the smarter parts of the city pushed middle-class professionals into the Jordaan from the early 1980s. This process of gentrification was at first much resented, but today the Jordaan is home to many young and affluent "alternative" Amsterdammers, who rub shoulders more or less affably with working-class Jordaaners with long-standing local roots.

Leidsegracht to Elandsgracht

The southern boundary of the Jordaan is generally deemed to be the **Leidsegracht**, though this is open to debate: according to dyed-in-the-wool locals the true Jordaaner is born within earshot of the Westerkerk bells, and you'd be hard-pushed to hear the chimes this far south. The narrow streets and canals just to the north of the Leidsegracht are routinely modern, but **Elandsgracht** does hold, at no.109, the enjoyable **De Looier antiques market** (daily except Fri 11am–5pm), which is good for picking up Dutch bygones including tiles and ceramics, with a few stalls dealing in particular items or styles such as silver trinkets or delftware. Footballophiles will also want to take a peek at the **sports shop** at Elandsgracht 96, where **Johan Cruyff** – star of Ajax in the 1970s and one of the greatest players of all time – bought his first pair of football boots.

The Jordaan's hofjes

One feature of the Jordaan's low-key architectural pleasures is its **hofjes** – almshouses built around a central courtyard and originally occupied by the city's elderly and needy. There were – and are – *hofjes* all over the city (most famously the Beginhof – see p.62), but there's a concentration here in the Jordaan. Most date back to the seventeenth or eighteenth centuries, but the majority have been rebuilt or at least revamped – and all are still lived in. The Jordaan's most diverting *hofje* is the **Karthuizerhofje**, on Karthuizersstraat (see p.89).

Elandsgracht to Rozengracht

The streets immediately to the north of Elandsgracht are unremarkable and easily the most agreeable route onwards is along the **Lijnbaansgracht** (Rope-walk Canal). This narrow canal threads its way round most of the city centre and here – in between Elandsgracht and Rozenstraat – it's cobbled and leafy, the lapping waters flanked by old brick buildings. On **Rozenstraat** itself, at no. 59, is an annexe of the Stedelijk Museum (see p.111), the **Stedelijk Museum Bureau** (Tues–Sun 11am–5pm; free; ❀www.smba.nl), which provides space for up-and-coming Amsterdam artists, with small-scale exhibitions, installations and occasional lectures and readings.

One block further north, **Rozengracht** lost its canal years ago and is now a busy main road of no particular distinction, though it was here at no. 184 that **Rembrandt** spent the last ten years of his life – a scrolled **plaque** distinguishes his old home. Rembrandt's last years were scarred by the death of his wife Hendrickje in 1663 and his son Titus five years later, but nevertheless it was in this period that he produced some of his finest work, including *The Return of the Prodigal Son*, which is displayed in the Hermitage, Leningrad. Also dated to these years is *The Jewish Bride*, a touchingly warm and heartfelt portrait of a bride and her father completed in 1668 and now in the Rijksmuseum. The other place of some interest hereabouts is **Coppenhagen**, a shop at Rozengracht 54, which is packed with every sort of bead imaginable – so much so that it has become something of an Amsterdam institution.

From Rozengracht, it's the shortest of walks to the Westerkerk and the Anne Frankhuis.

Rozengracht to Westerstraat

The streets and canals extending north from Rozengracht to Westerstraat form the heart of the Jordaan and hold the district's prettiest moments. Beyond Rozengracht, the first canal is the **Bloemgracht** (Flower Canal), a leafy water-way dotted with houseboats and arched by dinky little bridges, its network of cross streets sprinkled with cafés, bars and idiosyncratic shops. There's a warm, relaxed community atmosphere here which is really rather beguiling, not to mention a clutch of old and handsome canal houses. Pride of architectural place goes to **nos. 87–91** a sterling Renaissance building of 1642 complete with mullion windows, three crowstep gables, brightly painted shutters and distinc-tive facade stones, representing a *steeman* (city-dweller), *landman* (farmer) and a *seeman* (sailor). Next door, **nos. 83–85** were built a few decades later – two immaculately maintained canal houses adorned by the bottleneck gables typical of the period.

From Bloemgracht, it's a few metres north to the prettiness of **Egelantiers-gracht** (Rose-Hip Canal), where, at no. 12, the **Café 't Smalle** is one of Amsterdam's oldest cafés, opened in 1786 as a *proeflokaal* – a tasting house for the (long-gone) gin distillery next door. In the eighteenth century, when qual-ity control was partial to say the least, each batch of *jenever* (Dutch gin) could turn out very differently, so customers insisted on a taster before they splashed out. As a result, each distillery ran a *proeflokaal* offering free samples, and this is a rare survivor. The café's waterside terrace remains an especially pleasant spot to take a tipple (see p.184).

A narrow cross street – 1e Egelantiersdwarsstraat and its continuation 1e Tuindwarsstraat and 1e Anjeliersdwarsstraat – runs north from Bloemgracht to workaday **Westerstraat**, a busy thoroughfare, which is home to the small but

△ Bloemgracht houses

fascinating **Pianola Museum** (Sun 11.30am–5.30pm; €4; ⓦwww.pianola.nl), at no. 106, whose collection of pianolas and automatic music-machines dates from the beginning of the twentieth century. Fifteen have been restored to working order. These machines, which work on rolls of perforated paper, were the jukeboxes of their day, and the museum has a vast collection of 15,000 rolls of music, some of which were "recorded" by famous pianists and composers – Gershwin, Debussy, Scott Joplin, Art Tatum and others. The museum runs a programme of pianola music concerts throughout the year (except July/Aug), where the rolls are played back on restored machines (exact times are listed on their website). Nearby, and also of some interest, is the largest of the Jordaan's *hofjes*, the **Karthuizerhofje**, Karthuizersstraat 89–171, a substantial courtyard complex established as a widows' hospice in the middle of the seventeenth century, though the present buildings are much later.

The Noorderkerk and the Noordermarkt

At the east end of Westerstraat, overlooking the Prinsengracht, is Hendrik de Keyser's **Noorderkerk** (March–Nov Sat 11am–1pm; free), the architect's last creation and probably his least successful, finished two years after his death in 1623. A bulky, overbearing brick building, it represented a radical departure from the conventional church designs of the time, having a symmetrical Greek cross floor plan, with four equally proportioned arms radiating out from a steepled centre. Uncompromisingly dour, it proclaimed the serious intent of the Calvinists who worshipped here in so far as the pulpit – and therefore the preacher – was at the centre and not at the front of the church, a symbolic break with the Catholic past. Nevertheless, it's still hard to understand quite how Keyser, who designed such elegant structures as the Westerkerk, could have ended up designing this.

The **Noordermarkt**, the somewhat inconclusive square outside the church, holds a **statue** of three figures bound to each other, a poignant tribute to the bloody Jordaanoproer riot of 1934, part of a successful campaign to stop the government cutting unemployment benefit during the Depression; you'll find the statue just in front of the church's west door. The inscription reads "The strongest chains are those of unity". The church also boasts a **plaque** honouring those Communists and Jews who were rounded up here by the Germans in February 1941. More cheerfully, the square hosts two of Amsterdam's best open-air **markets** (see p.230). There's an antiques and general household goods market on Monday mornings (9am–1pm) plus a popular Saturday farmers' market, the **Boerenmarkt** (9am–3pm), a lively affair with organic fruit and vegetables, freshly baked breads and a plethora of oils and spices for sale. Cross an unmarked border though, and you'll find yourself in the middle of a Saturday bird market, which operates on an adjacent patch at much the same time, and, if you're at all squeamish, is best avoided – the brightly coloured birds squeezed into tiny cages are not for everyone. Incidentally, the *Lunchcafé Winkel*, beside the Noordermarkt at the corner with Westerstraat, sells huge wedges of home-made **apple pie**, which many Jordaaners swear is the best in town.

The Lindengracht and Brouwersgracht

Just to the north of the Noorderkerk, the **Lindengracht** ("Canal of Limes") lost its waterway decades ago, but has had a prominent role in local folklore since the day in 1886 when a policeman made an ill-advised attempt to stop an eel-pulling contest. Horrible as it sounds, **eel-pulling** was a popular pastime hereabouts: a live eel, preferably smeared in soap to make the entertainment last a little longer, was suspended from a rope strung across a canal. Teams took to their boats and tried to pull the poor creature off the rope, the fun being who would end up in the water; the winner came away with the eel – or at least a good piece of it. In 1886, the crowd unceremoniously bundled the policeman away, but when reinforcements arrived, the whole thing got out of hand and there was a full-scale **riot** – the Paling-Oproer ("Eel Uprising") – which lasted for three days and cost 26 lives.

The east end of the Lindengracht intersects with leafy **Brouwersgracht**, which marks the northerly limit of both the Jordaan and the Grachtengordel (see Chapter Two). In the seventeenth century, Brouwersgracht lay at the edge of Amsterdam's great harbour, one of the major arteries linking the open sea with the city centre. Thronged by vessels returning from – or heading off to – every corner of the globe, it was lined with storage depots and warehouses. Breweries flourished here too – hence its name – capitalizing on their ready access to shipments of fresh water. Today, the harbour bustle has moved way out of the city centre to the northwest, and the **warehouses**, with their distinctive spout-neck gables and shuttered windows, formerly used for the delivery and dispatch of goods by pulley from the canal below, have been converted into apartments, some of the most expensive in the city. There is an especially fine, uninterrupted row of these warehouses at **Brouwersgracht 172–212**, across the canal from the Lindengracht. You'll also find handsome merchants' houses on the Brouwersgracht, as well as moored houseboats and a string of quaint little swing bridges, making it altogether one of the most classically picturesque canals in the whole of the city.

The Scheepvaartsbuurt and the Westerdok

Brouwersgracht is also the southern boundary of the **Scheepvaartsbuurt** – the Shipping Quarter – an unassuming neighbourhood which focuses on **Haarlemmerstraat** and its continuation **Haarlemmerdijk**, a long, rather ordinary thoroughfare lined with bars, cafés and food shops. In the eighteenth and nineteenth centuries, this district boomed from its location between the Brouwersgracht and the **Westerdok**, a narrow parcel of land dredged out of the River IJ immediately to the north and equipped with docks, warehouses and shipyards. The construction of these artificial islands took the pressure off Amsterdam's congested maritime facilities and was necessary to sustain the city's economic success. Stretching from the Westerdok to the Oosterdok, Amsterdam's riverside wharves functioned as the heartbeat of the city until the city's shipping facilities began to move away from the centre, a process accelerated by the construction of Centraal Station, slap in the middle of the old quayside in the 1880s. The Westerdok hung on to some of the marine trade until the 1960s, but today – bar the odd small boatyard – industry has to all intents and purposes disappeared and the area is busy reinventing itself. There is still a vague air of faded grittiness here, but the old forgotten warehouses – within walking distance of the centre – are rapidly being turned into bijou studios and dozens of plant-filled houseboats are moored alongside the tiny streets.

Haarlemmerdijk and the Haarlemmerpoort

Before World War II the **Haarlemmerstraat** and its westerly extension, the **Haarlemmerdijk**, was a congested thoroughfare, but the trams that once ran here were rerouted and now it's a pleasant if unremarkable pedestrianized strip flanked by shops and cafés. The only architectural high point is the meticulously restored Art Deco interior of **The Movies** cinema (see p.214), near the west end of the street at Haarlemmerdijk 161. Just metres away, the busy Haarlemmerplein traffic junction sports the grandiose Neoclassical **Haarlemmerpoort**, built on the site of a medieval gateway in 1840 for the new king

△ Brouwersgracht

William II's triumphal entry into the city. The euphoria didn't last long. William was a distinguished general, who had been wounded at Waterloo, but as a king he proved much too crusty and reactionary to be popular, only accepting mild liberal reforms after extensive rioting in Amsterdam and elsewhere.

The Westerdok

Proceeding north from the near (east) side of the Haarlemmerpoort, walk through the tunnel beneath the railway lines and then turn right along Sloterdijkstraat, which soon crosses the canal over onto **Galgenstraat** (Gallows Street), once the sight of the municipal gallows, which were clearly visible to passing ships – to discourage potential law-breakers. Galgenstraat bisects the smallest of the Westerdok islands, pint-sized **Prinseneiland**, a pleasing mix of houseboats, former warehouses and old canal houses, guarded by a pair of dinky little bridges.

Keep going straight along Galgenstraat, over the next canal, and then turn north up Grote Bickersstraat for the bridge over to another Westerdok island, **Realeneiland**, whose houseboats, ex-warehouses and mini-boatyards give it a distinctly nautical flavour. On the island, tiny **Zandhoek** once offered an uninterrupted view over the harbour and was long a favourite with the city's sea captains, who constructed a clutch of fine old canal houses here in the seventeenth and eighteenth centuries. A number of them have survived and several are decorated with distinctive facade stones, including **De Gouden Reael**, at no.14, whose stone sports a gold coin. Before Napoleon introduced a system of house numbers, these stones were the principal way that visitors could recognize one house from another, and many homeowners went to considerable lengths to make theirs unique. Jacob Real, the Catholic tradesman who owned this particular house, also used the image of a *real* – a Spanish coin – to discreetly advertise his sympathies for the Catholic Habsburgs.

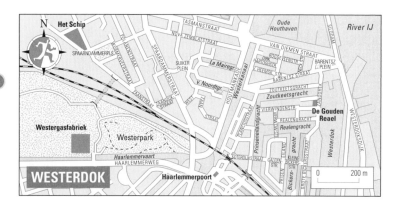

At the top of Zandhoek, cross over the canal and then turn left along Zout-keetsgracht; another left turn, this time onto Planciusstraat, returns you to the pedestrian tunnel near the Haarlemmerpoort.

Westerpark and Het Schip

Heading west from the Haarlemmerpoort along the main road, cross the canal, take the first right turn and on the other side of the road you'll come to the east entrance to the **Westerpark**, one of the city's smaller and more enticing parks, running alongside a narrow sliver of a canal. At the far end of the park you bump into the old gas factory, the **Westergasfabriek**, a sprawling jumble of neo-Gothic buildings dating from the 1880s. Currently being developed as a leisure complex, it had a brief reincarnation as the city's prime venue for Acid House parties in the early 1990s.

On the north side of the park, about halfway along, a pedestrian tunnel leads under the railway lines to **Zaanstraat**, the southern edge of a working-class neighbourhood that stretches north to the busy Spaarndammer Dijk boulevard. Taken as a whole, this part of the city is really rather glum, but hang a left on Zaanstraat and you soon reach Spaarndammerplantsoen, the site of **Het Schip**, a municipal housing block which is a splendid – and pristine – example of the Expressionistic Amsterdam School of architecture. Seven years in the making, from 1913 to 1920, the complex takes its name from its ship-like shape and is graced by all manner of fetching decorative details – from the funnel-like main tower and the intriguing mix-and-match windows through to the sweeping brick facades and balconies. The architect responsible was **Michael de Klerk** (1884–1923), who also designed the two other housing blocks on Spaarndammerplantsoen, though Het Schip is easily the most striking. De Klerk reacted strongly against the influence of Berlage, whose style – exemplified by the Beurs – favoured clean lines and functionality, opting instead for much more playful motifs. De Klerk also installed a post office in Het Schip and this, with its superb multicoloured tiling, now serves as the **Museum Het Schip** (Thurs–Sun 1–5pm; €5; @www.hetschip.nl), which looks at the living conditions of the city's proletariat at the start of the twentieth century, relating it to the history of the Amsterdam School. Politically motivated, De Klerk and his architectural allies were eager to provide high-quality homes for the working class, though their laudable aims were often undermined – or at least diluted

△ Het Schip

- by a tendency to over-elaborate. For details of De Klerk's other major commission in Amsterdam, the De Dageraad housing project, see p000.

Het Schip is at the terminus of **bus** #22, which will whisk you back to Centraal Station in no time at all.

The Old Jewish Quarter and eastern docks

Originally one of the marshiest parts of Amsterdam, the narrow slab of land between the curve of the River Amstel, Kloveniersburgwal and the Nieuwe Herengracht was the home of Amsterdam's Jews from the sixteenth century up until World War II. By the 1920s, this Old Jewish Quarter, aka the **Jodenhoek** (pronounced "yo-den-hook", "Jews' Corner"), had become one of the busiest parts of town, crowded with tenement buildings and smoking factories, its main streets holding scores of open-air stalls, selling everything from pickled herrings to pots and pans. The war put paid to all this and in 1945 it lay derelict – and neither has postwar redevelopment treated it kindly. Its focal point, **Waterlooplein**, has been overwhelmed by a domineering town and concert hall complex, which caused much controversy at the time of its construction, and the once-bustling Jodenbreestraat is now bleak and very ordinary, with **Mr Visserplein**, at its east end, one of the city's busiest traffic junctions. Picking your way round these obstacles is not much fun, but persevere – amongst all the cars and concrete are several moving reminders of the Jewish community that perished in the war. For reasons that remain unclear, the Germans did not destroy all the Jodenhoek's synagogues, and the late seventeenth-century **Esnoga** (Portuguese synagogue) is one of the finest buildings in the city. Close by, four other synagogues have been merged into the fascinating **Joods Historisch Museum** (Jewish Historical Museum), celebrating Jewish culture and custom. As a footnote, Rembrandt spent the best years of his life living in the Jodenhoek and the restored **Het Rembrandthuis** (Rembrandt House) contains a large collection of his etchings.

Immediately to the east of the Old Jewish Quarter lies the **Plantagebuurt**, a well–heeled residential area that's home to the city's botanical gardens, the **Hortus Botanicus**, as well as the **Artis Zoo** (see p.106), the excellent **Verzetsmuseum** (Dutch Resistance Museum), and, just to the west, **Hermitage Amsterdam**, a brand new gallery which is used for lavish temporary exhibitions of fine and applied art on loan from the Hermitage Museum in St Petersburg. From the Plantagebuurt it's a short hop north to the reclaimed islands of the **Oosterdok** (East Dock), dredged out of the River IJ to accommodate warehouses and docks in the seventeenth century. The Oosterdok's nautical heyday is recalled by the **Nederlands Scheepvaartmuseum** (Netherlands Maritime Museum), whilst the old railway yards to the east of Centraal station along **Oosterdokskade** are in the throes of a huge development, with the old postal sorting office now holding – at least for the next year or two – the modern and contemporary art of the **Stedelijk Museum.** The Oosterdok once formed part of a vast maritime complex that spread right along the River IJ, from the Westerdok (see p.91) east to the clutter of nineteenth–century artificial islands that comprise **Zeeburg**. Industrial decline set in during the 1880s, but Zeeburg is currently being redefined as residential and leisure district, featuring funky bars, some startling modern architecture and a several award–winning, prestige buildings.

The Old Jewish Quarter

Throughout the nineteenth century and up until the German occupation, the **Old Jewish Quarter** – the Jodenhoek – was a hive of activity, its main streets lined with shops and jam–packed with open-air stalls, where Jews and Gentiles traded in earnest. Fatefully, it was also surrounded by canals and it was these the Germans exploited to create the ghetto that foreshadowed their policy of starvation and deportation. They restricted movement in and out of the quarter by raising most of the swing bridges (over the Nieuwe Herengracht, the Amstel and the Kloveniersburgwal) and imposing stringent controls on every other access route. The Jews, readily identifiable by the yellow Stars of David they were obliged to wear, were not allowed to use public transport, ride bicycles or own telephones, and were placed under a rigorously imposed curfew. Meanwhile, roundups and deportations had begun shortly after the Germans arrived and continued into 1945. At the end of the war, the Jodenhoek was deserted and, as the need for wood and raw materials intensified in the cold winter that followed, many of the houses were dismantled for fuel. The Jodenhoek remained a neglected corner of the city well into the 1970s when the battered remains took another hit with the large–scale demolition that preceded the sinking of the metro beneath Waterlooplein. By these means, the prewar Jodenhoek disappeared almost without trace, the notable exception being the imposing **Esnoga** (Portuguese Synagogue) and the four connected synagogues of the Ashkenazi Jews, now the **Joods Historisch Museum**. The district's other main sight is **Het Rembrandthuis**, which holds an outstanding collection of the artist's etchings.

St Antoniesbreestraat

Stretching south from the Nieuwmarkt (see p.57), **St Antoniesbreestraat** once linked the city centre with the Jewish quarter, but its huddle of shops and houses was mostly demolished in the 1980s to make way for a main road. The plan was subsequently abandoned, but the modern buildings that now line most of the street hardly fire the soul, even if the modern symmetries – and cubist, coloured panels – of the apartment blocks that spill along part of the street are at least visually arresting. One of the few survivors of all these municipal shenanigans is the **Pintohuis** (Pinto House; Mon & Wed 2–8pm, Fri 2–5pm, Sat 11am–4pm; free), at no. 69, which is now a public library. Easily spotted by its off-white Italianate facade, the mansion is named after Isaac de Pinto, a Jew who fled Portugal to escape the Inquisition and subsequently became a founder of the East India Company (see p.108). Pinto bought this property in 1651 and promptly had it remodelled in grand style, the facade interrupted by

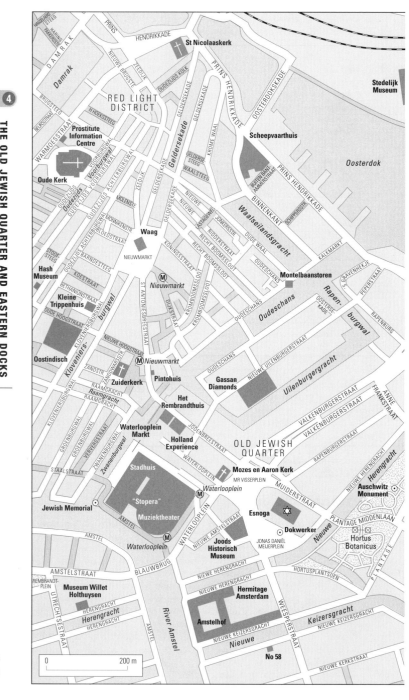

PIET HEINKADE

DIJKSGRACHT

NEMO

N

OOSTERDOK

Oosterdok

De Amsterdam

Nederlands
Scheepvaart-
museum

ARCAM

PRINS HENDRIKKADE

FOELIESTRAAT

NIEUWE FOELIEDWARS-
STRAAT

RAPENBURG

RAPENBURGER-
PLEIN

SCHIPPERSGRACHT

KADIJKSPLEIN

HOOGTE KADIJK

Dutch East India
Compound

LAAGTE KADIJK

ENTREPOTDOK

Wertheim-
park

PLANTAGEKADE

PLANTAGE DOKLAAN

PARKLAAN

Vakbondsmuseum

HENRI POLAKLAAN

Verzetsmuseum

PLANTAGEBUURT

KERKLAAN

Artis Zoo

De Hollandsche
Schouwburg

PLANTAGE

PLANTAGE

PLANTAGE MIDDENLAAN

ROETERSSTRAAT

Plantage Muidergracht

PLANTAGE WESTERMANLAAN

PLANTAGE MUIDERGRACHT

PLAN TEPELLAAN

NIEUWE PRINSENGRACHT

KATTENBURGERSTRAAT

BLUKERGRACHTSTR

OLIFANTSWERF

KATTENBURGERKADE

Kattenburgervaart

KATTENBURGERKADE

BIJLMESPAD

KATTENBURGER-
PLEIN

KATTENBURGERGRACHT

Nieuwevaart

NIEUWEVAART

WITTENBURGERKADE

GROTE WITTENBURGERSTRAAT

KLEINE
WITTENBURGERSTRAAT

PAREL STRAAT

KLEINE
STRAAT

POOLSTR

WAAIGAT

WITTENBURGERGRACHT

OVERHAALSGANG

Entrepotdok

ENTREPOTDOK

Museum Werf
't Kromhout

HOOGTE KADIJK

SARPHATISTRAAT

▶ De Gooyer Windmill

six lofty pilasters, which lead the eye up to the blind balustrade. The mansion was the talk of the town, even more so when Pinto had the interior painted in a similar style to the front – pop in to look at the birds and cherubs of the original painted ceiling.

Across the street, through the old archway, the **Zuiderkerk** (Mon 11am–4pm, Tues–Fri 9am–4pm, Sat noon–4pm; free), dating from 1611, was the first Amsterdam church built specifically for the Protestants. It was designed by the prolific architect and sculptor, Hendrick de Keyser (1565–1621), whose distinctive – and very popular – style extrapolated elements of traditional Flemish design, with fanciful detail and frilly towers added wherever possible. The basic design of the Zuiderkerk is firmly Gothic, but the soaring tower is typical of his work, complete with balconies and balustrades, arches, urns and columns. Now deconsecrated, the church has itself been turned into a municipal information centre with displays on housing and the environment, plus temporary exhibitions revealing the city council's future plans. The **tower**, which has a separate entrance, can be climbed during the summer (June–Sept Wed–Sat 2–4pm; €3) and from the top there are wide views over the city centre.

Jodenbreestraat and Het Rembrandthuis

St Antoniesbreestraat runs into **Jodenbreestraat**, the "Broad Street of the Jews", at one time the main centre of Jewish activity. Badly served by postwar development, this ancient thoroughfare is now short on charm, but in these unlikely surroundings, at no. 6, stands **Het Rembrandthuis** (Rembrandt House; Mon–Sat 10am–5pm, Sun and public holidays 11am–5pm; €7.50; ⓦwww .rembrandthuis.nl), an intriguing building whose intricate facade is decorated by pretty wooden shutters and a dinky pediment. Rembrandt bought this house at the height of his fame and popularity, living here for over twenty years and spending a fortune on furnishings – an expense that ultimately contributed to his bankruptcy (see box, p.121). An inventory made at the time details the huge collection of paintings, sculptures and art treasures he'd amassed, almost all of which was confiscated after he was declared insolvent and forced to move to a more modest house on Rozengracht in the Jordaan in 1658. The city council bought the Jodenbreestraat house in 1907 and has revamped the premises on several occasions, most recently in 1999.

A visit begins in the modern annexe, but you're soon into Rembrandt's old house, where a string of **period rooms** have been returned to something of their appearance when the artist lived here – the reconstruction being based on the inventory. The period furniture is enjoyable enough, especially the two dinky box-beds, and the great man's studio is surprisingly large and well-lit, but the paintings that adorn the walls are mostly second-rate and none of them Rembrandts. The most interesting paintings are those by Rembrandt's master in Amsterdam, Pieter Lastman (1583–1633) – not because of their quality, but rather because their sheer mawkishness demonstrates just how far Rembrandt towered above his artistic milieu. More positively, two rooms beyond the period rooms hold an extensive collection of **Rembrandt's etchings** as well as several of the original copper plates on which he worked. The biblical illustrations attract the most attention, though the studies of tramps and vagabonds are equally appealing. Beyond, two further rooms are used for well-judged temporary displays of **prints**, usually – but not exclusively – by Dutch artists. To see any of Rembrandt's paintings, however, you'll have to go to the Rijksmuseum.

△ Rembrandthuis

Holland Experience and Gassan Diamonds

Next door to Het Rembrandthuis, the multimedia **Holland Experience** (daily 10am–6pm; €8.50, under-16s & over-65s €7.25; @www.holland -experience.nl) is a kind of sensory-bombardment movie about the Netherlands, with synchronized smells and a moving floor – not to mention the special 3D glasses. The experience lasts thirty minutes and is (allegedly) popular with young kids. From here, it's a couple of minutes' walk to the **Gassan Diamonds** factory (frequent guided tours daily 9am–5pm; free; @www.gassandiamonds .com), which occupies a large and imposing brick building dating from 1897 on Nieuwe Uilenburgerstraat. Before World War II, many local Jews worked as diamond cutters and polishers, though there's little sign of the industry here today, Gassan being the main exception. Traditionally, the city's diamond workers were poorly paid and endured foul working conditions, but all this changed after the creation of the Diamond Workers' Association, the ANDB, at the end of the nineteenth century. Unionised, the diamond workers transformed their pay and conditions, becoming the vanguard of the working class under the leadership of the socialist rabbi **Henri Polak** (1868–1943). The ANDB also pushed education and did more to integrate the city's Jews into the mainstream than any other organisation; predictably, the Germans made short work of the union during the occupation. **Tours** of the Gassan factory include a visit to the cutting and polishing areas as well as a gambol round the diamond jewellery showroom; there is also a Royal Delftware gift shop in the factory compound, just outside the main doors.

④

From the late sixteenth century onwards, Amsterdam was the refuge of Jews escaping persecution throughout the rest of Europe. The **Union of Utrecht**, ratified in 1579, signalled the start of the influx. Drawn up by the largely Protestant northern Dutch provinces in response to the invading Spanish army, the treaty combined the United Provinces (later to become the Netherlands) in a loose federation, whose wheels could only be greased by a degree of religious toleration then unknown elsewhere across the Continent. Whatever the Protestants may have wanted, they knew that the Catholic minority (around 35 percent) would only continue to support the rebellion against the Spanish Habsburgs if they were treated well – the Jews benefited by osmosis and consequently immigrated here in their hundreds.

This **toleration** did, however, have its limits: Jewish immigrants were forced to buy citizenship; Christian-Jewish marriages were illegal; and, as with the Catholics, they were only allowed to practise their religion discreetly behind closed doors. A proclamation in 1632 also excluded them from most guilds – effectively withdrawing their right to own and run businesses. This forced them to either excel in those trades not governed by the guilds or introduce new non-guild trades into the city. Nonetheless, by the middle of the eighteenth century the city's Jewish community was active in almost every aspect of the economy, especially in bookselling, tobacco, banking and commodity futures.

The first major Jewish influx was of **Sephardic** Jews from Spain and Portugal, where persecution had begun in earnest in 1492 and continued throughout the sixteenth century. In the 1630s the Sephardim were joined in Amsterdam by hundreds of (much poorer) **Ashkenazi** Jews from German-speaking central Europe. The two groups established separate synagogues and, although there was no ghetto as such, the vast majority settled on and around what is now Waterlooplein, then a distinctly unhealthy tract of low–lying land that was subject to regular flooding by the River Amstel. Initially known as **Vlooyenburg**, this district was usually referred to as the **Jodenhoek**, or "Jews' Corner", though this was not, generally speaking, a pejorative term and neither did the Dutch eschew living here: Rembrandt, for instance, was quite happy to take up residence and frequently painted his Jewish neighbours. Indeed, given the time, the most extraordinary feature of Jewish settlement in Amsterdam was that it occasioned mild curiosity rather than outright hate, as evinced by contemporary prints of Jewish religious customs, where there is neither any hint of stereotype nor discernible demonization.

The restrictions affecting both Jews and Catholics were removed during **Napoleon**'s occupation of the United Provinces, when the country was temporarily renamed the Batavian Republic (1795–1806). Freed from official discrimination, Amsterdam's Jewish community flourished and the Jewish Quarter expanded, nudging northwest towards Nieuwmarkt and east across Nieuwe Herengracht, though this was just the focus of a community whose members lived in every part of the city. In 1882 the dilapidated houses of the Jodenhoek were razed and several minor canals filled in to make way for **Waterlooplein**, which became a largely Jewish marketplace, a bustling affair that sprawled out along St Antoniesbreestraat and Jodenbreestraat.

At the turn of the twentieth century, there were around 60,000 Jews living in Amsterdam, but **refugees** from Hitler's Germany swelled this figure to around 120,000 in the 1930s. The disaster that befell this community during the **German occupation** is hard to conceive, but the bald facts speak for themselves: when Amsterdam was liberated, there were only 5000 Jews left and the Jodenhoek was, to all intents and purposes, a ghost town. At present, there are about 25,000 Jews resident in – and spread out across – the city, but while Jewish life in Amsterdam has survived, its heyday is gone forever.

Waterlooplein

Jodenbreestraat runs parallel to the **Stadhuis en Muziektheater** (Town Hall and Concert Hall), a sprawling complex whose indeterminate modernity dominates **Waterlooplein**, a rectangular parcel of land that was originally swampy marsh. This was the site of the first Jewish Quarter, but by the late nineteenth century it had become an insanitary slum, home to the poorest of the Ashkenazi Jews. The slums were cleared in the 1880s and thereafter the Waterlooplein and its open–air market became the centre of Jewish life in the city. In the war, the Germans used the square to round up their victims, but despite these ugly connotations the Waterlooplein was revived in the 1950s as the site of the city's main **flea market** and remains so to this day (Mon–Sat 9am–5pm; see also p.230), albeit a much smaller affair. The market's reappearance was, as far as the city council was concerned, only a stopgap while they mulled over plans to entirely reinvent the depopulated Jodenhoek; for starters, whole streets were demolished to make way for the motorist – with Mr Visserplein (see below), for example, becoming little more than a traffic intersection – and then, warming to their theme in the late 1970s, the council announced the building of a massive new Waterlooplein concert-and-city-hall complex. Opposition was immediate and widespread, but attempts to prevent the building failed, and the Muziektheater opened in 1986, since when it has established an international reputation for the quality of its performances (see above). One of the story's abiding ironies is that the title of the protest campaign – "**Stopera**" – has passed into common usage to describe the complex.

Inside, amidst all the jaded concrete, there are a couple of minor attractions, beginning with the **glass columns** in the glass-roofed public passageway towards the rear of the complex. These give a salutary lesson on the fragility of the Netherlands: two contain water indicating the sea levels at high and low tide in the Dutch towns of Vlissingen and IJmuiden, while another records the levels experienced during the 1953 flood disaster (way above head height). Down the stairs, a concrete pile shows what is known as "Normal Amsterdam Level" (NAP), originally calculated in 1684 as the average water level in the River IJ and still the basis for measuring altitude above sea level across Europe. Metres away, in the foyer of the Muziektheater, is a forceful and inventive **memorial** to the district's Jews, in which a bronze violinist bursts through the floor tiles. Outside, at the very tip of Waterlooplein, where the River Amstel meets the Zwanenburgwal canal, there is another memorial – a black stone tribute to the dead of the Jewish resistance; the inscription from Jeremiah translates as "If my eyes were a well of tears, I would cry day and night for the fallen fighters of my beloved people."

Mr Visserplein

Just behind the Muziektheater, on the corner of Mr Visserplein, is the **Mozes en Aaron Kerk**, a rather glum Neoclassical structure built on the site of a clandestine Catholic church in the 1840s. It takes its unusual name from a pair of facade stones bearing effigies of the two prophets that decorated the earlier building. Earlier still, the site was occupied by the house where the philosopher and theologian **Spinoza** was born in 1632. Of Sephardic descent, Spinoza's pantheistic views soon brought him into conflict with the elders of the Jewish community. At the age of 23, he was excommunicated and forced out of the city, moving into a small village where he survived by grinding lenses. After an attempt on his life, Spinoza moved again, eventually ending up in The Hague, where his free-thinking ways proved more acceptable. He produced his most famous treatise, *Ethics Demonstrated in the Geometrical Order*, in 1674, three years before his death.

Next door to the church, **Mr Visserplein** is a busy junction for traffic speeding towards the IJ tunnel. It takes its name from **Lodewijk Ernst Visser** (1871–1942), President of the Supreme Court of the Netherlands in 1939. He was dismissed the following year when the Germans occupied the country, and became an active member of the Jewish resistance, working for the illegal underground newspaper *Het Parool* ("The Password") and refusing to wear the yellow Star of David. He vehemently opposed the Nazi–appointed Judenrat (Jewish Council), publicly – and famously – denouncing all forms of collaboration and arguing that the Dutch government should take responsibility for all Dutch citizens, Jew and Gentile alike. Visser died from a heart attack shortly after he was threatened with deportation to a concentration camp.

The Esnoga

Unmissable on the corner of Mr Visserplein is the brown and bulky brickwork of the **Esnoga** or **Portugees Synagoge** (Portuguese Synagogue; Sun–Fri 10am–4pm; closed Yom Kippur; €6.50; ⍟www.esnoga.com), completed in 1675 for the city's Sephardic Jews. One of Amsterdam's most imposing buildings, the central structure, with its grand pilasters and blind balustrade, was built in the broadly Neoclassical style that was then fashionable in Holland. It is surrounded by a courtyard complex of small outhouses, where the city's Sephardim have fraternized for centuries. Barely altered since its construction, the synagogue's lofty interior follows the Sephardic tradition in having the Hechal (the Ark of the Covenant) and *tebah* (from where services are led) at opposite ends. Also traditional is the seating, with two sets of wooden benches (for the men) facing each other across the central aisle

△ Inside the Esnoga

△ Dockwerker statue

– the women have separate galleries up above. A set of superb brass chandeliers holds the candles that remain the only source of artificial light. When it was completed, the synagogue was one of the largest in the world, its congregation almost certainly the richest; today, the Sephardic community has dwindled to just six hundred-odd members, most of whom live outside the city centre. In one of the outhouses, a video sheds light on the history of the synagogue and Amsterdam's Sephardim; the mystery is why the Germans left it alone – no one knows for sure, but it seems likely that they intended to turn it into a museum once all the Jews had been polished off.

Jonas Daniel Meijerplein

Next to the synagogue, on the south side of its retaining outhouses, is **Jonas Daniel Meijerplein**, a scrawny triangle of gravel named after the eponymous lawyer, who in 1796, at the age of just 16, was the first Jew to be admitted to the Amsterdam Bar. It was here in February 1941 that around 400 Jewish men were forcibly loaded up on trucks and taken to their deaths at Mauthausen concentration camp, in reprisal for the killing of a Dutch Nazi during a street fight. The arrests sparked off the **February Strike** (Februaristaking), a general strike in protest against the Germans' treatment of the Jews. It was organized by the outlawed Communist Party and spearheaded by Amsterdam's transport workers and dockers – a rare demonstration of solidarity with the Jews whose fate was usually accepted without visible protest in all of occupied Europe. The strike was quickly suppressed, but is still commemorated by an annual wreath-laying ceremony on February 25, as well as by Mari Andriessen's **statue** of the **Dokwerker** (Dockworker) here on the square.

Joods Historisch Museum

Across the square, on the far side of the main road, the **Joods Historisch Museum** (Jewish Historical Museum; daily 11am–5pm; closed Yom Kippur; €6.50; ⓦwww.jhm.nl) is cleverly shoehorned into four Ashkenazi synagogues dating from the late seventeenth century. For years after the war these buildings lay abandoned, but they were finally refurbished – and connected by walkways – in the 1980s to accommodate a Jewish resource centre and exhibition area. The museum is currently undergoing a major revamp, the first part of which has seen a well-considered exhibition entitled "Religion and History of the Jews in the Netherlands, 1600–1890" installed in the handsome **Grote Synagoge** of 1671. This features a fairly small but wide-ranging collection covering most aspects of Dutch Jewish life, beginning downstairs, in the main body of the synagogue, with a fine collection of religious silverware, plus antique artefacts illustrating religious customs and practices. The gallery above holds a finely judged social history of the country's Jewish population, tracing their prominent role in a wide variety of industries, both as employers and employees, up until 1890.

The next part of the museum's redevelopment will see the **Nieuwe Synagoge** used to display a complementary history of the Jews in the Netherlands from 1890 until today, focusing, inevitably, on the trauma of World War II. Another part of the complex will become a Children's Museum, and the resource centre, with its myriad books, periodicals, and photographs, mostly chronicling the Jewish experience in the Netherlands, will be allocated a home. Space will also be found for the moving gouaches of the German Jewess **Charlotte Salomon** (1917–1943), who died in Auschwitz. Salomon painted several hundred pieces in her short life and the museum owns a large sample of them, though they are currently not on display.

For more on Amsterdam during the German occupation, visit the Dutch Resistance Museum (see p.107).

The Plantagebuurt

Developed in the middle of the nineteenth century, the **Plantagebuurt**, whose comfortable, leafy streets are spined by **Plantage Middenlaan** boulevard, was built as part of a concerted attempt to provide good-quality housing for the city's expanding middle classes. Although it was never as fashionable as the older residential parts of the Grachtengordel, the new district did contain elegant villas and spacious terraces, making it the first suburban port of call for many aspiring Jews. Nowadays, the Plantagebuurt is still one of the more prosperous parts of the city, in a modest sort of way, and boasts two especially enjoyable attractions – the **Hortus Botanicus** (Botanical Gardens) and the **Verzetsmuseum** (Dutch Resistance Museum). Just over the **Plantage Muidergracht** canal, and stretching west to the River Amstel, is a small parcel of old Amsterdam, developed in the late seventeenth century. The main attraction here is the newly opened **Hermitage Amsterdam**, which showcases temporary exhibitions of fine and applied art loaned from St Petersburg's Hermitage Museum..

The Amstelhof and Hermitage Amsterdam

With the second phase of the digging of the Grachtengordel, the three main canals that ringed the city centre were extended beyond the River Amstel up towards the Oosterdok – hence "Nieuwe" Herengracht, Keizersgracht and Prinsengracht. At first, takers for the new land were few and far between and the city had no option but to offer it to charities at discount prices. One result was the establishment of the **Amstelhof**, a large *hofje* (alms house) built for the care of elderly women (and ultimately men and women) in the 1680s on behalf of the Dutch Reformed Church. In time, the Amstelhof, a singularly stern-looking structure, grew to fill out the entire chunk of land between Nieuwe Herengracht and Nieuwe Keizersgracht, becoming a fully fledged hospital on the way, but in the 1980s it became clear that its medical facilities were outmoded and it went up for sale. Much municipal huffing and puffing ensued until the director of the Hermitage Museum in St Petersburg and his Dutch contacts dreamed up a real cultural wheeze: they proposed that the Amstelhof be turned into a museum for the display of items loaned from the Hermitage. It was – and is – a very ambitious scheme, with work on the Amstelhof scheduled to continue until the end of the decade. The first phase, however, has been completed with six, medium-sized galleries spread over two floors now comprising **Hermitage Amsterdam**, at Nieuwe Herengracht 14 (daily 10am–5pm; €6; ⓦwww.hermitage.nl). Exhibitions, which usually last about five months, have included "Nicholas & Alexandra" and "Venezia! Art of the 18th Century".

Nieuwe Keizersgracht

In the nineteenth century, many better-off Jews escaped the crowded conditions of the Old Jewish Quarter to live along Nieuwe Keizersgracht and Nieuwe Prinsensgracht, but this community did not survive World War II. One painful reminder of the occupation still stands at **Nieuwe Keizersgracht 58**, across the canal from the back of the Amstelhof. From 1940, this house, with its luxurious Neoclassical double doorway and twin caryatids, was the headquarters of the **Judenrat** (Jewish Council), through which the Germans ran the ghetto and organized the deportations. The role of the Judenrat is extremely controversial. Many have argued that they were tainted collaborators, who hoped to save their own necks by working with the Germans and duping their fellow Jews into thinking that the deportations were indeed – as Nazi propaganda insisted – about the transfer of personnel to new employment in Germany. Just how much the council leaders knew about the gas chambers remains unclear, but after the war the surviving members of the Jewish Council successfully defended themselves against charges of collaboration, claiming that they had been a buffer against the Germans rather than their instruments. Vindicated or not, the Judenrat foolishly refused to destroy the registration cards that were a key feature of the Germans' ability to round up Jews at will, seemingly deceived by the occupiers' assurances regarding "work redeployment". Neither did the Dutch police shirk their new responsibilities: Adolf Eichmann later declared that the Amsterdam round–ups went "like clockwork" and, in the whole of the city, the Germans only needed to post fifty to sixty men to assist.

Hortus Botanicus

From Nieuwe Keizersgracht, it's a hop, skip and a jump to the lush **Hortus Botanicus** (Mon–Fri 9am–5pm, Sat & Sun 10am–5pm; €6; ⓦwww.hortus-botanicus.nl), an appealing if smallish botanical garden accessed via Plantage Middenlaan. Founded in the late seventeenth century, the gardens have seen several botanical coups: in 1848, for instance, two oil palms left the gardens for Java, where they were used to establish the first of many oil-palm plantations. Today, the gardens contain around 6000 plant species, on display both outside and in a series of hothouses. Most of the outdoor sections are covered by plants, trees and shrubs from temperate and Arctic zones with many of the more established trees dating back to a major replanting in 1895. The largest of the hothouses is the **Three-Climates Glasshouse**, which is partitioned – as you might expect from the name – into three climate zones, sub-tropical, tropical and desert. The gardens also hold an orchid nursery, a butterfly house and a capacious palm house with a substantial collection of cycad palms. The orangery has been turned into a **café** (same hours), which serves tasty lunches and a simply wonderful blueberry cheesecake.

Starting at Centraal Station, **trams** #9 and #14 run along Plantage Middenlaan, passing by – or near – all the district's main attractions.

Wertheimpark and De Hollandsche Schouwburg

Across the street from the botanical gardens, beside the canal, is the pocket-sized **Wertheimpark**, where the **Auschwitz monument** is a simple affair with symbolically broken mirrors and an inscription that reads *Nooit meer Auschwitz* ("Auschwitz – Never Again"); it was designed by the Dutch writer Jan Wolkers. Continue down the right-hand side of Plantage Middenlaan to reach another sad relic of the war, **De Hollandsche Schouwburg**, at no. 24 (daily 11am–4pm; closed Yom Kippur; free). Formerly a Jewish theatre, the building became the main assembly point for Amsterdam Jews prior to their deportation. Inside, there was no daylight and families were interned in conditions that foreshadowed those of the camps they would soon be taken to. The front of the building has been refurbished to house a list of the dead and an eternal flame on the ground floor and a small but excellent exhibition on the plight of the city's Jews up on the first floor. The exhibition, complete with lots of occupation photographs, is only labelled in Dutch, but an English translation is available at reception. By contrast, the old auditorium at the back of the building has been left as an empty, roofless shell. A memorial column of basalt on a Star of David base stands where the stage once was, an intensely mournful monument to suffering of unfathomable proportions.

Vakbondsmuseum

From De Hollandsche Schouwburg, it's a brief walk northeast to both the **Artis Zoo**, on Plantage Kerklaan (see p.241), and the **Vakbondsmuseum** (Trade Union Museum; Tues–Fri 11am–5pm, Sun 1–5pm; €2.50), at Henri Polaklaan 9. The museum building is a handsome structure, built for the Diamond Workers' Union in 1900 to a distinctive design by Hendrik Petrus Berlage (1856–1934), who incorporated Romanesque features – such as the castellated balustrade and the deeply recessed main door – within an Expressionist framework. From the outside, it looks very much like a fortified mansion, hence its nickname **De Burcht** ("Stronghold"), but this design was not just about Berlage's architectural whims. Acting on behalf of the employers, the police – and sometimes armed scabs – were regularly used to break strikes, and the union believed members could, in emergency, retreat here to hold out in relative safety. On a number of occasions this proved to be the case, leading to the idea being copied elsewhere, especially in Berlin, where it had disastrous consequences for the Left: in the 1930s the National Socialists simply surrounded the trade union strongholds and captured many of the leading activists in one fell swoop.

The museum's striking, brightly coloured **interior** develops the stylistic themes with a beautiful mixture of stained-glass windows, stone arches, painted brickwork and patterned tiles. In the foyer is a bust of the remarkable **Henri Polak** (1868–1943), both a part-time rabbi and founder of the ANDB, the Diamond Workers' Association (Algemene Nederlandse Diamantbewerkersbond), which became the city's most powerful union. A Socialist, committed to change via constitutional means, Polak organized the diamond workers as never before and was evangelical about his members' self-improvement, arranging all manner of reading and discussion groups. Up the stairs from the foyer, Floor 1 holds the handsome, wood-panelled **Bestuurskamer** (union boardroom), which is kitted out in classic Arts and Crafts style. The room sports three paintings on asbestos cement – one each for sleep, work and relaxation – which celebrate the introduction of the eight-hour working day in 1911, the union's most famous victory. Floor 2, the top floor, is given over to temporary exhibitions.

Verzetsmuseum

From the Vakbondsmuseum, double back along Henri Polaklaan and take the first left for the excellent **Verzetsmuseum**, at Plantage Kerklaan 61 (Dutch Resistance Museum; Tues–Fri 10am–5pm, Mon, Sat & Sun noon–5pm; €5; ⓦwww.verzetsmuseum.org), which tells the story of the German occupation of the Netherlands in World War II from the invasion of May 1940 to the liberation of 1945. Thoughtfully presented, the main gangway examines the experience of the majority of the population, dealing honestly with the fine balance between cooperation and collaboration. Side rooms are devoted to different aspects of the Resistance, from the brave determination of the Communist Party, who went underground as soon as the Germans arrived, to more ad hoc responses like the so-called **Melkstaking** (Milk Strike) in the spring of 1943, when hundreds of milk producers refused to deliver, in protest to the Germans' threatened deportation of 300,000 former (demobilized) Dutch soldiers to labour camps in Germany. Interestingly, the Dutch Resistance proved especially adept at forgery, forcing the Germans to make the identity cards they issued more and more complicated – but without much success. Fascinating old photographs illustrate the (English and Dutch) text along with a host of original artefacts, from examples of illegal newsletters to signed German death warrants. Apart from their treatment of the Jews, which is detailed here, perhaps the most chilling feature of the occupation was the use of indiscriminate reprisals to terrify the population. For the most part it worked, though there was always a minority courageous enough to resist. The museum has dozens of little metal sheets providing biographical sketches of the members of the Resistance – and it's this mixture of the general and the personal that is its real strength.

The Oosterdok

Just to the north of the Plantagebuurt lies the **Oosterdok**, whose network of artificial islands was dredged out of the River IJ to increase Amsterdam's shipping facilities in the seventeenth century. By the 1980s, this mosaic of docks, jetties and islands had become something of a post-industrial eyesore, but since then an ambitious redevelopment programme has turned things around and parts of the area are now reckoned to be some of the most up-and-coming in the city. The obvious sights here are the **Nederlands Scheepvaartmuseum** (Netherlands Maritime Museum) and the **Stedelijk Museum**, which holds the city's prime collection of modern and contemporary art, though the collection is scheduled to return to its former – and fully revamped – premises next door to the Van Gogh Museum (see p.122–124) in 2008.

Entrepotdok

At the northern end of Plantage Kerklaan, just beyond the Verzetsmuseum, a footbridge leads over to **Entrepotdok**, on the nearest, and most interesting, of the Oosterdok islands. On the far side of the bridge old brick **ware-**

4

The Dutch East India Company

Founded in 1602, the Dutch East India Company (or VOC – Verenigde Oostin-dische Compagnie) was the chief pillar of Amsterdam's wealth for nearly two hundred years. Its high-percentage profits came from importing spices into Europe, and to secure them the company's ships ventured far and wide, establishing trading links with India, Sri Lanka, Indo-China, Malaya, China and Japan, though modern-day Indonesia was always the main event. Predictably, the company had a cosy relationship with the merchants who steered the Dutch government: the company was granted a trading monopoly in all the lands east of the Cape of Good Hope and could rely on the warships of the powerful Dutch Navy if they got into difficulty. Neither was their business purely mercantile: the East India Company exercised unlimited military, judicial and political powers in those trading posts it established, the first of which was Batavia in Java in 1619. In the 1750s, the Dutch East India Company went into decline, partly because the British expelled them from most of the best trading stations, but mainly because the company borrowed too extensively. The French army of occupation had little time for the privileges and pretensions of the VOC, abolishing its ruling council and ultimately dissolving the company in 1799.

houses stretch right along the quayside, distinguished by their spout gables, multiple doorways and overhead pulleys. Built by the **Dutch East India Company** (see box above) in the eighteenth century, they were once part of the largest warehouse complex in continental Europe, a gigantic customs-free zone established for goods in transit. On the ground floor, above each main entrance, every warehouse sports the name of a town or island; goods for onward transportation were stored in the appropriate warehouse until there were enough to fill a boat or barge. The warehouses have been tastefully converted into offices and apartments, a fate they share with the central **Dutch East India Company compound**, whose two, modest brick wings culminate in a chunky Neoclassical entrance at the west end of Entrepotdok on Kadijksplein.

The Nederlands Scheepvaartmuseum

The **Nederlands Scheepvaartmuseum** (Netherlands Maritime Museum; Tues–Sun 10am–5pm; mid-June to mid-Sept also Mon 10am–5pm; €7.50, €4 for kids; ⊛www.scheepvaartmuseum.nl), occupies the old arsenal of the Dutch Navy, a vast sandstone structure built on the Oosterdok beside Kattenburger-plein. It's underpinned by no less than 18,000 wooden piles driven deep into the river bed at enormous expense in the 1650s. The building's four symmetrical facades are dour and imposing despite the odd stylistic flourish, principally some dinky dormer windows and Neoclassical pediments, and they surround a central, cobbled courtyard under which was kept a copious supply of freshwater to victual the ships. It's the perfect location for a Maritime Museum, but although parts of the collection are enjoyable and interesting in equal measure, the accumulated aretefacts, which spread over three main floors, don't quite live up to the setting, and the English-language labelling, where it exists, is often cursory.

The **ground floor** features temporary exhibitions and displays a flashy gilded barge built for King William I in 1818. The **first floor** is much more diverting, concentrating on shipping in the seventeenth and eighteenth centuries. It includes garish ships' figureheads, examples of early atlases, globes and navigational equipment, and finely detailed models of the clippers of the East India Company, then the fastest ships in the world. The officers' quarters were at the stern and contemporary shipbuilders tried hard to make them as domestic as possible – literally a home-from-home – right down to their mullion windows. There are many nautical paintings too, some devoted to the achievements of Dutch trading ships, others showing heavy seas and shipwrecks and yet more celebrating the successes of the Dutch Navy. Honed by the long and bloody struggle with Habsburg Spain, the Navy was the most powerful fleet in the world for about thirty years from the 1650s to the 1680s. Commanded by a series of brilliant admirals – principally Tromp and De Ruyter – the Dutch even inflicted several defeats on the British navy, infuriating Charles II by a spectacu-

△ De Amsterdam

From the Maritime Museum, there's a choice of several routes: if you're heading **west**, both the Canal Bus (see p.32) and the Museumboot (see p.32) will speedily return you to Centraal Station via the NEMO centre (see below). Alternatively, you can walk back to Centraal Station in about fifteen minutes either along Prins Hendrikkade or rather more appealingly via the footbridge which spans the water between NEMO and the Oosterdokskade, the location of the Stedelijk Museum. Finally, diligent sightseers can either venture **southeast** to the De Gooyer windmill (see opposite) or **northeast** – from either the Stedelijk Museum or Centraal Station – to the jangle of River Ij islands that comprise Zeeburg (see pp.113–115).

lar raid up the Thames in 1667. **Willem van de Velde II** (1633–1707) was the most successful of the Dutch marine painters of the period and there's a good sample of his work here – canvases that emphasize the strength and power of the Dutch warship, often depicted in battle.

The **second floor** focuses on shipping in the nineteenth and early twentieth centuries with yet more precise models and an enjoyable selection of romantic maritime paintings. There's also a cabinet of commemorative souvenirs devoted to **Jan Carel Josephus van Speijk**, whose misguided heroism made him a folk hero. An Amsterdam orphan, Speijk joined the Dutch Navy, rising through the ranks to become the commander of a munitions ship. In 1830, Speijk and his ship were in Antwerp harbour when that city joined the rebellion against the United Kingdom of the Netherlands (1815–1830), the short-lived attempt to combine modern-day Belgium and the Netherlands. The rebellion was to prove successful – leading to the creation of an independent Belgium – but Speijk, seeing the rebels approaching, decided to blow his ship up rather than allow its munitions to fall into their hands, killing himself and most of his crew in the process.

Outside, moored at the museum jetty, is a full-scale replica of an East India-man, the 78-metre **De Amsterdam**. The original ship first set sail in 1748, but came to an ignominious end, getting stuck on the British coast near Hastings. The ship is crewed by actors, and visitors can wander its decks and galleys, storerooms and gun bays at their leisure.

ARCAM, NEMO and around

Strolling west from the Maritime Museum along the waterfront Prins Hendrikkade, you soon reach **ARCAM** (Tues–Sat 1–5pm; free; ⓦwww.arcam.nl), the Amsterdam Centre for Architecture, housed in a distinctive aluminium and glass structure recently designed by the Dutch architect René van Zuuk. The building is the big deal here, but inside a small gallery area is used for an imaginative programme of temporary exhibitions on contemporary architecture.

Moored behind ARCAM are twenty antique **boats and barges**, which together make up an informal record of the development of local shipping; the earliest vessels date from the middle of the nineteenth century, and plaques, in English and Dutch, give the historical low-down on the more important. The boats lead towards the massive elevated hood that rears up above the entrance to the River IJ tunnel. A good part of this hood is now occupied by **NEMO** (Tues–Sun 10am–5pm, plus Mon 10am–5pm during school holidays and in July & Aug; €11, under-4s free; ⓦwww.e-nemo.nl), a (pre-teenage) kids' attraction par excellence, with all sorts of interactive science and technological exhibits spread over six decks. For more on NEMO, see p.241.

From NEMO, a footbridge leads over the harbour to the Stedelijk Museum or you can double back to Prins Hendrikkade for the short walk west to the **Oude Schans** canal, which serves as an attractive introduction the Old Centre.

Stedelijk Museum

Amsterdam's number-one venue for modern art, the **Stedelijk Museum** (daily 10am–6pm, Thur till 9pm; €8; ⓦwww.stedelijk.nl) currently occupies part of the city's former postal sorting office, a routine modern tower block near Centraal Station on the Oosterdokskade. These new premises have proved very popular with Amsterdammers, so although the original plan was to return the collection to its old home adjacent to the Van Gogh Museum in 2008, once the refurbishment has been completed, it's possible that the museum (or parts of it) will stay here on the Oosterdokskade, which is itself set to be colonised by glass and concrete office and apartment blocks.

In the meantime, the museum has taken to its new surroundings with aplomb, spreading itself over two large and well-appointed floors. **Floor 2** features a lively programme of temporary exhibitions drawn from both its wide-ranging permanent collection and loaned pieces, featuring everything from oil paintings through to photography and installations. Upstairs, **Floor 3** is devoted to a regularly rotated selection from the permanent collection. Broadly speaking, this starts off with drawings by Picasso, Matisse and their contemporaries, and moves on to paintings by Manet, Monet, Bonnard, Ensor and Cézanne. Piet Mondriaan (1872–1944) is well represented too, holding sway among the De Stijl group, from his early, muddy-coloured abstractions to the cool, boldly coloured rectangular blocks for which he's most famous. The museum also owns a goodly sample of the work of the Russian Kasimir Malevich (1878–1935), his dense attempts at Cubism leading to the dynamism and bold, primary tones of his "Suprematist" paintings – slices, blocks and bolts of colour that shift around as if about to resolve themselves into some complex computer graphic. Other highlights of the Stedelijk collection include several Marc Chagall paintings, and a number of pictures by American Abstract Expressionists Mark Rothko, Ellsworth Kelly and Barnett Newman, plus the odd work by Lichtenstein, Warhol, Robert Ryman, Kooning and Jean Dubuffet. Incidentally, *Eleven*, on the top floor of the same block is presently one of the city's most fashionable restaurants – and it offers wide views over the centre; for more details, see p.184.

From in front of the Stedelijk Museum, a long footbridge sticks to the edge of the harbour on its way back to Centraal Station.

Museum Werf 't Kromhout and De Gooyer windmill

Heading east from the Nederlands Scheepvaartmuseum along Kattenburgergracht, you soon reach the footbridge that spans the Nieuwevaart canal over to Hoogte Kadijk, where, at no. 147, the **Museum Werf 't Kromhout** (Tues 10am–3pm, €4.75) is one of the city's few remaining shipyards. In its heyday, the Oosterdok was littered with shipyards like this one. The first major contraction came at the back end of the nineteenth century when steel and steam replaced timber and few of the existing yards were big enough to make the switch successfully. A number struggled on, including this one, by concentrating on the repair and construction of smaller inshore and canal boats. Even so, 't Kromhout almost went bust in 1969 and was only saved by turning into a combination of operating shipyard and tourist attraction, its yard full of old boats, its museum strewn with ancient engines and shipyard tools.

Continuing east along Hoogte Kadijk from 't Kromhout, it's about 500m to **De Gooyer windmill**, standing tall between two canals at Funenkade 5. Amsterdam was once dotted with windmills, used for pumping water and grinding corn, but most were demolished years ago and this is a rare survivor. If you have come this far, you'll be pleased to discover that the bar and mini-brewery in the old public baths adjoining the windmill – the **Brouwerij Het Ij** (Wed–Sun 3–8pm) – is a good old-fashioned place with an excellent range of beers and ales. They brew a head-stomping, amber ale called Columbus (9%) as well as less frightening stuff, such as the creamy Natte (6.5%).

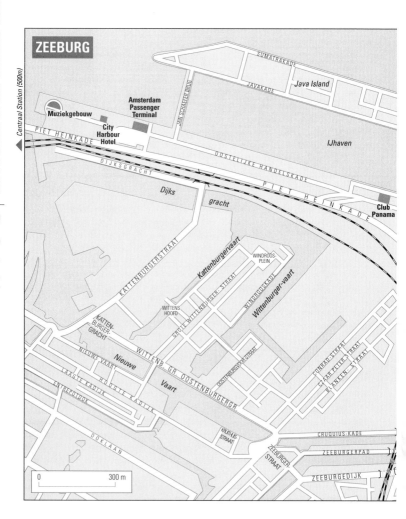

It takes about ten minutes to walk back from the windmill to the The Nederlands Scheepvaartmuseum

Zeeburg

To the north and east of the Oosterdok, the **Zeeburg** district or **Oostelijk Havengebied** – basically the old docks between the Stedelijk Museum (see p.111) and the island of Zeeburg – have taken over as the city's most up-and-coming district. Actually a series of islands and peninsulas connected by bridges, the docks here date back to the end of the nineteenth century, but like dockland

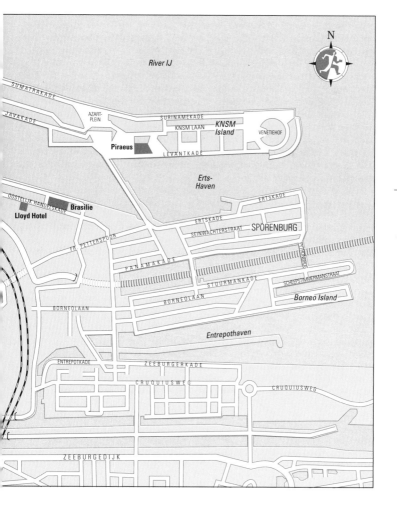

areas all over Europe they fell into disuse and disrepair during the last century due to the advent of large container ships, which couldn't travel this far up river. They were virtually derelict by the early 1990s, when the city began a massive renovation that has been going on for the past ten years or so, with the result that it's now one of the most densely populated parts of the city, and architecturally its fastest-growing and most resurgent area, with a mixture of renovated dockside structures and new landmark buildings that give it a feel that's far removed from the city centre – despite being just a twenty-minute walk from Centraal Station. To save your legs for exploring once there, take bus #32 from Centraal Station, or the **free ferry** that runs to Java island from behind the station, which takes about ten minutes.

Oostelijke Handelskade

The mainland quayside of the **Oostelijke Handelskade** is perhaps the best place to start, stretching for about a mile from its starting point ten minutes' walk east from Centraal Station. There has been and still is a lot of large development here, most notably the spanking new **Amsterdam Passengers' Terminal**, a glass-walled monster that is the new venue for cruise ships to berth – it's also due to be a major transport hub, with a stop on the new IJ tram, with a taxi stand, carparks and shops. Close by, they're building a hotel – the **City Harbour** – and a state-of-the-art music auditoreum, the **Muziekgebouw**, which will feature an eclectic range of contemporary music and events (see also p.210). Both the hotel and the Musiekgebouw are due to open in late 2005. You can follow Oostelijke Handelskade east from here, where, a kilometre or so further on, it is more quietly residential, home to the **Brasilie** shopping centre, housed in an old cocoa warehouse, and a number of cafés and restaurants, including a couple of moored boats, the *Odessa* and *Lizboa*, not to mention the super-chic *Lloyd Hotel* (see p.171).

Java and KNSM islands

From Oostelijke Handelskade you could walk on to the main islands of the district, or, from close by the cruise terminal, you can cross by way of the 200m-long Jan Schaeferbrug to **Java island**, where the tall houses that line the canals that cross it – each crossed by quirky wrought iron bridges – are a successful contemporary take on the seventeenth-century canal houses of the city centre, each of them strikingly modern and completely individual. Stop off for dinner at the sleek *Voorbij het Einde* restaurant, named after the squat that used to be here in the days when Java island was a remote refuge from city centre prices.

The far end of Java island is connected to **KNSM island** named after the shipping company (the Royal Dutch Steamboat Company) that used to be based here. Running down the centre of the island, **KNSM Laan** has a number of big warehouses housing design and art, most of them situated in the enormous **Loods 6** shed that faces onto the northern waterfront, while on the other side of the island the **Piraeus** apartment building looks south across the water to the mainland and gives perhaps the best impression of the monumental stature of some of the architecture here. **Levantkade**, which runs alongside, is lined with houseboats and old moored ships and also has a number of decent bars and restaurants.

Sporenburg and Borneo island

A bridge connects KNSM island to the **Sporenburg** peninsula, where there is more fancy modern residential architecture, most conspicuous of which is an enormous structure known as **The Whale** due to its bizarre shape, the sharp outlines of which apparently allow the sun to better warm the building. Follow Ertskade east from here and cross over to **Borneo island** by way of the pedestrian **Pythonbrug**, so called for its curvy, snakelike shape. On Borneo, you can admire more modern canalside dwellings on **Scheepstimmerman-straat**. Like those on Java island, these again follow their seventeenth-century predecessors in the conformity of their height and plot size but otherwise each is utterly unique.

Across the bridge from Borneo island, the recently refurbished **Nederlands Persmuseum** or Dutch Press Museum (Tues–Fri 10am–5pm & Sun noon–5pm; €3.50; @www.persmuseum.nl), housed in the International Institute for Social History at Zeeburgerkade 10, focuses on the history of the Dutch press since 1618, as revealed in newspapers, leaflets, posters and political cartoons. The collection of the institute itself holds original letters and writings from many of the leading figures of the left including Marx, Lenin and Bakunin. Bus #32 drops you nearby, as do buses #43 and #59.

5

The Museum Quarter and Vondelpark

During the nineteenth century, **Amsterdam** burst out of its restraining canals, gobbling up the surrounding countryside. These newish outlying neighbourhoods are mostly described in Chapter Six, but Amsterdam's two leading **museums**, packed into a relatively small area around the edge of Museumplein, deserve their own chapter. The larger of the two, the **Rijksmuseum**, is in the throes of a major revamp (see below), but the kernel of the collection – a superb sample of **Dutch paintings** from the so–called Golden Age (the seventeenth century) – is still on display in the Philips Wing, the only part of the museum to remain open during the refurbishment. Similarly superb is the nearby **Van Gogh Museum** which boasts the most satisfying collection of Van Gogh paintings in the world, with important works representative of all his artistic periods. Taken together, the two museums form one of Amsterdam's biggest pulls.

Museumplein itself, extending south from Stadhouderskade to Van Baerlestraat, is one of Amsterdam's largest open spaces, its wide lawns used for a variety of outdoor activities, from visiting circuses to political demonstrations. At the far end of Museumplein is the **Concertgebouw**, the city's most prestigious classical music concert hall, from where it's a short walk to the sprawling greenery of the **Vondelpark**, Amsterdam's loveliest park.

The Rijksmuseum

Facing onto the Singelgracht, at the head of Museumplein, the **Rijksmusem** (daily 9am–6pm, €9, under-18s free; audio guide €4; ⏎www.rijksmuseum.nl) is an imposing pile, built in an inventive historic style by Petrus Josephus Hubertus **Cuypers**, also the creator of Centraal Station, in the early 1880s. The leading Dutch architect of his day, Cuypers (1827–1921) specialized in neo-Gothic churches, but this commission called for something more ambitious, the result being a permutation on the neo-Renaissance style then popular in the Netherlands, an intricate structure complete with towers and turrets, galleries, dormer windows and medallions. More importantly, the museum possesses an extravagant collection of paintings from every pre-twentieth-century period of **Dutch art** together with a vast hoard of applied art and sculpture. The problem is that the museum is in the middle of an extensive (€272 million) revamp, which will last until 2008, and until this is finished only one part of the museum, the **Philips**

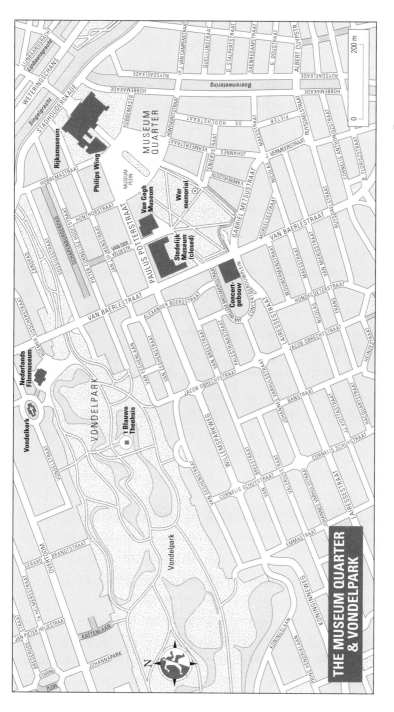

THE MUSEUM QUARTER
& VONDELPARK

Wing, will remain open. The good news is that the wing's thirteen rooms are used to good effect to display the kernel of the permanent collection under the title "**The Masterpieces**" – a splendid selection of seventeenth-century Dutch paintings, from the Dutch **Gouden Eeuw** (Golden Age) as well as delftware, silver and icons from Dutch history. There is some rotation, but you can count on seeing all the leading **Rembrandts** plus a healthy sample of canvases by Steen, Hals, Vermeer and their leading contemporaries. The clearly signposted entrance is round the back of the main body of the building on Jan Luijkenstraat.

Rooms 1 to 5

The Philips Wing begins in style with two large galleries – Rooms 1 and 2 – giving the historical background to the Dutch Golden Age with features on the count ry's success as a trading nation and its naval prowess. Amongst the paintings on display here is a breezily self-confident *The Celebration of the Peace of Münster*, by **Bartholomeus van der Helst** (1613–1670), who became one of Amsterdam's most popular portraitists after Rembrandt abandoned the normal protocols of portraiture to adopt an introspective, religious style that did not please the city's burghers at all. For the Dutch at least, the treaty was well worth celebrating: signed in 1648, it ended the Thirty Years' War and recognised the United Provinces (now the Netherlands) as an independent state, free of Habsburg control. The Thirty Years' War had convulsed most of western Europe by pitting Catholic against Protestant and **Adriaen van de Venne** (1589–1662) was quite clear what side he was on: his curious *Fishing for Souls*, in Room 2, has the disorganised Catholics on the right river bank, the Protestants merrily heaving in souls on the left.

Moving on, Room 3 holds several antique dolls' houses, Room 4 is mostly silverware and Room 5 showcases a large assortment of **delftware**, from plates and tiles through to vases, chargers and flower holders. Dating from the late sixteenth century, the earlier pieces are comparatively plain, typically decorated with rural, classical or Biblical scenes, whereas the later porcelain is more elaborate and often copied from – or in imitation of – Chinese ceramics (see box below).

Rooms 7 and 8

Upstairs, Room 7 holds several superb canvases by **Frans Hals** (1582–1666), most notably his expansive *Marriage Portrait of Isaac Massa and Beatrix Laen*. Relaxing beneath a tree, a portly Isaac glows with contentment as his new

Delftware

Named after the Dutch city of Delft, where it was manufactured, **delftware** traces its origins to fifteenth–century Mallorca, where craftsmen developed **majolica**, a type of porous pottery that was glazed with bright metallic oxides. During the Renaissance, these techniques were exported to Italy from where they spread north, first to Antwerp and then to the United Provinces (aka the Netherlands). Initially, delft pottery **designs** featured landscapes, portraits and bible stories, whilst the top–end of the market was dominated by more ornate Chinese porcelain imported by the Dutch East India Company. However, when a prolonged civil war in China broke the supply line, Delft's factories quickly took over the luxury side of the market by copying Chinese designs. By the 1670s, Delft was churning out blue-and-white tiles, plates, panels, jars and vases of all descriptions by the thousand, even exporting to China, where they undercut Chinese producers. The delft factories were themselves undercut from the 1760s by the British and the Germans, and by the time Napoleon arrived they had all but closed down.

wife sits beside him in a suitably demure manner. An intimate scene, the painting also carries a detailed iconography: the ivy at Beatrix's feet symbolizes her devotion to her husband, the thistle faithfulness, the vine togetherness and in the fantasy garden behind them the peacock is a classical allusion to Juno, the guardian of marriage. In the same room, look out also for the cool church interiors of **Pieter Saenredam** (1597–1665), whose *Old Town Hall of Amsterdam* is a characteristically precise work in which the tumbledown predecessor of the current building (now the Royal Palace) witnesses the comings and goings of black-hatted townsmen in the stilted manner of a Lowry.

In Room 8, examples of the work of **Salomon van Ruysdael** (1602–1670), a Haarlem artist with a penchant for soft, tonal river scenes, share space with some of Rembrandt's better-known pupils, including **Nicholas Maes** (1632–1693), whose caring *Young Woman by the Cradle* is not so much a didactic tableau as an idealization of motherhood. Another pupil, **Ferdinand Bol** (1616–1680) painted *Portrait of Elizabeth Bas* in a style so close to that of his master that it was regarded as a Rembrandt until the director of the museum proved it otherwise in 1911. Perhaps the most talented of the Rembrandt's pupils was **Carel Fabritius**, who was killed in 1654 at the age of 32, when Delft's powder magazine exploded. His *Portrait of Abraham Potter*, a restrained, skilful work of soft, delicate hues, contrasts with the same artist's earlier *The Beheading of St John the Baptist*, where the head is served on a platter in piercingly grisly style.

Room 9

Rembrandt's *The Night Watch* is displayed in Room 12 (see p.120), but Room 9 has several fine examples of his work, notably a late *Self-Portrait*, with the artist caught in mid-shrug as the Apostle Paul, a self-aware and defeated old man. There's also the artist's touching depiction of his cowled son, *Titus*, and *The Jewish Bride*, one of his very last pictures, finished in 1667. No one knows who the couple are, nor whether they are actually married (the title came later), but the painting is one of Rembrandt's most telling, the paint dashed on freely and the hands touching lovingly, as the art historian Kenneth Clark wrote, in a "marvellous amalgam of richness, tenderness and trust".

Room 10

In Room 10, **Johannes Vermeer** (1632–1675) is well represented by both *The Love Letter*, which reveals a tension between servant and mistress – the lute on the woman's lap was a well-known sexual symbol – and *The Kitchen Maid*, an exquisitely observed domestic scene, right down to the nail – and its shadow – on the background wall. Similarly, in the precise *Young Woman Reading a Letter*, the map behind her hints at the far-flung places her loved one is writing from. What you won't get, however, is Vermeer's *Girl with a Pearl Earring* as that is on display in the Mauritshuis gallery in Den Haag (The Hague). **Gerard ter Borch** (1617–1681) also depicted apparently innocent scenes, both in subject and title, but his *Woman at a Mirror* glances in a meaningfully anxious manner at her servants, who look on with delicate irony from behind dutiful exteriors. The paintings of **Pieter de Hooch** are less symbolic, more exercises in lighting, but they're as good a visual guide to the everyday life and habits of the seventeenth-century Dutch bourgeoisie as you'll find – as evidenced by his *Woman with a Child in a Pantry*.

Room 11

From the latter half of the seventeenth century come **Gerrit Berckheyde**'s (1638–1698) crisp depictions of Amsterdam and Haarlem and the carous-

△ *The Night Watch*, Rijksmuseum

ing peasants of **Jan Steen** (1625–1679). Steen's *Feast of St Nicholas*, with its squabbling children, makes the festival a celebration of disorderly greed, while the drunken waywardness of his *Merry Family* and *Family Scene* verge on the anarchic. Steen knew his bourgeois audience well: his caricatures of the proletariat blend humour with moral condemnation – or at least condescension – a mixture perfectly designed to suit their tastes. Steen was also capable of more subtle works, a famous example being his *Woman at her Toilet* (in Room 10), which is full of associations, referring either to sexual pleasures just had or about to be taken. For example, the woman is shown putting on a stocking in a conspicuous manner, the point being that the Dutch word for stocking, *kous*, is also a slang word for a woman's genitalia. By contrast, **Willem van de Velde II**'s (1633–1707) preoccupations were nautical, his canvases celebrating either the power of the Dutch navy or the seaworthiness of the merchant marine, as in the churning seas of the superbly executed *Gust of Wind*, whose counterpoint is to be found in the calm waters and gunfire of *The Cannon Shot*.

Room 12: The Night Watch

Dominating Room 12, **Rembrandt**'s *The Night Watch* (*De Nachtwacht*) of 1642 is the most famous of all the artist's pictures. Restored after being slashed in 1975, the painting is of a Militia Company – the **Kloveniersdoelen company** – and as such celebrates one of the companies formed in the sixteenth century to defend the United Provinces against Spain. As the Habsburg threat receded, so the militias became social clubs for the well-heeled, who were eager to commission their own group portraits as signs of their prestige. Rembrandt charged the princely sum of 100 guilders for each member of the company who wanted to be in the picture and sixteen – out of a possible two hundred – stumped up the cash, including its well–heeled captain, Frans Banningh Cocq, whose disapproval of Rembrandt's live–in relationship with Hendrickje Stoffels (see box below) was ultimately to polish off their friendship. Curiously, *The Night Watch* is, in fact, a misnomer – the painting got the tag in the eighteenth century when the background darkness was misinterpreted. There were other misconceptions about the painting too, most notably that it was this work that led to the downward shift in Rembrandt's standing with the Amsterdam elite; in fact, there's no evidence that the militia men weren't pleased with the picture, or that Rembrandt's commissions flowed in any more slowly after it was completed.

Though not as subtle as much of the artist's later work, *The Night Watch* is an adept piece, full of movement and carefully arranged. Paintings of this kind were collections of individual portraits as much as group pictures, and for the artist their difficulty lay in including each single face while simultaneously producing a coherent group scene. Abandoning convention in vigorous style, Rembrandt opted to show the company preparing to march off, a snapshot of military activity in which banners are unfurled, muskets primed and drums rolled. There are a couple of allegorical figures as well, most prominently a young, spotlit woman who has a bird hanging from her belt, a reference to the Kloveniersdoelen's

Rembrandt's progress

Born in Leiden to a family of millers, **Rembrandt Harmenszoon van Rijn** (1606–1669) picked up his first important artistic tips as an apprentice to Pieter Lastman in Amsterdam in the early 1620s. It was here that Rembrandt developed a penchant for mythological and religious subjects. After his apprenticeship, in around 1625, Rembrandt went back to Leiden to establish himself as an independent master painter and, this achieved, he returned to Amsterdam some six years later; Rembrandt stayed in Amsterdam for the rest of his life. In the early 1630s Rembrandt concentrated on **portrait painting**, churning out dozens of pictures of the burghers of his day, a profitable business that made him both well-to-do and well known. In 1634 he married **Saskia van Uylenburch** and five years later the couple moved into a smart house on Jodenbreestraat, now the Rembrandthuis museum (see p.000). Things seemed set fair, and certainly Rembrandt's portraits of his wife are tender and loving, but these years were marred by the death of all but one of his children in infancy, the sole survivor being his much loved **Titus** (1641–1668).

In 1642 Rembrandt produced what has become his most celebrated painting, *The Night Watch*, but thereafter his career went into decline, essentially because he forsook portraiture to focus on increasingly sombre and introspective **religious works**. Traditionally, Rembrandt's change of artistic direction has been tied in with the death of Saskia in 1642, but although it is certainly true that Rembrandt was grief-stricken, he was also facing increased competition from a new batch of portrait artists, primarily Bartholomeus van der Helst, Ferdinand Bol and Govert Flinck. Whatever the reason, there were few customers for Rembrandt's religious works and he made matters worse by refusing to adjust his spending. The crunch came in 1656, when he was formally declared insolvent, and four years later he was obliged to sell his house and goods, moving to much humbler premises in the Jordaan (see p.000). By this time, he had a new cohabitee, **Hendrickje Stoffels** (a clause in Saskia's will prevented them from ever marrying), and, in the early 1660s, she and Titus took Rembrandt in hand, sorting out his finances and making him their employee. With his money problems solved, a relieved Rembrandt then produced some of his finest paintings – for example *The Jewish Bride* – emotionally deep and contemplative works with a rough finish, the paint often daubed almost trowel-like. Hendrickje died in 1663, Titus in 1668, a year before his father.

traditional emblem of a claw. Militia portraits commonly included cameo portraits of the artist involved, but in this case it seems that Rembrandt didn't insert his likeness, though some art historians insist that the pudgy-faced figure peering out from the back between the gesticulating militiamen is indeed the great man himself.

Museumplein

The pancake–flat lawns and footpaths of **Museumplein** stretch out behind the Rijksmuseum and about halfway along, on the east side, are the slim steel blocks of a **war memorial** commemorating the women of the wartime concentration camps, particularly the thousands who died at Ravensbruck. The text reads: "For those women who defied fascism until the bitter end". The Van Gogh Museum overlooks the north side of the Museumplein.

The Van Gogh Museum

Vincent van Gogh (1853–1890) is arguably the most popular, most reproduced and most talked about of all modern artists, so it's not surprising that the **Van Gogh Museum** (daily 10am–6pm, Fri till 10pm; 𝗪www.vangoghmuseum .nl; €9, children 13–17 years €2.50), comprising a fabulous collection of the artist's work, is one of Amsterdam's top attractions. The museum occupies two modern buildings on the north edge of Museumplein, with the key paintings housed in an angular building designed by a leading light of the De Stijl movement, Gerrit Rietveld, and opened to the public in 1973. Well-conceived and beautifully presented, this part of the museum provides an introduction to the man and his art based on paintings that were mostly inherited from Vincent's art-dealer brother Theo. To the rear of Rietveld's building, and connected by a ground-floor-level escalator, is the ultramodern annexe, an aesthetically controversial structure completed in 1998. The annexe was financed by a Japanese insurance company – the same conglomerate who paid $35 million for one of Van Gogh's *Sunflowers* canvases in 1987 – and provides temporary exhibition space. Most of these exhibitions focus on one aspect or another of Van Gogh's art and draw heavily on the permanent collection, which means that the paintings displayed in the older building are regularly rotated. As you might expect, the museum can get very crowded, so come early to avoid the crush.

The collection

The museum starts on the **ground floor** with a group of paintings by some of Van Gogh's well-known friends and contemporaries, many of whom influenced his work – Gauguin, Decamps, Anton Mauve, Charles Daubigny and others. It then moves on to the works of the man himself, presented for the most part chronologically on the **first floor**. The first paintings go back to the artist's **early years** (1880–1885) in Holland and Belgium, dark, sombre works in the main, ranging from an assortment of drab grey and brown still-lifes to the gnarled faces and haunting, flickering light of *The Potato Eaters* – one of Van Gogh's best-known paintings, and the culmination of hundreds of studies of the local peasantry.

Further along, the sobriety of these early works is easily transposed onto the **Parisian** (1886–1888) urban landscape, particularly in the *View of Paris*, where the city's domes and rooftops hover below Montmartre under a glowering, blustery sky. But before long, under the sway of fellow painters and – after the bleak countryside of Holland – the sheer colour of the city itself, Van Gogh's approach began to change. This is most noticeable in two of his many self-portraits – the almost–cheerful *Self–portrait with Straw Hat* and *Self-portrait with Felt Hat* – and in the pictures from Asnières, just outside Paris, where the artist used to travel regularly to paint. In particular, look out for the surprisingly soft hues and gentle tones of his *Courting Couples* and the disturbing yellows of *Still Life with Quinces and Lemons.*

In February 1888 Van Gogh moved to **Arles**, inviting Gauguin to join him a little later (see box, p.124). With the change of scenery came a heightened interest in colour, and the predominance of yellow as a recurring motif: it's represented best in such paintings as the *Harvest*, and most vividly in the disconcerting juxtapositions of *The Yellow House*. Also from this period comes a striking canvas from the artist's *Sunflowers* series, justly one of his most lauded works, intensely, almost obsessively, rendered in the deepest oranges, golds and ochres he could find. Gauguin told of Van Gogh painting these flowers in a near trance; there were usually sunflowers in jars all over their house.

In 1889 Van Gogh committed himself to the asylum in **St Rémy** and, while there, his approach to nature became more abstract as evidenced by his unsettling *Wheatfield with a Reaper* and the sinister shapes and purple and yellow sky of the *Garden of St Paul's Hospital*. Van Gogh is at his most expressionistic here, the paint applied thickly, often with a palette knife, a practice he continued in his final, tortured paintings done at **Auvers–sur–Oise**, where he lodged for the

△ Van Gogh Museum

Van Gogh's ear

In February 1888, **Vincent van Gogh** left Paris for **Arles**, a small town in the south of France. At first the move went well with Van Gogh warming to the open vistas and bright colours of the Provençal countryside. In September, he moved into the house he nicknamed the "Yellow House", where he hoped to establish an artists' colony, gathering together painters of like mind. Unfortunately for Van Gogh, his letters of invitation were ignored by everyone except **Gauguin**, who arrived in Arles in late October. Initially the two artists got on well, hunkering down together in the Yellow House and sometimes painting side by side, but the bonhomie didn't last. They argued long and hard about art, an especially tiring business for Van Gogh, who complained "Sometimes we come out of our arguments with our heads as exhausted as a used electric battery". Later, Gauguin would claim that Van Gogh threatened him during several of these arguments, but true or not it is certainly the case that Gauguin had decided to return to Paris by the time the two had a ferocious quarrel on the night of December 23. The quarrel was so bad that Gauguin hot–footed to the local hotel and when he returned in the morning, he was faced by the police. After Gauguin's exit, a deeply disturbed Van Gogh had taken a razor to his **ear**, severing part of it before presenting the selected slice to a prostitute by the name of Rachel at the local brothel. Presumably, this was not an especially welcome gift, but in Van Gogh's addled state he may well have forged some sort of connection with bullfighting, where the dead bull's ears are cut off and given as a prize to the bullfighter.

Hours after Gauguin's return, Van Gogh was admitted to hospital, the first of several extended stays before, fearing for his sanity, he committed himself to the asylum of **St Rémy** in May 1889. Here, the doctor's initial assessment described him as suffering "from acute mania, with hallucinations of sight and hearing"; Van Gogh attributed his parlous state to excessive drinking and smoking, though he gave up neither during his year–long stay. In May 1990, feeling lonely and homesick, Van Gogh discharged himself from St Rémy and headed north to Paris before proceeding on to the village of Auvers–sur–Oise. At first, Van Gogh's health improved and he had even began to garner critical recognition for his work. However, the twin ogres of depression and loneliness soon returned to haunt him and in despair Van Gogh shot himself in the chest. This wasn't, however, the end: Van Gogh had not managed to kill himself outright, but took two days to die, even enduring a police visit when he refused to answer any questions, pronouncing that he was "...free to do what I like with my own body".

last three months of his life. It was at Auvers that he painted the frantic *Wheatfield with Crows*, in which the fields swirl and writhe under weird and dark skies, as well as the equally deranged *Tree Roots*. The two floors above provide a back-up to the lead collection. The **second floor** has a study area with PC access to a detailed computerized account of Van Gogh's life and times, plus a number of dark and sombre paintings from his early years in Holland. It's here you're likely to find *A Pair of Shoes*, an idiosyncratic painting that used to hang in the house Van Gogh shared with Gauguin in Arles. The **third floor** features several less familiar Van Gogh paintings as well as temporary exhibitions illustrating his influences, and his influence on other artists.

The Concertgebouw

Across Van Baerlestraat just to the southwest of the Van Gogh Museum is the **Concertgebouw** (Concert Hall), home of the famed – and much recorded – Royal Concertgebouw Orchestra. When the German composer Brahms visited Amsterdam in the 1870s he was scathing about the locals' lack of culture and, in particular, their lack of an even halfway suitable venue for his music. In the face of such ridicule, a consortium of Amsterdam businessmen got together to fund the construction of a brand-new concert hall and the result was the Concertgebouw, completed in 1888. An attractive structure with a pleasingly grand Neoclassical facade, the Concertgebouw has become renowned among musicians and concertgoers for its marvellous acoustics, though it did have to undergo major repairs when it was discovered that the wooden piles on which it rested were rotting away. The overhaul included the addition of a new glass gallery that contrasts nicely with the red brick and stone of the rest of the building. Although the Concertgebouw attracts the world's best orchestras and musicians, ticket prices can be surprisingly inexpensive – the venue operates an arts-for-all policy – and from September to May there are often free walk-in concerts at lunchtime. For more on Concertgebouw tickets and performances, see p.210.

△ Concertgebouw

The Vondelpark

Amsterdam is short of green spaces, which makes the leafy expanse of the **Vondelpark**, a short stretch from both Museumplein and the Concertgebouw, doubly welcome. This is easily the largest and most popular of the city's parks, its network of footpaths used by a healthy slice of the city's population. The park dates back to 1864, when a group of leading Amsterdammers clubbed together to transform the soggy marshland that lay beyond the old Leidsepoort gateway, on the western edge of Leidseplein, into a landscaped park. The group, who were impressed by the contemporary English fashion for natural (as distinct from formal) landscaping, gave the task of developing the new style of park to the Zocher family, big-time gardeners who set about their task with gusto, completing the project in 1865. Named after the seventeenth-century poet **Joost van den Vondel** (see p.54), the park proved an immediate success and was expanded to its present size (45 hectares) in 1877. It now possesses over 100 species of tree, a wide variety of local and imported plants, and – amongst many incidental features – a **bandstand** and excellent **rose garden**. Neither did the Zochers forget their Dutch roots: the park is latticed with ponds and narrow waterways, home to many sorts of wildfowl. There are other animals too: cows, sheep, hundreds of squirrels, plus, bizarrely enough, a large colony of bright-green parakeets. The Vondelpark has several different children's **play areas** and during the summer regularly hosts free **concerts** and theatrical performances, mostly in its own specially designed open-air theatre.

The Nederlands Filmmuseum and Vondelkerk

Housed in a glum, nineteenth-century building near the northeast corner of the Vondelpark is the **Nederlands Filmmuseum** (Netherlands Film Museum; ☏020/589 1400, ⓦwww.filmmuseum.nl), which possesses a large archive of old films and is a dab hand at celluloid restoration. It also acts as a showcase for avant-garde films, most of which are shown in their original language, plus subtitles in Dutch (and occasionally English). There are several screenings nightly, plus a matinée on Wednesday afternoons, and the programme often follows a prescribed theme or subject. Check their website for news of the free outdoor screenings of classic movies on Saturday nights in summer. Metres away, at Vondelstraat 69, the museum's **film library** (Mon–Fri 1–5pm) has a well-catalogued collection of books, magazines and journals, some in English, though they are for reference only and are not loaned out.

Across the street is the lugubrious brown brick hull and whopping spire of the **Vondelkerk**, which has had more than its share of bad luck. Work on the church, which was designed by Cuypers – the architect of Centraal Station and the Rijksmuseum – began in 1872, but the finances ran out the following year and the building was not completed until the 1880s. Twenty years later it was struck by lightning and in the ensuing fire its tower was burnt to a cinder – the present one was added much later. The church always struggled to find a decent-size congregation, but limped on until it was finally deconsecrated in 1979, being turned into offices thereafter.

From the Vondelkerk, it takes between five and ten minutes to walk back to the Rijksmuseum.

The outer districts

Amsterdam is a small city, and the majority of its residential **outer districts** are easily reached from the city centre. The **south** holds most interest, made up of the **Oude Zuid** (Old South), at the heart of which is the raucous **De Pijp** quarter, home to the Heineken Experience, sited in the company's old brewery, and the 1930s architecture of the **Nieuw Zuid** (New South), which also contains the enjoyable woodland area of the **Amsterdamse Bos**. As for the other districts, you'll find a good deal less reason to make the effort. Multicultural influences in the **east** give this part of the city some diversity, and this is also the location of the excellent **Tropenmuseum**, and, further south, the **Amsterdam ArenA**, but the **west** has nothing special at all. Finally, the **north** of the city, on the other side of the IJ, reachable by way of short (free) ferry ride from behind Centraal Station, is again almost entirely residential, but it's pleasant enough if you're cycling through on the way to open country.

De Pijp

Amsterdam's city centre is ringed by the Singelgracht, beyond which lies the so-called **Oud Zuid**, and, its most authentic district, **De Pijp** ("The Pipe"), Amsterdam's first suburb. New development beyond the Singelgracht began around 1870, but after laying down the street plans, the city council left the actual house-building to private developers, who constructed the long rows of cheaply built and largely featureless five- and six-storey buildings that still dominate the area today – and whose sombre canyons of brick tenements give the district its name (the apartments here were said to resemble pipe-drawers, since each had a tiny street frontage but extended deep into the building). De Pijp remains a largely working-class neighbourhood, which despite some gentrification remains one of the city's more closely knit communities, and home to a large proportion of new immigrants – Surinamese, Moroccan, Turkish and Asian. To get here on public transport, take either tram #16 or #24, beginning at Centraal Station, which go past the junction of Albert Cuypstraat and De Pijp's main drag, Ferdinand Bolstraat.

The Wetering circuit

Just off Weteringschans, on the city centre side of Singelgracht, the **Wetering circuit** roundabout has two low-key **memorials** to World War II. On the southwestern corner of the roundabout, by the canal, is a sculpture of a wound-

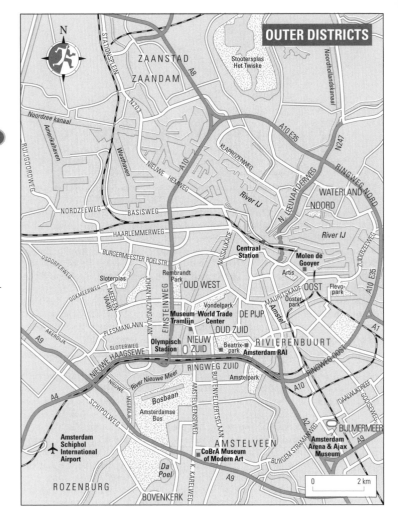

ed man holding a bugle: it was here, on March 12, 1945, that thirty people were shot by the Germans in reprisal for acts of sabotage by the Dutch Resistance – given that the war was all but over, it's hard to imagine a crueller or more futile action. Across the main street, the second memorial commemorates H.M. van Randwijk, a Resistance leader. The restrained wording on the monument translates as:

When to the will of tyrants,
A nation's head is bowed,
It loses more than life and goods –
Its very light goes out.

The Heineken Experience

On the far side of the Singelgracht, on the northern edge of De Pijp at Stadhouderskade 78, the **Heineken Experience** (Tues–Sun 10am–6pm; €10; ®www.heinekenexperience .com) is housed in the former Heineken brewery, a whopping building that was company's headquarters from 1864 to 1988, at which time the firm restructured and its brewing moved to a more efficient location out of town. Since then, Heineken has developed the site as a tourist attraction, with displays on the history of beer-making in general and Heineken in particular. The old brewing facilities are included on the tour, but for many the main draw is the beer itself – although the days when you could quaff unlimited quantities are long gone. It's an expensive attraction, no question, but it's undeniably well done, and considering it's not a real brewery any more, Heineken make a decent stab at both entertaining you and informing at the same time – as well as of

△ Vintage poster, Heineken Experience

course promoting the brand. There are lots of gimmicky but fun attractions. Initial displays take in advertising since the war, how beer is made, and a weird show on what it's like to be a bottle of Heineken, from bottling plant to delivery. You can also do a virtual reality tour of Amsterdam by shire horse and drey, you can lie back and watch five decades' worth of Heineken TV ads, and even send a video email to a friend. You also get three drinks vouchers, at bar stops that punctuate the tour, the first of which takes place after the impressive brewing hall, with its great brass vats overlooking the old (still inhabited) stables, and the last of which forms a convivial end to the proceedings (they throw in a Heineken glass souvenir on the way out, incidentally). All in all not a bad way to pass an hour or two.

Albert Cuypstraat, the Sarphatipark and Gemeentearchief

Ferdinand Bolstraat, running north–south, is De Pijp's main street, but the long, slim east–west thoroughfare of **Albert Cuypstraat** (pronouced "cowp-straat") is its heart. The daily general **market** held here – which stretches for over a kilometre between Ferdinand Bolstraat and Van Woustraat – is the largest in the city (in fact it claims to be the largest in Europe), with a huge array of stalls selling everything from cut-price carrots and raw-herring sandwiches to saucepans and day-glo thongs. Check out, too, the bargain-basement and ethnic shops that flank the market on each side, and the Indian and Surinamese restaurants down the side streets – they're often cheaper than their equivalents in the city centre. The market is open every day except Sunday, 10am until 5pm.

A couple of blocks south of the Albert Cuypstraat market is the leafy **Sarphatipark**, a welcome splash of greenery amongst the surrounding brick and concrete. The park, complete with footpaths and a sinewy lake, was laid out before the construction of De Pijp got underway, and was initially intended as

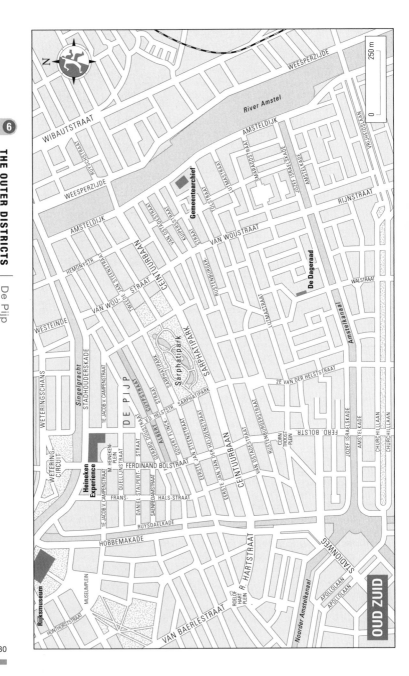

N

WIBAUTSTRAAT
River Amstel
WEESPERZIJDE
AMSTELDIJK
WEESPERZIJDE
AMSTELDIJK
RUYSCHSTRAAT
SMARAGDSTRAAT
VRIJHEIDSLAAN
JOZEF ISRAELSKADE
AMSTELKADE
RIJNSTRAAT
Gemeentearchief
VAN WOUSTRAAT
HEMONYSTR
VAN WOUSTRAAT
UITMASTRAAT
TOLSTRAAT
VAN WOU STRAAT
WEED JAN STEENSTRAAT
CENTUURBAAN
KUIPERSTRAAT
VAN OSTADESTRAAT
RUSTENBURGER
De Dageraad
WALSTRAAT
WESTEINDE
UITMASTRAAT
Amstelkanaal
WETERINGSCHANS
Singelgracht
STADHOUDERSKADE
SARPHATIPARK
Sarphatipark
SARPHATIPARK
2E VAN DER HELSTSTRAAT
DE PIJP
WETERING-
CIRCUIT
1E JACOB V CAMPENSTRAAT
TE JACOB V. CAMPENSTRAAT
M HEINEKEN-
PLEIN
Heineken
Experience
QUELLIJNSTRAAT
FERDINAND BOLSTRAAT
FRANS-
HALS-STRAAT
DANIEL STALPERT-
STRAAT
SARPHEDAMSTRAAT
GERARD DOUSTRAAT
ALBERT CUYPSTRAAT
JO HELSTR
GOVERT FLINCK
STRAAT
EERSTE JAN STEENSTRAAT
EERSTE JAN VAN DER HEIJDENSTRAAT
RUSTENBURGERSTRAAT
CORN
TROOST
PLEIN
VAN OSTADESTRAAT
CENTUURBAAN
FERD BOLSTR
JOZEF ISRAELSKADE
AMSTELKADE
CHURCHILLLAAN
CHURCHILLLAAN
RUYSDAELKADE
HOBBEMAKADE
Rijksmuseum
HONTHORSTSTRAAT
MUSEUMPLEIN
ROELOF
HART
PLEIN
R. HARTSTRAAT
VAN BAERLESTRAAT
STADIONWEG
APOLLOLAAN
APOLLOLAAN
Noorder Amstelkanaal
OUD ZUID

0   250 m

△ De Pijp shop

a place for the bourgeoisie to take a picnic. Heading east from the Sarphati-park, the main **Ceintuurbaan** artery crosses **Van Woustraat** – a long, unremarkable shopping street, though with a number of speciality ethnic food shops – before it reaches the River Amstel. At the river, turn right along Amsteldijk for the short walk south to the **Gemeentearchief** or Municipal Archives at Amsteldijk 67 (Daily 11am–5pm during exhibitions, otherwise Mon–Fri 10am–5pm; ☎020/572 0202; free), on the corner with Tolstraat. Housed in a large and flashy neo-Gothic confection built as the district's town hall in 1895, the archives provide extensive research facilities: all births, marriages and deaths from the early sixteenth century onwards are on record here, and there's also an enormous collection of newspapers, posters, plans and documents. Of more general interest, however, are the temporary exhibitions on the city's past that are held here regularly.

The Nieuw Zuid

Southwest of De Pijp and the Oud Zuid, the **Nieuw Zuid** (New South), reach-able direct from the city centre by trams #5 or #24, encompasses the whole area south of the Noorder Amstel canal to the railway tracks, as well as the old

Rivierenbuurt district wedged in between the railway track, the River Amstel and the Amstel canal. By contrast with the Oud Zuid, this was the first properly planned extension to the city since the concentric canals of the seventeenth century. The Dutch architect, Hendrik Petrus Berlage (1856–1934), was responsible for the relatively sober overall plan, but after his death much of the implementation passed to a pair of prominent architects of the **Amsterdam School**, Michael de Klerk (1884–1923) and Piet Kramer (1881–1961), who added a playfulness to the scheme – turrets and bulging windows, sloping roofs and frilly balustrades – that you can still see in the buildings here today. Neither was this architectural virtuosity confined to the houses of the well-to-do. In 1901 a reforming Housing Act forced the city council into a concerted effort to clear Amsterdam's slums, a principal result being several quality public housing projects designed by De Klerk and Kramer. There's one extant example in the Westerdok (see p.92) and another here in the Nieuw Zuid, **De Dageraad**, though neither is as fanciful as the duo's phantasmagorical Scheepvaarthuis (see p.69). Cutbacks in the city's subsidy meant that the more imaginative aspects of Berlage's original scheme for the Nieuw Zuid were toned down, but the area's wide boulevards and narrower side streets were completed as conceived. In this, Berlage wanted to reinterpret the most lauded feature of the city's seventeenth-century canals: their combination of monumental grandeur and picturesque scale.

Nowadays the Nieuw Zuid is one of Amsterdam's most sought-after addresses. **Apollolaan**, **Stadionweg** and, a little way to the east, **Churchilllaan** are especially favoured, and are home to some of the city's most sumptuous prop-

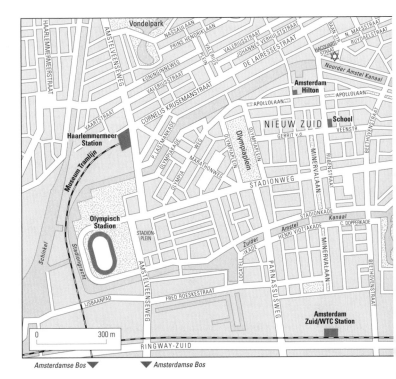

erties – huge idiosyncratic mansions set back from the street behind trees and generous gardens. Locals pop to the shops on **Beethovenstraat**, the main drag running south right through the district from the Noorder Amstel canal. Nonetheless, posh residential areas are rarely much fun for the casual visitor and the Nieuw Zuid is no exception. More enticing is the pleasant greenery of the **Beatrixpark**, and, slightly further out beyond the railway tracks, the sprawling parkland of the **Amsterdamse Bos** – both providing a pleasant interlude from the network of suburban streets.

Apollolaan and around

Apollolaan, a wide residential boulevard just south of the Noorder Amstel canal, is representative of Berlage's intended grand design, but despite its obvious gracefulness, the Nieuw Zuid was far from an instant success with the Dutch bourgeoisie. Indeed, in the late 1930s the district became something of a Jewish enclave – the family of Anne Frank, for example, lived for a time on Merwedeplein just off Churchilllaan. This embryonic community was swept away during the German occupation, their sufferings retold in Grete Weil's (Dutch language) novel *Tramhalte Beethovenstraat*. A reminder of those terrible times is to be found at the intersection of Apollolaan and Beethovenstraat, where a **monument**, built in 1954, commemorates the reprisal shooting of 29 resistance fighters here in 1944 in retribution for the killing of German security officer – a striking monument showing three desperate figures.

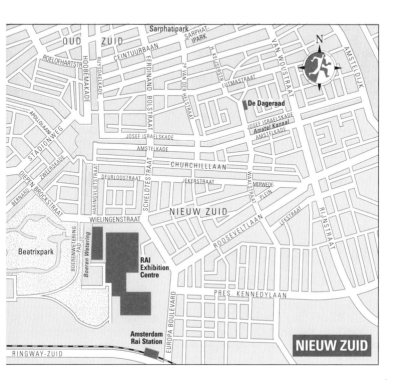

Another reminder is the **school** just off Apollolaan on Rubenstraat – itself named after an Amsterdam Resistance fighter who was shot for organizing false identity papers – which was once the headquarters of the Gestapo, and where the Frank family were brought after their capture.

On a different note, Apollolaan is also known for the **Amsterdam Hilton** at no. 138, where John Lennon and Yoko Ono staged their famous week-long "Bed-In" for peace in 1969. Part celebrity farce, part skilful publicity stunt, the couple's anti-war proclamations were certainly heard far and wide, but in Britain the press focused on the supposed evil influence of Yoko on John, which satisfied at least three subtexts – racism, sexism and anti-Americanism.

Beatrixpark to De Dageraad

From Apollolaan, head south down **Beethovenstraat**, and beyond the Amstel canal, take the first left, Cornelius Dopperkade, for the nearest of several entrances into the **Beatrixpark** (daily dawn to dusk; free). Recently renovated, this appealing park, with its footpaths and walled garden, is latticed by narrow waterways fed by the Amstel canal. It's a pleasant place for a stroll and in summer you can catch free open-air concerts. The park's eastern perimeter is marked by the Boeren Wetering canal, beyond which rises the clumpy **RAI exhibition centre**, a trade and conference complex that was built as part of the city's plan to attract more business trade. It's of little interest in itself, but if you're at a loose end, you might want to check out one of the centre's many exhibitions. To get there, leave the Beatrixpark at Boerenweteringpad and then follow Wielingenstraat across the canal.

A more appealing option is to take a left off Wielingenstraat up Haringvlietstraat, which leads after about 350m to the west end of **Churchilllaan**. This wide and well-heeled boulevard leads in its turn to Waalstraat, which, after crossing the Amstel canal, band ecomes Pieter Lodewijk Takstraat, a short narrow street that is home to **De Dageraad** ("The Dawn") housing project, completed in 1923 and one of the most successful examples of the Amsterdam School of architecture. Architects De Klerk and Kramer used a reinforced concrete frame as an underlay to the structure, thus permitting folds, tucks and curves in the brick exterior – a technique known as "apron architecture" (*Schortjesarchitectuur*). The facades are punctuated by strong, angular doors, sloping roofs and turrets, and you'll find a corner tower at the end of every block.

From De Dageraad, you can either walk up to the Albert Cuypstraat market (see above), about 800m away to the north, or return to the Churchilllaan to catch tram #12 northwest to the Concertgebouw, and then tram #16 heading west to the Haarlemmermeer Station – for the Amsterdamse Bos.

The Amsterdamse Bos

With almost ten square kilometres of wooded parkland, the **Amsterdamse Bos** is the city's largest open space. Planted during the 1930s, the park was a laudable, large-scale attempt to provide gainful work for the city's unemployed, whose numbers had risen alarmingly following the Wall Street Crash of 1929. Originally a bleak area of flat, marshy fields, it's a mixture of well-tended city park, leafy waterways, and deep woodland and grassy meadows, cut by footpaths and cycleways.

The main **entrance** to the Bos is in the northeast corner of the park, close to the junction of Amstelveenseweg and Van Nijenrodeweg, around 500m south of the main southern ringroad and some 3km south of the west end of the Vondelpark. **Buses** #142, #170 and #172, from Centraal Station and the Leidseplein, ply Amstelveenseweg; or you can take the #222 Schiphol bus, which runs from Centraal Station via Leidsplein and Haarlemmermeer Station. Once there you can rent a **bike** (March–Oct) just inside the park entrance – much the best way of getting around. Canoes and pedaloes can be rented here too. The **Bezoekerscentrum het Bosmuseum**, just inside the main entrance at Koenenkade 56 (daily 10am–5pm; free; ⓦwww.amsterdamsebos.nl), is a visitor information centre that provides maps and basic information on the park's facilities, and has an exhibition on its history and widlife upstairs. Also here is the convivial **café-restaurant**, *Grand Café Bosbaan* (☎020 404.4869), which does drinks, snacks and full meals, and whose terrace overlooks the **Bosbaan** – a kilometre-long dead-straight canal, popular for boating and swimming. Elsewhere in the park there are children's playgrounds and spaces for various sports, including ice skating. There's also a reserve in the south containing bison, buffalo and deer. Or just walk, jog or cycle your way around by way of the wide choice of clearly marked trails.

The Museum Tramlijn

It's a little more convoluted, but you can also get to the Amsterdamse Bos on the vintage trams of the **Museumtramlijn** (May–Oct Sun 11am–5pm, July–Aug also Wed at 1.45pm & 3.15pm; ☎0900 423 1100; €3.50 return). The trams depart from the Haarlemmermeer Station, located beside Amstelveenseweg, about 600m south of the western tip of the Vondelpark. To get to Haarlemmermeer Station, catch buses #170, #172 or #222, or trams #6 or #16 from Centraal Station. The Museumtramlijn trams, imported from as far away as Vienna and Prague, clank south along the eastern edge of the Bos to the suburb of Bovenkerk on its southeast corner –a forty-minute journey in all, although you can get off earlier, at the main entrance to the park, or at other stops along the way.

The CoBrA Museum of Modern Art

A little way east of the Amsterdamse Bos is the **CoBra Museum of Modern Art**, bang next to Amstelveen station at Sandbergplein 13 (Tues–Sun 11am–5pm; €7; ⓦwww.cobra-museum.nl), and also reachable by metro to Amstelveen, or a #5 tram (it's a ten-minute walk from the metro station, slightly less from the tram stop). This bright modern gallery displays the works of the artists of the post-war **CoBra movement**, founded in 1948, which grew out of the cities of Copenhagen, Brussels and Amsterdam – hence the name. CoBrA were kind of post-war European art punks, and their first exhibition, held at Amsterdam's Stedelijk Museum, not surprisingly caused controversy, their big colourful canvases, with bold lines and confident forms, displaying a spontaneity and inclusivity that was unusual for the art world at the time. You'll only find a scattering of their work here – the museum's soothing white galleries, flanked with glass and looking out onto the canal behind also host regular temporary exhibitions of contemporaneous works and artists – but there's enough to get an idea of what CoBrA was about, not least Karel Appel's weird, junky bird sculpture outside the front (a model of which you can see inside) and the brash, childlike paintings of Appel (in many ways the movement's leading light), Constant, Corneille and others in the rest of the gallery. There's a good shop, too, with plenty of prints and books on the movement and the times.

Amsterdam Oost

Next door to Amsterdam's Old South, **Amsterdam Oost** (East) is another rough-and-ready working-class quarter stretching out beyond the Singelgracht, although it's less gentrified than de Pijp. The area begins with Amsterdam's old eastern gate, the **Muiderpoort** (pronounced "mao-der-port"), overlooking the canal at the end of Plantage Middenlaan (p.104). In the 1770s the gate was revamped in pompous style, a Neoclassical refit complete with a flashy cupola and grandiosely carved pediment. Napoleon staged a triumphal entry into the city through the Muiderpoort in 1811, but his imperial pleasure was tempered by his half-starved troops, who could barely be restrained from helping themselves in a city of (what was to them) amazing luxury. Despite its general lack of appeal the Oost district does have one obvious attraction – the **Tropenmuseum**, near the Muiderpoort and perched on the corner of another of the city's municipal parks, the **Oosterpark**.

The Tropenmuseum

Across the Singelgracht canal on Mauritskade rises the gabled and turreted **Royal Tropen Instituut** – formerly the Royal Colonial Institute – a sprawling complex which contains the **KIT Tropenmuseum** (Daily 10am–5pm; €7.50, 6- to 17-year-olds €3.75; @www.tropenmuseum.nl; tram #9 from Centraal Station), whose entrance is around the side at Linnaeusstraat 2. With its cavernous central hall and three floors of gallery space, this is Amsterdam's ethnographic museum, focusing on all the world's tropical and subtropical zones – and doing so incredibly well, with a spectacular collection of art, applied art and other exhibits, displayed in an engaging, modern, yet entirely gimmick-free way. Among many artefacts, there are Javanese stone friezes, elaborate carved wooden boats from the Pacific, a Thai temple, a gamelan orchestra, a whole room of masks, and some incredible ritual totem poles cut from giant New Guinea mangroves. The collection is imaginatively presented through a variety of media – slides, videos and sound recordings – and you can watch everything from film of Dutch colonials meeting the natives over 100 years ago to video footage of Bob Marley and other cultural icons; and there are

△ The Tropenmuseum

creative and engaging displays devoted to such subjects as music-making and puppetry, and traditional storytelling. Perhaps best of all are the museum's great, studiously authentic reconstructions of contemporary life around the world – a mock-up of a Nigerian bar and residential compound, a Middle Eastern teahouse, a south American café, a Filipino Jeepney – plus its candid expositions on the problems besetting the developing world, both urban (Manila, Mumbai) and rural, such as the destruction of the world's tropical rainforests. The permanent collection is also enhanced by an ambitious programme of temporary exhibitions; there's a great **shop**, with crafts and music from and books about the developing world, and downstairs the **Tropen Instituut Theater**, which specializes in Third World cinema, music and dance. Part of the museum is also geared up for children under the age of 12, with a section known as the **Tropenmuseum Junior** that takes a hands-on approach to the same themes as the main museum but operates restricted opening hours (see p.24, 'Kids' Amsterdam').

The Oosterpark and beyond

Behind the Royal Tropen Instituut, the manicured greenery of the **Oosterpark** is a pleasant introduction to the massed housing that extends south and east. A working-class district for the most part, particularly on the far side of Linnaeusstraat, the area also has a high immigrant presence, and the street names – Javastraat, Balistraat, Borneostraat – recall Holland's colonial past. This is one of the city's poorer neighbourhoods, with a sea of ageing terraced houses, though whole streets have been torn down to make way for new and better public housing – and there's the inevitable creeping gentrification. One of the few reasons to venture out this way is the **Dapperstraat market** (Mon–Sat 9am–5pm), one block east of Linnaeusstraat. This eastern equivalent to the Albert Cuypstraat market (see p.129) is a diverse affair, where you can pick up a quarter-kilo of Edam at one stall and fragrant Vietnamese *loempia* at the next.

The Amsterdam ArenA

Not strictly in Amsterdam Oost, but nonetheless on this side of town, the new home ground of Ajax, the **Amsterdam ArenA** (April–Sept daily 10am–6pm; Oct–March Mon–Sat 10am–5pm; museum and stadium tour €8.50, museum only €3.50), is well worth the fifteen-minute metro trip down to visit both the Ajax Museum and to take a tour of the stadium itself. Either take the metro to Strandvliet and walk around the stadium to the main entrance on the far side, or a stop further on to Bijlmer station, from which the so-called ArenA Boulevard, lined with new shops and cafés, leads to the main entrance. Much as you would expect, the museum is a historical homage to Holland's most successful club side, Ajax, charting its origins at the turn of the century – lots of photos of men in big shorts in muddy fields – through its various stadia and the evolution of the famous red-and-white strip. There are special shrines to two of the clubs's most illustrious players – Cruyff and Van Basten – and the centrepiece, true to the club's obvious self-image as one of the big hitters of European football (there's relatively little on the domestic league), is a display describing Ajax's European campaigns, with tickets, programmes, shirts and footage of the key moments from each final, taking in their first victory – in 1971 against Panathinaikos – to their most recent, against AC Milan in 1995. As for the stadium, tours are conducted in Dutch and English about every 45 minutes between 11am and 4.30pm and last about an hour. They take in main concourses, the press room, where you can snap yourself in front of the sponsors logos, and the view from up in the press box – as well as allowing you onto a corner of the hallowed turf. Actually the pitch is perhaps the most remarkable thing about the Amsterdam ArenA: the stadium is built in such a way that the grass receives no sunlight and not a lot of wind, which means that it doesn't drain or grow very well and has to be relaid at least two or three times a year, sometimes more. (See p.245 for more on seeing a game at the ArenA.)

△ Amsterdam ArenA

Amsterdam west

Of all Amsterdam's outer districts, **Amsterdam west** is probably the least interesting for the visitor, as it's primarily a residential area with only a couple of minor parks as possible attractions. That said, the **Oud West** (Old West), beyond the Singelgracht and north of the Vondelpark, does have a busy Turkish and North African street life, which is seen at its most vigorous at the daily **Katestraat market**, about halfway down **Kinkerstraat** (trams #7 and #17). Beyond, in the **Nieuw West** (New West) districts of Bos en Lommer, De Baarsjes and Overtoomse Veld, the best you'll do is the large but really rather ordinary **Rembrandtpark**.

Amsterdam Noord

Solidly residential, **Amsterdam Noord** (North), on the far side of the River IJ, has flourished since the construction of the IJ tunnel linked it with the city centre in the 1960s. A modern suburban sprawl, the district is short on charm, but the determined can weather the aesthetic gloom to reach the open countryside beyond. The area to head for is the **Waterland**, an expanse of peat meadows, lakes, polders and marshland to the northeast of the built-up area. Until the turn of the twentieth century, this parcel of land was a marshy fen, whose scattered population made a healthy living raising and grazing cattle to be sold in Amsterdam. The Waterland was then made much more tractable by the digging of drainage canals, prompting wealthy Amsterdammers to build their summer residences here. These myriad waterways still pattern the Waterland and are home to a wide range of **waterfowl**, as are the many lakes, the largest of which – abutting the Markermeer, formerly part of the Zuider Zee – is the **Kinselmeer**. Easily the best way to explore the Waterland is by **bike** and the VVV sells a Waterland leaflet, which outlines a circular, 38-kilometre bike tour. The recommended route begins at the **Adelaarswegveer ferry dock** (see box below) on the north side of the IJ, from where you follow Meeuwenlaan to the large roundabout at the start of Nieuwendammerdijk. This long thin lane leads east, running parallel to the river, before it meets Schellingwoudedijk and then Durger Dammerdijk at the southern tip of the long dike that stretches up the coast, with the polders and a scattering of tiny villages just inland.

Ferries across the IJ

GVB operates two **ferries** across the IJ from De Ruijterkade, behind Centraal Station. Neither ferry (*veer*) takes cars but both carry foot passengers, bicycles and motorbikes for free. Of the two, the **Buiksloterwegveer** (Mon–Sat 6.30am–10.54pm, till 9pm from Buiksloterweg, Sun 11.06am–6.54pm) shuttles back and forth every six minutes or so, running to the foot of Buiksloterweg. The smaller **Adelaarswegveer** (Mon–Sat 6.27am–11.57pm, Sun 9.12am–11.57pm) connects with the southern end of Meeuwenlaan, the starting point of the Waterland bike tour; it runs roughly every ten to fifteen minutes.

7

Day-trips from the city

Although Amsterdammers may try to persuade you that there's nothing remotely worth seeing outside their own city, the truth is very much the opposite – indeed, you're spoilt for choice. The fast and efficient Dutch railway network puts a whole swathe of the Netherlands within easy reach, including all of the **Randstad** (ring city), a sprawling conurbation that stretches south of Amsterdam and encompasses the country's other big cities, primarily The Hague, Utrecht and Rotterdam. Amidst this urban pile-up, and very close to Amsterdam, is one especially appealing medium-sized town – **Haarlem**, whose attractive centre is home to the outstanding Frans Hals Museum. Not only that but Haarlem is also the briefest of train rides from the wide sandy beaches of **Zandvoort**, one of Holland's most popular resorts, and but a short bus ride from the pristine coastal dunes, woods and beaches of the **Nationaal Park Zuid–Kennemerland**, which stretches north from Zandvoort to the ugly port of Ijmuiden. Further south – about 40km from Amsterdam and 15km from Haarlem – is another enticing attraction, the world–famous **Keukenhof gardens**, the springtime showcase for the country's flower growers, the land striped by long lines of brilliant blooms.

To the north of Amsterdam, there's more countryside and less city. The most obvious targets are the old seaports bordering the freshwater **Markermeer**, which forms part of the Ijsselmeer, created when the Afsluitdijk dam cut the former Zuider Zee off from the North Sea in 1932 (see box on p.150). No trains venture out along this coast, but it's an easy bus ride from Amsterdam to the nearest three: the former fishing village of **Marken**, the port of **Volendam** and – best of the lot – the beguiling, one-time shipbuilding centre of **Edam**. Edam is, of course, famous for its cheese, but its open-air **cheese market** is not a patch on that of **Alkmaar**, itself an amiable small town forty minutes by train north from Amsterdam. Alkmaar is also within easy striking distance of another stretch of undeveloped coastline, protected as the **Noordhollands Duin-reservaat**, extending north from Ijmuiden to the hamlet of Camperduin.

Public transport to all these destinations from Amsterdam is fast, frequent and inexpensive.

Haarlem and around

Though only fifteen minutes (and €3.20) from Amsterdam by train, amiable **HAARLEM** has a very different pace and feel from its big-city neighbour and it's well worth an afternoon in itself – maybe an overnight stay if you're tired of

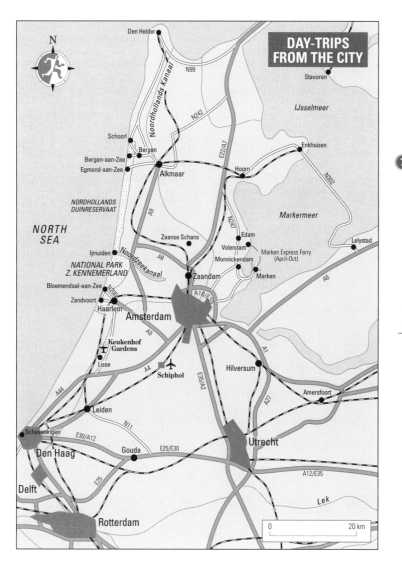

the crowded capital. Founded on the banks of the River Spaarne in the tenth century, the town first prospered when the counts of Holland decided to levy shipping tolls here, but later it developed as a cloth-making centre. In 1572 the townsfolk sided with the Protestant rebels against the Habsburgs, a decision they must have regretted when a large Spanish army led by Frederick of Toledo besieged them in December of the same year. The siege was a desperate affair that lasted for eight months, but finally the town surrendered after receiving various assurances of good treatment – assurances which Frederick promptly broke, massacring over two thousand of the Protestant garrison and all their

Calvinist ministers. Recaptured in 1577 by the Protestant army of William the Silent, Haarlem went on to enjoy its greatest prosperity in the seventeenth century, becoming a centre for the arts and home to a flourishing school of **painters**. Nowadays, it's an easily absorbed town of around 150,000 people, with a good-looking centre studded with fine old buildings and home to the wonderful **Frans Hals Museum**, located in the almshouse where the artist spent his last years.

Haarlem is also a short train ride from one of the country's busiest coastal resorts, the clumpy modern town of **Zandvoort**, where the long sandy beach is the main event. More enticing still is the **Nationaal Park Zuid–Kennemerland**, a slab of wood, dune and beach that stretches north along the coast from Zandvoort. Criss-crossed by hiking trails, the park has several entrances, but the most appealing are reached along the **N200** linking Haarlem with the seaside shacks of tiny **Bloemendaal–aan–Zee**.

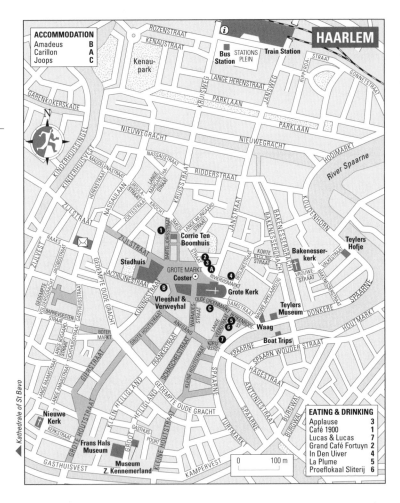

△ Haarlem riverfront houses

The Town

At the heart of Haarlem is the **Grote Markt**, a wide and attractive open space flanked by an appealing ensemble of neo–Gothic, Gothic and Renaissance architecture, including an intriguing if exceptionally garbled **Stadhuis**, whose turrets and towers, balconies, gables and galleries were put together in piecemeal fashion between the fourteenth and the seventeenth centuries. At the other end of the Grote Markt stands a **statue** of a certain Laurens Coster (1370–1440), who, Haarlemmers insist, is the true inventor of printing (despite most historians agreeing that it was the German Johannes Gutenberg). Legend tells of Coster cutting a letter "A" from the bark of a tree, dropping it into the sand by accident, and, hey presto, he realised how to create the printed word – the statue has him holding the wooden letter up in an enthusiastic pose.

The Grote Kerk

The Coster statue stands in the shadow of the **Grote Kerk** or **Sint Bavokerk** (Mon–Sat 10am–4pm; €1.50), a soaring Gothic structure supported by mighty buttresses that dwarfs the surrounding clutter of ecclesiastical outhouses. If you've been to the Rijksmuseum in Amsterdam (see p.116), the church may seem familiar, at least from the outside, since it turns up in several paintings of Haarlem by the seventeenth-century artist Gerrit Berckheyde – only the black-coated burghers are missing. Finished in 1538, and 150 years in the making, the church is surmounted by a good-looking lantern tower, which perches above the transept crossing; the tower is made of wood clad in lead, a replacement for a much grander stone tower that had to be dismantled in 1514 when its supports began to buckle.

Entry to the church is round the back, on Oude Groenmarkt, with a humble passageway leading to the southeast end of the **nave**, whose towering beauty is enhanced by the creaminess of the stone and the bright simplicity of the whitewashed walls. The Protestants cleared the church of most of its decoration during the Reformation, but the splendid wrought-iron **choir screen** has survived as have the choir's wooden **stalls** with their folksy misericords. In front of the screen is the conspicuous Neoclassical **tomb** of Haarlem's own Christiaan Brunings (1736–1805), a much–lauded hydraulic engineer and director of Holland's water board, who devised a detailed strategy for controlling the waters of the the lower Rhine.

Close by, next to the south transept, is the **Brewers' Chapel**, where the central pillar bears two black markers – one showing the height of a local giant, the 2.64m-tall Daniel Cajanus, who died in 1749, the other the 0.84m-high dwarf Simon Paap from Zandvoort. Further west still, on the north side of the nave, is the pocket–sized **Dog Whippers' Chapel**, built for the men employed to keep dogs out of the church, and now separated from the nave by an iron grille. At the west end of the church, the mighty Christian Müller **organ** was manufactured in Amsterdam in the 1730s. It is said to have been played by Handel and Mozart (the latter on his tour of the country in 1766, at the age of 10) and is one of the biggest in the world, with over five thousand pipes and loads of snazzy Baroque embellishment. Hear it at work at one of the free organ recitals held in the summer (mid-May to mid-Sept Tues 8.15pm, July & Aug also Thurs 3pm; free). Beneath the organ, Jan Baptist Xavery's lovely group of draped marble figures represent Poetry and Music offering thanks to the town, which is depicted as a patroness of the arts – in return for its generous support in the purchase of the organ.

The Vleeshal, Verweyhal and Corrie Ten Boomhuis

Back outside, just beyond the western end of the church, the rambling **Hallen** divides into two: first up is the old meat market, the **Vleeshal**, which boasts a flashy Dutch Renaissance facade and a basement given over to a modest **Archeologisch Museum** (Wed–Sun 1–5pm; free). A couple of doors along is the **Verweyhal** (Tues–Sat 11am–5pm, Sun noon–5pm; €4), where the emphasis is on temporary exhibitions of modern and contemporary art and photography.

After these modest attractions, you'll probably want to push on south to Haarlem's star turn, the Frans Hals Museum (see below), but you might consider the brief detour north from the Grote Markt to the **Corrie Ten Boomhuis**, Barteljorisstraat 19 (Tues–Sat: April–Oct 10am–3.30pm; Nov–March 11am–2.30pm; 50min guided tours only; free; ⊛www.corrietenboom.com), where a Dutch family – the Booms – hid fugitives, Resistance fighters and Jews alike, above their watchmaking shop during World War II. There is not too much to actually look at, but the guided tour is instructive and moving if a tad drawn out. The family, whose bravery sprang from their Christian faith, was betrayed to the Gestapo in 1944 and only one, Corrie Boom, survived.

The Frans Hals Museum

Haarlem's biggest pull, the **Frans Hals Museum**, at Groot Heiligland 62 (Tues–Sat 11am–5pm, Sun noon–5pm; €5.40; ⊛www.franshalsmuseum.nl), is a five-minute stroll south from the Grote Markt – via a pleasant pedestrianized shopping street, Schagchelstraat. The museum occupies an old almshouse complex, a much modified red-brick *hofje* with a central courtyard, where the aged Hals lived out his last destitute years on public funds. The collection comprises a handful of prime works by Hals along with a small but eclectic sample of Dutch paintings from the fifteenth century onwards, all immaculately presented and labelled in English and Dutch. There's also a small separate section consisting of a life-size, replica, seventeenth-century Haarlem street.

Little is known of **Frans Hals** (c.1580–1666). Born in Antwerp, the son of Flemish refugees who settled in Haarlem in the late 1580s, his extant oeuvre is relatively small – some two hundred paintings, and nothing like the number of sketches and studies left behind by his contemporary, Rembrandt. His outstanding gift was as a portraitist, showing a sympathy with his subjects and an ability to capture fleeting expression that some say even Rembrandt lacked. Seemingly quick and careless flashes of colour characterize his work, but they are always blended into a coherent and marvellously animated whole.

The museum begins with the work of other artists: first comes a small group of early sixteenth-century paintings, the most prominent of which, displayed in Room 2, is a triptych from the **School of Hans Memling**. In the same room is a curious painting by Haarlem-born **Jan Mostaert** (1475–1555), his *West Indian Scene* depicting a band of naked, poorly armed natives trying to defend

△ Frans Hals Museum

themselves against the cannon and sword of their Spanish invaders; the comparison with the Dutch Protestants was obvious. Next door, Room 3 displays a polished *Adam and Eve* by **Jan van Scorel** (1495–1562) and the same artist's *Pilgrims to Jerusalem*, one of the country's earliest group portraits.

The adjacent Room 4 displays **Cornelis Cornelisz van Haarlem**'s (1562–1638) *Wedding of Peleus and Thetis*, an appealing rendition of what was then a popular subject, though Cornelisz gives as much attention to the arrangement of his elegant nudes as to the subject. This marriage precipitated civil war amongst the gods and was used by the Dutch as a warning against discord, a call for unity during the long war with Spain. Similarly, and also in Room 4, the same artist's *Massacre of the Innocents* connects the biblical story with the Spanish siege of Haarlem in 1572. Moving on, Room 6 features several paintings by the **Haarlem Mannerists**, including three tiny and precise works by **Karel van Mander** (1548–1606), leading light of the Haarlem School and mentor of many of the city's most celebrated painters. There's more Cornelis Cornelisz van Haarlem in Room 7, most notably an early militia group portrait and a Mannerist Biblical work entitled *Worshipping the Golden Calf*.

The **Hals paintings** begin in earnest in **Room 14** with a set of five "Civic Guard" portraits – group portraits of the militia companies initially formed to defend the country from the Spanish, but which later became social clubs for the gentry. Getting a commission to paint one of these portraits was a well-paid privilege – Hals got his first in 1616 – but their composition was a tricky affair and often the end result was dull and flat. With great flair and originality, Hals made the group portrait a unified whole instead of a static collection of individual portraits, his figures carefully arranged, but so cleverly as not to appear contrived. For a time, Hals himself was a member of the Company of St George, and in the *Officers of the Militia Company of St George* he appears in the top left-hand corner – one of his few self-portraits. Hals' later paintings are darker, more contemplative works, closer to Rembrandt in their lighting and increasingly sombre in their outlook. In **Room 18**, amongst several portraits of different groups of regents, is Hals' *Regents of St Elizabeth Gasthuis*, a serious but benign work of 1641 with a palpable sense of optimism, whereas his twin *Regents* and *Regentesses of the Oudemannenhuis*, currently displayed in **Room 19**, is deep with despair. The latter were commissioned when Hals was in his eighties, a poor man despite a successful painting career, hounded for money by the town's tradesmen and by the mothers of his illegitimate children. As a result he was dependent on the charity of people like those depicted here: their cold, self-satisfied faces staring out of the gloom, the women reproachful, the men only marginally more affable. The character just right of centre in the *Regents* painting has been labelled (and indeed looks) drunk, although it is inconceivable that Hals would have depicted him in this condition; it's more likely that he was suffering from some kind of facial paralysis, and his jauntily cocked hat was simply a popular fashion of the time. There are those who claim Hals had lost his touch by the time he painted these pictures, yet their sinister, almost ghostly power, suggests quite the opposite. Van Gogh's remark that "Frans Hals had no fewer than 27 blacks" suddenly makes perfect sense.

Near the end of the museum, Room 23 displays several raucous peasant and tavern scenes by **Adriaen van Ostade** (1610–1684) and **Adriaen Brouwer** (1605–1638). Brouwer could paint from experience: fond of a drink, he had a roller-coaster life, even being arrested by the Spanish as a spy, before his untimely death from the plague in Antwerp. Finally, just before you exit, look out for Room 24's berserk *Dutch Proverbs* by **Pieter Brueghel the Younger** (1564–1638).

Excursions from Harlem

In the summertime, **Woltheus Cruises**, by the river at Spaarne 11 (☎023/535 77 23, ⊛www.woltheus-haarlem.nl), operates several boat trips from Haarlem, including excursions to Artis zoo in Amsterdam and a local Molen (windmill) cruise (mid–May to Sept 1 weekly; 4hr 30min; €20). Advance reservations are recommended.

To the River Spaarne

Back up the street from the Frans Hals Museum, at Groot Heiligland 47, stands the **Historisch Museum Zuid–Kennemerland** (Tues–Sat noon–5pm, Sun 1–5pm; €1), which tracks through a really rather pedestrian history of Haarlem in premises that were once used as a women's almshouse. From here, stroll south down Groot Heiligland and turn left at the end along the canal and you soon reach the **River Spaarne**, whose gentle curves mark the eastern periphery of the town centre. Turn left here, along riverside Turfmarkt and its continuation Spaarne, to reach the surly stonework of the **Waag** (Weigh House) and then the country's oldest museum, the **Teylers Museum**, located in a grand Neoclassical building at Spaarne 16 (Tues–Sat 10am–5pm, Sun noon–5pm; €5.50). Founded in 1774 by a wealthy local philanthropist, one Pieter Teyler van der Hulst, the museum should appeal to scientific and artistic tastes alike. It contains everything from fossils, bones and crystals, to weird, H.G. Wells-type technology and sketches and line drawings by Raphael, Rembrandt and Claude, among others. Look in, too, on the rooms beyond, filled with work by eighteenth- and nineteenth-century Dutch painters, principally Breitner, Israëls, Weissenbruch and, not least, Wijbrand Hendriks, who was once the keeper of the art collection here. Teyler also bestowed his charity on the riverside **Teylers Hofje**, a little way east around the bend of the Spaarne at Koudenhorn 64. With none of the cosy familiarity of the town's other *hofjes*, this is a grandiose affair, a Neoclassical edifice dating from 1787 and featuring solid columns and cupolas. Nearby, the elegant fifteenth-century tower of the **Bakenesserkerk** (no public access), on Vrouwestraat, is a flamboyant, onion–domed affair poking high above the Haarlem skyline.

Practicalities

With fast and frequent services from Amsterdam, Haarlem's handsome **train station**, in a Dutch version of the Arts and Crafts style, is located on the north side of the city centre, about ten minutes' walk from the main square, the Grote Markt. **Cycle rental** is available at the train station for about €6 per day. The **bus station** is in front of the train station on Stationsplein and the **VVV** is adjacent (April–Sept Mon–Fri 9am–5.30pm, Sat 10am–4pm; Oct–March Mon–Fri 9.30am–5pm, Sat 10am–2pm; ☎0900/61 61 600, premium line).

The VVV issues free city maps and brochures, sells hiking and cycling maps of the Nationaal Park Zuid–Kennemerland (see next page), and, although there's no strong reason to overnight here, it also has a small supply of **rooms in private houses**, mostly on the outskirts of town and costing in the region of €40 per double per night. Alternatively, Haarlem has three recommendable central **hotels** (see overleaf). The pick of the town's **restaurants** and **bars** are conveniently clustered around the Grote Markt and on Oude Groenmarkt, round the back of the Grote Kerk.

Hotels

Amadeus Grote Markt 10 ⊕023/532 45 30, ⓦwww.amadeus-hotel.com. Homely, medium–sized hotel with plain but perfectly comfortable en-suite rooms. The front bedrooms have enjoyable views over the main square. Doubles from €70.

Carillon Grote Markt 27 ⊕023/531 05 91, ⓦwww.hotelcarillon.com. Inexpensive place with spartan modern rooms, but friendly atmosphere. Opposite the Grote Kerk. Doubles with shared facilities €60, en suite €75.

Joops Oude Groenmarkt 20 ⊕023/532 22 08, ⓕ023/532 95 49. Large if somewhat austere modern rooms in a recently renovated building immediately behind the Grote Kerk. Doubles from €85.

Eating and drinking

Café 1900 Barteljorisstraat 10. With a smashing 1930s interior, right up to the swishing ceiling fans, this has long been a popular café-bar, serving drinks and light meals.

Applause Grote Markt 23a ⊕023/531 1425. A chic little bistro serving up Italian food with excellent main courses hovering around €20. Closed Mon & Tues.

Grand Café Fortuyn Grote Markt 21. A quiet, cosy café-bar with charming 1930s decor, including a tiled entrance and dinky little glass cabinets preserved from its days as a shop.

In Den Uiver Riviervismarkt 13. Just off the Grote Markt, this lively and extremely appealing bar is decked out in traditional Dutch brown style; showcases occasional live music too.

Lucas & Lucas Korte Veerstraat 1 ⊕023/534 18 55. Upmarket Italian restaurant with a menu that covers all the favourites and then some. Main courses from €15, pizzas from €12. Open Mon–Wed 4pm–2am, Thurs–Sun 2pm–2am.

Proeflokaal Sliterij Lange Veerstraat 7. Intimate and amenable bar – typically Dutch.

Restaurant La Plume Lange Veerstraat 1 ⊕023/531 32 02. A popular and very affordable restaurant with a range of tasty dishes from pastas through to traditional Dutch.

Around Haarlem: Zandvoort and the Nationaal Park Zuid–Kennemerland

The suburbs of Haarlem ramble out almost as far as **ZANDVOORT**, a major seaside resort just 5km away to the west. As Dutch resorts go, Zandvoort is pretty standard – packed in summer, dead and gusty in winter – and its agglomeration of modern apartment blocks hardly cheers the heart, but the beach is wide and sandy, it musters up a casino and a car-racing circuit and it is one of the few places in the Netherlands where the rail network reaches the coast: there's a half-hourly service from Haarlem, the journey only takes ten minutes, and Zandvoort train station is merely a five-minute walk (if that) from the beach.

If, however, you're after more than just a few hours sunbathing, the better option when it comes to exploring the coast is to delve into the pristine woods, dunes and lagoons of the **Nationaal Park Zuid–Kennemerland**, which stretches north from Zandvoort all the way up to the industrial town of **Ijmuiden**, at the mouth of the Nordzeekanaal (maps of the park are available at Haarlem VVV). Hourly **bus #81** from Haarlem bus station travels west to cut across the national park along the **N200** before reaching the coast at the huddle of fast–food joints that make up **BLOEMENDAAL–AAN–ZEE**; it then proceeds the 4km south to Zandvoort bus station, on Louis Davidsstraat, a short, signposted walk from the train station. En route, between Haarlem and Bloemendaal-aan-Zee, several bus stops give access to the clearly marked **hiking trails** that pattern the national park, but the best option is to get off at the **Koevlak** entrance – ask the driver to put you off. Three colour–coded **hiking routes** are posted at Koevlak and the most appealing is the 9km (3hr) jaunt west through wood and dune to the seashore at the **Parnassia café** (April–Nov), where you can wet your whistle gazing out across the North Sea. From the café, it's 2km by minor road to Bloemendaal-aan-Zee, where you can catch bus #81 back to Haarlem.

The Dutch bulbfields

The pancake-flat fields extending southwest from Amsterdam Schiphol airport towards Leiden are the heart of the Dutch **bulbfields**, whose bulbs and blooms support a massive industry and some ten thousand growers, as well as attracting tourists in their droves. Bulbs have flourished here since the late sixteenth century, when a certain **Carolus Clusius**, a Dutch botanist and one-time gardener to the Habsburg emperor, brought the first **tulip bulb** over from Vienna, where it had – in its turn – been brought from modern-day Turkey by an Austrian aristocrat. The tulip flourished in Holland's sandy soil and was so highly prized that it fuelled a massive **speculative bubble**. At the height of the boom – in the mid-1630s – bulbs were commanding extraordinary prices: the artist Jan van Goyen, for instance, paid 1900 guilders and two paintings for ten rare bulbs, while another set of one hundred bulbs was swapped for a coach and pair of horses. The bubble burst in 1636, thanks to the intervention of the government, and the bulb industry returned to normal, though it left hundreds of investors ruined, much to the satisfaction of the country's Calvinist ministers who had railed against the excesses.

Other types of bulb were introduced after the tulip and today the **spring flowering sequence** begins in mid-March with crocuses, followed by daffodils and yellow narcissi in late March, and hyacinths and tulips in mid- and late April through to May. Gladioli flower in August.

The Keukenhof gardens

The views of the bulbfields from any of the trains heading southwest from Schiphol airport can often be sufficient in themselves, the fields divided into stark geometric blocks of pure colour, but, with your own transport, you can take in their full beauty by way of special routes marked by hexagonal signposts; local VVVs sell pamphlets listing the best vantage points. Alternatively, you can make a beeline for the bulb growers' showcase, the **Keukenhof gardens** (late March to late May daily 8am–7.30pm; €12.50, ⓦwww.keukenhof.com), located on the edge of the little town of **LISSE**, beside the N208 about 40km southwest of Amsterdam. The largest flower gardens in the world, and dating back to 1949, the Keukenhof was designed by a group of prominent bulb growers to convert people to the joys of growing flowers from bulbs in their own gardens. Literally the "kitchen garden", its site is the former estate of a fifteenth-century countess, who used to grow herbs and vegetables for her dining table. Several million flowers are on show for their full flowering period, complemented, in case of especially harsh winters, by thousands of square metres of glasshouse holding indoor displays. You could easily spend a whole day here, swooning with the sheer abundance of it all, but to get the best of it you need to come early, before the tour buses pack the place. There are several restaurants in the grounds and a network of well-marked footpaths explore every horticultural nook and cranny.

To get to the Keukenhof by **public transport** from Amsterdam, take the train to Leiden Centraal (every 30min; 40min) and then catch bus #54, the *Keukenhof Express* (every 30min; 30min), from the adjacent bus station.

Marken, Volendam and Edam

The placid, steel-grey waters of the freshwater **Markermeer** and **IJsselmeer** lakes are popular with day-tripping Amsterdammers, who come here in their droves to sail boats, observe the waterfowl, and visit a string of dinky little towns and villages. These begin on the coast just a few kilometres north of Amsterdam with the picturesque old fishing village of **Marken** and the former seaport of **Volendam**, which is itself just a couple of kilometres from **Edam**, the pick of the bunch, a small and infinitely pretty little town of narrow canals and handsome old houses. You don't necessarily need to make a choice though, since all three places can comfortably be visited in a day.

There are fast and frequent **buses** from Amsterdam's Centraal Station to Marken, Volendam and Edam, but travelling between the three is a tad more complicated. To get from Marken by bus to both Volendam and Edam, you have to change at Monnickendam, easy enough except on Saturdays when the two buses do not pass through the same Monnickendam bus stop (see p.152). More poetically, a seasonal **passenger ferry**, the Marken Express (⊕029/936 33 31, ⓦwww.markenexpress.nl; April–Oct daily 10.30am–5.30pm every 30–45min; €6.25 return, €4 single, bikes an extra €1 one-way), shuttles along the coast between Marken and Volendam, giving a taste of the pond-like Markermeer.

Marken

Once an island in the Zuider Zee, **Marken** was, until its road connection to the mainland in 1957, pretty much a closed community, supported by a small fishing industry. Despite its proximity to Amsterdam, its biggest problem was the genetic defects caused by close and constant intermarrying, but now it's how to contain the tourists, whose numbers on summer weekends can reach alarming proportions. That said, there's no denying the picturesque charms of the island's one and only village – also called **MARKEN** – where the immaculately maintained houses, mostly painted in deep green with white trimmings, cluster on top of artificial mounds raised to protect them from the sea. There are two main parts to the village, **Havenbuurt**, behind the harbour, and **Kerkbuurt** around the **church** (mid-May to Oct Mon–Sat 10am–5pm; free), an ugly 1904 replacement for its sea–battered predecessor. Of the two, Kerkbuurt is the less touristy, its narrow lanes lined by ancient dwellings and a row of old eel-smoking houses, now the **Marker Museum**, Kerkbuurt 44 (April–Sept Mon–Sat 10am–5pm, Sun noon–4pm; Oct Mon–Sat 11am–4pm; €2), devoted to the history of the former island and its fishing industry. Across in the Havenbuurt, one or two of the houses are open to visitors, proclaiming themselves to be "typical" of Marken, and the waterfront is lined by snack bars and souvenir shops, often staffed by locals in traditional costume. It's all a tad prosaic, but now and again you get a hint of how hard life used to be – many of the houses on the waterfront are raised on stilts and although these are now panelled in, they were once open, allowing the sea to roll under the floors in bad weather, enough to terrify most people half to death.

Practicalities

Marken is accessible direct from Amsterdam on **bus #111**, departing from outside Centraal Station (every 20–30min; 30min journey). The bus drops pas-

---

The closing of the Zuider Zee

The ports, towns and villages that string along the east coast of **Noord Holland** (North Holland) flourished during Amsterdam's Golden Age, their economies buoyed up by shipbuilding, the Baltic sea trade and the demand for herring. Indeed, the Baltic trade was the lynchpin of Holland's prosperity, an immensely profitable business revolving around the import of huge quantities of grain, the supply of which was municipally controlled to guarantee against famine. The east coast had access to the open sea via the turbulent waters of the **Zuider Zee** (Southern Sea) and, to the north, the connecting **Waddenzee** (Mud Sea). Both seas were comparatively new, created when the North Sea broke through from the coast in the thirteenth century – the original coastline is marked by Texel and the Frisian Islands. However, the Zuider Zee was shallow and tidal, part salt and part freshwater, and accumulations of silt began to strangle its ports from the end of the seventeenth century. As a result, the Zuider Zee ports were effectively marooned by the 1750s, the Baltic trade slumped, and the only maritime activity was fishing – just enough to keep a cluster of tiny hamlets ticking over, from Volendam and Marken on the sea's western coast, to Stavoren and Urk on the eastern side.

The Zuider Zee may have provided a livelihood for local fishermen, but most of the country was more concerned by the flood danger it posed, as time and again storms and high tides combined to breach the east coast's defences. The first plan to seal off and reclaim the Zuider Zee was proposed in 1667, but the rotating-turret windmills that then provided the most efficient way of drying the land were insufficient for the task and matters were delayed until suitable technology arrived – in the form of the steam-driven pump. In 1891 one **Cornelis Lely** (1854–1929) proposed a retaining dike at the mouth of the Zuider Zee and his plans were finally put into effect after devastating floods hit the area in 1916. Work began on this dike, the **Afsluitdijk**, in 1920 despite some uncertainty among the engineers, who worried about a possible rise in sea level around the islands of the Waddenzee. In the event, their concerns proved groundless and, on May 28, 1932, the last gap in the dike was closed and the Zuider Zee simply ceased to exist, replaced by the freshwater **IJsselmeer**.

The original plan was to reclaim all the land protected by the Afsluitdijk, turning it into farmland for settlers from the country's overcrowded cities, and as starters three large-scale land reclamation schemes were completed over the next forty years. In addition, a complementary dike linking Enkhuizen with Lelystad was finished in 1976, thereby creating lake **Markermeer** – a necessary prelude to the draining of another vast stretch of the IJsselmeer. The engineers licked their contractual lips, but they were out of sync with the majority of the population, who were now opposed to any further draining of the lake. Partly as a result, the grand plan was abandoned and, after much governmental huffing and puffing, the Markermeer was left alone.

There are many economic benefits to be had in the closing of the Zuider Zee. The threat of flooding was removed, the country gained great chunks of new and fertile farmland and the roads that were built along the top of the two main retaining dikes brought North Holland within twenty minutes' drive of Friesland. The price was the demise of the old Zuider Zee **fishing fleet**. Without access to the open sea, it was inevitable that most of the fleet would become redundant, though some skippers wisely transferred to the north coast before the Afsluitdijk was completed. Others learnt to fish the freshwater species that soon colonized the Markermeer and IJsselmeer, but in 1970 falling stocks prompted the government to ban trawling. This was a bitter blow for many **fishermen** and there were several violent demonstrations before they bowed to the inevitable. Today, villages such as Marken and Urk are shadows of their former selves, forced to rely on tourism to survive.

sengers beside the car park on the edge of Marken village, from where it's a five-minute walk to the centre. Marken does not have a **VVV**. In season a **passenger ferry** links Marken with Volendam (see p.150), but otherwise it's a fiddly bus trip: take bus #111 back towards Amsterdam, but get off at the **Swaensborch stop** on the edge of Monnickendam village. At Swaensborch, change to bus #110, which runs from Amsterdam to Volendam and Edam. Note, however, that on Saturday bus #110 does not stop at Swaensborch, and instead you have to walk across Monnickendam to the Bernhardbrug bridge stop.

Volendam

Larger but not nearly as quaint as Marken, the old fishing village of **VOLENDAM** has had, by comparison with its neighbour, some rip-roaring cosmopolitan times. In the early years of the twentieth century it became something of an artists' retreat, with both Picasso and Renoir spending time here, along with their assorted acolytes. The artists are, however, long gone and nowadays Volendam is crammed with day-tripping tourists bobbing in and out of the souvenir stalls that run the length of the cobbled main street, whose perky gables line up just behind the harbour. It's a pleasant enough scene, if you don't mind crowds, and the antique public rooms of the *Best Western Hotel Spaander*, on the waterfront at Haven 15 (☎029/936 3595, ℻029/936 9615, ⊛www .hotelspaander.com; doubles €75), with their creaking wooden floors, low ceilings, paintings and sketches, are pleasant reminders of more artistic times. The hotel was opened in 1881 and its first owner, Leendert Spaander, was lucky to have seven daughters, quite enough to keep a whole bevy of artists in lust for a decade or two. Some of the artists paid for their lodgings by giving Spaander paintings – hence today's collection.

Practicalities

In Volendam **bus** #110 from Amsterdam and Monnickendam drops passengers on Zeestraat, just across the street from the **VVV**, at Zeestraat 37 (mid–March to Sept daily 10am–5pm; Oct to mid–March Mon–Sat 10am–3pm; ☎029/936 37 47, ⊛www.vvvvolendam.nl). From the VVV, it's a five–minute walk to the waterfront, from where, in the summertime, there is a regular **passenger ferry** to Marken (see p.150).

Edam

Just 3km from Volendam – and further up along the #110 bus route from Amsterdam – you might expect **EDAM** to be jammed with tourists considering the international fame of the rubbery red balls of cheese that carry its name. In fact, Edam usually lacks the crowds and remains a delightful, good-looking and prosperous little town of neat brick houses, high gables, swing bridges and slender canals. Founded by farmers in the twelfth century, it experienced a temporary boom in the seventeenth as a shipbuilding centre with river access to the Zuider Zee. Thereafter, it was back to the farm – and the excellent pasture land surrounding the town is still grazed by large herds of cows, though nowadays most Edam cheese is produced elsewhere, even in Germany ("Edam" is the name of a type of cheese and not its place of origin). This does, of course, rather undermine the authenticity of Edam's open-air **cheese market**, held every Wednesday morning in July and August on the Kaasmarkt (see below), but it's still a popular attraction and the only time the town heaves with tourists.

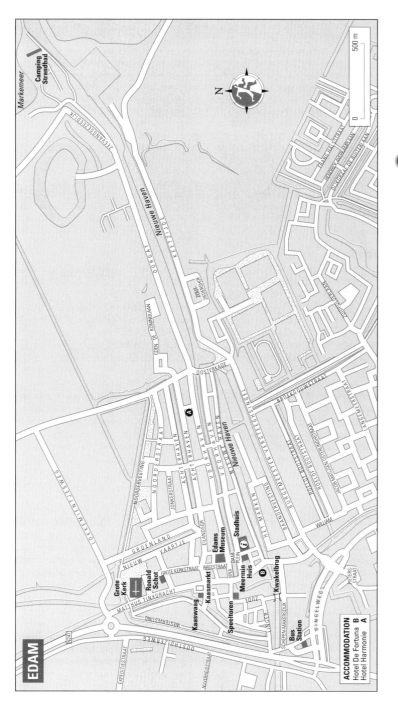

EDAM

ACCOMMODATION
Hotel De Fortuna **B**
Hotel Harmonie **A**

The mermaid of Edam

A number of **mermaid legends** have their grown up around the coastal towns of northern Holland, but Edam's is the best. In 1403, two milkmaids were rowing across the lake to the north of Edam to get to their cows, when they spied a mermaid, who they agreed must have been washed up over the sea dyke during a storm. Later, they returned to fish the mermaid out of the lake and, in the way of such things, blushes were saved all round by the layer of seaweed and moss hiding the creature's remarkable curves and contours. Back in town, the mermaid slipped into a dress willingly enough and soon picked up all the necessary domestic and devotional skills, learning how to spin, cook and kiss the crucifix, though some versions of the legend feature a less obliging mermaid who didn't take kindly to her chores and was forever trying to escape. The mermaid is supposed to have lived on in Edam for fifteen years and one of the now–demolished town gates was decorated with a mermaid statue. More important was the municipal sub–text: as the legend confirmed, the women of Edam were so kind and the town so pleasant that even a slippery siren was prepared to hole up here.

The Town

At the heart of Edam is the **Damplein**, a pint-sized main square where an elongated humpbacked bridge has long vaulted the Voorhaven **canal**, which connects the town with the Markermeer and formerly linked it to the Zuider Zee. At a stroke, the bridge stopped the canal flooding the town, as it had done with depressing regularity, but local ship builders hated the thing as it restricted navigation and on several occasions they launched night–time raids to break it down. Facing the bridge is Edam's eighteenth-century **Stadhuis**, a severe Louis XIV-style structure whose plain symmetries culminate in a squat little tower. The Stadhuis is home to the VVV (see opposite) and stands across the street from a newly opened museum, **Het huis van de Meermin** (House of the Mermaid; April–Sept Tues–Sun 11am–5pm; €5), which occupies a large and distinctive red- and white-striped, neo-Gothic building. The museum's main display features one of the region's most enduring mermaid legends (see box above) and there's another mildly enjoyable section devoted to the local painter, explorer, writer and ethnographer, **Wynand Nieuwenkamp** (1874-1950).

On the other side of Damplein is the **Edams Museum** (early April to late Oct Tues–Sat 10am–4.30pm, Sun 12–4.30pm; €3), which occupies an attractive house whose crow-stepped gables date from 1530. Inside, a modest assortment of local bygones is redeemed by the curious floating cellar, supposedly built by a retired sea captain who could not bear the thought of sleeping on dry land.

From Damplein, it's a short walk along Grote Kerkstraat to the rambling **Grote Kerk** (April–Oct daily 2–4.30pm; free), on the edge of the fields to the north of town. This is the largest three-ridged church in Europe, with a huge organ built in 1663 and a vaulted ceiling constructed in wood in an attempt to limit the subsidence caused by the building's massive weight. A handsome, largely Gothic structure, it contains several magnificent **stained-glass windows** dating from 1606 to 1620, mostly heraldic but including historical scenes too. Unfortunately, the church's strong lines are disturbed by the almost comically stubby spire, which was shortened to its present height after a lightning strike started a fire in 1602.

Stroll back from the church along Matthijs Tinxgracht, just to the west of Grote Kerkstraat, and you soon reach the **Kaasmarkt**, site of the summer **cheese market** (July & Aug Wed 10.30am–12.30pm). It's is a good deal more humble than Alkmaar's (see p.156), but follows the same format, with the cheeses laid out in rows before the buyers sample them. Once a cheese has been purchased,

△ Damplein, Edam

the cheese porters, dressed in the traditional white costumes and straw boaters, spring into action, carrying them off on their gondola-like trays. Overlooking the market is the **Kaaswaag** (Cheese Weighing House), whose decorative panels celebrate – you guessed it – cheese-making and also sport the town's coat of arms, a bull on a red field with three stars. From here, it's a couple of hundred metres to the sixteenth-century **Speeltoren**, an elegant tower which is visible from all over town, and roughly the same distance again – south along Lingerzijde – to the impossibly picturesque **Kwakelbrug** bridge. This leads over to **Schepenmakersdijk**, from where it takes about five minutes to regain Damplein.

Practicalities

Leaving Amsterdam every half hour from outside Centraal Station, **bus #110** takes 25 minutes to reach Volendam and 10 minutes more to get to Edam. Edam's **bus station** is on the southwest edge of town, on Singelweg, a five- to ten–minute walk from Damplein, where the **VVV** (mid–March to mid–Oct Mon–Sat 10am–5pm, plus Sun 1–4.30pm in July & Aug; mid–Oct to mid–March Mon–Sat 10am–3pm; ☎029/931 5125, ⊛www.vvv-edam.nl) issues town maps and sells *A Stroll through Edam* (€2.25), a leaflet exploring Edam's every architectural peccadillo. The VVV also has details of the town's **boat trips**, which coincide with the cheese market – a quick, 90–minute gambol out into the Markermeer every Wednesday in July and August. **Bike rental** is available at Ronald Schot, in the town centre at Grote Kerkstraat 7 (Tues–Fri 8.30am–6pm & Sat 8.30am–5pm; ☎029/937 2155); a one-day rental costs about €7.

In addition, the VVV has a small supply of **rooms in private houses** (averaging €40 per double), which they will book on your behalf for no extra charge. Otherwise, there are four **hotels**, easily the pick being the charming *De Fortuna*, just round the corner from the Damplein at Spuistraat 3 (☎029/937 16 71, ☎029/937 14 69, ⊛www.fortuna-edam.nl; doubles €90). This three-star hotel, abutting a narrow canal, is the epitome of cosiness, its 24 guest rooms distributed amongst two immaculately restored old houses and three cottage–like buildings round the back. A reserve choice is the much more modest, one-star *Harmonie*, in a plain and modern but fairly pleasant canalside house a couple of hundred metres east of the VVV at Voorhaven 92 (☎029/937 16 64; ⓦwww .harmonie-edam.nl; doubles €45). The nearest **campsite**, *Strandbad*, is east of town on the way to the lakeshore at Zeevangszeedijk 7A (☎029/937 19 94; April–Sept) – a twenty-minute walk east along the canal from Damplein.

For **food**, *De Fortuna* has a first–rate restaurant, a lively and eminently agreeable spot decorated in traditional style and with an imaginative, modern menu featuring local ingredients; main courses average around €20; reservations, especially on the weekend, are well–nigh essential.

Alkmaar and around

Forty minutes from Amsterdam by train, the amenable little town of **ALKMAAR** was founded in the tenth century in the middle of a marsh. It takes its name from the auk, a diving bird which once hung around here in numbers, as in *alkeen meer*, or auk lake. Just like Haarlem, the town was besieged by Frederick of Toledo, but heavy rain flooded its surroundings and forced the Spaniards to withdraw in 1573, an early Dutch success in their long war of independence. Alkmaar's attractive, partially canalized centre is still surrounded by its medieval moat, a segment of which has been incorporated into the Noordhollandskanaal, itself part of a longer network of waterways running north from Amsterdam to the open sea.

Alkmaar has a cluster of impressive medieval buildings, but is best known for its much-touted **cheese market** (see box, p.159), an ancient affair that these days ranks as one of the most extravagant tourist spectacles in Holland. Finally, Alkmaar is within easy striking distance of the coastal resort of **Bergen–aan-Zee**, from where you can hike out into the woods and sand dunes of the **Noordhollands Duinreservaat**.

The Town

Even if you've only come for the cheese market, it's well worth seeing something of the rest of the town before you leave. On the main square, the **Waag** (Weighing House) was originally a chapel dedicated to the Holy Ghost – hence the imposing tower – but was converted and given its delightful east gable shortly after the town's famous victory against the Spanish. This gable is an ostentatious Dutch Renaissance affair bedecked with allegorical figures and decorated with the town's militant coat of arms. Nowadays, the Waag holds the **VVV** (see p.159) and the **Kaasmuseum** (Cheese Museum; April–Oct Mon–Sat 10am–4pm, Fri 9am–4pm; €2.50), with displays on the history of cheese, cheese-making equipment and such like. Rather less predictable is the **Biermuseum de Boom**, housed in the old De Boom brewery just off the north side of the square at Houttil 1 (Tues–Sat 10am–4pm, Sun 1.30–4pm; €3). This museum has displays tracing the brewing process from the malting to the bottling stage, aided by authentic props from this and other breweries. There's lots of technical equipment, enlivened by mannequins and empty bottles from once innumerable Dutch brewers – though few, curiously, from De Boom itself. It's an engaging museum, put together by enthusiasts, and there's a shop upstairs where you can buy a huge range of beers and associated merchandise, as well as a downstairs bar serving many varieties of Dutch beer.

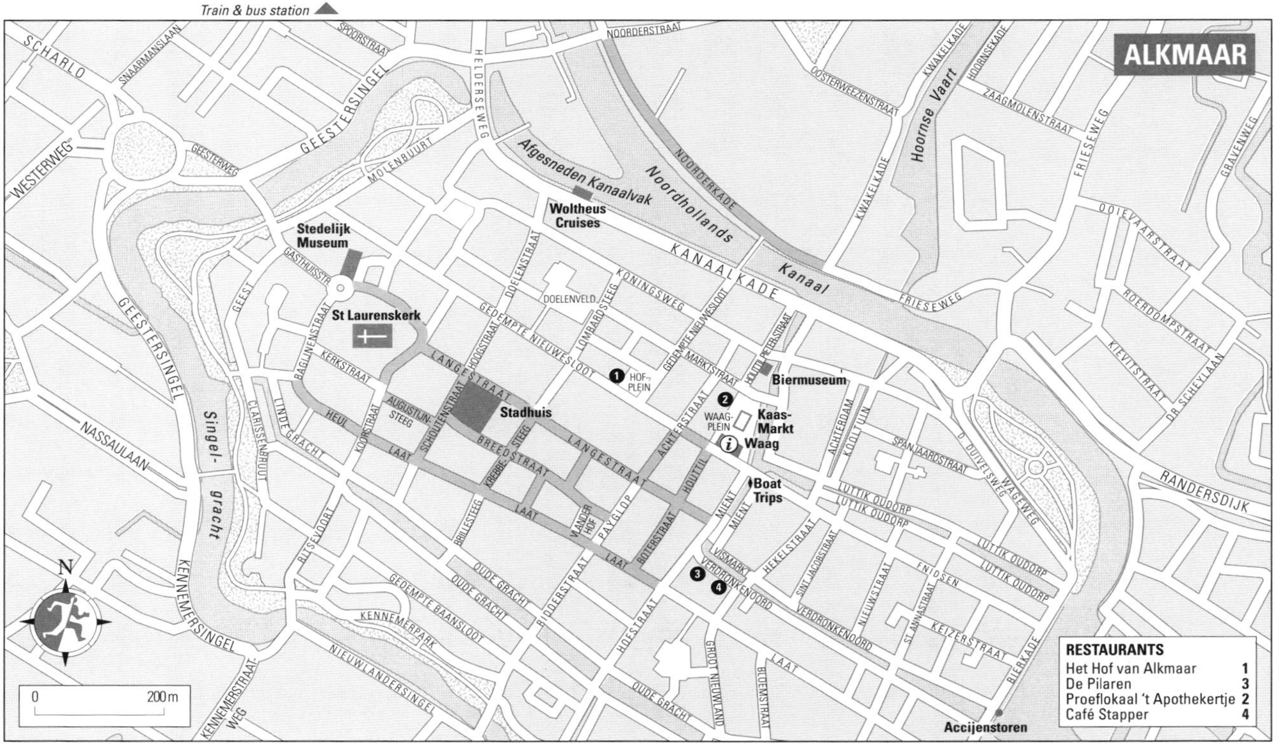

ALKMAAR
Train & bus station
RESTAURANTS
Het Hof van Alkmaar 1
De Pilaren 3
Proeflokaal 't Apothekertje 2
Café Stapper 4
Stedelijk Museum
St Laurenskerk
Stadhuis
Woltheus Cruises
Biermuseum
Kaas-Markt
Waag
Boat Trips
Accijnstoren
Noordhollands Kanaal
Afgesneden Kanaalvak
Hoornse Vaart
Singel-gracht
KANAALKADE
NOORDERKADE
KWAKELKADE
HOORNSEKADE
FRIESEWEG
GRAVENWEG
OOIEVAARSTRAAT
ROERDOMPSTRAAT
KIEVITSTRAAT
DR SCHEYLAAN
RANDERSDIJK
ZAAGMOLENSTRAAT
OOSTERWEEZENSTRAAT
NOORDERSTRAAT
SPOORSTRAAT
SNAARMANSLAAN
SCHARLO
WESTERWEG
GEESTERWEG
GEESTERSINGEL
HELDERSEWEG
MOLENBUURT
KENNEMERSINGEL
KENNEMERSTRAAT-WEG
NASSAULAAN
GEEST
CLARISSENBRUUT
LINDEGRACHT
GASTHUISSTR
BAGIJNENSTRAAT
KERKSTRAAT
HEUL
LAAT
KOORSTRAAT
AUGUSTIJN-STEEG
SCHOUTENSTRAAT
HOOGSTRAAT
LANGESTRAAT
BREEDSTRAAT
KREBBE-STEEG
BRILLESTEEG
VLANDER HOF
PAYGLOP
BOTERSTRAAT
RIDDERSTRAAT
HOESTRAAT
OUDE GRACHT
GEDEMPTE BAANSLOOT
KENNEMERPARK
NIEUWLANDERSINGEL
RITSEVOORT
DOELENSTRAAT
DOELENVELD
LOMBARDSTEEG
GEDEMPTE NIEUWESLOOT
KONINGSWEG
MARKTSTRAAT
HOUTTIL
PIETERSTRAAT
HOF-PLEIN
WAAG-PLEIN
ACHTERSTRAAT
MIENT
VISMARKT
VERDRONKENOORD
HEKELSTRAAT
SINT JACOBSTRAAT
NIEUWSTRAAT
ST ANNASTRAAT
FNIDSEN
KEIZERSTRAAT
BIERKADE
LUTTIK OUDORP
SPANJAARDSTRAAT
D. DUIVELSWEG
WAGEWEG
ACHTERDAM
KOOLTUIN
GROOT NIEUWLAND
BLOEMSTRAAT
N
0
200m

Heading south from the Waag along Mient, it's a few metres to the jetty from where boat trips (see box below) leave for a quick zip round the town's central canals – an enjoyable way to spend 45 minutes. At the south end of Mient, the open-air **Vismarkt** (Fish Market) marks the start of the **Verdronkenoord** canal, whose attractive medley of facades and gables leads down to the spindly **Accijenstoren** (Excise Tower), part harbour master's office, part fortification built during the long struggle with Spain in 1622. Turn left at the tower along Bierkade and you'll soon reach **Luttik Oudorp**, another attractive corner of the old centre, a slender canal jammed with antique barges that leads back to the Waag.

The Stadhuis and St Laurenskerk

One block southwest of the Waag, pedestrianized **Langestraat** is Alkmaar's main and mundane shopping street, whose only notable building is the **Stadhuis**, a florid affair, half of which (the Langestraat side) dates from the early sixteenth century. At the west end of Langestraat lurks **St Laurenskerk** (June to mid-Sept Mon–Sat noon–5pm; free), a Gothic church of the late fifteenth century whose pride and joy is its **organ**, commissioned at the suggestion of the diplomat and political bigwig Constantijn Huygens in 1645. The case was designed by Jacob van Campen, the architect who was later to design Amsterdam's town hall (see p.51), and decorated with paintings illustrating the triumph of David by Caesar van Everdingen (1617–1678). The artist's seamless brushstrokes and willingness to kowtow to the tastes of the burgeoning middle class were to make him a wealthy man. In the apse is the tomb of Count Floris V, penultimate in the line of medieval counts of North Holland, who did much to establish the independence of the towns hereabouts; he was murdered for his trouble by jealous nobles in 1296.

The Stedelijk Museum

Across from the church, Alkmaar's Cultureel Centrum holds a theatre, offices and a mildly diverting museum, the **Stedelijk Museum** (Municipal Museum; Tues–Fri 10am–5pm, Sat & Sun 1–5pm; €4), whose three floors hone in on the history of the town. Well displayed, but almost entirely labelled only in Dutch, the collection begins with two floors devoted to Alkmaar's seventeenth–century Golden Age. In the basement, a large assortment of archeological finds is divided up by theme – "Light and Warmth", "Blue and White Porcelain" and so forth – while, up above, the ground floor has sections on different aspects of the town, from trade, war and the militias through to replica scenes and scenarios. Many of the exhibits are illustrated by paintings and highlights among them include a typically precise interior of Alkmaar's St Laurenskerk by Pieter Saenredam (1597–1665), a striking *Holy Family* by the Mannerist Gerard van Honthorst (1590–1656), who usually kept to

---

Boat trips

Canal trips around Alkmaar leave from the jetty on Mient (April–Oct daily, hourly 11am–5pm, plus additional departures during the cheese market; 30min; €4) and the VVV sells the tickets. There are also longer **boat trips** organised by **Woltheus Cruises** (℡072/511 48 40; ⊛www.woltheuscruises.nl) and departing from the Kanaalkade jetty, on the north side of the centre. Amongst the company's several offerings is an excursion to Amsterdam (April to Oct 1 weekly; 9hr; €19) and a Molen (windmill) cruise (Nov–Dec I weekly; 2hr; €10).

Alkmaar's cheese market

Cheese has been sold on Alkmaar's main square since the 1300s, and although it's no longer a serious commercial concern, the **kaasmarkt** (cheese market; every Friday 10am–12.30pm, from the first Friday in April to the first Friday in Sept) remains popular and continues to draw the crowds. If you want a good view be sure to get there early, as by opening time the crowds are already thick on the ground. The ceremony starts with the buyers sniffing, crumbling, and finally tasting each cheese, followed by intensive bartering. Once a deal has been concluded, the cheeses – golden discs of Gouda mainly, laid out in rows and piles on the square – are borne away on ornamental carriers by groups of four **porters** (*kaasdragers*) for weighing. The porters wear white trousers and shirt plus a black hat whose **coloured bands** – green, blue, red or yellow – represent the four companies that comprise the cheese porters' guild. Payment for the cheeses, tradition has it, takes place in the cafés around the square.

glossy portraits of high officials, and a huge canvas depicting the bloody siege of 1573 by the medievalist Jacobus Hilverdink (1809–1864). The top floor explores the history of the town during the twentieth century.

Practicalities

From Alkmaar's **train** and **bus station**, it's a ten–minute walk to the centre of town: keep straight outside the station along Spoorstraat, hang a left at the end onto Geestersingel and then turn right over the bridge onto Kanaalkade; keep going along Kanaalkade until you reach Houttil Pieterstraat, which leads straight to the Waagplein. where the **VVV** occupies the Waag (April–Sept Mon–Wed 10am–5.30pm, Thurs 10am–9pm, Fri & Sat 9am–5.30pm; Oct–March Mon–Fri 10am–5.30pm & Sat 9.30am–5.30pm; ☎072/511 42 84, ⊚www.vvvalkmaar.nl). Alkmaar only takes an hour or two to explore, but if you decide to stay the VVV has plenty of **rooms in private houses** for €40 per double per night, including breakfast, though most places are on the outskirts of town and en-suite rooms are a rarity; there are no recommendable central hotels.

For **food**, Alkmaar is well served by *Het Hof van Alkmaar*, which occupies delightful old premises just off Nieuwesloot at Hof van Sonoy 1 (☎072/512 12

22). During the day this restaurant offers inexpensive sandwiches, snacks and pancakes, and at night they serve up tasty Dutch cuisine – it's the best place in town by a long chalk. Alkmaar has two main groups of **bars**, one on Waagplein, the other just a couple of minutes' walk away around the Vismarkt. Among the former, the pick is *Proeflokaal 't Apothekertje*, an old-style bar, open until 2am, with an antique-cluttered interior and a laid-back atmosphere. On the Vismarkt, *De Pilaren* is a livelier, more youthful spot catering to a cooler crowd, some of whom take refuge in the *Café Stapper* next door, if the music gets too much.

Around Alkmar: Bergen and the coast

Heading west, **bus #160** leaves Alkmaar train station every thirty minutes or so – hourly on Sunday – for the ten-minute ride to **BERGEN**, a cheerful, rambling, leafy village whose main square, the **Plein**, is an amiable affair crowded by cafés and restaurants. From the Plein, it's about 700m southwest to the **Museum Kranenburgh**, a fine-arts museum housed in a handsome Neoclassical villa at Hoflaan 26 (Tues–Sun 1–5pm; €5). Bergen has been something of an artists' retreat since the late nineteenth century and the museum features the work of the Expressionist Bergen School, which was founded here in 1915. Greatly influenced by the Post-Impressionists, especially Cézanne, none of the group is original enough to stand out, but taken as a whole it's a delightful collection and one that is supported by an imaginative programme of temporary exhibitions. These often focus on the two contemporaneous Dutch schools that were to have much more impact – De Ploeg (see p.282) and De Stijl (see p.281). Warming to this artistic heritage, the local council organizes all sorts of cultural events in Bergen, including open-air sculpture displays and concerts, and the village also boasts a scattering of chi-chi art-for-sale galleries.

If you are intending to do some **walking** in the coastal dunes to the west of Bergen, pick up a trail map at Bergen **VVV**, Plein 1 (Mon–Sat 10am–5pm; ☎072/581 31 00, ⊛www.vvvnoordzeekust.nl).

Bergen–aan-Zee and the Noordhollands Duinreservaat

Travelling west from Bergen, **bus #262** (daily, every hour) takes ten minutes to travel the 5km to the coast at **BERGEN-AAN-ZEE**, a sprawling, modern resort that dips and bucks over the dunes. There's little reason to hang around, unless you're after the beach, but to north and south lie the pristine woods and dunes of the **Noordhollands Duinreservaat**, with its abundance of footpaths and cycle trails.

Listings

Listings

Accommodation

Accommodation in Amsterdam can be difficult to find, and is often a major expense: even hostels are pricey for what you get, and the hotels are among the most expensive in Europe. At peak times of the year – July and August, Easter and Christmas – you'd be advised to book well ahead as hotel rooms and even hostel beds can be swallowed up remarkably quickly, and if you arrive without a reservation at any time of the year you may be hard pushed to find somewhere decent. On the bonus side, at least the city's compactness means that you'll almost inevitably end up somewhere central and/or convenient. Most of the places we've listed – even the larger hostels – will accept bookings from abroad by fax or email, although the cheaper ones may require some guarantee of payment (such as a credit card number). Telephone bookings are not always accepted, particularly at many of the hostels during peak season. You can also reserve rooms in advance by contacting the **Netherlands Reservations Centre** (T0031/299 689 144, Wwww.hotelres.nl) or Wwww.bookings.nl, both of which allow you to view availability and prices before making a booking. Once you've arrived, the city's VVVs (tourist offices) will make hotel reservations on your behalf either in advance or on the same day for a €3.50 fee, but note that during peak periods and weekends they get extremely busy with long and exhausting queues. They also sell a booklet on hotels in Amsterdam for €3.50. For VVV locations and opening times, see p.28.

Accommodation prices and touts

The hotel and guesthouse prices in this book are given for the **cheapest double room available during the high season**, and unless indicated otherwise, include breakfast. Single rooms, where available, usually cost between sixty and eighty percent of a double. For hostel accommodation we've specified the price per person for a dorm bed. Note that in the low season hotel prices can drop by as much as 50 percent and dorm beds can be up to €5 cheaper; note also that most of the larger hotels will offer rooms at various prices.

Touts

If, like most visitors, you arrive at Amsterdam's Centraal Station, you may well be approached outside by touts offering rooms or beds in hostels and cheap hotels. Usually they welcome you to the place and claim a fee from the management. Despite the fact that most of them are genuine enough, our advice is to steer clear. If the place they're offering is in our listings you can phone it directly yourself, and if it isn't, it's probably been left out for a reason. Although the possibility of encountering unpleasantness is small, it does exist and anyway there are plenty of good, cheap and reliable places within five minutes' walk of Centraal Station.

Where to stay

To help you choose a place to stay, we've **divided our listings by area**, using the same headings as in the guide chapters – "The Old Centre", "The Grachtengordel", etc. All the hostels, hotels and B&Bs we describe are marked on the **colour maps** at the end of the book.

If you choose to stay in the **Old Centre**, you'll never have to search for nightlife. Cheap hotels abound in the Red Light District, as you might expect – and this is the first place to start looking if money is tight, although women travellers may find it intimidating. However, there's also a good selection of quiet, reasonably priced places in more agreeable locations on and near the canals, close to restaurants and shopping areas.

The **western section** of the **Grachtengordel** is only a few minutes' walk from the bustle of Dam square, but it has a number of quiet canalside hotels; the Anne Frank House and several of the city's smaller museums are here too. The least expensive places in this area are concentrated along Raadhuisstraat, one of the city's busiest streets. **Grachtengordel south** is not as appealing a district as its neighbour, but it is ideally positioned for the plethora of nightclubs, bars and restaurants on and around Leidseplein and Rembrandtplein. There are plenty of hotels for all budgets here, including a number of very pleasant, occasionally stylish options along the surrounding canals.

Staying in the **Jordaan** puts you in among the locals and well away from the hustle and bustle of the main tourist zones. There's no shortage of bars and restaurants in this up-and-coming area either – and some of the most beautiful of the city's canals are here too – but you'll be at least fifteen minutes' walk from the bright lights. Beware that Marnixstraat and Rozengracht are busy traffic streets.

Very few tourists venture out to the **Old Jewish Quarter**: the streets and canals off the main traffic arteries of Weesperstraat and Plantage Midden-laan are purely residential, with very few bars or restaurants. Consequently, although you're pretty much guaranteed a quiet night's sleep here, you'll be a tram ride away from any of the main sights.

The main reason for staying out of the centre in the **Museum Quarter** is to be close to the city's two leading museums – the Van Gogh and the Rijksmuseum – although the nightlife around Leidseplein is also within easy striking distance. There are no canals in the area, and two of the main drags, Overtoom and 1e Constantijn Huygensstraat constantly rumble with traffic, but there are plenty of quiet and comfortable hotels in the smaller side streets, as well as two of the city's best hostels on the edge of the leafy expanse of the Vondelpark. There's not too much reason to venture out into the city's far-flung suburbs, but the **outer districts** do possess two noteworthy hotels (see p.172). For specifically **gay** or gay-friendly hotels, see Chapter 12.

Many of Amsterdam's buildings have narrow, very steep **staircases**, and many do not have lifts; indeed in the older houses, the insertion of lifts is actually illegal. If this is a consideration for you, check before you book. Finally, note that all directions and trams given are from Centraal Station (abbreviated as "CS") unless otherwise indicated.

Hotels and B&Bs

Aside from a couple of ultra-cheap places, Amsterdam's **hotels** start at around €90 for a double and can represent pretty poor value for money, even though some form of breakfast – "Dutch" (ham, bread and jam) or "English" (eggs) – is normally included in the price. Given this state of affairs, it's advisable to ask to see the room first before you slap down any money, and if you don't like it refuse it. Note too that with some of the independently run hotels the cheapest rooms often have shared facilities, and rooms with en suite could be an extra €5–15. A number of hotels in Amsterdam have large three- or four-bed family rooms available from €150. Most hotel prices include the 5 percent city tax, but some of the more expensive places charge it on top of quoted prices.

There are relatively few **bed-and-breakfasts** in Amsterdam, although they are on the increase and we've listed some of the best. Holiday Link, Postbus 70-155, 9704 AD Groningen (☎050/313 3535, ☻www.holidaylink.com), can send you a book for €15 plus p&p that lists reputable B&Bs throughout the country.

The Old Centre

Botel Amstel Moored at Oosterdokskade 2 ☎020/626 4247, ☻www.amstelbotel.com. The idea of a floating hotel may seem romantic – or at least perfect in house-boat-heaven Amsterdam – but the 175 identically decorated rooms here are poky and connected by claustrophobic corridors. Something a bit different certainly, but you might find staying here is a bit like spending your holiday on a cross-Channel ferry. Bar stays open till 12.45am. Minimum three-night stay at weekends. Breakfast €10. Prices depending on view €87–97.

The Crown Oudezijds Voorburgwal 21 ☎020/626 9664, ☻www.hotelthecrown.com. Friendly hotel over a busy "smoker friendly" bar overlooking a canal that's very safe despite the location. Rooms with large twin beds and shared facilities; no breakfast. Triples, quads and six-person rooms also available, some with a view. Late bar with pool table until 3am. Higher weekend rates. Two-night minimum stay at weekends. Payment upon arrival. €45 per person.

Delta Damrak 42 ☎020/620 2626, ☻www .delta-hotel.com. If you really want to stay on Damrak, try this place first – uninspired, plain and characterless, but comfortable enough, all 48 rooms have private bathroom, TV and safe; one of the better options on a generally unappealing street. €90 midweek; €125 weekends.

France Oudezijds Kolk 11 ☎020/535 3777, ☻www.francehotel.nl. Friendly but rather characterless hotel on a tiny, beautiful and little-used canal in the heart of the Old Centre. All rooms are slowly being updated and are small, but perfectly adequate. All have TV and en suite. Payment on arrival. €80.

De Gerstekorrel Damstraat 22–24 ☎020/624 1367, ☻www.gerstekorrel.nl. Tram #4, #16, #24 or #25 to Dam square. Simple hotel situated along a busy shopping street steps away from the Dam. Large, brightly decorated and well-lit doubles; rooms at the back are quieter. Discounts often available. €140

Grand Oudezijds Voorburgwal 197 ☎020/555 3111, ☻www.thegrand.nl. Tram #4, #9, #16, #24 or #25 to Dam square. Originally a Royal Inn dating from 1578, and after that the Amsterdam Town Hall, this fine Classical building is one of the city's architectural high points. The rooms are large and well-appointed and boldly decorated in crisp, modern style. All the usual facilities you would expect from a five-star hotel including a spa with inside pool and Turkish bath. Prices exclude tax and breakfast, which is a whopping €25 extra. €420

Grand Hotel Krasnapolsky Dam 9 ☎020/554 9111, ☻www.nh-hotels.com. Occupying a huge and strikingly good-looking, mid-nineteenth-century building, this luxurious hotel occupies an entire side of Dam square. 5-star facilities plus a lounge overlooking the Royal Palace and a monumental Winter Garden. Rack-rate €270; online rates as low as €190.

Hotel de l'Europe Nieuwe Doelenstraat 2–8 ☎020/531 1777, ☻www.leurope.nl. Tram #4, #9, #16, #24 or #25 to Muntplein. Very central hotel which retains a wonderful fin-de-siècle charm, with large, well-furnished rooms and a very attractive riverside terrace. Liveried staff and a red carpet on the pavement

▽ Hotel de l'Europe

outside complete the picture. Tax and breakfast (€22.50) extra. €360

Misc Kloveniersburgwal 20 ☎020/330 6241, Ⓦwww.hotelmisc.com. Small, intimate hotel well-positioned close to the Waag and recently taken over by two young business partners. Six well-sized en suite rooms individually themed with names such as Dolly, Rembrandt and Design. The bright breakfast area overlooks the canal and is great for people watching (also has wireless Internet connection). Breakfast is a freshly prepared affair of eggs, jams, croissants and a choice breads. An extremely pleasant experience. €145.

Nes Kloveniersburgwal 137–139 ☎020/624 4773, Ⓦwww.hotelnes.nl. Tram #4, #9, #16, #24 or #25 to Muntplein. Attractive and quiet hotel with helpful staff; well-positioned near the Muziektheater away from noise but close to shops and nightlife. Lift access. Prices vary depending on the view, and exclude tax. €165.

Rho Nes 5 ☎020/620 7371, Ⓦwww.rhohotel .com. Tram #4, #9, #16, #24 or #25 to Dam square. A very comfortable hotel in a quiet alley off Dam square. The place appears somewhat unenticing from the outside, but it's still a fine city-centre option, with helpful and welcoming staff, and the reception, originally built as a theatre in 1908, boasts an extraordinary Art Deco ceiling. Lift access. Bike rental available. Large, pleasant rooms €120 (€145 weekend).

Rokin Rokin 73 ☎020/626 7456, Ⓦwww .rokinhotel.com. Tram #4, #9, #16, #24 or #25 to Rokin. Three-star family hotel which has recently had a facelift and undergone major expansion. Small, modern doubles with

exposed beams some singles and two triples also available. Basement breakfast room. Lift access to three of the four floors. Private car park. €145.

Tourist Inn Spuistraat 52 ☎020/421 5841, Ⓦwww.tourist-inn.nl. Popular four-floor budget hotel, with clean and comfortable non-smoking rooms. Bright orange six-person dorms with TV (€25), Triples and quads also available. Downstairs bar, breakfast and lounge area. A cut above the rest of the budget hotels in the area. Lift access. Doubles with shower from €65, €90 on the weekend.

Travel Beursstraat 23 ☎020/626 6532, Ⓦwww .travelhotel.nl. Small, simple hotel on a dingy street that backs onto busy Warmoesstraat. Inside, the rooms are not exactly luxurious but it's very clean and comfortable and considering the area it's light years away from the backpacker places nearby. Quiet 24-hour bar and no curfew. One five-bed room €250. Doubles from €85.

Utopia Nieuwezijds Voorburgwal 132 ☎020/626 1295, Ⓦwww.hotelutopia.nl. Self-proclaimed "smokers' hotel" above a coffeeshop with tiny, musty rooms over the street, reached by a near-vertical staircase. Basic, and generally welcoming, though we've had complaints about unhelpful staff during peak season. Payment upon arrival. Doubles without bathroom €70.

Victoria Damrak 1–5 ☎020/623 4255, Ⓦwww .parkplaza.com. The Victoria is one of the landmarks of the city – a tall, elegant building, wonderfully decorated throughout – and one of the classiest hotels, with every possible amenity (despite its grimy location opposite CS). Rack rate €300, though online prices can be as low as €190.

Vijaya Oudezijds Voorburgwal 44 ☎020/626 9406, Ⓦwww.hotelvijaya.com. Stately old canal house in the heart of the Red Light District, with drab but clean rooms and accommodating management, who also own an Indian restaurant of the same name (guests receive ten per cent discount). Doubles €95, quads €155 and five-bed room €185.

Winston Warmoesstraat 129 ☎020/623 1380, Ⓦwww.winston.nl. Popular but noisy hotel designed for an arty crowd. Rooms (sleeping from one to six) are light and airy, some en-suite, some with a communal balcony, and many are specially commissioned "Art" rooms, including the Durex

Room, Heineken Room and Schiffmacher Room. Erotic images abound in many, though, so if you're travelling as a family you might want to check first to prevent any embarrassing questions. Lift and full disabled access. High season discounts available. Basic rooms with shower and shared toilet €85. Art rooms with private facilities €90.

Grachtengordel west

Ambassade Herengracht 341 ☎020/555 0222, ⓦwww.ambassade-hotel.nl. Tram #1, #2 or #5 to Spui. Elegant canalside hotel made up of ten seventeenth-century houses, with friendly staff, attractive furnished lounges, a well-stocked library and comfortable en-suite rooms. Free internet access. Breakfast is an extra €16, but well worth it. Doubles from €195. Family rooms from €350.

Brian Singel 69 ☎020/624 4661, ⓦwww .hotelbrian.com. Still one of the cheapest hotels for this area and has friendly staff. Doubles are very basic but clean and there's free tea and coffee throughout the day. Triples and quads also available. All rooms have shared facilities. Less positively, its compact rooms and narrow stairways means it suffers from "slamming door syndrome" late at night; not the best place if you're looking for somewhere peaceful. €54.

Canal House Keizersgracht 148 ☎020/622 5182, ⓦwww.canalhouse.nl. Tram #13 or #17 to Westermarkt. Magnificently restored seventeenth-century building, centrally located on one of the principal canals. Comfortable rooms, but generally brusque staff. Prices from €160.

Clemens Raadhuisstraat 39 ☎020/624 6089, ⓦwww.clemenshotel.com. Tram #13 or #17 to Westermarkt. Excellent, friendly, budget hotel, close to the Anne Frank House with a very knowledgeable owner. Individually decorated doubles, some with en-suite. All rooms offer free Internet connection, and you can rent laptops for €8. One of the better options along this busy main road. Rooms without shower start from €75.

The Dylan Keizersgracht 384 ☎020/530 2010, ⓦwww.dylanamsterdam.com. Tram #1, #2 or #5 to Keizersgracht. Formerly *Blakes*, this stylish hotel housed in a seventeenth-century building and centred on a beautiful courtyard has been rebranded and is now part of the Stein Group. The decor and the restaurant menu remain quintessentially the same, combining Oriental and European styles, and each of the rooms is opulently decorated, featuring exposed beams, natural fabrics and a flatscreen TV. There's now a new bar, open to non-guests, and plans are afoot for a spa and gym. Luxury suites overlook the Keizersgracht canal. Hip without being pretentious. Doubles from €390.

Estherea Singel 303–309 ☎020/624 5146, ⓦwww.esterea.nl. Tram #1, #2 or #5 to Spui. Appealing, low–key hotel converted from a pair of old canal houses. Great location and, although the rooms lack the personal touch, they are all perfectly adequate; the best overlook the canal. Prices exclude tax and breakfast (€14). €242

Hegra Herengracht 269 ☎020/623 7877, ⓦwww.hegrahotelamsterdam.com. Tram #1, #2 or #5 to Spui. Welcoming atmosphere and relatively inexpensive for the location, on a beautiful stretch of the canal. Rooms are small but comfortable; some with en suite. Prices with shared facilities start from €65.

Hoksbergen Singel 301 ☎020/626 6043, ⓦwww.hotelhoksbergen.nl. Tram #1, #2 or #5 to Spui. Friendly, standard-issue hotel, with a light and open breakfast room overlooking the canal. Basic en-suite rooms, all with telephone and TV. Self-catering apartments also available. Prices start from €85 for smallest room.

't hotel Leliegracht 18 ☎020/422 2741, ⓦwww .thotel.nl. Tram #13 or #17 to Westermarkt. Extremely pleasant hotel located along a quiet canal. Owned by the proprietors of the downstairs design shop, who believe in making people feel at home. Eight spacious rooms, large beds, TV, fridge and either bath or shower. No groups. Minimum three-night stay at the weekend. Doubles from €134.

New Amsterdam Herengracht 13–19 ☎020/522 2345, ⓦwww.hotelnewamsterdam. nl. Small, ultra-friendly hotel overlooking a quiet stretch of the canal on the edge of the Jordaan, now lovingly revamped having stood vacant for a number of years. All 25 rooms are comfortably furnished with TV, Internet connection and have either a bath or shower. Buffet breakfast is provided downstairs along with tea and coffee making facilities. There's also a TV lounge area with daily newspapers. Higher weekend rates. Doubles without a canal view from €100.

NH City Centre Spuistraat 288 ☎020 420 4545, ⓦwww.nh-hotels.com. Tram #1, #2 and #5 to Spui. Built in the 1920s, this appealing chain hotel occupies an intelligently renovated Art Deco former textile factory. Well situated for the cafes and bars around the Spui, and the Museum Quarter. Rooms vary in size, some have canal view, and all boast extremely comfy beds and good showers. The buffet breakfast is an extra €16, but it will set you up for the day. Doubles from €135.

Pax Raadhuisstraat 37 ☎020/624 9735, ⓕ624 9735. Tram #6, #13 or #17 to Westermarkt. Straightforward city-centre cheapie, owned by two brothers. A mixture of fair-sized rooms sleeping one to four persons; plans are afoot to refurbish the rooms in the minimalist white style of room no.19 – the large double on the top floor. In the meantime, as with most of the hotels along here, ask for a room at the back. Credit cards 3.5 per cent charge. En-suite doubles €85.

Pulitzer Prinsengracht 315 ☎020/523 5235, ⓦwww.starwood.com. Tram #6, #13 or #17 to Westermarkt. An entire row of seventeenth-century canal houses creatively converted into a five-star Sheraton hotel. Very popular with visiting businessfolk, but although the public areas are tastefully decorated and the breakfasts very good, the modern rooms lack character and some – considering the price – are very disappointing. Doubles from €260.

Toren Keizersgracht 164 ☎020/622 6033, ⓔhotel.toren@tip.nl. Tram #6, #13 or #17 to Westermarkt. Fine example of an imagina-

▽ Toren

tively revamped seventeenth-century canal house, once the home of a Dutch prime minister and now popular with American visitors. Friendly and efficient staff. Opulently designed en-suite doubles with a touch of class as well as some deluxe rooms with a Jacuzzi (€230). From €195.

Wiechmann Prinsengracht 328–332 ☎020/626 3321, ⓦwww.hotelwiechmann.nl. Tram #1, #2 or #5 to Spui. Canal-house restoration, family-run for fifty years, with dark wooden beams and restrained style throughout. Large, bright rooms with TV and shower, kept in perfect condition. Close to the Anne Frank House. Prices stay the same throughout the year. €125.

Grachtengordel south

De Admiraal Herengracht 563 ☎020/626 2150, ⓔde-admiraal-hotel@planet.nl. Tram #4, #9 or #14 to Rembrandtplein. Small hotel with a laid-back and likeable owner sited in a seventeenth-century canal house close to the bars and clubs of Rembrandtplein. Nine rooms with somewhat dated décor and uneven floors, but somehow these just add to the quirky charm of the place. Reception sometimes closes during the day; hotel closes for a few weeks in Feb. Pleasant attic room for four people with its own private balcony €190. Breakfast an extra €5. Rooms from €86.

Agora Singel 462 ☎020/627 2200, ⓦwww.hotelagora.nl. Tram #1, #2 or #5 to Koningsplein. Nicely located, small and amiable hotel right near the flower market and close to the Spui, with a large breakfast room. Pleasantly decorated doubles and three- and four-bed rooms also available. All rooms have en suite, but some have bath instead of shower. Same rates throughout the year. Rooms without a canal view cost upwards of €120.

American Leidsekade 97 ☎020/556 3000, ⓦwww.amsterdam-american.crowneplaza.com. Tram #1, #2 or #5 to Leidseplein. This landmark Art Deco hotel, dating from 1902, was once chic and fashionable in equal measure. The high rollers have moved on, and the bed rooms are now standard-issue modern affairs, but they are large, double-glazed and comfortable. The hotel is just off Leidseplein. Discounts are available if you book online. Doubles from €270.

Dikker & Thijs Fenice Prinsengracht 444 ☎020/620 1212, ⓦwww.dtfh.nl. Tram #1, #2 or #5 to Prinsengracht. Small and stylish hotel on a beautiful canal close to all the shops. Rooms feature exposed beams and vary in decor but all include a minibar, telephone and TV – and those on the top floor give a good view of the city; lift access. €180.

Jolly Hotel Carlton Vijzelstraat 4 ☎020/622 2266, ⓦwww.jollyhotels.nl. Next door to the flower market, this large, four–star chain hotel has well-appointed bedrooms kitted out with standard modern fittings and furnishings. From €200

Maas Leidsekade 91 ☎020/623 3868, ⓦwww .hemhotels.nl. Tram #1, #2 or #5 to Leidseplein. Modern hotel on a quiet stretch of water just a short hop from Leidseplein and the Melkweg. Clean, inoffensively decorated and well-equipped, en-suite rooms – some with Jacuzzi and waterbed. Doubles without a canal view start from €145.

Marcel van Woerkom Leidsestraat 87 ☎020/622 9834, ⓦwww.marcelamsterdam .com. Tram #1, #2 and #5 to Prinsengracht. Well-known, popular B&B run by an English-speaking graphic designer and artist, who attracts like-minded people to this stylish restored house. Four en-suite doubles available for two, three or four people sharing. Relaxing and peaceful amidst the buzz of the city, with regulars returning year after year, so ring well in advance in high season. No breakfast, but there are

▽ American Hotel

tea- and coffee-making facilities. Prices start from €100.

De Munck Achtergracht 3 ☎020/623 6283, ⓦwww.hoteldemunck.com. Tram #4 to Prinsengracht. Fine, family-run hotel in a quiet spot by the Amstel, with clean, light and well-maintained rooms. The Sixties-style breakfast room sports a Wurlitzer jukebox with a good collection of 1960s hits. Booking recommended. En-suite rooms from €105.

Op de Gracht Prinsengracht 826 ☎020/626 1937, ⓦwww.opdegracht.nl. Tram #4 from CS to Prinsengracht. B&B in a good-looking canal house on one of the main canals; run by the very pleasant Jolanda Schipper. Two rooms tastefully decorated, both with en suite. Minimum stay two nights. Prices €90 and €100,

Prinsenhof Prinsengracht 810 ☎020/623 1772, ⓦwww.hotelprinsenhof.com. Tram #4 to Prinsengracht. One-star hotel with smartly decorated rooms, some en suite, and a bright breakfast room. This is one of the city's top budget options, usually booked months in advance so reservations are essential. Doubles without shower €60.

Quentin Leidsekade 89 ☎020/626 2187, ⓦwww.quentinhotels.com. Tram #1, #2 or #5 to Leidseplein. Very friendly small hotel, often a stopover for artists performing at the Melkweg. Welcoming to all, and especially well-regarded among gay and lesbian visitors. Higher weekend rates. Doubles €95.

Schiller Rembrandtplein 26–36 ☎020/554 0700, ⓦwww.nh-hotels.com. Tram #4, #9 or #14 to Rembrandtplein. Once something of a hangout for Amsterdam's intellectuals, the Schiller, named after the painter and architect, still has one of the city's better-known and more atmospheric brasseries on its ground floor kitted out in fetching Art Deco style. The drawback is its location – on tacky Rembrandtplein – but if you're here to sample a few of the city's nightclubs, the Muziektheater or the shops along Leidsestraat you couldn't be better situated. Rates without breakfast begin at around €230.

Seven Bridges Reguliersgracht 31 ☎020/623 1329. Tram #4 or #9 to Prinsengracht. Perhaps the city's most charming hotel – and certainly one of its better-value ones. Takes its name from its canalside location, which affords a view of no less than seven dinky little bridges. Beautifully decorated, its spotless rooms are regularly revamped.

Small and popular, so often booked solid. Breakfast is served in your room and prices vary depending on the view. From €100.

▽ Seven Bridges

The Jordaan and the Westerdok

Acacia Lindengracht 251 ☎020/622 1460, ⓦwww.acaciahotel.nl. Fifteen-minute walk from CS or bus #18 to Willemstraat. Well-kept hotel situated in the heart of the Jordaan, along a quiet canal. Situated right on a corner, so some of the rooms have panoramic views of the water and streets below. They also let self-catering apartments. Three- and four-bed rooms also available. Doubles from €82.

Calendula's Guest House Goudsbloemstraat 132 ☎020/428 3055, ⓦwww.calendulas.com. Bus #18 to Willemstraat. Comfortable and well-furnished guesthouse, off an unassuming street, close to the Noordermarkt. Has a couple of double rooms both with TV and shared bathroom. Bright, spacious front room with polished beech floorboards and large windows, sleeps up to four people. Back room overlooking garden and with a small balcony sleeps up to three people. Large, open kitchen and pleasant terrace area. Three-night minimum stay. Double €90, €25 for extra bed.

Johanna's B&B Van Hogendorpplein 62 ☎62/413 3056 (mobile), ⓦwww.johannasbnb.com.

Tram #10 from Leidseplein to Van Limburg Stirumplein. A privately run B&B, very friendly and helpful to newcomers. It's a little difficult to get to, situated out near the Westergas-fabriek, but is excellent value. Two double rooms only, so be sure to call before you set out. €90.

La Boheme Marnixstraat 415 ☎020/624 2828, ⓦwww.labohemeamsterdam.nl. Tram #1, #2 or #5 to Leidseplein. One of the best of the many, many hotels spreading up the Marnixstraat from Leidseplein, and just along from the Melkweg. This small establishment with super-friendly staff has basic, but bright en-suite doubles for €105. Key deposit €20

Mark's Studio Van Beuningenstraat 80a ☎020/776 0056, ⓦwww.marksamsterdam .com. Bus #18 or #22, or a five-minute taxi ride from CS. Comfortable and stylishly decorated B&B/apartment situated northwest of the city centre. Sleeps up to four people but can be booked as a single. Facilities include TV and DVD player, private car parking for €17.50. No breakfast but use of fridge provided along with tea and coffee facilities. There's a pleasant garden terrace too. Online bookings only; minimum stay two nights. Price depends on length of stay and number of people staying, around €40–45 per person.

Van Onna Bloemgracht 102 ☎020/626 5801, ⓦwww.hotelvanonna.com. Tram #13 or #17 to Westermarkt. A quiet, well-maintained, family-run place on a tranquil canal, still retaining some of its original fixtures dating back over three hundred years. Simple setup, no TV, no smoking and cash payment only. Booking advised. Rooms sleeping up to four people for €40 per person.

The Old Jewish Quarter and the eastern docks

Adolesce Nieuwe Keizersgracht 26 ☎020/626 3959, ⓦwww.adolesce.nl. Tram #9 or #14 to Waterlooplein. Quiet and welcoming family-run hotel, with ten neat, airy if unspectacular rooms and a large dining room and bar. All day breakfast available. Rooms with private facilities €95.

Amstel Inter-Continental Professor Tulpplein 1 ☎020/622 6060, ⓦwww.interconti .com /amsterdam. Metro Weesperplein. The absolute top-of-the-range – one of the best and most luxurious hotels in the country. Favoured by visiting celebrities and treated in the late nineties to a sumptuous renovation to the tune of €50 million. If you have the money, splash out on a night of ultimate style and class; cheapest doubles from €395.

Arena 's-Gravesandestraat 51 ☎020/850 2410, ⓦwww.hotelarena.nl. Metro Weesperplein, then walk, or tram #9 or #14 to Tropenmuseum. A little way east of the centre, in a renovated old convent on the edge of the Oosterpark, this place has been stylishly revamped, transforming a popular hostel into a hip three-star hotel. Despite the odd pretentious flourish (Playstation upon request) it manages to retain a relaxed vibe attracting both businessfolk and travellers alike. Lively bar, intimate restaurant, and late-night club (Fri & Sat). Six split-level designer suites available for €195. Doubles start from €125.

Fantasia Nieuwe Keizersgracht 16 ☎020/623 8259, ⓦwww.fantasia-hotel.com. Tram #9 or #14 to Waterlooplein. Nicely situated family-run hotel in a handsome old canal house overlooking a quiet stretch of canal; the rooms are well-maintained, connected by quaint, narrow corridors, and there are also some very attractive attic rooms, including triples (€124) as well as a family room (€195) available. Rooms from €86.

De Hortus Plantage Parklaan 8 ☎020/625 9996, ⓦwww.hotelhortus.com. Tram #9 to Artis Zoo. Smoker-friendly hotel-cum-hostel close to the Hortus Botanicus gardens. Rooms vary in size, from two- to twelve-person, and maintenance is kept to a minimum, but they're clean, and the common room, equipped with free Internet access, pool table and coffee machine, has a good atmosphere. Note that you need to confirm your booking two days prior, otherwise you'll lose the room. All rooms €25 per person.

Lloyd Hotel Oostelijke Handelskade 34 ☎020/561 36 36; ⓦwww.lloydhotel.com. Take the free ferry from Centraal Station (see p.114). Recently renovated, the sleek re-modelled interior of this former immigrant hostel and – chillingly – Nazi-era prison, is perfectly in tune with the renaissance of the Eastern Docklands, with 120 or so rooms and two restaurants and a bar that are striving hard to set the standards for new Amsterdam. The rooms have bright, white interiors and range from small doubles with shared bathroom (€80) to very large rooms with views (€300) – well worth the money if you don't mind being this far out of the centre. From €80

Rembrandt Plantage Middenlaan 17 ☎020/627 2714, ⓦwww.hotelrembrandt.nl. Tram #9 to Artis Zoo. Elegant hotel with a dining room dating from the sixteenth century, though the building itself is nowhere near as old. Rooms are decorated in crisp modern style, with wood interiors and are en suite; €110.

The Museum Quarter and Vondelpark

Acro Jan Luyckenstraat 44 ☎020/662 5538, ⓦwww.acro-hotel.nl. Tram #2 or #5 to Hobbemastraat. Excellent, modern hotel with stylish rooms, a plush bar and self-service restaurant (breakfast only). Well worth the money; reserve at least two months in advance. €100.

AMS Hotel Holland P.C. Hooftstraat 162 ☎020/676 4253, ⓦwww.ams.nl. Tram #2 or #5 to Van Baerlestraat. Comfortable, quiet and welcoming hotel at the end of the street near the Vondelpark. Price excludes tax and breakfast (€10). €120.

Bema Concertgebouwplein 19b ☎020/679 1396, ⓦwww.bemahotel.nl. Tram #16 to Museumplein. Large, clean rooms within a huge house under the canny eye of the friendly manager-owner. The rooms aren't modern but they're full of funky character. Handy for the Concertgebouw and the main museums. Dutch breakfast delivered to your room. Triples and quads available. Minimum two nights weekends. En-suite doubles €85.

Fita Jan Luyckenstraat 37 ☎020/679 0976, ⓦwww.fita.nl. Tram #2 or #5 to Van Baerlestraat. Mid-sized, friendly family-run hotel in a quiet spot between the Vondel-park and the museums. Sixteen comfortable en-suite doubles, all rooms non-smoking. Discounts for longer stays; free phone calls within Europe and to America. €120 (extra bed €25).

Jan Luycken Jan Luyckenstraat 58 ☎020/573 0730, ⓦwww.janluyken.nl. Tram #2 or #5 to Hobbemastraat. Part of the Bildergerg hotel group, this elegant hotel is located in an imposing nineteenth-century town house, and has a lounge bar. Stylish and comfort-able in equal measure. Price of standard doubles excludes tax and breakfast (€17). €175.

Karen McCusker Zeilstraat ☎020/679 2753 (mornings), ⓦwww.bedandbreakfastamsterdam .net. Tram #2 to Amstelveenseweg. Small B&B run by an Englishwoman who moved to Amsterdam in 1979. Two cosy and clean, Laura Ashley-style (non-smoking) double rooms in her home, close to the Vondelpark. Suite available with bathroom, kitchen and private balcony, suitable for longer stays. Ring first, because the owner isn't always around and you'll also need to reserve well in advance. Doubles with shared bathroom cost around €75.

Parkzicht Roemer Visscherstraat 33 ☎020/618 1954, ℉020/618 0897. Tram #1, #2 or #5 to Leidseplein. Quiet, unassuming hotel on a pretty backstreet near the Vondelpark and museums, with an appealingly lived-in look. Clean and characterful, some rooms have fireplaces and each are furnished with old Dutch wood funiture. Singles, doubles, triples and quads with a mixture of shared and en-suite facilities. Closed end Nov to mid March. €80 plus tax.

Piet Hein Vossiusstraat 53 ☎020/662 7205, ⓦwww.hotelpiethein.nl. Tram #1, #2 or #5 to Leidseplein. Calm, low-key and stylish, tucked away on a quiet street running past the Vondelpark, midway between Leidseplein and the Concertgebouw. Bar with white leather couches open till 1am. Lift access. Doubles with bath or shower €140.

Prinsen Vondelstraat 38 ☎020/616 2323, ⓦwww.prinsenhotel.nl. Tram #2 and #5 to Leidseplein, or #1 to Stadhouderskade. Family-run hotel built in the nineteenth century by Dutch architect P.J.H. Cuijpers (he of Centraal Station fame) on the edge of the Vondelpark. Quiet and with a large, secluded back garden. Marginally higher rates at the weekend. En-suite doubles with all mod cons €135.

Toro Koningslaan 64 ☎020/673 7223, ℉020/675 0031. Tram #2 to Emmastraat. Lovely hotel in two very comfortably furnished early twentieth-century town houses on a peaceful residential street by the southern reaches of the Vondelpark. At the time of writing it had just reopened under the same owners as the Toren hotel (see p.168) and

possesses much of the same charm and lavishness. Has its own garden and terrace overlooking a lake in the park. Tax extra and breakfast €12 Prices start from €145.

Verdi Wanningstraat 9 ☎020/676 0073, ℉020/673 9070. Tram #5 to Museumplein. Small and simple hotel with large, basic but bright and comfortable rooms near the Concertgebouw. Doubles with shower €120, excluding tax.

Zandbergen Willemsparkweg 205 ☎020/676 9321, ⓦwww.hotel-zandbergen.com. Tram #2 to Emmastraat. Light, airy, family-run hotel on a busy street near the Vondelpark; eighteen non-smoking rooms are clean, spacious and tastefully decorated with minibar and free internet connection. Minimum two-night stay during high season. Closed for two weeks in Dec and Jan. Price excluding tax, €135.

The outer districts

Hilton Apollolaan 138 ☎020/710 6000, ⓦwww .amsterdam.hilton.com. Tram #5 or #24 to Apollolaan. Way outside the centre in the distinctly upmarket Nieuw Zuid, with everything you'd expect, lounge bar, health club and a fine Italian restaurant. Only really worth considering if you can afford to soak up a bit of 1960s nostalgia in its (admittedly stunning) Lennon and Ono suite, where the couple held their famous 1969 "Bed-In" for peace; one night here will set you back €920, otherwise doubles hover around the €260 mark.

Van Ostade Van Ostadestraat 123 ☎020/679 3452, ⓦwww.bicyclehotel.com. Tram #25 to Ceintuurbaan. Friendly, youthful place not far from the Albert Cuyp market in the Pijp, it bills itself as a "bicycle hotel", renting bikes (€5 per day) and giving advice on routes and suchlike. Good breakfast. Garage parking for cars (€17.50), though you'll need to book in advance. Basic but clean rooms with shared facilities start at €70.

Hostels

If you're on a tight budget, the cheapest central option is to take a dormitory bed in a **hostel**, and there are plenty to choose from: Hostelling International places, unofficial private hostels, even Christian hostels. Most hostels will either provide (relatively) clean bed linen or charge a few euros for it; your own sleeping bag might be a better option. Many hostels also lock guests out for a short period each day to clean the place; and some set a nightly curfew, though these are usually late enough not to cause too much of a problem. Some hostels don't accept reservations from June to August.

The cheapest **dorms** you'll find are the "Shelter" Christian-run hostels, between €16–19 per person per night; although the average elsewhere is closer to €22. A few otherwise friendly, good-value places have a policy of **charging more at the weekends** than during the week – a price hike of as much as €5 that can come as an unpleasant surprise. Note that you can pay the same for a bed in a sixteen-person dorm as you'd pay to be in a four-person dorm elsewhere: any place that won't allow you to see the dorm before you pay is worth avoiding. If you want a little extra privacy, many hostels also offer triples, doubles and singles for much less than you'd pay in a regular hotel, though the quality and size of rooms can leave a lot to be desired.

The Old Centre

Anna Youth Hostel Spuistraat 6 ☎020/620 1155, ⓦwww.annayouthhostel.com. Small ground floor hostel, with two large seventeen-bed dorms. Decorated Bedouin-style, though rooms are rather dark and impersonal; shower rooms are curtained off to the side at reception. OK for short stays. No bookings. €20.

Bob's Youth Hostel Nieuwezijds Voorburgwal 92 ☎020/623 0063, ⓦwww.bobsyouthhostel.nl. An old favourite with backpackers and a grungy crowd, Bob's is lively and smoky. Dorms are a little on the poky side, but they're clean, and at this price per person, including breakfast, you can't expect luxuries. Ground floor coffeeshop stays open to 3am and does cheap snacks. They also let four apartments (€70 for two people, €80 for three). However, they kick everyone out between 10am–12.30pm to clean, which is not so good if you want a lie in. €19.

Bulldog Hotel Oudezijds Voorburgwal 216–220 ☎020/620 3822, ⓦwww.bulldog.nl. Tram #4, #9, #16 or #24 to Dam, then a 3-min walk. Part of the Bulldog coffeeshop chain, this low-budget hotel has all the amenities of "a five-star hotel for backpackers". Bar and DVD lounge downstairs complete with leather couches and soft lighting. Price of dorms with TV and shower includes breakfast, linen and wake-up service. Also double rooms for €85, as well as fully equipped luxury apartments available from €135. From €26.

Durty Nelly's Warmoesstraat 115–117 ☎020/638 0125, ⓦwww.xs4all.nl/~nellys. A rabbit warren of a hostel situated above a packed Irish pub. Dorms are rather over-priced but the sheets are clean, and a large Dutch breakfast and lockers are included. Street-side dorms are better lit and airier. €25 (€30 weekends).

Flying Pig Downtown Nieuwendijk 100 ☎020/420 6822, ⓦwww.flyingpig.nl. Clean, large and well run by ex-travellers familiar with the needs of backpackers. Free use of kitchen facilities and internet, and there's a late-night coffeeshop next door. Hostel bar open till 4am. Justifiably popular, and a very good deal, with 22-bed dorms offering the cheapest price. Queensize bunks sleeping two also available. Female dorm available in summer. €10 deposit for sheets and keys. During the peak season you'll need to book well in advance. See also the Flying Pig Palace, p.175. Dorms start at €22.60.

The Globe Oudezijds Voorburgwal 3 ☎020/421 7424, ⓦwww.hostel-theglobe.nl. A popular hostel with a 24-hr sports-screen bar that's a favourite with those on all-day drinking binges. Twins (a steep €95) triples and quads also available. €5 key deposit.

▽ Bulldog Hotel

Breakfast is an extra €4.50. Dorm beds from €22; weekends €28.

Kabul Warmoesstraat 38–42 ☎020/623 7158, 📧kabulhotel@hotmail.com. Large and bustling hostel in the middle of the Red Light district with basic rooms sleeping between one and sixteen people. Not always as clean as it might be, but there's no lockout or curfew and you can book in advance. Groups welcome. Cost of a dorm bed including use of all facilities start from €22.

Meeting Point Warmoesstraat 14 ☎020/627 7499, 🌐www.hostel-meetingpoint.nl. Warm and cosy central hostel with space in twelve- to eighteen-bed dorms. Four-person dorms also available (€85). Breakfast of bread, jam and eggs €2.50. As with most of the City's hostels checkout is 10am. Private bar and pool table for guests is open 24-hours. Cash payment only. Midweek dorms go for €16.

The Shelter City Barndesteeg 21 ☎020/625 3230, 🌐www.shelter.nl. Metro Nieuwmarkt. A non-evangelical Christian youth hostel smack in the middle of the Red Light District. These are some of the best-value beds in Amsterdam, with bed linen, shower and sizeable breakfast included. Four- and eight–bed dorms are single-sex, lockers require a €5 deposit and there's a midnight curfew (1am at weekends). You might be handed a booklet on Jesus when you check in, but you'll get a quiet night's sleep and the sheets are clean. €19 (€16 winter).

Stay Okay Stadsdoelen Kloveniersburgwal 97 ☎020/624 6832, 🌐www.stayokay.com /stadsdoelen. Metro Nieuwmarkt, or tram #4, #9, #16, #24 or #25 to Muntplein. The closest to Centraal Station of the two official hostels, with clean eight- to twenty-bed dorms. Two-bed rooms also available (€63). Prices include linen, breakfast and locker, plus use of communal kitchen. Also offers a range of discounts on city activities and travel for HI card holders. The bar overlooks the canal and serves good-value if basic food, and there's a 2am curfew (though the door opens for three 15min intervals between 2am and 7am). The other HI hostel is the Stay Okay Vondelpark, which is equipped for large groups (see opposite). Members get priority in high season. Members €21; non-members €23.50.

Grachtengordel south

Hans Brinker Budget Hotel Kerkstraat 136 ☎020/622 0687, 🌐www.hans-brinker.com. Tram #1, #2 or #5 to Prinsengracht. Well-established and raucously popular Amsterdam cheapie, which has over 550 beds. Singles and doubles also available. The facilities are good: breakfast, free Internet after 10pm, disco every night, and dorms are basic and clean; near to the buzz of Leidseplein too. A hostel to head for if you're out for a good time (and not too bothered about getting a good night's sleep), though be prepared to change dorms several times during your stay to accommodate larger groups. Walk-in policy only. Dorm beds go for around €24.

▽ Hans Brinkner Budget Hotel

International Budget Hotel Leidsegracht 76 ☎020/624 2784, 📠626 1839. Tram #1, #2 or #5 to Prinsengracht. An excellent budget option on a peaceful little canal in the heart of the city. Small, simple rooms sleeping up to four with shared bathroom Breakfast in the café is extra and is around €2–4. Singles and twin rooms with private facilities (€65) also available. Young, friendly staff. Prices from €30 per person.

The Jordaan and the Westerdok

The Shelter Jordan Bloemstraat 179 ☎020/624 4717, 🌐www.shelter.nl. Tram #6, #13 or #17 to Marnixstraat. The second of Amsterdam's two Christian youth hostels (the other is Shelter City, see above). Great value beds, with breakfast and bed linen included. Non-smoking dorms are single-sex, lockers require a €5 deposit and there's a 2am curfew. Friendly and helpful staff, plus a decent café. Sited in a particularly attractive part of the Jordaan, close to the Lijnbaansgracht canal. €19.

The Museum Quarter and Vondelpark

Flying Pig Palace Vossiusstraat 46 ⊤ 020/400 4187, ⓦ www.flyingpig.nl. **Tram #1, #2 or #5 to Leidseplein, then walk.** The better of the two Flying Pig hostels, facing the Vondel-park and close to the city's most important museums. Immaculately clean and well maintained. Free use of kitchen facilities, the Internet and skates hire, no curfew and good tourist information. A few two-person queensize bunks at €33, as well as double rooms. €10 deposit for sheets and key. Great value. Ten-bed dorms start at €22.20.

Stay Okay Vondelpark Zandpad 5 ⊤ 020/589 8996, ⓦ www.stayokay.com/vondelpark. **Tram #1, #2 or #5 to Leidseplein, then walk.** A large modern hostel next to the Vondelpark with friendly and efficient staff and, for facilities, the better of the city's two HI hostels. There's a bar, restaurant, TV lounge, free Internet access and bicycle shed, plus various discount facilities for tours, museums and bike hire. Rooms are spacious and clean and have small lockers with hangers; all have en-suite facilities. Singles, doubles and rooms sleeping up to six are available. Downstairs brasserie offers cheap meals and stays open till 1am. Secure pin lockers; lift and disabled access; no curfew. To be sure of a place in high season you'll need to book at least two months ahead. Price of dorms includes use of all facilities, sheets and a good buffet breakfast. HI members have priority in high season and pay €2.50 less than non-members. Non-member rates are €24.

Apartments and houseboats

For groups or families, short-term **apartment** rentals can work out cheaper than staying in a hotel, with the further advantages of privacy and the conven-ience (or at least economy) of self-catering. Apartments sleeping four or five can often be found for the same price as a double room in a hotel. **Houseboats** tend to be significantly more luxurious and expensive. Both are often organized through local hotels.

Acacia Lindengracht 251, 1015 KH Amsterdam ⊤ 020/622 1460, ⓦ www.hotelacacia.nl. Studios sleeping two people €90 per night; houseboats from €95.
Amsterdam House 's Gravelandseveer 7, 1011 KN Amsterdam ⊤ 020/626 2577, ⓦ www .amsterdamhouse.com. Two-person apartments start from €115 per night; houseboats €150.

Cafeine Korte Lijnbaanssteeg 1 ⓦ www .amsterdamapartment.com. Apartments for rent above an Italian-style coffee bar.
Hoksbergen Apartments Singel 301, 1012 WH Amsterdam ⊤ 020/626 6043, ⓦ www .hotelhoksbergen.nl. Apartments sleeping up to five from €120.

Campsites

There are a number of **campsites** in and around Amsterdam, most of them readily accessible by car or public transport. The three listed below are recom-mended by the VVV, which divides them into two self-explanatory classifica-tions, "youth" and "family" campsites. The latter is more suitable for touring caravans and mobile homes. For information on city campsites throughout the Netherlands check out ⓦ www.stadscampings.nl.

Youth campsites

Vliegenbos Meeuwenlaan 138 ⓣ020/636
8855, ⓦwww.vliegenbos.com. Bus #32, #36 or
nightbus #361 from CS; drivers take Exit S116
off the A10. A relaxed and friendly site, just a
ten-minute bus ride into Amsterdam North
from CS. Facilities include a general shop,
bar and restaurant. Rates are between
€4.60–7.60 per night per person with hot
showers included. There are also huts with
bunk beds and basic cooking facilities, for
€65 per night for four people; phone ahead
to check availability. Car park is €8. Under-
16s need to be accompanied by an adult;
no pets. Open April to Oct.

Zeeburg Zuider IJdijk 20 ⓣ020/694 4430,
ⓦwww.campingzeeburg.nl. Bus #22 to
Kramatweg, or nightbus #359 both from CS, or
tram #14 from Dam square and a 10 min walk;
drivers take Exit S114 off the A10. Slightly better equipped than the Vliegenbos, but a bit
more hassle to get to. Rates are €2–4.50
per person, plus €4 for a tent, €2.50 for a
motorbike and €4 for a car. Hot showers
are an extra 80 cents. Cabins sleeping two

and six people are €18.25 per person per
night, including bed linen; minimum two
night stay in high season. The shop sells
freshly baked bread, and the bar has has
live music in high season. Winter discounts.
Open all year.

Family campsite

Amsterdamse Bos Kleine Noorddijk 1, Aalsmeer
ⓣ020/641 6868, ⓦwww.campingamsterdambos
.nl. Bus # 172 from CS to Amstelveen then bus
#171; by car take Exit 6 off the A9 towards
Aalsmeer and follow N231 to Bosrandweg.
Facilities include a bar, shop and restaurant,
but this campsite is a long way out, on the
southern reaches of the lush and well-kept
Amsterdam Bos (forest). Rates are from
€2.50–5 per person per night (children
under 4 are free), hot showers included;
tents are €3, plus a car is €3, €6 for a
camper van and €3.50 for a caravan. Huts
sleeping up to four cost €45 a night, which
includes a gas stove. Open April to mid-Oct.

9

Eating and drinking

A
msterdam is not by any means Europe's culinary capital. But the **food** in the average Dutch restaurant has improved by leaps and bounds in recent years, and there are any number of places serving a good, inventive, take on homegrown cuisine. The capital also has a good assortment of ethnic restaurants, especially Indonesian, Chinese and Thai, most of which serve food at prices that (by big-city standards) are hard to beat. Like the rest of Holland, there are also lots of cafés and bars that serve adventurous food for a decent price in a relaxed and unpretentious setting – often known as *eetcafés*. Amsterdam is also, of course, a great city to **drink**, with a selection of bars that is one of the city's real pleasures. Holland's proximity to the great beer-drinking nation of Belgium, where monks more or less invented modern beer, helps explain the variety on offer.

For such a small city, Amsterdam is filled with places to eat and drink, and you should have no trouble finding somewhere convenient and enjoyable to suit your budget. On Friday and Saturday nights it's advisable to start early (between 6pm and 7pm) or make a reservation, if you want to find a place at a popular **restaurant**. Dutch mealtimes are a little idiosyncratic: breakfast tends to be later than you might expect, and other meals tend to be eaten earlier. If you choose to eat breakfast away from your hotel, you'll find few cafés open before 8am or 8.30am. The standard Dutch lunch hour is from noon to 1pm, and most restaurants are at their busiest between 7pm and 8pm, and may stop serving altogether by 10pm. If you just want lunch, or a bite between sights, there are plenty of places throughout the city – **cafés and tearooms** – where you can sit just grab a cup of coffee and a sandwich or light lunch. And of course **bars** almost always serve sandwiches, and usually something more substantial as well – we've indicated in the text which ones serve food.

With Amsterdam's singular approach to the sale and consumption of cannabis, you might choose to enjoy a joint after your meal rather than a beer: we've included in this chapter a selection of **"coffeeshops"** where you can buy and smoke grass or hash. Don't, however, assume that you can light up a joint anywhere else – almost everywhere else you can't, even though it's almost impossible to avoid cigarette smoke.

What to eat

Dutch restaurant food tends to be higher in protein content than imagination: steak, chicken and fish, along with filling soups and stews, are staple fare, although in recent years the local cuisine has absorbed other influences and can now vary quite a lot. There's more of an emphasis on well prepared fresh ingredients and, as in Britain, a parade of adventurous young chefs who take pride in what they

Dutch cheese

Holland's **cheeses** have a somewhat unjustified reputation abroad for being bland and rubbery, possibly because they only export the nastier products and keep the best for themselves. In fact, Dutch cheese can be delicious, although there isn't the variety you get in, say, France or Britain. Most are based on the same soft, creamy *Goudas*, and differences in taste come with the varying stages of maturity – young, mature or old (*jong*, *belegen* or *oud*). *Jong* cheese has a mild flavour, *belegen* is much tastier, while *oud* can be pungent and strong, with a flaky texture not unlike Italian Parmesan. Generally, the older they get, the saltier they are. Among the other cheeses you'll find are the best-known round, red *Edam*, made principally for export and (quite sensibly) not eaten much by the Dutch; *Leidse*, which is simply *Gouda* with cumin seeds; *Maasdammer* and *Leerdammer*, strong, creamy and full of holes; and Dutch-made *Emmentals* and *Gruyères*. The best way to eat cheese here is the way the Dutch do it, in thin slices cut with a special cheese knife (*kaasschaaf*) rather than large hunks. See p.225 for recommended cheese shops. Street markets are a good place to shop too; try the organic farmers' produce market on Saturday at the Noordermarkt, or of course the markets outside Amsterdam at Edam and Alkmaar.

do. Most bars serve food, too, and most will offer a dagschotel (dish of the day, generally available for as long as the restaurant is open), for which you'll pay around €12 bottom line, for what tend to be enormous portions. Otherwise reckon on spending around €15 for a main course, maybe more for fish which tends to be expensive. A wide selection of vegetarian restaurants offer full-course set meals for around €12, or hearty dishes for €10 or less, but bear in mind that they often close early. Another cheap stand-by is Italian food: pizzas and pasta dishes start at a fairly uniform €8–10 in all but the ritziest places. Chinese and Thai restaurants are also common, as are (increasingly) Spanish ones, all of which serve well-priced, filling food. But Amsterdam's real speciality is its **Indonesian restaurants**, a consequence of the country's imperial adventures and well worth checking out. You can eat à la carte – nasi goreng and bami goreng (rice or noodles with meat) are ubiquitous dishes, and chicken or beef in peanut sauce (sateh) is available everywhere too. Alternatively, order a rijsttafel – boiled rice and/or noodles served with a number of spicy side dishes and hot sambal sauce on the side. Eaten with the spoon in the right hand, fork in the left, and with dry white or rosé wine or beer, this is delicious and normally more than enough for two.

In **bars** you can expect to find sandwiches and rolls (*boterhammen* and *broodjes*) – often open, and varying from a simple slice of cheese to something so embellished it's a complete meal – as well as more substantial fare. Dutch classics include *broodje halfom*, a roll with a combination of thinly sliced salted beef and liver eaten with mustard, and *broodje warm vlees*, thinly sliced warm pork served with *sateh* sauce. In the winter, *erwtensoep* (aka "snert") is available in most bars. At around €5 a serving, this thick pea soup with smoked sausage, accompanied by a portion of smoked bacon on pumpernickel, makes a great-value lunch. Or there's *uitsmijter*: one, two or three fried eggs on buttered bread, topped with a choice of ham, cheese or roast beef – at around €8, it's another good budget lunch.

What to drink

The beverage drunk most often in Amsterdam's bars is beer. The three leading Dutch brands – Amstel, Grolsch and Heineken – are worldwide bestsellers, but are available here in considerably more potent formats than the insipid varieties shunted out for export. Beer is usually served in small measures, around half a pint (ask for *een pils*), much of which will be a frothing head. Different beers come in different glasses – Oranjeboom, for instance, is served in a vaasje; white beer (*witbier*), which is light, cloudy and served with lemon, has its own tumbler; and most of the speciality Belgian beers have individual stemmed glasses.

Jenever, Dutch gin, is not unlike English gin but a bit weaker and a little oilier; it's made from molasses and flavoured with juniper berries. Served in small glasses it is traditionally drunk straight, often knocked back in one gulp with much hearty back-slapping. There are a number of varieties: oud (old) is smooth and mellow, jong (young) packs more of a punch – though neither is terribly alcoholic. Ask for a *borreltje* (straight jenever), a *bitterje* (with angostura bitters) or, if you've a sweeter tooth, try a *bessenjenever* – blackcurrant-flavoured gin; for a glass of beer with a jenever chaser, ask for a *kopstoot*.

Other drinks you'll see include numerous Dutch **liqueurs**, notably advocaat (eggnog), and the sweet blue *curaçao*; and an assortment of lurid-coloured **fruit brandies**, which are best left for experimentation at the end of an evening. There's also the Dutch-produced brandy, *Vieux*, which tastes as if it's made from prunes but is in fact grape-based.

Dutch **coffee** is black and strong, and comes in small cups, usually with *koffiemelk* (evaporated milk); ordinary milk is offered only occasionally. If you want white coffee (café au lait), ask for a *koffie verkeerd*. Most bars also serve cappuccino, although bear in mind that many stop serving coffee altogether around 11pm.

Tea generally comes with lemon, if anything; if you want milk you have to ask for it. **Hot chocolate** is also popular, served hot or cold: for a real treat, drink it hot with a layer of fresh whipped cream on top.

Breakfast, fast food and snacks

In all but the very cheapest hostels and the most expensive hotels, **breakfast** (*ontbijt*) will be included in the price of the room. Though usually nothing fancy, it's always very filling: rolls, cheese, ham, hard-boiled eggs, jam and honey or peanut butter are the principal ingredients. If you're not eating in your hotel, many bars and cafés serve breakfast, and those that don't invariably offer rolls and sandwiches.

For the rest of the day, eating cheaply and well, particularly on your feet, is no real problem, although those on the tightest of budgets may find themselves dependent on the dubious delights of **Dutch fast food**. Chips – *frites* – are the most common standby (*Vlaamse* or "Flemish" are the best), either sprinkled with salt or smothered with huge gobs of mayonnaise (sometimes known as *fritesaus*); alternative toppings are curry, goulash, peanut or tomato sauce. Chips are often complemented with *kroketten* – spiced meat (usually either veal or beef) in hash covered with breadcrumbs and deep-fried – or *fricandel*, a frank-furter-like sausage, made from offal. All these are available over the counter at evil-smelling fast-food places (FEBO is the most common chain), or from heat-ed glass compartments outside. Tastier, and good both as a snack and a full lunch, are the **fish specialities** sold from street kiosks – raw herrings (tip your head back and dangle the fish into your mouth, Dutch-style), smoked eel, mackerel in a roll, mussels, and various kinds of deep-fried fish – and there are also a number of **Indonesian take-aways**, serving *sateh* and noodle dishes in an "open-kitchen" atmosphere. Other, though less common, street foods include

FEBO Leidsestraat and Reguliersbreestraat (Grachtengordel south), Damrak (Old Centre) and other locations. The most obvious place to get a *kroket* or *fricandel*, but not a bad choice. Ask for it on a roll with some mustard.

Kwekkeboom Reguliersbreestraat 36 (Grachtengordel south). Bakery selling pastries, pies, rolls and *kroketten*. There are a couple of small tables out the back.

Van Dobben Korte Reguliersdwarsstraat 5 (Grachtengordel south). For most people this is *the* place to come for a *kroket*. Open till 1am during the week, 2am on Fri & Sat, Sun till 9pm.

Vlaamse Friethuis Voetboogstraat 33 (Old Centre). The best chips in town; takeaway only. Tues-Sat 11am–6pm, Sun & Mon noon–6pm.

pancakes (*pannekoeken*), sweet or spicy (more widely available at sit-down restaurants), **waffles** (*stroopwafels*) doused with maple syrup, and, in November and December, *oliebollen*, deep-fried dough balls with raisins and candied peel, traditionally eaten on New Year's Eve. Dutch **cakes and biscuits** are always good and filling, best eaten in a *banketbakkerij*; or buy a bag and eat them on the go. Apart from the ubiquitous *appelgebak* – a wedge of apple tart flavoured with cinnamon – other things to try include *spekulaas*, a cinnamon biscuit with a gingerbread texture, and *amandelkoek*, cakes with a biscuity outside and melt-in-the-mouth almond paste inside.

Bars

There are, in essence, two kinds of Amsterdam bar: the traditional, old-style bar or **brown café** – a *bruin café* or *bruine kroeg* – cosy places so called because of the dingy colour of their walls, stained by years of tobacco smoke; and the slick, self-consciously modern **designer bars**, many of them known as "grand cafés", which tend to be as un-brown as possible and geared towards a largely young crowd. We've included details of the more established of these, although these places come and go – something like seventy percent are said to close down within a year of opening. Bars, of either kind, **open** daily at around 10am or 5pm; those that open in the morning do not close at lunchtime, and both stay open until around 1am during the week, 2am at weekends (sometimes until 3am).

Another type of drinking spot – though there are very few of them left – is the **tasting houses** (*proeflokalen*), originally the sampling rooms of small private distillers, now tiny, stand-up places that sell only spirits – mainly Dutch gin or *jenever* – and close around 8pm. And as in the rest of Europe there's a growing number of **Irish pubs**, all featuring Guinness and other stouts on tap, Gaelic music of varying quality, and English football live via satellite most weekends. The clue to their success seems to lie much more in the football than the fiddlers – all have rapidly become "locals" for the relatively large numbers of British and Irish living and working in Amsterdam, and although at quiet times the clientele might include a smattering of Amsterdammers, most of the (generally male) drinkers in these places are expats rather than locals. For listings of **gay bars** see Chapter Twelve.

Many bars – often designated **eetcafés** – offer a complete food menu, and most will make you a sandwich or a bowl of soup; at the very least you can snack on hard-boiled eggs from the counter. Those bars that specialize more in food than drink are listed in our "Restaurants" section.

Prices are fairly standard everywhere, and the only time you'll pay through the nose is when there's music, or if you're desperate enough to step into the obvious tourist traps around Leidseplein and along Damrak. Reckon on paying roughly €1.70–2.00 for a standard-measure small beer, €2.40 for a glass of wine or a shot of *jenever*.

The Old Centre

Absinthe Nieuwezijds Voorburgwal 171. Small, late-night basement lounge bar, slightly hidden from the street but in a prime position close to the area's trendy bars and clubs. Not surprisingly it specializes in absinthe. Opens 10pm.

In 't Aepjen Zeedijk 1. This building has been a bar since the days when Zeedijk was the haunt of sailors gambling away their last few guilder and having to sometimes pay by barter rather than hard cash. Its name – literally 'In the Monkeys' – refers to the fact that monkeys were the stock in trade here. There are no monkeys now, but not much else has changed.

Belgique Gravenstraat 2. Tiny and very appealing bar behind the Nieuwe Kerk that specializes in brews from Belgium. Sample them with plates of Dutch and Trappist cheese.

Blincker St Barberenstraat 7. Squeezed between the top end of Nes and Oudezijds Voorburgwal, this hi-tech theatre bar, all exposed steel and hanging plants, is more comfortable than it looks.

▽ Blinckner

De Brakke Grond Nes 43. Modern, high-ceilinged bar and *eetcafé* often full of people discussing the performances they've just seen at the adjacent theatre. Belgian beer and food, as you might expect from somewhere next door to the Flemish Cultural Centre.

De Buurvrouw St Pieterspoortsteeg 29. Dark, noisy bar with a wildly eclectic crowd; a great alternative place to head for in the centre.

Dante Spuistraat 320. A would-be trendy bar-cum-art gallery right in the heart of the city's densest concentration of watering-holes. There are cosier places – but to peruse the art, and the people perusing the art, it's ok.

Dantzig Zwanenburgwal 15. Large and easy-going grand café, right on the water behind Waterlooplein, with comfortable chairs, friendly service and a low-key, chic atmosphere. Decent food, too: uitmijters, open sandwiches and salads at lunchtimes, and a simple French menu – steaks, fish, a veggie option – in the evenings.

De Drie Fleschjes Gravenstraat 16. Long-standing tasting house for spirits and liqueurs. No beer, and no seats either; its clients tend to be well heeled or well soused (often both). Closes at 8.30pm Monday to Saturday, at 7pm on Sundays.

De Engelbewaarder Kloveniersburgwal 59. Once the meeting place of Amsterdam's bookish types, this is still known as a literary café. It's relaxed and informal, with live jazz on Sunday afternoons.

De Engelse Reet Begijnensteeg 4. Also known as the Pilserner Club, this place is more like someone's front room than a bar – indeed, all drinks mysteriously appear from a back room. Photographs on the wall record generations of drinking – which has been going on here since 1893.

Gaeper Staalstraat 4. Convivial brown café packed during the school year with students from the university across the canal. Good food and seating outside for people-watching.

't Gasthuis Grimburgwal 7. Another brown café popular with students. Both this place and *Gaeper* are run by brothers, so it's in more or less the same style. It serves some of Amsterdam's cheapest hot food, both at lunchtime and in the evenings.

Gollem Raamsteeg 4. Small and cosy, split-level bar with rickety furniture, wood panelling and a comprehensive selection of Belgian beers plus a few Dutch brews for extra variety.

Harry's American Bar Spuistraat 285. Smoother than the average brown café, and, as you might guess from the name, rather self-consciously American in style. Not the hippest bar in town, but serving decent cocktails – though to a background of ear-shattering house music at weekends.

Het Doktertje Roozenboomsteeg 4. Small, dark, brown café with stained glass to keep you from being ogled by the world outside. Liqueurs fill the wall behind the tiny bar.

Het Paleis Paleisstraat 16. Bar that's a favourite with students from the adjoining university buildings. Refurbished in a trendy style, they also serve food – foccaccia sandwiches, salads, and suchlike.

Hoppe Spui 18. One of Amsterdam's longest-established and best-known bars, and one of its most likeable, popular with the city's businessfolk. Summer is especially good, when the throngs spill out onto the street.

▽ Hoppe

De Jaren Nieuwe Doelenstraat 20. One of the grandest of the grand cafés, overlooking the Amstel next to the university, with three floors, two terraces and a cool, light feel. A great place to nurse the Sunday paper – unusually you'll find English ones here. Reasonably priced food too, and a great salad bar.

De Koningshut Spuistraat 269. In the early evening, at least, it's standing room only in this small, spit-and-sawdust bar, popular with office folk on their way home or to dinner.

Lokaal 't Loosje Nieuwmarkt 32. Quiet old-style brown café that's been here for two hundred years and looks it, with a nice old tiled interior. Wonderful for late breakfasts and pensive afternoons.

Luxembourg Spui 22. The prime watering-hole of Amsterdam's advertising and media brigade. a long and deep café-bar with a pleasant pavement terrace and an elegant if faded area at the back. Competent, reasonably priced bar food – the house speciality, the Luxemburger (hamburger) really hits the spot. Very popular. Overlooks the Singel at the back.

Mercurius Prins Hendrikkade 20. Cool, spacious bar and restaurant that hosts live TV shows and Sunday-night jazz singers.

De Ooier Stolofspoort 1. Old *proeflokaal* that's a civilised escape from the nearby sleaze of the Red Light District – and handily situated for Centraal Station too. Boiled eggs on the bar go down well with the gin.

Scheltema Nieuwezijds Voorburgwal 242. Journalists' bar, now only frequented by more senior newshounds and their occasionally famous interviewees, since all the newspaper headquarters along here have since moved to the suburbs. Faded early twentieth-century feel, with a reading table and meals.

Schuim Spuistraat 189. Popular and spacious grand café with retro furniture, attracting an unpretentious crowd.

Tapvreugd Oude Hoogstraat 11. Far and away the most amicable of the loud, crowded music bars on this and surrounding streets.

In de Wildeman Kolksteeg 3. Lovely old-fashioned bar with a barely changed wood and tiled interior that still boasts the original low bar and shelving. A very peaceful escape from the generally loud and tacky shops of Niuewendijk too.

Wynand Fockink Pijlsteeg 31. Hidden just behind Dam square, this is one of the older *proeflokalen*, and perhaps its most authentic. Standing-room only, bend down at the bar to sip your *jenever* when it's poured.

Grachtengordel west

Café 't Arendsnest Herengracht 90. In a handsome old canal house, this bar boasts impressive wooden décor – from the longest of bars to the tall wood and glass cabinets – and specialises in Dutch beers, of which it has 130 varieties, twelve on tap. Rather surprisingly, it can, however, be very, very quiet. Open daily except Sun from 4pm till midnight, 2am on the weekend.

Brix Wolvenstraat 16 ☎020/639 03 51, ⊛www .cafebrix.nl. Chic bar-café featuring regular jam and jazz sessions two or three times a week from 8.30pm onwards. Open daily from 5pm.

Hegeraad Noordermarkt 34. Lovingly maintained, old-fashioned brown café-bar with a fiercely loyal, older clientele. The back room, furnished with red plush and paintings, is the perfect place to relax with a hot chocolate.

Het Molenpad Prinsengracht 653. This is one of the most appealing brown café-bars in the city – a long, dark, dusty bar that also serves remarkably good food. Fills up with a young, professional crowd after 6pm.

Het Papeneiland Prinsengracht 2. With its wood panelling, antique Delft tiles and ancient stove, this is one of the cosiest bars in the Grachtengordel, though it does get packed late at night with a garrulous crew. Popular with locals and tourists alike.

De Pieper Prinsengracht 424. Laid-back neighbourhood brown bar, with rickety old furniture and a mini-terrace beside the canal. Has a surprisingly large selection of liqueurs. At the corner of Leidsegracht.

De Prins Prinsengracht 124. With its well-worn décor and chatty atmosphere, this popular and lively bar is long, deep and brown. It offers a wide range of drinks and a well-priced bar menu with food served from 10am to 9pm. All in all, a good place to drink in an attractive part of town.

Spanjer & van Twist Leliegracht 60. Hip café-bar with an arty air and brisk modern fittings. Tasty snacks and light meals plus an outside terrace right on the canal. Lunch served daily 10am–4pm, evening meals from 6pm.

Van Puffelen Prinsengracht 377. Recently enlarged, this long-established and popular spot is divided into two with a brown café-bar on one side and a restaurant on the other. The café-bar (daily 3pm–1/2am) is an appealing place to drink, with a good choice of international beers, whilst the restaurant (Mon–Sat 6–11pm, Sun 5.30–10pm) concentrates on Dutch(ish) dishes with lots of organic frills – organic duck and bulgar wheat for example or smoked salmon

with beetroot chips. Main courses average around €18, but the daily specials are much more economical with a three-course meal costing just €20.

Grachtengordel south

Black & White Leidseplein 18. No-nonsense bar, whose "rolling stone" emblem at the front is a good indicator of the loud rock music within. A large good-time crowd on Saturday night.

Coco's Outback Thorbeckeplein 8 ☎020/627 24 23. Bustling, determinedly youthful and lively Aussie bar that's spread out over two floors with a pool table and Sky Sports. Cheap meals, mostly of the barbeque and meat variety (try the all-you-can-eat spare ribs). English and Aussie breakfast menu also available. Good selection of draught beers. Happy hour 5–6pm.

De Duivel Reguliersdwarsstraat 87. Tucked away on a street of bars and coffeeshops, this is the only hip-hop bar in Amsterdam, with continuous beats and a clientele to match. Daily 8pm–3/4am.

Het Hok Lange Leidsedwarsstraat 134. Games bar, where you can play backgammon, chess or draughts, or just drink against a backdrop of clicking counters. Pleasingly unpretentious after the plastic restaurants of the rest of the street, though women may find the overwhelmingly male atmosphere off-putting.

Huyschkaemer Utrechtsestraat 137. Careworn but hip café-bar, which is a favourite watering-hole of arty students. At weekends the some of the tables are cleared away to make room for a dance floor.

Lux Marnixstraat 403. À la mode designer bar with nightly DJs and a good line in house at full volume. Attracts a young alternative crowd. From 8pm till 3am, 4am on the weekend.

Morlang Keizersgracht 451. Lively, split-level bar-cum-restaurant decorated in soft modern style and attracting a prosperous crew. Good bar and occasional live music too. Next door to the Walem (see next page). Daily 11am–1am.

Oosterling Utrechtsestraat 140. Stone-floored, neighbourhood bar-cum-off-licence that's been owned by the same family for donkeys' years. Kitted out in attractive traditional style, it specialises in *jenever* (gin) with dozens of brands and varieties. No mobiles.

Schiller Rembrandtplein 26. Not an exciting choice perhaps, but the café-bar attached to the Schiller Hotel boasts splendid Art Deco furnishings and fittings in the manner of a cruise liner. Somewhere to warm up if you're out on the razzle.

Walem Keizersgracht 449. A chic bar-restaurant – cool, light, and vehemently un-brown, the sort of place where you can either eat in or chill out at the bar sipping a Mojito. The clientele is stylish, and the food is a hybrid of French-Dutch inspired dishes; their salmon trout and crème fraîche is particularly good; mains begin at €10. Breakfast in the garden during the summer is a highlight. Usually busy. Open daily 9.30am–1am.

▽ Walem

De Zotte Proeflokaal Raamstraat 29. Down a grubby alley not far from the Leidseplein, this cosy, laid-back bar specialises in Belgian beer of which it has dozens of brews. Open daily 4pm–1am, bar food served 6–9.30pm.

The Jordaan and the Westerdok

Chris Bloemstraat 42. Very proud of itself for being the Jordaan's (and Amsterdam's) oldest bar, dating from 1624. Comfortable, homely atmosphere.

Duende Lindengracht 62. Wonderful little tapas bar with good, cheap tapas (from €2.50) to help your drink go down. Also includes a small venue in the back for live dance and music performances, including regular flamenco. Opens 4pm.

Dulac Haarlemmerstraat 118. Very appealing Art Deco grand café housed in what used to be an old city bank – the metal cage

doors remain but nowadays the only money changing hands is at the bar, especially on weekends when it stays open till 3am. Open daily from noon. DJs Thurs, Fri & Sat playing a mixture of jazz, funk and '70s & '80s.

Festina Lente Looiersgracht 40b. Relaxed, mezzanine neighbourhood café-bar with mismatched furniture and armchairs to laze about on. The outside tables overlooking the canal are a suntrap in the summer when the locals come out to relax with friends for the afternnoon; inside is equally cozy in the winter. Good selection of board games. As for the cons – service at the weekend can be slow.

De Kat in de Wijngaert Lindengracht 160. With the enticing name "Cat in the Vineyard", this small local bar is quiet enough for conversation.

Nol Westerstraat 109. Probably the epitome of the jolly Jordaan singing bar, a luridly lit dive, popular with Jordaan streetsters and ordinary Amsterdammers alike. Opens 8pm and closes late, especially at weekends, when the back-slapping joviality and drunken singalongs keep you here until closing time.

De Reiger Nieuwe Leliestraat 34. The Jordaan's main meeting place, an old-style café filled with modish Amsterdammers. Affordable lunches from 11am, dinner twice that.

't Smalle Egelantiersgracht 12. Candle-lit and comfortable café-bar, with a barge out front for relaxed summer afternoons. One of the highlights of the city (see p.87).

De Tuin 2e Tuindwarsstraat 13. The Jordaan has some marvellously unpretentious bars, and this is one of the best: loud, agreeably unkempt and always filled with locals.

The Old Jewish Quarter and eastern docks

11 Oosterdokskade 3 ☎020/625 59 99. One of the hippest joints in town, this sprawling bar-club-restaurant has bare minimalist/industrial décor inherited from its previous incarnation as the top floor of the old postal building – the ground floor now holds the modern art of the Stedelijk Museum. The views out over the city centre are second to none and the journey up in one of the enormous old postal lifts is good fun, but the food doesn't match the setting and really the place is best used as a bar/club.

Open Sun–Wed 11am-10pm, Thurs–Sat – club nights – 11am–4am (kitchen till 10pm).

Brouwerij Het Ij Funenkade 5. Cosy, old-fashioned bar and mini-brewery in the old public baths adjoining the De Gooyer windmill. Serves up an excellent range of beers and ales, from the thunderously strong Columbus (9%) amber ale to the creamier, more soothing Natte (6.5%). Open Wed–Sun 3–8pm.

De Druif Rapenburgerplein 83. Possibly the city's first bar, and one of its most beguiling, yet hardly anyone knows about it. Its popularity with the locals lends it a village pub feel. Daily from noon (Sun 1pm).

Entredok Entrepotdok 64. Tucked-away basement bar along a canal lined with houseboats. The clientele hails from the surrounding hi-tech offices, though increasingly from the residential blocks in between, too. Tapas and antipasti available. Opens 4pm.

De Groene Olifant Sarphatistraat 126. Metres from the Muiderpoort, this is a characterful old wood-panelled brown café-bar, with floor-to-ceiling windows and an excellent, varied menu. From noon.

KHL Oostelijke Handelskade 44. Cosy dock-side bar and restaurant that serves decent and reasonably-priced food.

Tisfris St Antoniesbreestraat 142. Colourful, split-level café and bar near the Rembrandt House, and minutes from Waterlooplein. Youthful and popular. Closes 7pm.

The Museum Quarter and Vondelpark

't Blauwe Theehuis Vondelpark 5 ⊛www .blauwetheehuis.nl. Beautiful tearoom/bar housed in a circular building from the De Stijl period. A good place for breakfast and for open-air dancing in the summer with DJs on Fri, Sat and Sun nights; in winter dancing transfers to the inside bar.

Cobra Museumplein ⊛www.cobracafe.nl. A modern café set up during the renovation of the square, with paintings from the twentieth-century CoBrA movement and floor to ceiling glass walls which provide a pleasant view across the terrace, popular with Amsterdam's professional couples and their kids. The club sandwiches are pricey but good; the coffee could be better. The bar hosts monthly parties with DJs.

Ebeling Overtoom 52. Cosy lounge bar within a few minutes of Leidseplein, housed in an old bank – with the toilets in the vaults. Inexpensive snacks and long leather seats to sink into. Open till 3am Fri & Sat.

Vertigo Vondelpark 3. Attached to the Film Museum, this is a pleasant café to while away a sunny afternoon (or take refuge from the rain), with a spacious, but cosy interior and a large terrace overlooking the park. The apple pie is worth the visit alone. Open till 1am.

De Vondeltuin Vondelpark 7 ☎020/664 5091. Large, peaceful terrace on the Amstelveen side of the Vondelpark serving tapas, fresh salads and pancakes, next to the in-line skate rental. A picnic or barbeque in the park including skate hire can also be arranged. Mar–Oct daily from 11am.

Wildschut Roelof Hartplein 1–3. Congenial bar famous for its Art Deco trimmings. Has a mixture of long tables and cosy booths and serves well priced meals and snacks. Near the Concertgebouw.

The outer districts

Duvel 1e van der Helststraat 59. A bar and *eetcafé* on a pedestrianized Van der Helstraat, around the corner from Albert Cuypstraat. Handy if you've come to shop in the market, but a convivial stop at any time of day.

East of Eden Linnaeusstraat 11. A wonderfully relaxed café-bar across the road from the Tropenmuseum. Appealing combination of high-ceilinged splendour and gently waving palm trees, with James Dean thrown in on top. Well worth a sunny afternoon. Inexpensive food and cocktails from €4.

De Engel Albert Cuypstraat 182. This cavern-ous converted church is an excellent and very convenient choice if you're longing for some space while shopping in the crowded market. It does food too, though nothing to write home about. Closed Monday, other-wise open all day.

Kingfisher Ferdinand Bolstraat 24. A nice neighbourhood café, that's good for lunch or just a drink if you want to continue imbib-ing after the Heineken experience – it's right around the corner.

Café Krull Sarphatipark 2. On the corner of 1e van der Helststraat and the park, a few metres from the Albert Cuyp, this is an atmospheric place on a lively corner. The actual *krull* (curve) is the nearby men's urinal designed in a curve. Drinks, snacks and jazz all day long from 11am.

Ot en Sien Buiksloterweg 27. Brown café in a row of seventeeth-century *dijkhuisjes*, serving Dutch beers and filled with locals. A good stopoff when taking a cycling trip along the Noord-Hollandskanaal. Take the ferry from behind Centraal Station.

Coffeeshops

Amsterdam's pragmatic approach to cannabis (see box opposite) has led to the rise of licensed **coffeeshops**, selling bags of dope much in the same way as bars sell glasses of beer. The first thing you should know about coffeeshops is that locals use them too. The second thing you should know is that the only ones they use are outside the Red Light District. Practically all the coffeeshops you'll run into here are worth avoiding, either for their decor, their deals or their clientele. Plasticky, neon-lit dives abound, pumping out mainstream varieties of house, rock or reggae at ear-splitting level; the dope on offer is usually limited and of poor quality. A short time exploring the city will turn up plenty of more congenial, high-quality outlets for buying and enjoying cannabis, light years away from the tack of the city centre.

When you first walk into a coffeeshop, it isn't immediately apparent how to buy the stuff – it's illegal to advertise cannabis in any way, which includes calling attention to the fact that it's available at all. What you have to do is ask to see the **menu**, which is normally kept behind the counter. This will list all the different varieties on offer, along with (if it's a reputable place) exactly how many grams you get for your money. Most of the stuff is sold either per gram, or in bags worth €5 or €10 (the more powerful it is, the less you get). The in-house dealer will be able to help you out with queries. In theory, purchases of up to 5g of cannabis, are tolerated; in practice, most coffeeshops around the city offer discounted bulk purchases of 50g with impunity (though bear in mind that if the police do search you they're entitled to confiscate any amount they find).

The **hash** you may come across originates in various countries and is pretty self-explanatory, apart from *Pollem*, which is compressed resin and stronger than normal. **Grass** is a different story, and the old days of imported Colombian, Thai and sensimelia are fading away; taking their place are limitless, potent varieties of *Nederwiet*, Dutch grown under UV lights. Skunk, Haze and Northern Lights are all popular types of Dutch weed, and should be treated with caution – a single spliff can lay you low (or high) for hours. You would be equally well advised to take care with **space-cakes**, which are widely available: you can never be sure exactly what's in them; they tend to have a delayed reaction (up to two hours before you notice anything strange); and once they kick in, they can bring on an extremely intense, bewildering high – 10–12 hours is common. Some large coffeeshops, such as the *Bulldog*, refuse to sell them, and advise you against buying elsewhere. You may also come across cannabis seeds for growing your own. While Amsterdammers are permitted to grow five small marijuana plants for "domestic consumption", the import of cannabis seeds is illegal in any country – don't even think about trying to take some home.

Most coffeeshops open around 10am or 11am and close around midnight. Away from coffeeshops, always ask if smoking is OK in a given situation, the worst you'll get will be a "no".

Drugs in Amsterdam

Amsterdam has an international reputation as a haven for the dope smoker, though many visitors are surprised to find that **all drugs**, hard and soft, are technically illegal, the caveat being that since 1976 the possession of small amounts of **cannabis** (up to 30g/1oz) has been ignored by the police. From its inception, there have been problems with this policy. In part, this is because the Dutch have never legalized the supply chain – or more specifically that section of it within their national borders – and partly because the 30g rule has proved difficult to enforce. Other complications have arisen because of the difference between Holland's policy and that of its European neighbours. Inevitably, the relative "laxity" of the Dutch has made the country in general and Amsterdam in particular attractive to soft (and arguably hard) **drug dealers**. The Dutch authorities have tried hard to keep organized crime out of the soft drug market, but drug dealing and **drug tourism** – of which there is an awful lot – irritate many Amsterdammers no end.

In recent years, the French and German governments have put pressure on the Dutch to bring their drug policy into line with the rest of Europe – one concession obliged coffeeshops to choose between selling dope or alcohol, and many chose the latter. Overall, however, while the Dutch have found it prudent to keep a rigorous eye on the coffeeshops and emphasize their credentials in the fight against hard drugs, they have stuck to their liberal guns on cannabis. As justification, they cite the lack of evidence to **link soft- and hard-drug use** and indeed, the country's figures for hard-drug addiction are actually among the lowest in Europe. Furthermore, by treating drugs as a medical rather than criminal problem, Amsterdam's authorities have been able to pioneer positive responses to **drugs issues**. The city council runs a wide range of rehabilitation programmes and recently decided to overhaul the **methadone** programme it introduced for heroin addicts in 1979. Here as elsewhere, methadone is now discredited as a means of weaning addicts off heroin and as a result the Dutch began issuing free heroin in tightly controlled quantities to users in 1998, a nationwide policy that continues to this day.

The Old Centre

Abraxas Jonge Roelensteeg 12. Quirky, mezzanine coffeeshop with challenging spiral staircases, especially after a few hours. The hot chocolate with hash is not for the fainthearted.

The Bulldog Oudezijds Voorburgwal 90, 132 & 218. The biggest and most famous of the coffeeshop chains – see below for more.

Dampkring Handboogstraat 29. Colourful coffeeshop with loud music and laid-back atmosphere, known for its good-quality hash.

Extase Oude Hoogstraat 2. Part of a chain run by the initiator of the Hash Museum. Considerably less chichi than the better-known coffeeshops.

Grasshopper Oudebrugsteeg 16; Nieuwezijds Voorburgwal 57. One of the city's more welcoming coffeeshops, though at times overwhelmed by tourists. Mon–Sun 10am–1am.

Homegrown Fantasy Nieuwezijds Voorburgwal 87a. Attached to the Dutch Passion seed company, this sells the widest selection of marijuana in Amsterdam, most of it local.

Josephine Baker Oude Hoogstraat 27. Once known as the *Café de Dood* – "Café of the Dead" – after the studiously wasted youth who patronize it – this is the loudest hangout in the area.

Kadinsky Rosmarijnsteeg 9; Zoutsteeg 9; Grimburgwal 9. Strictly accurate deals weighed out to a background of jazz dance. Chocolate chip cookies to die for.

Rusland Rusland 16. One of the first Amsterdam coffeeshops, a cramped but vibrant place whose multi-levelled interior is a favourite with both dope fans and tea addicts (it has 43 different kinds). A cut above the rest.

Smoking Bull Lange Niezel 13. A relaxed place amongst the rumble of the Red Light District, with a good choice of music.

De Tweede Kamer Heisteeg 6. A friendly and rather cosy coffeeshop, in a tiny alley off Spui, with experienced staff and an enormous variety.

Grachtengordel west

Siberië Brouwersgracht 11. Bright, modern coffeeshop set up by the former staff of Rusland and notable for the way it's avoided the overcommercialization of the larger chains. Very relaxed, very friendly, and worth a visit whether you want to smoke or not; has a good selection of magazines as well as a chess board.

▽ Siberië

La Tertulia Prinsengracht 312. Tiny corner coffeeshop, complete with indoor rockery and tinkling fountain. Much better outside, though, as it's on a particularly beautiful stretch of the canal. Mon–Sat 11am–7pm.

Grachtengordel south

The Bulldog Leidseplein 17; Singel 12. The biggest and most famous of the coffeeshop chains, and a long way from its pokey Red Light District origins, The Bulldog's main branch is here on the Leidseplein, housed in a former police station. It has a large cocktail bar, coffeeshop, juice bar and souvenir shop, all with separate entrances. It's big and brash, not at all the place for a quiet smoke, though the dope they sell (packaged up in neat little brand-labelled bags) is reliably good. Coffeeshop open daily 9am–1am.

Free I Reguliersdwarsstraat 70. Tiny place that looks and feels like an African mud hut, except for the hip-hop beats. Grass specialists.

Global Chillage Kerkstraat 51. Celebrated slice of Amsterdam dope culture, always comfortably filled with stoners propped up against the walls. Many sentences go unfinished. Daily 11am–midnight.

Hemp Bar Frederiksplein 15. Welcoming and cozy marijuana-friendly hotel bar, which stays open until late, or until the last customer has gone upstairs to bed.

Mellow Yellow Vijzelgracht 33. Sparse but bright coffeeshop with a small but good-quality dope list. A little out of the way, but makes up for it in friendliness.

The Otherside Reguliersdwarsstraat 6. Popular with (but not exclusively occupied by) gay smokers, this is a crowded and fun coffeeshop near the Muntplein. In Dutch, "the other side" is a euphemism for gay.

Stix Utrechtsestraat 21. The quietest branch of an Amsterdam institution in dope-smoking. You can get it all here: a coffee, a newspaper and a smoke. Daily 11am–1am

The Jordaan and the Westerdok

Barney's Breakfast Bar Haarlemmerstraat 102. Something of an Amsterdam institution, this extremely popular café-cum-coffeeshop is simply the most civilized place in town to enjoy a big hit with a fine breakfast – at any time of the day.

Free City Marnixstraat 233. Dimly-lit and inviting coffeeshop with large sports screen. Favoured by local white-collar smokers. Open from 7am (Sun 1pm) till late.

Paradox 1e Bloemdwarsstraat 2. If you're fed up with the usual coffeeshop food offerings of burgers and chocolate, *Paradox* satisfies the munchies with outstanding natural food, including spectacular smoothies as well as veggie burgers. Closes 8pm.

The Old Jewish Quarter and eastern docks

Pollinator Company Nieuwe Herengracht 25, ⓦ www.pollinatorcompany.com. Not strictly a coffeeshop, this place is for those serious about growing their own marijuana. The owner, Mila, can tell you everything you need to know, and stocks the products you need to do it, from seeds to compost, as well as various peripherals such as pipes, cannabis lollies and hemp rock. The small chill-out area offers free tea and coffee and has a large collection of back issues of HighTimes, including numerous books Mila has written on the subject. Closes 7pm.

The outer districts

Greenhouse Tolstraat 91; Waterlooplein 345; OZ Voorburgwal 191. Consistently sweeps the boards at the annual Cannabis Cup, with medals for its dope as well as "Best Coffeeshop". Tolstraat is a way down to the south (tram #4), but worth the trek: if you're only buying once, buy here. Also an Old Centre branch at OZ Voorburgwal 191.

Yo-Yo 2e Jan van der Heijdenstraat 79. About as local as it's possible to get. Down in the Pijp, to the east of the Sarphatipark, a small, airy little place to seek out smoking solitude. Daily except Sun noon–7pm.

Cafés and tearooms

Amsterdam has plenty of **cafés and tearooms** which concentrate on serving good coffee, sandwiches, light snacks and cakes during the day. Some may serve alcohol but you wouldn't class them as "bars", and most don't allow dope-smoking. Usual opening hours are 9am or 10am to 5pm or 6pm; some are closed on Sundays. Along with *eetcafés* they make good places to stop off for lunch, or to spend a quiet time reading or writing without distractions.

The Old Centre

Arnots Singel 441. Just around the corner from Heiligeweg, a basement café serving some of the best coffee in town along with wholemeal sandwiches and freshly squeezed apples. A great summertime spot with people spilling out onto the pavement. Mon–Fri 11.30am–4.30pm.

Café Beurs van Belage Beurssplein 1. ☎020/638 39 14. Comfortable serving lunchtiume snacks in the old Beurs building (see Chapter 1) just off Damrak. Outside seating in summer. Tues–Sun 10am–6pm.

Cafeine Korte Lijnbaanssteeg 1. An Italian-style coffee bar where you can have a quick espresso standing at the counter. They also have apartments for rent (see p.175). Open from 8am.

Café Esprit Spui 10a. Attached to the euro-chain chlothes shop, this is a swish modern café, with wonderful sandwiches, rolls and superb salads.

Juicebar Tasty & Healthy Korte Lijnbaans-steeg 8. It looks like a snack bar but all they serve is fresh juice; good for a quick energy recharge.

Latei Zeedijk 174. A lovely shop and café in one, selling bric-a-brac and serving good espresso and lunches, with a different menu every week.

't Nieuwe Kafé Adjoining the Nieuwe Kerk, facing the Dam. Neat and trim, bistro-style café offering a tasty line in snacks, salads and pancakes plus mountainous sundaes and ice creams. Very popular with city-centre shoppers. Open daily 9am–6pm.

Puccini Staalstraat 21. Lovely café that serves great salads and sandwiches, wonderful handmade pastries and good coffee. A good lunchtime option, close to Water-looplein.

Villa Zeezicht Torensteeg 3. Small and central, this pastel-painted café serves excellent rolls and sandwiches, plus some of the freshest apple cake in the city. Open Mon–Fri 8am–6.30pm, Sat & Sun 9am–6.30pm.

▽ Villa Zeezicht

Grachtengordel west

Baton Espresso Herengracht 82. Bright, modern and cheerful café with a good selection of sandwiches, muffins and croissants. Corner of Herenstraat. Daily 10am–6pm.

Buffet van Odette & Yvette Herengracht 309. Neat little place decorated in attractive modern style and serving tasty snacks and light meals, from homemade quiches, soups and pastas through to fruit tarts; cheese omelettes are the house speciality. Open Mon–Fri 8.30am–5.30pm, Sat 10am–5.30pm & Sun noon–5.30pm.

Greenwood's Singel 103. Amenable, pocket-sized café serving up a tasty line in salads, omelettes and cakes. Look out for the daily specials and order up an English-style pot of tea. Daily 9.30am–6pm.

Lunchcafé Winkel Noordermarkt 43. Packed to the gunnels on Saturday and Monday, when there is a market, this popular café may be decorated in plain, modern style, but the food is tasty and wholesome: the salads are good, but the doorstep apple pie is better. On the corner with Westerstraat. Open 10am–6pm.

▽ Lunchcafé Winkel

Pompadour Patisserie Huidenstraat 12. This patisserie sells 50 different sorts of bonbon as well as a mouth–watering selection of cakes and candied fruits – either take out or eat in, with a drink. Mon–Sat 9am–6pm.

Grachtengordel south

Café Americain American Hotel, Leidseplein 28. There was a time when this café was the trendiest spot in the city, attracting – at one time or another – artists, poets and TV folk.

Nowadays, things are much more routine, even canteen-like, but the fanciful Art Nouveau décor, coordinated down to the doorknobs, has survived intact and makes a visit worthwhile.

Backstage Utrechtsedwarsstraat 67. Run by former cabaret stars the Christmas Twins (Greg and Gary), this offbeat café, with its cheerfully zany décor, also sells knitwear and African jewellery. Mon–Sat 10am–5.30pm.

Bagels & Beans Keizersgracht 504. Bagel specialist with all sorts of imaginative fillings and attracting a young clientele: their version of strawberries and cream cheese is a big favourite in the summer. The "Beans" part of the name refers to the coffee you can have to accompany your bagel. Has several other branches, including one in De Pijp (see below). This one is open Mon–Fri 9.30am–5.30pm, Sat & Sun 10am–6pm.

Gary's Muffins Prinsengracht 454. The first New York bagels in town, with big, American-style cups of coffee and freshly baked muffins. Also at Jodenbreestraat 15. Daily 9am–5pm.

Metz Leidsestraat 34. Pleasantly appointed café on the top floor of the Metz department store, offering panoramic views over the city centre. The food is, however, really rather routine. Mon 11am–6pm, Tues–Sat 9.30am–6pm & Sun noon–5pm.

Café Panini Vijzelgracht 3. Formica may be a thing of the past almost everywhere else, but not here, which gives this split-level, Italian café-cum-restaurant a vaguely Beatnik air. Great coffee, sandwiches and snacks during the day, reasonably priced meat and fish dishes at night. Café-cum-restaurant with good sandwiches, plus pasta dishes in the evening. Daily 9.30am–10pm.

The Jordaan and the Westerdok

Arnold Cornelis Elandsgracht 78. Long-established confectioner and patisserie with a snug tearoom. Mon–Sat 9.30am–5pm.

J.G. Beune Haarlemmerdijk 156. Age-old chocolatier with a tearoom attached. Mon–Sat 8.30am–5pm.

Jordino Haarlemmerdijk 25. Small tearoom with an enormous variety of mouth-watering chocolates, pastries and ice cream. Sun 1–5pm, Mon 1–7pm, Tues–Sat 10am–7pm.

The outer districts

Bagels & Beans Ferdinand Bolstraat 70. The southern branch of this popular coffee and bagel joint, just opposite the Albert Cuyp. Funny opening hours – Mon–Fri 8.24am–5.32pm. Sat 9.31am–6.03pm, Sun 9.29am–6.01pm.

Granny 1e van der Helststraat 45. Just off the Albert Cuyp market, with terrific *appelgebak* and *koffie verkeerd*.

Restaurants

Traditionally at least, **Dutch cuisine** lacks a certain finesse with its origins firmly rooted in the meat, potato and cabbage school of cooking. That said, things have improved markedly in the last few years with a slew of restaurants now offering tasty renditions of Dutch dishes plus a healthy selection of vegetarian and seafood places. Nonetheless, it's the city's non-Dutch restaurants which usually steal the gastronomic limelight, most especially in the abundance of outstanding **Indonesian** restaurants.

Intense competition keeps **prices** down to manageable proportions and in all but the ritziest of joints you can expect to pay no more than €20–25 for a main course, usually less. As for **opening hours**, the Dutch eat out early, with most restaurants opening at 5.30pm or 6pm and closing their doors around 10pm, though you'll still be served if you're already seated; vegetarian restaurants tend to close even earlier. At all but the least expensive places, it's a good idea to call ahead and **reserve** a table. Unless indicated otherwise, all the places we've listed are open seven days a week. Almost all of the larger/smarter restaurants take **credit cards**, but don't assume this to be the case at smaller/cheaper places. A fifteen percent service charge is included in the bill, but nonetheless a **tip** of between ten and fifteen percent is pretty much expected; the custom is generally to hand some change directly to your server rather than adding it to the bill.

The Old Centre

Chinese

Golden Chopsticks Oude Doelenstraat 1 ☎020/620 7040. Cheap and cheerful canteen-style Chinese food on the edge of the Red Light District. Very central, and, despite the spartan interior, among the best Chinese food you'll find in Amsterdam. No credit cards. Daily 11.30am–1pm.

Hoi Tin Zeedijk 122 ☎020/625 6451. Right in the heart of Amsterdam's Chinatown, this place – 'Sea Air' in Chjinese – is constantly busy. It has an enormous menu (in English

▽ Hoi Tin

too), including some vegetarian dishes, several floors, and a bakery at street level. Prices are moderate. Daily noon–midnight.

Wing Kee Zeedijk 76 ⊕020/623 5683. Simple Chinese restaurant that's popular with the local Chinatown community. Good food, and very cheap, too, although the service isn't great. Daily noon–11pm.

Dutch and Modern European

Brasserie Harkema Nes 67 ⊕020/ 428 2222. Very sleek, very stylish converted warehouse restaurant, whose moderately priced food – mains €10–15 – is sometimes good, and sometimes more variable than you might expect. The menu is nice, but service sometimes leaves something to be desired as well, delivered by fresh-faced youths who tend not to have a clue. Daily noon–11pm.

Hemelse Modder Oude Waal 9 ⊕020/624 3203. Sleek, modern restaurant serving a tasty menu of Dutch and vaguely European food food in an informal atmosphere. Service is very attentive, and despite the trendy environment, not at all precious, and the food is excellent and reasonably priced. Deservedly popular, especially among the gay community. Main courses around €12–15. Daily 6pm–10pm.

In de Waag Nieuwmarkt ⊕020/422 7772. Comfortable and stylish café-restaurant with uniformed staff. Main courses average €15, and some might say are over-priced given the sometimes variable quality. A nice building though, well converted. Daily 10am–midnight.

De Roode Leeuw Damrak 93–94 ⊕020/555 0666. Fusty old Dutch restaurant that's good for both a quick bit at lunchtimes on the street-facing terrace – pea soup, herrings, *uitsmijters* – or a full evening meal in the more formal main restaurant. A good place if you want to sample a traditional Dutch feed. Main courses go for €15–20. Daily 7am–10am & noon–10pm.

De Silveren Spiegel Kattengat 4 ⊕020/624 6589. There's been a restaurant in this location since 1614, and "The Silver Mirror" is one of the best in the city, with a delicately balanced menu of Dutch cuisine. The proprietor lives on the coast and brings in the fish himself. Spectacular food, with a cellar of 350 wines to complement it. Four-course dinner for two at a table set with silver is a cool €100, though you can get away with a main course for €28. Closed Sun.

Supper Club Jonge Roelensteeg 21 ⊕020/344 6400. A five-course set menu served at 8pm to customers lounging on mattresses, smoking joints and listening to a DJ on a raised stage. The fusion food is of a very high standard, though some may find the whole concept pretentious or downright disconcerting – it's not the most comfortable way to eat dinner. Diners have free entry to the members-only club downstairs. Booking is essential, but it's expensive, since there's no à la carte menu and you have to have the set dinner at €65 a pop. You can also try Supperclub Cruise, which leaves from pier 4, behind Centraal Station on Friday and Saturday nights (⊕020/344 64 03).

Van Beeren Koningsstraat 54 ⊕020/622 2329. This eetcafé used to serve simple Dutch food but has gone more upmarket – and the prices reflect this: around €15 for a main course. The food is good, though, and the setting still cosy – and it remains a moderately priced choice. Daily 5.30–9.30pm.

D' Vijff Vlieghen Spuistraat 294 ⊕020/624 8369, ⓦwww.thefiveflies.com. One of the city's best restaurants, the "Five Flies" occupies immaculate ground-floor premises kitted out in a smart version of traditional Dutch style from the tiled and wood panelled walls to the beamed ceiling and antique embossed

▽ De Silveren Spiegel

leather hangings. Intimate and very cosy, its enterprising menu features imaginative renditions of traditional dishes, with herrings and suckling pig being two favourites. Superb service too. Main courses €20–30. Daily 5.30-10pm.

Fish

Kopke Adega Koggestraat 1 ☎020/622 4587. Mediterranean-style fish restaurant that does a great *bouillabaise*, as well as some great, mainly Iberian fish and shellfish dishes – and you can sample them in the restaurant itself or in the more informal tapas bar. Decent prices too – you'll spend no more than about €25 for three course à la carte. Daily except Tues 6pm–10.30pm

Lucius Spuistraat 247 ☎020/624 1831. Old-established fish place that has been uneven over the years, but when it gets it right – as it usually does – it's excellent, if not especially cheap. Not a large restaurant, and reasonably informal, try the seafood platters, which can be superb. Daily 5pm–midnight.

French, Belgian, Swiss

Het Begijntje Begijnensteeg 8 ☎020/624 0528. A good, simple French kitchen, close to the most enchanting *hofje* in Amsterdam. Daily except Mon noon–2.30pm & 6–10.30pm.

Café Bern Nieuwmarkt 9 ☎020/622 0034. This place is really more of a bar, but it's better known, with some justification, for its food, which is, not surprisingly, given the name, excellent and alcoholic cheese fondue. Oh, and steaks too. All for around €10–15 a head. It's very cosy and usually extremely crowded, so it's probably best to book. If not, just get plastered at the bar while you wait for table. Daily 6–11pm.

De Compagnon Guldenhandsteeg 17 ☎020/620 4225. This rather traditional restaurant serves decent French food to a self-consciously discerning clientele in an old-fashioned atmosphere. A great, if not especially cheap, wine list, too. It's expensive – reckon €20-plus for a m ain course – and tends to be fully booked well in advance, but you might get in for lunch. Daily except Sun noon–2pm & 6–10pm; evenings only on Sat.

Luden Spuistraat 304 ☎020/622 8979. Excellent French restaurant (part of a Dutch chain) that does fine value *prix fixe* menus, for which you can expect to pay around €26 for three courses, as well as a more moderately priced à la carte menu and brasserie.

Palmers Zeedijk 4 ☎020/427 0551. French fusion restaurant (set up, according to the menu, by an ex-aviator who crashed over Greenland and married an Eskimo), and serving an interesting variety that includes burgers, swordfish sashimi, grilled tuna and chicken sate. Main course €10–15. Daily 5.30–10pm.

Indonesian

Kantjil en de Tijger Spuistraat 291 ☎020/620 0994. High-quality food averaging around €30 per person, served in a stylish wood-panelled grand café. Moderate–Expensive. Daily 4.30–11pm.

Sie Joe Gravenstraat 24 ☎020/624 1830. Small café-restaurant which is great value for money. The menu is far from extensive, but comprises well-prepared, simple dishes such as *gado gado*, *sateh*, *rendang* and soups. Mon–Sat 11am–7pm, Thurs till 8pm.

Italian

La Piccola Trattoria Nieuwezijds Voorburgwal 346 ☎020/627 1305. A small family-run Italian café serving good cheap Italian staples – authentically prepared. Daily except Mon 5.30–11pm. Cash only.

Mappa Nes 59 ☎020/528 9170. The old Frascati theatre bar has reinvented itself as a modern Italian restaurant that caters to a young, lively clientele. Good antipasti and pasta – and a great buzzy yet casual environment. Moderately priced. Daily noon–10pm.

Vasso Roozenboomsteeg 12 ☎020/626 0158. Genuine, creative restaurant off a corner of Het Spui, housed in three curvy sixteenth-century buildings. Polite and attentive service and moderate prices – around €20 for a main course. Daily 6–10.30pm.

Japanese

Kobe House Nieuwezijds Voorburgwal 77 ☎020/622 6458. Ultra-cool Japanese interior and a little overpriced, but serving good sushi and tepanyaki. Daily 5pm–midnight. Three courses will set you back around €30.

Pancakes

Pannekoekhuis Upstairs Grimburgwal 2 ☎020/626 5603. Minuscule place in a tumbledown house opposite the university buildings, with sweet and savoury pancakes at low prices. Student discount. Mon–Fri noon–7pm, Sat noon–7pm, Sun noon–6pm.

Spanish

Centra Lange Niezel 29 ☎020/622 3050. Canti-na with a wonderful selection of great-value Spanish food, masterfully cooked, genially served and in the running for Amsterdam's best. Daily 1–11pm. Cash only.

Thai

Bird Zeedijk 77 ☎020/420 6289. A packed canteen-like restaurant with good views of the hustle and bustle in the street. Quality food for a good price, served with a smile – and Thai versions of all your favourite European pop songs. Main courses around €10. Daily 3–10pm.

De Klaes Compaen Raamgracht 9 ☎020/623 8708. Good Thai food at affordable prices. Daily except Mon 5–9.45pm.

Lana Thai Warmoesstraat 10 ☎020/624 2179. Among the best Thai restaurants in town, with seating overlooking the water of Dam-rak. Quality food, chic surroundings but high prices. Expensive, compared to most Thai restaurants – reckon on €30-plus if you're hungry. Closed Tues.

Krua Thai Staalstraat 22 ☎020/622 9533. High-quality Thai restaurant that has replaced Tom Yam, which used to be here, and is much better on the whole. Excellent fish and seafood dishes, and moderate pric-es, with most main dishes going for around €15. Daily except Mon 5–10.30pm.

Vegetarian

Green Planet Spuistraat 122 ☎020/625 8280. First-rate mezzanine café-restaurant with lots of tofu dishes and a varied international menu from wraps through to couscous and ravioli. Main courses start at around €14; no cards. Open daily from 5.30pm.

Grachtengordel west

Dutch and Modern European

Bar-restaurant 5 Prinsenstraat 10 ☎020/428 2455. Stylish, split-level bar-cum-restaurant with high ceilings and oodles of antiques plus an imaginative menu featuring the likes of calf with onion compote and a red mustard jus. Main courses average a very reasonable €15–18. Daily from 6pm–1am.

Belhamel Brouwersgracht 60 ☎020/622 1095. Chichi, bistro-style restaurant with an Art Nouveau-style interior and an excellent Franco-Dutch menu featuring such delights

as suckling pig and perch. Main courses €20–25. Daily 6–10pm.

Damsteeg Reestraat 28 ☎020/627 8794. Superb French-inspired cuisine with more than the occasional Dutch gastronomic flourish. Candlelit tables in a charmingly renovated old canal house. Main courses hover around €25. Mon–Sat 2pm to midnight.

Dylan Keizersgracht 384 ☎020/530 2010. Lauded fusion restaurant decorated in crisp modern style and located inside the city's first – and arguably smartest (or most contrived) – boutique hotel, The Dylan, formerly Blakes. The food is a fusion of Japanese, Thai and European styles and main courses begin at €25, though you can pay a lot more. Open for lunch and dinner Mon–Sat noon–2.30pm and from 6.30pm, brunch on Sunday.

't Zwaantje Berenstraat 12 ☎020/623 2373. Traditional Dutch restaurant, down to the mini-rugs on the tables, that serves up well-cooked, reasonably priced food with main courses from €14. Well known for its liver and onions. Daily from 4.30pm to 11pm.

French and Belgian

Bordewijk Noordermarkt 7 ☎020/624 3899. A chic, well-lit and roomy restaurant decorated in relaxed modern/minimalist style and serving delicious French cuisine with Italian gastronomic flourishes. Open daily from 6.30pm except Mon. Mains start at €25.

Chez Georges & Betsie Herenstraat 3 ☎020/626 3332. Smart, split-level restaurant offering highly rated, upmarket Belgian cusine with the emphasis on meat dishes; mains €20–25. Open daily from 6pm, but closed Wed & Sun.

Christophe Leliegracht 46 ☎020/625 0807. Classic, Michelin-starred restaurant on a quiet canal, whose menu draws inspiration from the olive-oil-and-basil flavours of southern France and the chef's early years in North Africa. His aubergine terrine with cumin has been dubbed the best vegetarian dish in the world. Try for a table well in advance. Open Tues–Sat from 6.30pm. Main courses average €30.

D'Theeboom Singel 210 ☎020/623 8420. Smart and polished restaurant occupying the ground floor of a good-looking, old canalside warehouse and serving up classy and classic French cuisine with mains averaging around €25. Lunch Mon–Fri noon–3pm, dinner Tues–Sun from 6pm.

Greek

De Twee Grieken Prinsenstraat 20 ☎020/625 **5317**. In a tastefully and creatively renovated old shop, this very appealing Greek restaurant with its wood panelling and attractive outside terrace, offers all the favourites in an intimate, informal setting. Main courses average €13–17. Daily from 5pm to 10.30pm.

Indian

Purna Hartenstraat 29 ☎020/623 6772. With its traditional Indian décor, this well-established restaurant serves up all the standards and does a particularly good line in spicy tandoori. Main courses €11–15. Open daily except Tues from 7pm till late.

Italian

Prego Herenstraat 25 ☎020/638 0148. Small restaurant serving exceptionally high-quality Mediterranean cuisine with main courses hovering between €15 and €20. Polite and friendly staff. Daily from 6pm.

Indonesian

Cilubang Runstraat 10 ☎020/626 9755. Small and cosy restaurant, serving well-presented, spicy dishes at affordable prices – the *rijsttafel* kicks in at around €20. Tues–Sun from 6pm.

Pancakes

Pancake Bakery Prinsengracht 191 ☎020/625 **1333**. Located in the basement of an old canal house, this long-established restaurant offers a mind-boggling range of fillings for its pancakes. Very popular with tourists; pancakes from €7. Daily noon–9.30pm.

Thai

Top Thai Herenstraat 22 ☎020/623 4633. Popular restaurant serving up some of the best, spiciest and most authentic Thai food in the city – no mean feat given the quality of the opposition. Main courses average around €11. Daily from 4.30pm.

Vegetarian

Bolhoed Prinsengracht 62 ☎020/626 1803. Something of an Amsterdam institution, this popular vegan and vegetarian restaurant features a daily changing menu, plus organic beer to wash it all down with. New Age décor. Main courses average €12–20. Daily noon–10pm.

▽ Bolhoed

Grachtengordel south

African

Axum Utrechtsedwarsstraat 85 ☎020/622 **8389**. Small and inexpensive Ethiopian café-restaurant offering a choice of sixteen authentic dishes. Cosy decor; open daily except Monday from 5pm.

Pygmalion Nieuwe Spiegelstraat 5a ☎020/420 **7022**. Good spot for both lunch and dinner serving up South African dishes, including crocodile steaks, along with a tempting selection of sandwiches and authentic Afrikaner desserts. The premises are decorated in brisk, modern style. Main courses around €15–20. Tues–Sun 11am–10.30pm.

Dutch

Piet de Leeuw Noorderstraat 11 ☎020/623 **7181**. Arguably Amsterdam's best steakhouse, an old-fashioned, darkly lit, wood-panelled affair dating back to the 1940s. Doubles as a local bar – hence the smoky atmosphere – but the steaks, served in several different ways and costing around €15, are excellent. Mon–Fri noon–11pm, Sat & Sun 5–11pm.

Fish

Le Pêcheur Reguliersdwarsstraat 32 ☏ 020/624 3121. Smart, pastel-painted seafood restaurant with a lovely garden terrace in the summer. The fish arrives daily from the port of Ijmuiden and defines both the menu and the daily specials. Main courses average around €20–25. Open Mon–Fri noon–3pm & Mon–Sat 5.30–11pm.

De Sluizer Utrechtsestraat 41-45 ☏ 020/622 6376. Smart, bistro-style restaurant with an excellent range of seafood, though the sauces (which can be avoided) tend to overwhelm rather than enhance the flavour of the fish – the cheese sauces are the worst culprits. Main courses €16–22, daily specials €20. Daily 5–11pm.

French and Belgian

Bonjour Keizersgracht 770 ☏ 020/626 6040. Bistro-style, French restaurant in a cosy basement setting; particularly good charcoal-grilled dishes. Mains around €18. Wed–Sun 5–10pm.

Brasserie Schiller Rembradntplein 26–36 ☏ 020/554 0723. Good French-Dutch staples in a beautiful, turn-of-the-century bar/restaurant that's part of the hotel of the same name. Much the best choice among the tourist joints of Rembrandtplein. Main courses €15; open daily 7am–10.30pm.

Le Zinc... et les autres Prinsengracht 999 ☏ 020/622 9044. Wonderfully atmospheric little place decorated in rustic style and featuring imaginatively prepared French country ("peasant") food. Main courses in the region of €20 plus a particularly good wine list. Mon–Sat from 5.30pm.

Quartier Latin Utrechtsestraat 51 ☏ 020/622 7419. Split-level, intimate, bistro-style restaurant serving up a (broadly) French menu – for example, tournedos with Roquefort sauce. Main courses €16–19. Tues–Sun from 6pm.

Van de Kaart Prinsengracht 512 ☏ 020/625 9232. Excellent French/Mediterranean basement restaurant decorated in minimalist style and featuring an inventive menu, for instance lobster carpaccio, home cured bacon and pumpkin-stuffed ravioli. Main courses around €20. A good cellar too. Mon–Sat from 6.30pm, plus Wed–Fri 12.30–3.30pm.

Indian

Shiva Reguliersdwarsstraat 72 ☏ 020/624 8713. One of the city's best Indian restaurants in terms of quality and price, with a good selection of dishes, all expertly prepared. Vegetarians are well catered for too. Main courses from as little as €8. Daily 5–11pm.

Indonesian

Bojo Lange Leidsedwarsstraat 51 ☏ 020/622 7434. One of the best-value Indonesian places in town. Recommended for its young, lively atmosphere and late opening hours, though the food itself is very much a hit-and-miss affair, and you may have to wait a long time both for a table and service. Main courses average €9–13. Mon–Thurs 4pm–2am, Fri 4pm–3am, Sat noon–3am & Sun noon–2am.

Puri Mas Lange Leidsedwarsstraat 37 ☏ 020/627 7627. Exceptionally good value for money Indonesian restaurant near the Leidseplein. Friendly and informed service preludes spectacular *rijsttafels*, both meat and vegetarian. Main courses from €12. Recommended. Daily 5–11pm

Tempo Doeloe Utrechtsestraat 75 ☏ 020/625 6718. Reliable, cosy, top-quality place close to Rembrandtplein. As with all Indonesian restaurants, be guided by the waiter when choosing – some of the dishes are very hot indeed. Main courses from €18. Daily 6–11.30pm.

Tujuh Maret Utrechtsestraat 73 ☏ 020/427 9865. Impressive Indonesian food, notable for its rich combinations without compromising on authentic taste. Mains from €13–23. Mon–Sat 12.30pm–10pm & Sun 4–10pm.

Italian

D'Antica Reguliersdwarsstraat 80 ☏ 020/623 3862. Long-established restaurant serving authentic Italian cuisine in plain but pleasant premises; no pizza. Main courses cost anywhere between €11–25. Open Tues–Sat 5–11pm.

Japanese

Japan-Inn Leidsekruisstraat 4 ☏ 020/620 4989. Warm and welcoming restaurant in the middle of the Leidseplein buzz. Sushi and sashimi popular with Japanese tourists and Dutch business folk alike. Main courses cross the gamut from €10 to €35. Daily 5pm–midnight.

Tomo Sushi Reguliersdwarsstraat 131 ☎020/528 5208. Quality, hip Japanese grill and sushi place, popular with a young professional crew. Mains begin at €15. Daily 5.30–11.30pm

Pancakes

Le Soleil Nieuwe Spiegelstraat 56 ☎020/622 7147. Pretty little restaurant (once visited by the Queen), which makes a delicious range of pancakes – arguably the best in town – from as little as €5. No credit cards. Daily 10am–6pm.

South American

Iguazu Prinsengracht 703 ☎020/420 3910. For carnivores only: a first-rate Argentinian-Brazilian restaurant, with perhaps the best fillet steak in town. Main courses hover around €17. Daily from 5pm.

Thai

Dynasty Reguliersdwarsstraat 30 ☎020/626 8400. Lavishly appointed restaurant – all orchids and murals – offering a first-rate choice of Indochinese food, with both Vietnamese and Thai options. Main courses from €20. Daily except Tues 5.30–11pm.

Vegetarian and organic

Golden Temple Utrechtsestraat 126 ☎020/626 8560. Laid-back place with a little more soul than the average Amsterdam veggie joint. Well-prepared, lacto-vegetarian food and pleasant, attentive service. No alcohol and non-smoking throughout. Inexpensive. Daily 5–9.30pm.

The Jordaan and the Westerdok

African

Semhar Marnixstraat 259-261 ☎020/638 1634. Small and popular restaurant with a simple but authentic Ethiopian menu. Dishes consist of a meat or vegetable dish such as lamb, catfish or chickpeas soaked up with a large flat, spongy bread. The vegetarian dish of lentils, spinach and pumpkin is delicious. Try the local African beer served in a calabash. Mains from as little as €8. Daily from 1pm to 11pm.

Dutch and Modern European

Claes Claesz Egelantiersstraat 24 ☎020/625 5306. Exceptionally friendly Jordaan restaurant that attracts a good mixed crowd and serves excellent modern Dutch food. Choose between two- and four-courses (€23–28). Live music on Friday and Saturday, and from September to May there's also a "theatre-dinner" every last Sunday of month, which sees various Dutch theatrical/musical acts between the courses. Open 6–11pm. Closed Mon.

De Eettuin 2e Tuindwarsstraat 10 ☎020/623 7706, ⊛www.eettuin.nl. Hefty, inexpensive portions of Dutch food, with salad from a serve-yourself bar. Non-meat eaters can content themselves with a choice of three tasty vegetarian dishes such as the roasted vegetable and wild spinach pancakes. Daily from 5.30pm.

Jur Egelantiersgracht 72 ☎020/423 4287, ⊛www.eetcafejur.com. Friendly Jordaan restaurant serving fish, steaks and grilled fare to a wide-ranging clientele. Also has a bar with five draught beers on tap. Main courses average €10–15. Daily from noon.

Heerlijk! Palmgracht 39 ☎020/421 5528, ⊛www.restaurantheerlijk.nl. An intimate, stylish restaurant with an Asian/Mediterranean inspired menu, which – as the name suggests – is perfectly flavoured (*heerlijk* is Dutch for delicious). An open kitchen, so you can view the action. À la carte menu has mains from €21.50 or there's a three-course set menu for €34.50. Sunday's set menu is €29.50. From 6pm. Closed Mon & Tues.

Koevoet Lindenstraat 17 ☎020/624 0846. The "Cow's-Foot" – or, alternatively, the "Crowbar" – is a small, traditional Jordaan *eetcafé* with a creative French-influenced menu and some excellent sauces. Mains from €14. Open from 6pm. Closed Mon.

Fish

Albatros Westerstraat 264 ☎020/627 9932. Family-run restaurant serving some mouth-wateringly imaginative fish dishes. A place to splash out and linger over a meal; mains from €20 Open from 6pm. Closed Tues & Wed.

▽ Albatros

French and Belgian

De Gouden Reael Zandhoek 14 ☎020/623 3883, ⓦwww.goudenreael.nl. Fine French food in an attractive waterside setting in the Westerdok. The bar, as described in the novel of the same name by Jan Mens, has a long history of association with the dock workers. Main courses hover around €15–20. Mon–Fri 11am–1am, kitchen closes 11pm.

Indian

Himalaya Haarlemmerstraat 11 ☎020/622 3776. Cosy and welcoming atmosphere, with a good selection of dishes to choose from. Set menus from €8. Take away service available. Daily from 7pm.

Italian

Burgers Patio 2e Tuindwarsstraat 12 ☎020/623 6854. Despite the name (the site used to be occupied by a butcher's), there isn't a burger in sight in this young and convivial restaurant. The owner of twenty years has managed to retain its informal atmosphere

without compromising on service and taste. The food is wonderfully presented, with Italian inspired dishes and there are daily specials as well as vegetarian options. Mains from as little as €12. Daily from 6pm.
Capri Lindengracht 61 ☎020/624 4940. Good café-restaurant serving filling food at reasonable prices. Usually busy with much of the easygoing atmosphere of the neighbouring market on Saturday and popular with local families in the evenings. Open 5–11pm (Sat from 9am).
Cinema Paradiso Westerstraat 186 ☎020/623 7344, ⓦwww.cinemaparadiso.info. A romantic combination of an former Amsterdam moviehouse and a modern interior complete with subdued lighting and chandeliers, serving pizza, antipasti, risotto and a pasta of the day. Popular but no reservations. Main courses kick off at around €14. Open from 6pm.
Hostaria 2e Egelantiersdwarsstraat 9 ☎020/626 0028. A traditional Italian restaurant serving lovely food, expertly prepared. Main courses average around €20. Open 7–10.30pm. Closed Mon.
Da Noi Haarlemmerdijk 128 ☎020/620 1409. A friendly open-kitchen restaurant where two chefs prepare three- or five-course dinners, from an à la carte menu. A place to settle down for the evening and enjoy Italian food beyond pasta and pizza. Fixed priced menus begin at €27. Open daily from 6.30pm.
Toscanini Lindengracht 75 ☎020/623 2813. Authentic Italian-based food prepared in front of your eyes; Very popular, so be sure to book ahead. Mains €20–25. Try the guinea fowl. Daily 6–10.30pm.
Yam Yam Trattoria F. Hendrikstraat 90 ☎020/681 5097. Top pizzeria and trattoria in a simple 1950s traditional-style dining room. Classic pizzas with fresh rucola or truffle sauce attract all the hip young parents from the neighbourhood. Mains from €12. Open 6–10pm. Closed Mon.

Thai

Rakang Thai Elandsgracht 29 ☎020/620 9551. Richly decorated restaurant with striking paintings and riveting glassware. The Thai food is fresh and delicious and not too highly spiced. The adjacent takeaway is of similarly good quality. Main courses average around €16. Open from 6pm.

Vegetarian and organic

De Vliegende Schotel Nieuwe Leliestraat 162 ☎020/625 2041, ⓦ www.vliegendeschotel .com. Perhaps the best of the city's cheap and wholesome vegetarian restaurants, the "Flying Saucer" serves delicious food in large portions. Lots of space, a peaceful ambience and a good notice board. Daily from 4pm. Budget-inexpensive.

The Old Jewish Quarter and eastern docks

African and Middle Eastern

Kilimanjaro Rapenburgerplein 6 ☎020/622 3485. Bright African restaurant in a forgotten part of the town, serving such delicacies as West African antelope goulash, Moroccan *tajine* and crocodile steak. Vegetarian option available. Small, moderately priced, simple and super-friendly. Open from 5pm. Closed Mon.

King Salomon Waterlooplein 239 ☎020/625 5860. Approved by the Rabbi of Amsterdam, this restaurant has a straightforward and inexpensive kosher menu. Closed Sat and Yom Kippur. Open noon–10pm..

Dutch and Modern European

Odessa Veemkade 259 ☎020/419 3010. Boat restarant that does middling Dutch and international food, good cocktails, and turns itself into a club after 10pm. A nice place to hang out on a summer's evening – and reachable by boat from Centraal Station. Daily 11am–10.30pm for dinner.

Panama Oostelijke Handelskade 4 ☎020/311 8686. Long-standing restaurant and club that's benefitting from the trendification of the eastern docks area. The food is no more than ok, but it's a pleasant place to drink too, and hosts regular bands and club nights. Daily 6–11pm.

Voorbij het Einde Sumatrakade 613 ☎020/419 1143. The name means literally "Beyond the End" and refers to the name of a nearby former squat that was known as the "End of the World". It's still relatively hard to get to, although ferries leave regularly from Centraal Station, but this bar-restaurant couldn't be further away from the days when this part of town was the haunt of squatters, a modern, light eatery, housed in a glass cube, where the emphasis is on style and quality. The food is good, inventive – and not too

expensive either; reckon on €20 or so for a main course. Daily 6.30–11.30pm

Fish

éénvistwéévis Schippersgracht 6 ☎020/623 2894. An uncomplicated fish restaurant serving an interesting selection of seafood such as oyster and mussel soup for starters and seabass with rosemary and thyme for main courses. No menu – the waiters will tell you what's cooking. Mains at around €20. Open Tues–Sun 6–10pm.

French and Belgian

Koffiehuis van de Volksbond Kadijksplein 4 ☎020/622 1209, ⓦ www.koffiehuisvandenvolk sbond.nl. Formerly a Communist Party café and the place where the local dock workers used to receive their wages, this is now an Oosterdok neighbourhood restaurant with a varied and filling menu ranging from grilled steak to Thai green curry with mussels. Faded décor and inexpensive food. Opens 6pm. No credit cards.

Indonesian

Anda Nugraha Waterlooplein 369 ☎020/626 6064. Lively restaurant serving moderately spicy Indonesian food. Well-prepared dishes using fresh ingredients, but the selection is small. Vegetarian rijsttafel €13.50. There's a very pleasant terrace in the summer. Weekdays from 4pm, weekends 5pm.

Italian

Rosario Peperstraat 10 ☎020/627 0280. Very attractive restaurant serving good Italian food in a slightly out-of-the-way corner of the city. Simple and traditional décor with dark wood tables, brass candelabras and a small open kitchen. Mains from €21. Open from 6pm. Closed Sun & Mon.

The Museum Quarter and Vondelpark

African

Lalibela 1e Helmersstraat 249 ☎020/683 8332. First-rate Ethiopian restaurant, with a well-balanced menu and attentive service. Mains from €8. Tram #1 along Overtoom to Jan Pieter Heijstraat. Open daily from 5pm.

Dutch

Eetcafé Loetje Johannes Vermeerstraat 52 ☎020/662 8173. Arguably one of the two best steakhouses in town (the other one being *Piet de Leeuw*, see p.195). Bustling, smokey pub-like restaurant, with a large conservatory and a menu that's chalked up on the wall. Steaks from €12. Open Mon–Sat 11am–10pm, but no Sat lunch.

French and Belgian

Brasserie de Joffers Willemsparkweg 163 ☎020/673 0360. Small café-like brasserie with a terrace at the front, serving delicious soups and poultry dishes. Mains begin at €13. Mon–Fri 8am–10pm, Sat & Sun 9am–6pm.

Gent aan de Schinkel Theophile de Bockstraat 1 ☎020/388 28 51. Lovely corner restaurant on a busy canal. Belgian and fusion cuisine and a huge range of bottled Belgian beers to enjoy on their perfect summer terrace. Just outside the westerly entrance to the Vondelpark, across the cyclist bridge. Mains from €17. Daily from noon.

Le Garage Ruysdaelstraat 54 ☎020/679 7176. This elegant restaurant is popular with a media crowd largely because it's run by a well-known Dutch TV cook. An eclectic French set menu (two- or three-courses), that consists of mainly meat and fish dishes. Call to reserve a week ahead, dress to impress and bring at least €40 or so per person. Daily 6–11pm, Mon–Fri also noon–2pm. The adjoining cocktail bar serves finger food from (a much more economic) €7.

Greek

Dionysos Overtoom 176 ☎020/689 4441. Good Greek restaurant not far from the Leidseplein serving tasty, authentic food and excellent Greek tapas. Live music every first Sunday of the month. Mains from around €12. Daily 5pm–11pm.

Indian

Dosa Overtoom 146 ☎020/616 4838. Halfway along the Vondelpark, this brightly lit corner restaurant concentrates on Southern Indian dishes at moderate prices – mains begin at around €13. No cards; daily 5-11pm.

Indonesian

Orient Van Baerlestraat 21 ☎020/673 4958. Excellently prepared dishes from a wide

ranging menu; vegetarians are very well taken care of, and the service is generally good. Expect to pay €21.75 for a *rijsttafel*. Javanese menu every Wednesday. Daily from 5pm.

Sama Sebo P.C. Hooftstraat 27 ☎020/662 8146, ⓦwww.samasebo.com. Amsterdam's best-known Indonesian restaurant, especially for its *rijsttafel* (€26.50), although, if this seems a little pricey, it's easy to eat much more economically by choosing à la carte dishes, starting from just €2 for *nasi goreng* and €3.75 for *gado gado*. A set lunch costs €14.50 per person. The food is usually great, though the waiters can be extravagantly rude. Mon-Sat noon-3pm & 6-10pm.

Thai

Khorat Top Thai 2e Const. Huygenstraat 64 ☎020/683 1297. Small, simple restaurant serving generous helpings of inexpensive Thai food. Service is efficient, though not always with a smile. Mains from just €11. Open daily from 4pm.

The outer districts

Central American

Il Cantinero Marie Heinekenplein 4 ☎020/670 6921. Right beind the Heinken brewery, this place has a choice of good-value Mexican, Caribbean and Surinamese dishes. Tapas are good, although the food overall isn't special, and the service can be worse. But it can be worth a visit for its live salsa bands. Moderately priced too.

Dutch and Modern European

Tolhuis Buiksloterweg 7 ☎020/636 0270. Large Amsterdam Noord restaurant that's two minutes from the Buiksloterweg ferry terminal. A heartwarming place for a late breakfast, lunch or an early dinner. Not expensive, and open daily 9.30am–7.30pm except Sun.

Wilhelmina Dok Noordwal 1 ☎020/632 3468. A good place to get some fresh air on the waterfront and enjoy a good lunch or dinner while admiring the Amsterdam skyline from its fifties-style interior at its best on late summer evenings. Take the ferry to Adelaarsweg behind CS and walk to the orange building. Main courses €15–20. Daily noon–10pm.

Italian

L'Angoletto Hemonystraat 2 ☎ 020/676 4182.
Small De Pijp neighbourhood Italian that
has a reputation for simple, hearty food,
although it's not as inexpensive as the
cheap café interior might imply (mains €15
or so). Not everything they serve is on the
menu so keep an eye on the glass showcase in front of the kitchen for any specials.
No bookings, so just turn up and hope
for the best. Closed Sat. Daily except Sat
6–11.30pm.

Japanese

Teppanyaki Sazanka Ferdinand Bolstraat 333
☎ 020/678 7450. Situated in the swanky
Okura Hotel (take tram 25 from Centraal
Station to Cornelis Troostplein), this place
serves some of the best Japanese food in
the city, as does its sister sushi restaurant,
Yamazato. Reckon on paying at least €50
per person though, probably more. Daily
6.30–10pm.

Middle Eastern

Artist 2e Jan Steenstraat 1 ☎ 020/671 4264.
A small Lebanese restaurant just off Albert
Cuypstraat. Inexpensive, though not a place
to particularly linger. Daily 2–11pm.
Eufraat 1e van der Helststraat 72 ☎ 020/672
0579. Basic *eetcafé* in the midst of the
cosmopolitan Pijp district run by Assyrian
Christians. Inexpensive. Daily except Mon
11am–midnight.

Spanish

Mas Tapas Saenredamstraat 37 ☎ 020/664
0066. Moorish-style restaurant with mosaic
tiles everywhere, serving inexpensive tapas
and an interesting variety of main dishes.
Outside seating, too, on the leafy yet happening intersection. Daily 5–10.30pm.

Surinamese

Warung Marlon 1e van der Helststraat 55
☎ 020/671 1526. Surinamese takeaway and
popular hangout for lunch, rapidly gaining
a loyal clientele. Lively atmosphere. Very
cheap, though not especially welcoming.
Daily except Tues 11am–8pm.
Warung Swietie 1e Sweelinckstraat 1
☎ 020/671 5833. Cheap and cheerful Suri-
namese-Javanese *eetcafé*. Budget prices.
Daily except Wed 11am–9pm, Sun from
2pm.

Thai

Cambodja City Albert Cuypstraat 58–60
☎ 020/671 4930. Thai and Vietnamese restaurant serving delicious and affordable
meat fondues, soups and prawn dishes,
and run by a friendly, but no-nonsense,
lady who provides good service. Not at all
expensive – you can eat your fill for €10–
15. Tues–Sat 11am–10pm, Sun 2–10pm.

Turkish

Saray Gerard Doustraat 33 ☎ 020/671 9216.
Excellent Turkish eatery down in the Pijp
neighbourhood. Popular with students.
Cheap too, with a living room ambience and
main course for €10 or less.

Vegetarian and organic

De Waaghals Frans Halsstraat 29 ☎ 020/679
9609. Well-prepared organic dishes in this
cooperative-run restaurant near the Albert
Cuyp. Inexpensive. Tues–Sun 5–9.30pm.
De Witte Uyl Frans Halsstraat 26 ☎ 020/670
0458. Good restaurant serving free-range
poultry and meat and organic vegetables
when available. Three-course menus go for
€36.50. Tues–Sat 6–11pm.

Entertainment and nightlife

Athough Amsterdam is not generally considered one of the world's major cultural centres, the quality and quantity of music, dance and film on offer here are high – largely thanks to the government's long-term subsidy to the arts. With a youthful population the city is at the cutting edge in many ways, though its strengths lie in the graphic arts and new media rather than the performing arts. If you spend any time in Amsterdam you're bound to come across plenty of fringe and mainstream events, many of them spontaneous and entertaining, though lacking perhaps the inventiveness or perspective of New York and London. That said, however, Amsterdam buzzes with places offering a wide range of affordable entertainment and you'll never find yourself at a loss for something to do.

Information and tickets

For information about **what's on**, a good place to start is the **Amsterdam Uitburo**, or **AUB** (Mon–Sat 10am–6pm, Thurs until 9pm, Sun noon–6pm) the cultural office of the city council, which is housed in a corner of the Stadsschouwburg theatre on Leidseplein. You can get advice here on anything remotely cultural, as well as tickets and copies of what listings magazines there are. Critical English-language listings of clubs, live music gigs and film screenings are hard to find, and your best bet, until some enterprising publisher fills the obvious gap, is to keep an eye out for posters, billboards and notices advertising upcoming events in the city.

Of the **listings magazines**, there's a choice of the AUB's own monthly *Uitkrant*, which is comprehensive and free, but in Dutch; or you could settle for the VVV's bland and uncontroversial English-language *Day By Day* (also free) On Wednesdays and Saturdays, the newspaper *Het Parool* has an entertainment supplement – one of the most up-to-date reference sources. Take a look, too, at the AUB's *Uitlijst* notice boards, which include a weekly update on pop music events. Any cinema can provide the long, thin, fold-out *Film Agenda*, which gives details of all films showing in the city that week (Thursday to Wednesday). Bars and restaurants often stock similar fortnightly or monthly listings leaflets. *SHARK*, a monthly pamphlet listing Amsterdam's clubs, bars and cafés, each with a personal review, and including a gay supplement, is available at the Athenaeum News Centre at Spui and a few other cafés and bookshops around town.

Tickets for most things can be bought at the Uitburo and VVV offices (for a €2 fee), or reserved by phone through the **AUB Uitlijn** (☎0900/0191 daily 9am–8pm; €0.40 per min) for a one-percent booking fee. You can also buy tickets for any live music event in the country at the GWK bureau de change offices at the Leidseplein and larger train stations, and the post office at Singel 250, for a fee of around €3–4. Obviously the cheapest way to obtain tickets is to turn up at the venue itself. If you're under 26, the AUB is the place to go for a **Cultureel Jongeren Passport** (**CJP**), which costs €12.50 and gets you reductions on entry to theatres, concerts and *filmhuizen*. Generally the only people eligible for **discounts** at cultural events are students, over-65s (though most places will only take Dutch ID) and CJP card-holders.

Rock, folk and world music

As far as **live music** goes, Amsterdam is a regular tour stop for many major artists, and something of a testing ground for current rock bands. Until recently, **Dutch rock and pop** was almost uniformly dire, but mercifully times have changed, and Dutch groups nowadays can lay claim to both quality and originality. Look out for the celebrated Zuco 103 and other members of the dance/ hip-hop scene, or try to catch rock bands such as Bløf, Spinvis and Junky XL. Anouk is also a popular draw whenever she comes back home to play. Bear in mind, too, that Amsterdam is often on the tour circuit of up-and-coming British bands – keep an eye on the listings.

With the completion in 1996 of the 50,000-seat Amsterdam ArenA out in the southeastern suburbs, the city finally gained the **stadium** rock venue it has craved for years. However, it's been slow to catch on, and most major stadium acts still choose to play at Rotterdam's Ahoy sports hall. The Heineken Music Hall, a simple but acoustically impressive black box, close to the ArenA, hosts smaller acts, while the two dedicated **music venues** in Amsterdam city centre – the Paradiso and the Melkweg – are all much smaller, and supply a constantly changing seven-days-a-week programme of music to suit all tastes (and budgets). Alongside the main venues, the city's clubs, bars and multimedia centres sporadically host performances by live bands. As far as **prices** go, for big names you'll pay anything between €20 and €30 a ticket; ordinary gigs cost €7.50–12.50, although some places charge a membership (*lidmaatschap*) fee on top.

The Dutch **folk music** tradition in Amsterdam is virtually extinct, although interest has been revived of late by the new duo, Acda and de Munnik. There are still one or two touring folk singers who perform traditional *smartlappen* ("torchsongs") at the Carré Theatre and a few sympathetic venues, but the best place to catch these traditional songs – a brash and sentimental adaptation of French chansons – is still in the cafés of the Jordaan, such as *Nol*, where they sprang from (see p.184).

More accessible is **world music**, for which there are several good venues including the Tropenmuseum theatre, Akhnaton and the Melkweg, the latter being one of the venues for the Amsterdam Roots Festival held in June (see p.250). Amsterdam doesn't have many **outdoor music festivals**, but the few events that do take place are usually well attended. Aside from the summer concerts held in the Vondelpark, Oosterpark hosts the free Roots Open Air festival, a huge event that attracts over 50,000 people and kicks off the afore-mentioned Roots Festival. Of the music and dance festivals outside the city, the most famous is the Pinkpop Festival (@www.pinkpop.nl) in June, down in the south at the Draf en Renbaan in Landgraaf, near Maastricht. Others include the winter Dance Valley Festival (@www.udc.nl) in 's-Hertogenbosch, northwest of Eindhoven, in Brabant; A Campingflight to Lowlands (@www.lowlands.nl) held the last weekend of August in Flevoland; and Parkpop (@www.parkpop. nl), Europe's largest free festival, held in June at The Hague's Zuiderpark. Dates are variable, so check websites before making plans.

Major venues

Amsterdam ArenA ArenA Boulevard (outer districts; metro or train to Bijlmer station) ☏ 020/311 1333, @www.amsterdamarena .nl. The home soccer stadium for Ajax also plays host to world-class music acts such as the Rolling Stones and Eminem.

Heineken Music Hall ArenA Boulevard (outer districts; metro or train to Bijlmer station) ☏ 0900/68742 4255, @www.heineken-music-hall .nl. A high-tech music venue attracting inter-national bands ranging from Pink to Franz Ferdinand. The bar has an efficient system using plastic tokens.

Melkweg (Milky Way) Lijnbaansgracht 234a (Grachtengordel south) ☏ 020/531 8181, @www.melkweg.nl. Probably Amsterdam's most famous entertainment venue, often featuring on the itinerary of many touring international bands, and these days one of the city's prime arts centres, with a young, hip clientele. A former dairy (hence the name) just round the corner from Leidse-plein, it has two separate halls for live music, putting on a broad range of bands covering everything from reggae to rock, all of which lean towards the "alternative". There's also a theatre, gallery, and bar and restaurant (Marnixstraat entrance; Wed–Sun noon–9pm).

▽ Melkweg

Paradiso

Paradiso Weteringschans 6–8 (Grachtengordel south) ☏ 020/626 4521, @www.paradiso.nl. A converted church near the Leidseplein, with bags of atmosphere, featuring bands ranging from the newly signed to the more established, such as Groove Armada. It has been known to host classical concerts, as well as debates and multimedia events (often in conjunction with the nearby Balie centre).

Smaller venues

Akhnaton Nieuwezijds Kolk 25 (Old Centre) ☏ 020/624 3396, @www.akhnaton.nl. A "Cen-tre for World Culture", specializing in African and Latin American music and dance par-ties. On a good night, the place heaves with people.

AMP KNSM-laan 13 (Old Jewish Quarter and east-ern docks) ☏ 020/418 1111, @www .ampstudios.nl. Way out in the eastern harbour district, this rehearsal space and recording studio features live bands, a jazz and a per-cussion festival. Bus #32 or #59 from CS.

De Buurvrouw St Pieterspoortsteeg 29 (Old Centre) ☏ 020/625 9654. Eclectic alternative bar featuring loud local bands on a Sunday night.

Cruise Inn Zeeburgerdijk 271 (Old Jewish Quarter and eastern docks) ☏ 020/692 7188, @www.cruise-inn.com. Clubhouse run by volunteers which was set up over twenty years ago by a group of Rockabillys. Open Saturdays only and is off the beaten track, but with jam sessions and great music from the 1950s and 1960s. Due to relocate to new premises sometime in 2005 so check website or call before set-ting out.

De Heeren van Aemstel Thorbeckeplein 5 (Grachtengordel south) ☏ 020/620 2173, @www.deheerenvanaemstel.nl. Warm atmo-spheric café with swinging soul and funk gigs almost every night.

Maloe Melo Lijnbaansgracht 163 (Jordaan and the Westerdok) ☏ 020/420 4592, ⓦ www .maloemelo.nl. Dark, low-ceilinged bar, with a small back room featuring lively local blues acts every night. Wed, Fri & Sat €5 after 11pm. free all other times. Acoustic sessions Mon & Sun.

Meander Café Voetboogstraat 5 (Old Centre) ☏ 020/625 8430, ⓦ www.cafemeander.nl. Daily live music of the soul, funk and blues variety, as well as DJs playing funk and hip-hop.

Mulligan's Amstel 100 (Grachtengordel south) ☏ 020/622 1330, ⓦ www.mulligans.nl. Irish bar that is head and shoulders above the rest for atmosphere and authenticity, with Gaelic musicians and storytellers most nights for free.

OCCII Amstelveenseweg 134 (opposite western entrance of the Vondelpark) ☏ 020/671 7778, ⓦ www.occii.org. Cosy former squat bar at the far end of the Vondelpark, with live alternative music from indie pop to electro funk.

The Waterhole Korte Leidsedwarsstraat 49 (Grachtengordel south) ☏ 020/620 8904, ⓦ www.thewaterhole.nl. Late-night bar with live music every night that ranges from punk and rock to jazz and blues. Popular for its regular Monday jam sessions which attract a raucous but friendly crowd. Also has a pool table and serves cheap beer. Sunday night is ladies' night, with half price drinks.

Tropentheater Linnaeusstraat 2 (East of Artis Zoo; Tram #9, or #10 from Leidseplein) ☏ 020/568 8500, ⓦ www.tropentheater.nl. Part of the Tropical Institute, this formal theatre specializes in non-Western drama, dance, film and music. A great place to pick up on acts that you wouldn't normally get to see.

Winston International Warmoesstraat 123 (Old Centre) ☏ 020/623 1380, ⓦ www.winston .nl. Part of the art hotel (see p.166) this adventurous small venue attracts an eclectic crowd and does a good line in camp entertainment, with Sunday Club Vegas nights, as well as a mix of live bands, electro and cheesy 80s pop nights and the like. Hip-hop every Tues.

Clubbing

Clubbing in Amsterdam has become much more exclusive over the last couple of years. Where before it wasn't so much about what you were wearing or who you were with, you'll now find a growing number of the more intimate clubs are just as style-conscious and scrupulous as those in many other European capitals and even the larger, more commercial places will refuse entry to groups of men.

That said, there are still enough places around which don't require a huge amount of label-flashing to get past the door staff, and entry into most places won't be a problem.

The image of vast arenas for thousands of shaven-headed speed-freaks has all but disappeared, and nowadays most clubs play a mixture of house, techno and funk. The **music** policy in the city's trendier nightspots, despite their new-found exclusivity, is becoming rather more commercialized than it used to be. The majority of venues are open every night and there's usually something going on to suit all tastes, including DJs playing anything from retro funk to jazz and underground trance and lounge; Thursday's house night, RUSH, at the *Escape* club, is extremely popular as is Saturday night at *Sinners*, which plays an altogether more sophisticated selection of dance and club classics.

The best place to find out what's going on is the free weekly **listings** magazine *nl20*, available in restaurants, hotels and bars, or the printed "flyer-newspaper" *guestlist.nu*, (ⓦ www.guestlist.nu) from Conscious Dreams Kokopelli, Warmoesstraat 12 (Old Centre), carries most of the latest flyers for future events.

A number of large dance and techno **events** take place throughout the year, including the Dance Valley Festivals in August and December (see p.251). Check for flyers at Cyberdog, Herengracht 250 (Grachtengordel west), or Midtown Records, Nieuwendijk 104 (Old Centre) and expect to pay €45 or more for entry; although this seems rather hefty, events do go on until dawn and flyers for after-hours parties will circulate during the night. **Tickets** can be purchased at the in-store ticket office at Cyberdog.

Most clubs have **entry prices**, hovering between €8 and €12.50 at weekends and then dropping to €5 during the week. A singular feature of Amsterdam clubbing, however, is that you tip the bouncer: if you want to get back into the same place next week, €1 or €2 in the palm of his hand will do very nicely. Drinks prices are just slightly more expensive than in cafés at around €3–4 but not excessively hiked up and, as in the rest of the city, toilets cost €0.50. Most places don't have a specific **dress code**, though it is advisable to make an effort especially if you want to get into some of the smaller, hip clubs where space is limited and door staff have carte blanche about who they let in. As far as **drugs** go, smoking joints is generally fine – though if you can't see or smell the stuff, ask the barman if it's OK. Should you need reminding, ecstasy, acid, speed and cocaine are all completely illegal, and you can expect less than favourable treatment from the bouncers (and the law) if you're spotted with anything.

Although all the places listed below **open** at either 10pm or 11pm, there's not much point turning up anywhere before midnight; unless stated otherwise, everywhere stays open until 5am on Friday and Saturday nights, 4am on other nights.

Finally, there are a couple of clubs **outside Amsterdam** that you might see advertised around town. *Beachbop*, at Bloemendaal aan Zee (ⓦwww.beachbop .info), holds three events on the beach over the summer, while the equally popular *Hemkade* at Hemkade 48, Zaandam (ⓣ075/614 8154, ⓦwww .hemkade.nl), attracts British and European DJs to its weekend parties.

For gay and lesbian clubs see Chapter Twelve.

Clubs and venues

Arena Part of a large, hip hotel (see p.204), the club situated in the former chapel opens Friday and Saturday only, with special multi-media nights often held on a Monday and a Sunday. Occasionally hosts popular international club nights, such as Hed Kandi.

Bitterzoet Spuistraat 2 (Old Centre) ⓣ020/521 3001, ⓦwww.bitterzoet.com. Spacious but cosy two-floored bar and theatre hosting a mixed bag of events, often featuring DJs playing acid jazz, R&B, funk and disco. Films and occasionally urban poetry nights.

't Blauwe Theehuis Vondelpark 5 ⓦwww .blauwetheehuis.nl. Open-air dancing in the summer in Vondelpark with DJs on Friday and Saturday nights. Free.

Club Zyon Nieuwezijds Voorburgwal 161–165 (Old Centre) ⓣ020/423 1150, ⓦwww.clubzyon .com. Large and funky place, recently refurbished and divided into two rooms: Futuristic-style Zyon 1, and Zyon 2 with comfortable sofas and a lounge area. Two dancefloors play a mix of house, techno and R&B. The club also holds special events featuring international DJs. Over 21s. No trainers.

Dansen bij Jansen Handboogstraat 11 (Old Centre) ⓣ020/620 1779, ⓦwww .dansenbijjansen.nl. Founded by – and for – students, and very popular dance music nights. Open nightly; €2–4, but officially you need student ID to get in.

Escape Rembrandtplein 11 (Grachtengordel south) ⓣ020/622 1111, ⓦwww.escape.nl. What once used to be a tacky disco is now home to Amsterdam's hottest Thursday night, RUSH, hosted by Chemistry, which draws huge crowds. It's a vast place, with room for 2000 people, although you may still have to queue. Sunday is house, funk and club classics night, often featuring guest DJs including the Netherlands' top DJ, Dimitri.

Heineken Music Hall See p.204. Hosts dance events featuring well known Dutch DJs including Tiesto, who opened the 2004 Olympics.

Loveboat 2 Passenger Terminal, Piet Heinkade 27, behind Centraal Station (Old Centre) ⓦwww .loveboat2.nl. Famous DJ partyship giving monthly dresscoded parties.

Melkweg See p.204. After the bands have finished, excellent offbeat disco sessions go on well into the small hours, sometimes featuring the best DJs in town. Also plays host to some of the most enjoyable theme nights around, everything from African dance parties to experimental jazz-trance.

The Ministry Reguliersdwarsstraat 12 (Grachtengordel south) ☏ 020/623 3981. Small club playing mainly hip-hop, funk and R&B with a popular Jam Session night every Monday featuring local music talent. Dress to impress.

Nieuwezijds Lounge Nieuwezijds Voorburgwal 169 (Old Centre) ☏ 020/622 7510, ⓦ www .clubnl.nl. An average lounge club where everybody pretends to work for MTV. Mon–Thurs & Sun till 3am, Fri & Sat till 4am.

More Rozengracht 133 (Grachtengordel west) ☏ 020/344 6402, ⓦ www.expectmore.nl. Trying to be the coolest club in town, but not hitting the mark. Sunday's Paleis Soestdijk attracts an older, stylish crowd, with the restaurant open from 5pm.

Panama Oostelijke Handelskade 4 (Eastern docks, overlooking the IJ) ☏ 020/311 8686, ⓦ www.panama.nl. Host to a wide variety of live gigs from 9pm, followed by themed club nights from 11pm. There is a theatre and a restaurant too. Funky.

Paradiso Weteringschans 6–8 (Grachtengordel south) ☏ 020/626 4521, ⓦ www.paradiso.nl. One of the principal venues in the city, housed in what was once a church, which plays host to a varied line-up of (international) live bands in the early part of the evening before turning into a club later. Popular with a younger, alternative crowd on Thursday, while Saturday's Paradisco is friendly and gets packed. Also hosts one-off events.

The Powerzone Daniel Goedkoopstraat 1–3 (outer districts; metro Spaklerweg) ☏ 020/681 8866, ⓦ www.thepowerzone.nl. Weekend partyzone, with good trance and techno DJs and a capacity of 5000. Usual admission costs €12 (ladies free before midnight), and includes cloakroom and toilet fees – door staff are not allowed to accept tips. Entry cost varies for special events during the week.

Sinners Wagenstraat 3 (Grachtengordel south) ⓦ www.sinners.nl. Intimate, plush Rembrandtplein club with a small dance floor that gets packed early. Plays R&B (Thurs) and house, groove and club classics (Fri & Sat) to a well-dressed and affluent crowd. Choosy door staff.

Café Sol Rembrandtplein 18 (Grachtengordel south) ☏ 020/330 3279. ⓦ www.djcafesol.nl. DJ café where the emphasis is on loud music rather then anything else. Weekdays till 3am, Fri & Sat till 4am.

ENTERTAINMENT AND NIGHTLIFE | Jazz and Latin

Winston Kingdom Warmoesstraat 129 (Old Centre) ☏ 020/623 1380, ⓦ www.winston.nl. Small venue adjacent to the *Winston Hotel* (see p.166), with eclectic club nights and performances.

Jazz and Latin

For **jazz** fans, Amsterdam can be a treat. Since the 1940s and 1950s, when American jazz musicians began moving to Europe to escape discrimination back home, the city has had a soft spot for jazz. Paris stole much of the limelight, but Chet Baker lived and died in Amsterdam, and he and any number of legendary jazzbos could once be found jamming into the small hours at the

Casablanca on Zeedijk. Although Zeedijk has changed a lot since then, varying from tiny bars staging everything from Dixieland to avant-garde, to the *Bimhuis* – the city's major jazz venue – which plays host to both international names and homegrown talent. Pianist Michiel Borstlap, cellist Ernst Reijseger and sought after percussionist Han Bennink – member of the acclaimed contemporary jazz collective, ICP – are among the **Dutch musicians** you might come across, and they're well worth catching if you get the chance.

It's worth remembering, too, that the Netherlands has one of the best jazz festivals in the world, the **North Sea Jazz Festival**, held in the Congresgebouw in The Hague during July; information on the event is available from PO Box 3325, 2601 DH Delft (℡015/215 7756, ⓦwww.northseajazz.nl). Comprising three days and nights of continuous jazz on fifteen stages, the festival regularly involves over 1200 musicians, among them world-class performers from Oscar Peterson to James Brown, Chuck Berry to Guru's Jazzmatazz. Tickets cost from about €60 a day, with supplements for the big names. Special late-night trains are laid on to bring revellers back to Amsterdam after the gigs – hotel rooms in The Hague are booked up months in advance. The jazz season runs from September to July with concerts and small festivals being held all over the country.

The Dutch connection with **Surinam** – a former colony tucked in between Venezuela and Brazil – means that there is a sizeable **Latin American** community in the city, and plenty of authentic salsa and other Latin sounds to be discovered.

Venues

Akhnaton Nieuwezijds Kolk 25 (Old Centre) ℡020/624 3396, ⓦwww.akhnaton.nl. A crowded, lively venue that often puts on Latin music.

Café Alto Korte Leidsedwarsstraat 115 (Grachtengordel south) ℡020/626 3249, ⓦwww.jazz-cafe-alto.nl. It's worth hunting out this legendary little jazz bar just off Leidseplein for the quality modern jazz every night from 9pm until 3am (and often much later). It's big on atmosphere, though slightly cramped, but entry is free, and you don't have to buy a (pricey) beer to hang out and watch the band.

Bimhuis Piet Heinkade 3 (overlooking the IJ, east of Centraal Station) ℡020/623 1361, ⓦwww.bimhuis.nl. The city's premier jazz and improvised music venue for almost 28 years has only recently moved to its spanking new building next to the Muziekgebouw (see p.114), having been forced to find a new venue after years of complaints about noise pollution from local residents. This well-equipped concert hall offers spectacular views of the city and features a modern bar

and café, and has stepped up its program to five or six concerts per week including jam sessions and workshops.

Bourbon Street Leidsekruisstraat 6 (Grachtengordel south) ℡020/623 3440, ⓦwww.bourbonstreet.nl. Friendly bar with a relaxed atmosphere and quality blues and jazz nightly until 4am Mon–Thurs, 5am Fri & Sat. Free entry before 11pm.

Casablanca Zeedijk 26 (Old Centre) ℡020/625 5685, ⓦwww.casablanca-amsterdam.nl. A shadow of its former self, though still hosting live jazz every night and Sunday afternoon.

De Engelbewaarder Kloveniersburgwal 59 (Old Centre) ℡020/625 3772. Excellent live jazz sessions Sunday afternoon and evening.

't Geveltje Bloemgracht 170 (Jordaan and the Westerdok) ℡020/623 9983. A jazz café offering workshops on Tuesday and Thursday, and professional and beginners' jam sessions on Fridays and Mondays respectively. Open until 3am weekdays; 4am Sat & Sun.

Le Maxim Leidsekruisstraat 35 (Grachtengordel south) ℡020/624 1920. Lively piano bar that's been going since the Sixties, with live music nightly.

Classical, opera and contemporary music

There's no shortage of **classical music** concerts in Amsterdam, with two major orchestras based in the city, plus regular visits by other Dutch orchestras. The **Royal Concertgebouw Orchestra** remains one of the most dynamic in the world, and occupies one of the finest concert halls to boot. The other resident orchestra is the **Netherlands Philharmonic**, based at the Beurs van Berlage concert hall, which has a wide symphonic repertoire and also performs with the Netherlands Opera at the Muziektheater. Among visiting orchestras, the Rotterdam Philharmonic and the Utrecht Symphony have world-class reputations, as does the Radio Philharmonic Orchestra, based in Hilversum outside Amsterdam.

As far as **smaller classical ensembles** go, Dutch musicians pioneered the use of **period instruments** in the 1970s, and Ton Koopman's Amsterdam Baroque Orchestra and Frans Brüggen's Orchestra of the 18th Century are two internationally renowned exponents. Koopman's Amsterdam Baroque Choir and the Amsterdam Bach Soloists are also pre-eminent. As well as the main concert halls, a number of Amsterdam's churches (and former churches) host regular performances of classical and chamber music – both types of venue are listed here. Others, including the huge Nieuwe Kerk on Dam square, the Westerkerk, the Noorderkerk, the Mozes en Aaronkerk on Waterlooplein, and the tiny Amstelkerk on Kerkstraat, as well as numerous small churches out in the residential south and west, occasionally put on one-off concerts, often at very reasonable prices (check venues for program). The popular Grachtenfestival, held at the end of August, is a week-long classical music festival (see p.251).

The most prestigious venue for **opera** is the Muziektheater (otherwise known as the Stopera) on Waterlooplein, which is home to the Netherlands Opera company – going from strength to strength under the guidance of Pierre Audi – as well as the National Ballet. Visiting companies sometimes perform here, but more often at the Stadsschouwburg and the Carré Theatre.

As far as **contemporary music** goes, the brand new Muziekgebouw, when it opens in September 2005 overlooking the IJ, has been designed as the leading showcase for musicians from all over the world. Local talent is headed by the Asko and Schoenberg ensembles, as well as the Nieuw Ensemble and the Volharding Orchestra. Look out also for Willem Breuker and Maarten Altena, two popular musicians who successfully combine improvised jazz with composed new music.

The most prestigious multi-venue Dutch festival for this type of music by far is the annual **Holland Festival** every June (info ☎020/530 7110), which attracts the best domestic mainstream and fringe performers in all areas of the arts, as well as an exciting international line-up. Otherwise, one of the more interesting music-oriented events is the **piano recital** held towards the end of August on a floating stage outside the *Pulitzer Hotel* on the Prinsengracht – with the whole area floodlit and filled with small boats, and every available spot on the banks and bridges taken up, this can be a wonderfully atmospheric evening. Also around this time – and from two ends of the musical spectrum – Utrecht plays host to the internationally renowned **Early Music Festival** (ⓦwww .oudemuziek.nl), and Amsterdam holds the **International Gaudeamus Music Week** (ⓦwww.gaudeamus.nl), a forum for debate and premier performance of cutting-edge contemporary music.

All the major venues listed below, as well as some of the churches, have wheelchair access, though you should call ahead if you need assistance.

Venues

Beurs van Berlage Damrak 277 (Old Centre) ☎020/530 4141, ⓦwww.beursvanberlage.nl. The splendid interior of the former stock exchange (see p.49) has been put to use as a venue for theatre and music. The resident Netherlands Philharmonic and Netherlands Chamber Orchestra rehearse in the huge but comfortable AGA Zaal, the former Corn Exchange room, a very strange, glassed-in room-within-a-room, while the Yakult Zaal (Main Hall) was the location for the royal wedding of Prince Willem-Alexander and Princess Máxima in 2002.

Carré Theater Amstel 115–125 (Grachtengordel south) ☎0900/252 5255, ⓦwww.theatercarre .nl. A splendid hundred-year-old structure (originally built for a circus) which represents the ultimate venue for Dutch folk artists, and hosts all kinds of top international acts: anything from Russian folk dance to *West Side Story* with reputable touring orchestras and opera companies squeezed in between.

Concertgebouw Concertgebouwplein 2–7 (Museum Quarter and Vondelpark) ☎020/671 8345, ⓦwww.concertgebouw.nl. Having undergone a much-needed face-lift and replacement of its crumbling foundations, the Concertgebouw remains one of the most impressive looking – and sounding – venues in the city. The acoustics of the Grote Zaal (Large Hall) are unparalleled, and a concert here is a wonderful experience, especially when the Netherlands Philharmonic Orchestra put on one of their regular performances. The smaller Kleine Zaal regularly hosts chamber concerts, often by the resident Borodin Quartet. Though both halls boast a star-studded international programme, prices very reasonable, ranging between €25 and €35, and €13 for the sponsored Sunday morning events. Free Wednesday lunchtime concerts are held from Sept to May (doors open 12.15pm, arrive early), and in July and August there's a heavily subsidized series of summer concerts. Look out also for occasional world music and swing/jazz nights.

Engelse Kerk Begijnhof 48 (Old Centre) ☎020/624 9665. The church with the biggest programme – three to four performances a week, lunchtime, afternoon and evening, with an emphasis on period instruments. Tickets are available from the church thirty minutes before the start of performance or in advance from the Uitburo (see p.202).

Marionette Theater Nieuwe Jonkerstraat 8 (Old Centre) ☎020/620 8027, ⓦwww.marionet .demon.nl. Continues an old European tradition with its performances of operas by Mozart and Offenbach. Although they're touring the Netherlands and the rest of Europe for most of the year, the wooden marionettes return to Amsterdam around May, October and Christmas. Call for details of performances, and to find out about their opera dinners.

Muziekgebouw Piet Heinkade 1(on the IJ, east of Centraal Station) ☎020/788 2000, ⓦwww .muziekgebouw.nl. The "Music Building", with its imposing glass facade and foyer overlooking the IJ, is due to open its doors in September 2005, and is Amsterdam's first new concert hall for a hundred years. Occupying a large site east of Centraal Station (and next door to the newly housed *Bimhuis*; see p.208), it was constructed for a cool €52 million and houses two halls, a café and state-of-the-art acoustics. The hall is set to put on a varied programme of musical events including multimedia concerts, contemporary music – ranging from electronic to world – as well as opera, chamber and early music performances.

Muziektheater Waterlooplein (Old Jewish Quarter and eastern docks) ☎020/625 5455, ⓦwww.hetmuziektheater.nl. Part of the €150 million complex that includes the city hall. The theatre's resident company, Netherlands Opera, offers the fullest, and most

▽ Concertgebouw

ENTERTAINMENT AND NIGHTLIFE | Classical, opera and contemporary music

reasonably priced, programme of opera in Amsterdam. Tickets go very quickly. Look out for free lunchtime concerts Sept–May.
Oude Kerk Oudekerksplein 23 (Old Centre) ℡020/625 8284. Hosts organ and carillon recitals, as well as occasional choral events. In summer, in conjunction with the Amstelkring Museum, the church organizes a series of "walking" concert evenings, consisting of three separate concerts at different venues, with time for coffee and a stroll between each.

Stadsschouwburg Leidseplein 26 (Grachtengordel south) ℡020/624 2311, Ⓦwww.ssba .nl. These days somewhat overshadowed by the Muziektheater, but still staging significant opera, theatre and dance, as well as occasionally hosting visiting English-language theatre companies.
Waalse Kerk Oudezijds Achterburgwal 159 (Old Centre) ℡020/623 2074. Weekend afternoon and evening concerts of early music and chamber music.

Theatre, cabaret and comedy

Surprisingly for a city that functions so much in English, there is next to no **English-language drama** to be seen in Amsterdam. A tiny handful of part-time companies put on two or three English productions during the summer; there are also performances by touring groups at the theatres listed below and at other venues dotted around town.

English-language **comedy** and **cabaret**, on the other hand, has become a big thing in Amsterdam, spearheaded by the resident and extremely successful "Boom Chicago" comedy company. During the summer in particular, a number of small venues host mini-seasons of English-language stand-up comedy and cabaret, with touring British performers, and material that's generally targeted at visitors to the city.

Most of Amsterdam's larger theatre companies concentrate either on foreign works in translation or Dutch-language theatre, neither of which is likely to be terribly interesting for the non-Dutch speaker. However, there are plenty of **avant-garde** theatre groups in the city, much of whose work relies on visual rather than verbal impact, as well as one or two companies devoted to **mime**. Look out also for performances at the Amsterdam Marionette Theatre (see opposite page). The Amsterdamse Bos Theatre (℡020/643 3286, Ⓦwww.bostheater.nl) might also be worth checking out, performing summertime, open-air Shakespeare plays (in Dutch). It's an atmospheric evening, with audiences picknicking before the show.

The main event to watch out for, apart from the mainstream Holland Festival (see p.250), is the summer-long **Over Het IJ Festival** (info ℡020/624 6380, Ⓦwww.overhetij.nl), a showcase for all kinds of theatre and performance arts at big, often outdoor locations in Amsterdam North (thus "over the IJ"). With a great many interesting fringe companies taking part, productions are often surprising and exciting. In June there is also the **International Theatre School Festival** (info ℡020/530 5566, Ⓦwww.itsfestival.nl), when the four theatres on Nes, a tiny alley running from Dam square parallel to Rokin, host productions by local and international theatre schools.

Major venues

De Balie Kleine Gartmanplantsoen 10 (Grachtengordel south) ℡020/553 5100, Ⓦwww.balie .nl. A multimedia centre for culture and the arts, located off the Leidseplein, which often plays host to drama, debates, international symposia and the like, sometimes in conjunction with the Paradiso next door.

Boom Chicago Leidseplein 12 (Grachtengordel south) ℡020/423 0101, Ⓦwww.boomchicago .nl. Something of a phenomenon in Amsterdam, this rapid-fire improv comedy troupe hailing from America performs at the Leidseplein Theater nightly to crowds of both tourists and locals, and has received rave reviews from *Rough Guide* readers, the Dutch press and *Time* magazine alike. With inexpensive food, the cheapest beer in town (in pitchers, no less!), and a "Smoke Boat Cruise" following the show, the comedy need not be funny – but it is.

Carré Theatre See p.210. A chunky old building on the eastern bank of the Amstel that, aside from its folk associations, hosts all kinds of top international acts, with the emphasis on hit musicals.

Comedy Café Max Euweplein 43 (Grachtengordel south) ⊕ 020/638 3971, ⓦ www .comedycafe.nl. Small cabaret theatre with a bar and restaurant that sometimes hosts English-language acts. "Without Ties" every Sunday is an improv and sketch night performed by English and American comedians.

Kleine Komedie Amstel 56 (Grachtengordel south) ⊕ 020/624 0534, ⓦ www .dekleinekomedie.nl. One of Amsterdam's oldest theatres, established in 1786, which occasionally hosts English-language shows, and performances by the odd pop megastar.

Melkweg See p.207. At the centre of the city's cultural scene, this is often the first-choice venue for foreign touring companies.

Stadsschouwburg See p.211. Occasionally hosts productions on tour from London or New York.

Avant-garde and mime

De Brakke Grond Nes 45 (Old Centre) ⊕ 020/626 6866, ⓦ www.brakkegrond.nl. See also ⓦ www.nestheaters.nl. Mainly Flemish productions.

Cosmic Theater Nes 75 (Old Centre) ⊕ 020/626 6866, ⓦ www.cosmictheater.nl. Cross-cultural productions.

DasArts Mauritskade 56 (east of the centre, past Artis Zoo) ⊕ 020/586 9636, ⓦ www .dasarts.nl. Not a venue as such but a global clubhouse for theatremakers, a think-tank and postgraduate institute, with international workshops and performances.

Felix Meritis Keizersgracht 324 (Grachtengordel south) ⊕ 020/626 2321, ⓦ www.felix.meritis .nl. Hosts theatre, debate, music and visual arts events.

De Nieuw Amsterdam Grote Bickersstraat 2 (Jordaan and the Westerdok) ⊕ 020/627 8672, ⓦ www.denieuwamsterdam.nl. Multicultural focus on non-Western productions.

Dance

Of the major **dance companies** based in Amsterdam, the largest and most prestigious is the Muziektheater's National Ballet, under Wayne Eagling. Also working regularly in Amsterdam are the noted Dutch choreographers Toer van Schayk and Rudi van Dantzig, while for **folk dance** fans the excellent Internationaal Danstheater is based in the city. However, a constant feature of dance in the Netherlands is the prevalence of non-Dutch choreographers and dancers, and the work of William Forsyth, Lloyd Newson, Saburo Teshigawara and others is regularly on show.

Of the other major Dutch dance companies, which can be seen on tour in Amsterdam – or in nearby Rotterdam and The Hague – the most innovative is The Hague's Netherlands Dance Theatre, with a repertoire of ballet and modern dance featuring inspired choreography by Jiří Kylian and Hans van Manen. The oldest company in the country, the Scapino Ballet (based in Rotterdam), has spruced up its image under artistic director Ed Wubbe and choreographer Nanine Linning and is gathering a new generation of admirers.

On a smaller scale, Amsterdam is particularly receptive to the latest trends in **modern dance**, and has many experimental dance groups, often incorporating other media into their productions; small productions staged by dance students also abound. Look out for performances by the Dans Werkplaats Amsterdam and the extraordinary Cloud Chamber company, as well as the mime specialists Griftheater and Shusaku Takeuchi's vast, open-air water-based extravaganzas. Modern dance and movement theatre companies from outside Amsterdam that often perform in the city include the Rotterdamse Dansgroep, who mainly focus on New York modern dance; Introdans, similar in style to the Netherlands Dance Theatre; and Djazzex, fine exponents of jazz dance.

Dance festivals are a little thin on the ground: **Julidans** (Ⓦwww.julidans.com), which is held in theatres around the Leidseplein area every July, is the leading event in the city. Two festivals in The Hague to watch for are the **Holland Dance Festival** (Ⓦwww.hollanddancefestival.com), which takes place every two years (October 2005 and 2007) and attracts many leading international companies; and **CaDance** (Ⓦwww.cadance.nl), which premieres contemporary dance works. (The Hague is just 45 minutes away from Amsterdam by regular trains from Centraal Station.)

Venues

Cosmic Theater See p.212. A modern dance and theatre company featuring young professionals with a multicultural background.

Dans Werkplaats Amsterdam Arie Biemondstraat 107 (Jordaan and the Westerdok) Ⓣ020/689 1789, Ⓦwww.danswerkplaats.nl. A dance studio staging occasional productions at its own studio, Het Veem and other locations in the city.

Internationaal Danstheater Kloveniersburgwal 87 (Old Centre) Ⓣ020/623 9112, Ⓦwww .intdanstheater.nl. Original folk dance from around the world, with international choreographers brought in to work with the dancers.

Het Veem Van Diemenstraat 410 (Tram #3 to Zoutkeetsgracht) Ⓣ020/626 0112, Ⓦwww .hetveemtheater.nl. Old warehouse, west of the centre, converted into dance studios and a theatre.

Melkweg See p.204. Upstairs in this pop- and world-music venue, there is a little theatre putting on modern and funky productions.

Muziektheater See p.210. Home of the National Ballet, but with a third of its dance schedule given over to international companies.

Stadsschouwburg See p.211. Principal host to the Julidans dance festival in July as well as staging regular productions.

Film

Most of Amsterdam's commercial **cinemas** are huge, multiplex affairs showing a selection of general releases. There's also a scattering of film houses (*filmhuizen*) showing **revival and art films** and occasional retrospectives, and Amsterdam's multimedia centres often organize film and video workshops and screenings too. Two Amsterdam cinemas worth a visit no matter what's showing are the extravagantly Art Deco Tuschinski and the atmospheric The Movies (see p.215 and p.214).

Pick up a copy of the weekly **Film Agenda** from any cinema for details of all films showing in the city, or check Ⓦwww.filmladder.nl. For details of gay and lesbian film programmes see Chapter Twelve. Weekly programmes change on Thursdays.

All foreign movies playing in Amsterdam (almost no Dutch movies turn up, anyway) are shown in their **original language** and subtitled in Dutch – which is fine for British or American fare, but a little difficult if you fancy Tarkovsky or Pasolini. If you're interested in seeing a non-English-language movie, check with the venue whether it's been **subtitled** in English (*Engels Ondertiteld*) before you go. Films are almost never dubbed into Dutch: if they are, *Nederlands Gesproken* will be printed in the listings. Most major cinemas have four showings a day: two in the afternoon, two in the evening; some also have midnight shows on Fridays and Saturdays.

Tickets can cost around €8 for an evening show Friday to Sunday, though it's not hard to find a ticket for €6 during the week. Prices at the *filmhuizen* are slightly lower, and can drop to as little as €4.50 for a 10/11am Sunday showing. Aside from occasional film festivals held by the likes of Amnesty International, Amsterdam's only regular event is the fascinating **International Documentary**

Film Festival in November/December (info ☎020/627 3329, ⓦwww .idfa.nl), where around 250 documentaries from all over the world are shown in ten days. The festival has established itself as the biggest international documentary festival in the world. Simultaneously, there's the **Shadowfestival** (ⓦwww.shadowfestival.nl), which showcases alternative documentaries and is held at three locations: Melkweg, de Uitkijk and the Filmmuseum. Whereas the **Netherlands Film Festival** (ⓦwww.filmfestival.nl), held each September in Utrecht, features only homegrown productions, January's **Rotterdam Film Festival** (info ☎010/890 9090, ⓦwww.filmfestivalrotterdam.com) is truly international, with screenings of well over a hundred art movies from all parts of the world, as well as the usual accompanying lectures and seminars.

Cinemas

De Balie Kleine-Gartmanplantsoen 10, off Leidseplein (Grachtengordel south) ☎020/553 5100, ⓦwww.debalie.nl. Cultural centre for theatre, politics, film and new media, showing movies at 1pm on Sunday and selected evenings during the week, often with English subtitles.

De Munt Vijzelstraat 15 (Grachtengordel south) ☎0900/1438 ⓦwww.pathe.nl/demunt. Huge multi-screen cinema with up to six showings a day of mainstream films, as well as a few homegrown productions.

Cavia Van Hallstraat 52 ☎020/681 1419, ⓦwww.filmhuiscavia.nl. Incongruously sited above a martial arts centre, this is one of the best of the small *filmhuizen*, with an eclectic and non-commercial programme of international movies.

Cinecenter Lijnbaansgracht 236 (Grachtengordel south) ☎020/623 6615, ⓦwww.cinecenter.nl. Opposite the Melkweg, this shows independent and quality commercial films, the majority originating from non-English-speaking countries, shown with an interval.

Filmmuseum Vondelpark 3 (Museum Quarter and Vondelpark) ☎020/589 1400, ⓦwww .filmmuseum.nl. Subsidized by the government since the 1940s, the Filmmuseum holds literally tens of thousands of prints. Dutch films show regularly, along with all kinds of movies from all corners of the world. Silent movies often have live piano accompaniment, and on summer weekend evenings there are free open-air screenings on the terrace. Also many cheap matinees. Most movies have English subtitles.

Kriterion Roeterstraat 170 (Old Jewish Quarter and eastern docks; tram #6, #7, #10) ☎020/623 1708, ⓦwww.kriterion.nl. Stylish duplex cinema close to Weesperplein metro. Shows arthouse and quality commercial films,

with late-night cult favourites. Friendly bar attached.

Melkweg See p.207. As well as music, art and dance, the Melkweg manages to maintain a consistently good monthly film and video programme, ranging from mainstream fodder through to obscure imports.

The Movies Haarlemmerdijk 161 (Jordaan and the Westerdok) ☎020/638 6016, ⓦwww .themovies.nl. A beautiful Art Deco cinema, and a charming setting for independent films. Worth visiting for the bar and restaurant alone, fully restored to their original sumptuousness. "Filmdinner" nights (Mon–Thur) include a three-course meal and film from €29. Late shows at the weekend.

▽ Filmmuseum

Rialto Ceintuurbaan 338 (De Pijp) ☎020/676 8700, ⓦ www.rialtofilm.nl. The only fully authentic arthouse cinema in Amsterdam, showing an enormously varied programme of European and World movies supplemented by themed series and classics. The cinema boasts a large café open to the public, and, thanks to the set-up of volunteer staff, the place has a friendly and welcoming atmosphere.

Smart Cinema 1e Const. Huygensstraat 10 (Museum Quarter and Vondelpark; tram #3 or #12 to Overtoom) ☎020/427 5951, ⓦ www .smartprojectspace.net. Small cinema showing the best non-mainstream and experimental Arthouse movies and free video slideshows on Wednesday and Sunday at 5pm. There's also a trendy international restaurant and bar with DJs, and occasional exhibitions.

Tropentheater See p.205. Attached to the Tropenmuseum, this theatre concentrates mostly on music and dance, but puts on ad hoc themed film shows and culture festivals from around the world.

Tuschinski Theater Reguliersbreestraat 26 (Grachtengordel south) no phone, ⓦ www .tuschinski.nl. Fabulous Art Deco theatre, famous for its handwoven carpet and painted wallpaper, this film house shows the more arty offerings from the mainstream list.

De Uitkijk Prinsengracht 452 (Grachtengordel south) ☎020/623 7460 ⓦ www.uitkijk.nl. The oldest cinema in the city (pronounced "out-kike"), in a converted canal house with no bar, no ice cream and no popcorn – but low prices. Shows popular movies for months on end.

Shops and markets

Variety is the essence of Amsterdam **shopping**. Whereas in other capitals you can spend days trudging around in search of something interesting, here you'll find every kind of store packed into a relatively small area. Throw in a handful of great **street markets**, and Amsterdam's shopping possibilities look even better. There are, of course, the obligatory generic malls and pedestrianized shopping streets, where you can find exactly the same stuff you'd see at home, but where Amsterdam scores is in its excellent, unusual **speciality shops** – designer clocks, rubber stamps, Indonesian arts, condoms, to name just a few, and almost always owned by a family or individual.

Shopping in Amsterdam can be divided roughly by **area**, with similar shops often huddled together in neighbouring streets. While exploring, bear in mind that the major canals are mostly given over to homes and offices, and it's along the small radial streets that connect them that many of the most interesting and individual shops are clustered. Broadly speaking, the **Nieuwendijk/Kalverstraat** strip running through Dam square in the Old Centre is home to high-street fashion and mainstream department stores – crowded Saturday afternoons here can be a hellish experience – and nearby **Koningsplein** and **Leidsestraat** offers a good selection of affordable designer shoe and clothes stores. The **Jordaan**, to the west, is where many local artists ply their wares: you can find individual items of genuine interest here, as well as more specialized and adventurous clothes shops and some affordable antiques. Less affordable antiques – the cream of Amsterdam's renowned trade – can be found in the Spiegelkwartier, centred on **Nieuwe Spiegelstraat**, while to the south, **P.C. Hooftstraat**, **Van Baerlestraat** and, further south still, **Beethovenstraat** play host to designer clothiers, upmarket ceramics stores, confectioners and delicatessens.

As regards **opening hours**, many shops take Monday morning off, not opening up until noon or 1pm and closing again at 6pm. On Tuesday, Wednesday and Friday, hours are the standard 9am to 6pm, although the larger shops in the centre have shifted towards a 7pm closing time. Thursday is late-opening night (*koopavond*), with most places staying open from 9am until 9pm. Saturday hours are normally 8.30 or 9am to 5 or 5.30pm, and most shops stay closed on Sundays, though this is changing fast with noon to 5pm the common formula. A few "night shops" are open between roughly 4pm and 1am – see the box on p.226.

Most small and medium-sized shops – and even some of the larger ones – won't accept **payment by credit card**: don't take it for granted in anywhere but the biggest or most expensive places. Shops that do will accept the usual range of major cards, but never travellers' cheques.

Shops

Antiques

By necessity, this is only a sample of what's on offer – you'll find **antiques** shops in every corner of Amsterdam, though the chicest cluster is undoubtedly in the **Spiegelkwartier** along Nieuwe Spiegelstraat and Spiegelgracht.

Affaire D'Eau Haarlemmerdijk 150 (Jordaan and the Westerdok) ℡020/422 0411. Antique bathtubs, taps, sinks and toilets, as well as boxed and embossed Thomas Crapper toilet paper. Mon–Fri 10.30am–6pm, Sat 10.30am–5pm.

Jan Beekhuizen Nieuwe Spiegelstraat 49 (Grachtengordel south) ℡020/626 3912. European pewter from the fifteenth century onwards. Tues–Sun 10.30am–6pm.

Jan Best Keizersgracht 357 (Grachtengordel west) ℡020/623 2736. Famed antique lamp shop, with some wonderfully kitsch examples. Offbeat new lamps and lights too. Corner Huidenstraat. Mon–Fri 10.30am–6pm & Sat 10am–5pm.

Blitz Nieuwe Spiegelstraat 37a (Grachtengordel south) ℡020/623 2663. Specialises in antique ceramics from China. Tues–Sun 10.30am–6pm.

Van Dreven Nieuwe Spiegelstraat 38 (Grachtengordel south) ℡020/428 8442. Antique clocks, barometers and music boxes. Tues–Sun 10.30am-6pm.

Gallery de Munt In the Munttoren, Muntplein 12 (Old Centre) ℡020/623 2271. One of the best outlets for gifts of antique delftware, pottery, hand-painted tiles and the like. Mon–Sat 10am–6pm.

Harrie van Gennip Govert Flinckstraat 402 (De Pijp) ℡020/679 3025. A huge collection of old and antique stoves from all parts of Europe, lovingly restored and all in working order. Only open Thurs 1–6pm & Sat 11am–4pm.

Eduard Kramer Nieuwe Spiegelstraat 64 (Grachtengordel south) ℡020/623 0832, Ⓦwww.antique-tileshop.nl. Holds a wonderful selection of Dutch tiles from the fifteenth century onwards. Operates an online ordering service too. Tues–Sun 10.30am–6pm.

Dick Meijer Keizersgracht 539 (Grachtengordel south) ℡020/624 9288. Egyptian, Roman and pre-Columbian antiquities. Just off Spiegel-straat. Tues–Sun 10.30am-6.30pm.

Thom & Lenny Nelis Keizersgracht 541 (Grachtengordel south) ℡020/623 1546. Medical antiques and spectacles. Just off Spiegelstraat. Thurs–Sat 11am–5pm.

Tóth Ikonen Nieuwe Spiegelstraat 68 (Grachtengordel south) ℡020/420 7359. Antique Russian icons from the sixteenth to the nineteenth century. Tues–Sun 11am–5.30pm.

Van Hier tot Tokio Prinsengracht 262 (Grachtengordel west) ℡020/428 2682. Modern and antique Japanese furniture, crafts, kimonos and the like. A split-level store with a good variety of quality items. Just south of Reestraat. Tues–Fri noon–6pm, Sat 11am–6pm & Sun noon–7pm.

Art supplies, postcards and posters

Art Unlimited Keizersgracht 510 (Grachtengordel south) ℡020/624 8419. Sprawling postcard, card and poster shop, with excellent stock. All kinds of images: good for communiqués home that avoid windmills and clogs. Near the corner of Leidsestraat. Mon–Sat 10am–6pm (Thurs till 9pm) & Sun noon-5pm.

De Lach 1e Bloemdwarsstraat 14 (Jordaan and the Westerdok) ℡020/626 6625, Ⓦwww .moviepostersdelach.com. Movie poster shop that also stocks Hollywood classics and some international films. An original *Barbarella* poster will set you back no less than e*250. Tues–Sat 11am–6pm.

Van Beek Stadhouderskade 62–65 (De Pijp) ℡020/662 1670. Long-established outlet for art materials of all kinds. Mon 1–6pm, Tues–Sat 9am–6pm, Sat 10am–5pm.

Van Ginkel Bilderdijkstraat 99 (Oud West) ℡020/618 9827. Supplier of art materials, with an emphasis on print-making. Mon–Fri 10am–5.30pm, Sat 10am–4pm.

Vlieger Amstel 52 (Grachtengordel south) ℡020/623 5834. Every kind of paper downstairs, every kind of paint upstairs.

Bikes

Bikes can be **rented** from a veritable raft of outlets all over town – see "Directory" (p.253) for further details. If you're **buying a bike**, don't be tempted by anything you're offered on the street or in a bar – more often than not you'll end up with a

stolen bike. Try instead the shops listed below, which rent, sell and repair
bikes of all qualities. If you find that
no one in the shop speaks English,
check out the glossary of basic bike
terms on p.293.

**Bike City Bloemgracht 70 (Jordaan and the
Westerdok)** ☎020/626 3721, ⓦwww.bikecity
.nl. The best of the sale-and-rental shops
for service and quality – try here first. Daily
9am–6pm, but closed late Dec to late Feb.
**Damstraat Rent-a-Bike Damstraat 20 (Old Cen-
tre)** ☎020/625 5029. Bike repair and rental.
**Freewheel Akoleienstraat 7 (Jordaan and the
Westerdok)** ☎020/627 7252. Women-run bike
repairs and sales. Tues–Fri 9am–6pm, Sat
9am–5pm.
**Kronan Tesselschadestraat 1E (Museum Quarter
and Vondelpark)** ☎020/627 0005. More of
a craze than a cycling revolution. Kronan
builds good-looking, if heavy and rather
slow bikes featuring a very small main cog-
wheel.
**Ligfietswinkel Waterspiegelplein 10H (Oud
West)** ☎020/686 9396. Bike shop which also
arranges cycling tours to the green areas
just outside Amsterdam on the first Sunday
of every month. Wed–Sat 10am–6pm.
't Mannetje Kastanjeweg 20 ☎020/665 1137,
ⓦwww.tmannetje.nl. This shop makes
bicycles to personalized designs, whether
you want to get your kids on board too or
indulge in some extreme sports. They have
dealers in London, Berlin and Brussels as
well. Mon–Fri 9am–6pm, Sat 10am–5pm.
**MacBike Centraal Station (Eastpoint), Stations-
plein 12; Mr Visserplein 2; and Weteringschans
2, on the edge of Leidseplein** ☎020/620 0985,
ⓦwww.macbike.nl. Several locations (but
one central phone number) for this well–
established and very popular bike rental
and sales firm, though the circular MacBike
disks carried by every one of their bikes do
look distinctly un-cool. They also organize
city tours. Daily 9am–5.45pm.

Books and comics

Virtually all of Amsterdam's many
bookshops stock at least a small
selection of **English–language
books**, though prices are always
inflated (sometimes dramatically). A
particular speciality is the city's range
of **secondhand** and **antiquarian**

bookshops, several of which are listed
below, but for a comprehensive list
pick up the free *Antiquarian & Secondhand Bookshops of Amsterdam* leaflet
at any of them. For gay and lesbian
bookstores see Chapter Twelve.

General bookstores

**American Book Center Kalverstraat 185 (Old
Centre)** ☎020/625 5537. Vast stock, all in
English, with lots of imported US magazines and books. Students get ten percent
discount. Mon–Wed, Fri & Sat 10am–8pm,
Thurs10am–9pm, Sun 11am–6.30pm.
Athenaeum Spui 14 (Old Centre) ☎020/622
6248. Excellent all-round bookshop with an
adventurous stock. Also the best source of
international newspapers and magazines.
Mon–11am–6pm, Tues–Sat 10am–8pm,
Thurs until 9pm, Sun 11am–6.30pm.
**The English Bookshop Lauriergracht 71 (Jor-
daan and the Westerdok)** ☎020/626 4230. A
small but quirky collection of titles on a wide
range of subjects. Tues–Sat 11am–6pm.
**Scheltema Koningsplein 20 (Grachtengordel
south)** ☎020/523 1411. Amsterdam's biggest
and best bookshop. Six floors of absolutely
everything (mostly in Dutch). Daily 10am–
6pm (Thurs till 9pm).
De Slegte Kalverstraat 48–52 (Old Centre)
☎020/622 5933. The Amsterdam branch of
a nationwide chain specializing in new and
used books at a discount. Mon 11am–6pm,
Tues–Sat 9.30am–6pm, Thurs until 9pm,
Sun noon–5pm.
Waterstone's Kalverstraat 152 (Old Centre)
☎020/638 3821. Amsterdam branch of the
UK high-street chain, with four floors of
books and magazines. A predictable selection, but prices are sometimes cheaper here
than elsewhere. Mon & Sun 11am–6pm,
Tues & Wed 9am–6pm, Thurs 9am–9pm, Fri
9am–7pm, Sat 10am–7pm.

Secondhand and antiquarian

**The Book Exchange Kloveniersburgwal 58 (Old
Centre)** ☎020/626 6266. Large and rambling
old shop with a crusty but friendly American
proprietor, and a great selection of English
secondhand books. Mon–Fri 11am–6pm,
Sat 11am–5.30pm, Sun 11.30am–4pm.
Boekenmarkt Spui (Old Centre). Open-air book
market every Friday.
**Book Traffic Leliegracht 50 (Grachtengordel
west)** ☎020/620 4690. An excellent and well-

organized selection of mostly secondhand books. Mon–Fri 11am–6pm, Sat 11am–6pm & Sun noon–5pm.

Brinkman Singel 319, Corner Ramsteeg. (Grachtengordel west) ☎020/623 8353. A stalwart of the Amsterdam antiquarian book trade, Brinkman has occupied the same premises for forty years. Lots of good local stuff. Mon–Fri 10am–5pm & Sat 11am–5pm.

Egidius Haarlemmerstraat 87 (Jordaan and the Westerdok) ☎020/624 3255. A good selection of literature, art and poetry, plus a gallery selling lithographs. Mon–Fri 11am–6pm, Sat 11am–5pm.

Fenix Frans Halsstraat 88 (De Pijp) ☎020/673 9459. General secondhand bookstore, with a good range of books in English, and with the emphasis on Celtic literature, history and culture.

De Kloof Kloveniersburgwal 44 (Old Centre) ☎020/622 3828. Enormous higgledy-piggledy used bookshop on four floors. Great for a rummage. All in English and mostly science and philosophy. Only open Thurs– Sat 1–6pm

A. Kok Oude Hoogstraat 14 (Old Centre) ☎020/623 1191. Vintage and secondhand bookstore, especially strong on prints and maps.

Magic Galaxies Oude Schans 140 (Old Centre) ☎020/627 6261. Run from home by a couple whose spare time is spent collecting science fiction, fantasy and other esoteric books, many of which are in English. Call first.

Oudemanhuispoort Book Market See p.59.

Art and architecture

Architectura & Natura Leliegracht 22 (Grachtengordel west) ☎020/623 618 6. Books on architecture and interior design. An eclectic collection with many English titles. Mon noon–6pm & Tues–Sat 9am–6pm.

Art Book Van Baerlestraat 126 (Museum Quarter and Vondelpark) ☎020/644 0925. The city's best source of high-gloss art books. Check out also the shops of the main museums, particularly the Rijksmuseum. Mon 1–6pm, Tues–Sat 10am–6pm.

Boekie Woekie Berenstraat 16 (Grachtengordel west) ☎020/639 05 07. Books on – and by – leading Dutch artists and graphic designers. Entertaining postcards too. Tues–Fri noon–6pm & Sat noon–6pm.

Nijhoff en Lee Staalstraat 13a (Old Centre) ☎020/620 39 80. This small corner store specializes in art, architecture and design titles, and is especially good on the art of printing, typography and lithography. Mon–Fri noon–6pm, Tues–Fri 9am–6pm, Sat 10–5.30pm.

Comics and graphic novels

Gojoker Zeedijk 31a (Old Centre) ☎020/620 5078. Classic and contemporary comic store. Tues–Sat 11am–7pm, Thurs until 9pm.

Lambiek Kerkstraat 132 (Grachtengordel south) ☎020/626 75 43, ⓦ www.lambiek.nl. The city's largest, oldest and best comic bookshop and gallery, with an international stock. Their website features the biggest comiclopedia in the world. Mon–Fri 11am–6pm & Sat 11am–5pm.

Stripwinkel Kapitein Rob 2e Egelantiersd-warsstraat 7 (Jordaan and the Westerdok) ☎020/622 3869. Alternative Dutch comics old and new. Not a superhero in sight. Mon–Fri noon–6pm (Thurs 8pm), Sat 11am–5pm.

Vandal Com-x Rozengracht 31 (Jordaan and the Westerdok) ☎020/420 21 44, ⓦ www .vandalcomx.com. US comic imports, as well as related toys, games and masks. Mon 1–5.30pm, Tues–Thurs 11am–5.30pm, Sat 11am–5pm, Sun noon–5pm.

Computer

Boek N Serve Ferdinand Bolstraat 151–153 (De Pijp) ☎020/664 3446. Good range of computer literature and travel guides. You can get coffee and surf the Internet too.

Computer Collectief Amstel 312 (Grachtengordel south) ☎020/638 9003. Vast collection of books, software and magazines, and an eminently knowledgeable staff. Metres from the Amstel sluizen (sluice gates, see p.82). Mon noon–6pm, Tues–Fri 10am–6pm & Sat 10am–5pm.

Language

Intertaal Van Baerlestraat 76 (Museum Quarter and Vondelpark) ☎020/575 6756. Teach-your-self books and dictionaries in every language you can think of. Mon–Fri 9am–6pm (Thurs till 9pm) & Sat 10am–5pm.

Scheltema See p.218. Amsterdam's biggest and best bookshop has an excellent range of language books and all sorts of stuff on the Dutch and their habits.

Politics and society

Fort van Sjakoo Jodenbreestraat 24 (Jewish Quarter and the and eastern docks) ☎020/625 8979, ⑩www.fortvansjakoo.nl. Anarchist bookshop stocking a wide selection of radical political publications. Mon–Fri 11am–6pm, Sat 11am–5pm.

Religion and occult

Au Bout du Monde Singel 313 (Grachtengordel west) ☎020/625 1397. Astrology, philosophy, psychology and mysticism, with classical music playing while you browse. Near Raamsteeg. Mon 1–6pm & Tues–Sat 10am–6pm.

International Evangelist Bookshop Raadhuisstraat 14 (Grachtengordel west) ☎020/620 1859. Bibles and Christian books. Mon 1.30–6pm, Tues–Fri 9.30am–6pm & Sat 9.30am–5pm.

Theatre and film

Cine-Qua-Non Staalstraat 14 (Old Centre) ☎020/625 5588. Film and cinema history books, posters and other film paraphernalia. **International Theatre and Film Bookshop** Leidseplein 26a (Grachtengordel south) ☎020/622 6489. Books and magazines on all aspects of the stage and screen. Mon–Fri 10am–6pm & Sat 10am–5pm. Beside the Stadsschouwburg.

Travel

A la Carte Utrechtsestraat 110 (Grachtengordel south) ☎020/625 0679. Large and friendly travel bookshop. Mon 1–6pm, Tues–Fri 10am–6pm & Sat 10am–5pm.

Evenaar Singel 348 (Grachtengordel west) ☎020/624 6289. Concentrates less on guidebooks than travel literature of which it has an exemplary selection in both English and Dutch. Near Raamsteeg. Mon–Fri 12.15–6pm & Sat 11am–5pm.

Jacob van Wijngaarden Overtoom 97 (Museum Quarter and Vondelpark) ☎020/612 1901. The city's best travel bookshop, with knowledgeable staff and a huge selection of books and maps. Also inflatable and illuminated globes. Mon 1–6pm, Tues–Fri 10am–6pm (Thurs till 9pm) & Sat 10am–5pm.

Pied-à-Terre Singel 393 (Grachtengordel west) ☎020/627 4455, ⑩www.piedaterre.nl. Hiking maps for Holland and beyond, mostly in English. Also adventure holiday guides. Mon–Fri 10am–6pm & Sat 10am–5pm.

Stadsboekwinkel Amsteldijk 67 (De Pijp) ☎020/572 0202. Part of the city archive, this is the shop for all books on Amsterdam: architecture, transport, history, urban planning, geography, etc. Mon–Fri 10am–5pm.

Women's

Vrouwen in Druk Westermarkt 5 (Grachtengordel west) ☎020/624 5003. "Women in Print" stocks secondhand books by female authors, with a large English selection. Mon–Fri 11am–6pm, Sat 11am–5pm.

Xantippe Unlimited Prinsengracht 290 (Grachtengordel west) ☎020/623 5854. Amsterdam's foremost women's bookshop, with a wide selection of new feminist titles in English. At Berenstraat. Mon 1–7pm, Tues–Fri 10am–7pm, Sat 10am–6pm, Sun noon–5pm.

Clothes and accessories

Amsterdam is in many ways an ideal place for **clothes** shopping: prices aren't too high and the city is sufficiently compact to save lots of shoe leather. On the other hand, don't expect the huge choice of, say, London or New York. There are are good-value, if somewhat dull, mainstream styles along Kalverstraat and Nieuwendijk, with better stuff along Rokin and Leidsestraat, and the really fancy goods down in the south of the city on P.C. Hooftstraat, Van Baerlestraat and Beethovenstraat. More interestingly, there's a fair array of one-off youth-oriented and secondhand clothing shops dotted around the Jordaan, on Oude and Nieuwe Hoogstraat, and along the narrow streets that connect the major canals west of the city centre. For **secondhand clothes** the Waterlooplein flea market (see p.230) is a marvellous hunting ground. For children's clothes, see "Kids' Amsterdam", p.243.

New and designer clothes

Agnès B Rokin 126 (Old Centre) ☎020/627 1465. Amsterdam city centre shop of the chic French designer.

America Today Magna Plaza (Old Centre)
☎020/638 8447; also at Sarphatistraat 48
(Amsterdam Oost). Popular outlet for classic
and modern US brands – sold at decent
prices.
Antonia Gasthuismolensteeg 18–20 (Grachtengordel west) ☎020/320 9443. High–fashion
shoes, slippers and handbags spread over
two smallish shops. Tues–Sat 10am–6pm
(Thurs till 9pm).

▽ Antonia

Azzurro P.C Hooftstraat 142a (Museum Quarter
and the Vondelpark) ☎020671 6804. Dutch–
owned fashion house which has five shops in
total, four along this street, including Azzurro
Kids (see p.243). Stocked full of the latest
designs from the hippest designers, including
Mui Mui, D&G and Stella McCartney. Mon
1–6pm, Tues–Fri 10am–6pm (Thurs 9pm),
Sat 10am–5.30pm, Sun noon–5pm.
Cora Kemperman Leidsestraat 72 (Grachtengordel south) ☎020/625 1284. Well-made,
elegantly relaxed designer clothes for
women that won't break the bank. Mon
noon–6pm, Tues–Sat 10am–6pm (Thurs till
9pm) & Sun noon–6pm.
Cyberdog Spuistraat 250 (Old Centre) ☎020/330
6385. Cutting-edge creations for clubbing.
Mon–Sat 10am–6pm, Thurs until 9pm.
Diversi 1e Leliedwarsstraat 6 (Jordaan and
the Westerdok) ☎020/625 0773. Small but
inspired collection of reasonably priced,
Dutch and Italian clothes for women.
Good selection of sunglasses and belts.
Mon–Fri 11am–6pm (closed Tues), Sat
11am–5.30pm.

Raymond Linhard Van Baerlestraat 50 (Museum
Quarter and Vondelpark) ☎020/679 0755.
Cheerful, well-priced separates. Mon
1–6pm, Tues–Fri 9.30am–6pm (Thurs 9pm),
Sat 9.30am–5.30pm.
Hemp Works Nieuwendijk 13 (Old Centre)
☎020/421 1762. Not all hemp is like sack-
cloth – check out the silky hemp shirts,
fleeces and jeans in this clothing store that
sells nothing but clothes made from the
stuff.
Laundry Industry Spui 1 (Old Centre) ☎020/420
2554. On the corner of Rokin, this Dutch
clothing brand does cool, chic, youthful
clothes for women and men. Mon 11am–
6.30pm, Tues–Fri 10am–6.30pm, Thurs
until 9pm, Sat 10am–6pm, Sun noon–6pm.
There's another branch in Magna Plaza.
Local Service Keizersgracht 400 (Grachtengordel west) ☎020/626 6840. Men's and
women's fashions. Ultra-trendy in an alternative, funky kind of way and expensive. At
Runstraat. Mon–Fri 10am–6pm, Sat 10am-
5pm & Sun 1–5pm.
Margriet Nannings Prinsenstraat 8 (Grachtengordel west) ☎020/620 7672. Pricey designer
clothes for women, mostly casual chic.
Classy handbags and jewellery too. Also
Nannings mens' shop just along the street
at Prinsenstraat 15 ☎020/420 20 97. Mon
1–6pm, Tues–Sat 10.30am–6pm & Sun
10.30am–8pm.
Mateloos Bilderdijkstraat 62; Kinkerstraat
77 (Oud West) ☎020/683 2384. Clothes for
women in larger sizes. Mon–Fri 10am–6pm,
Sat 10am–5pm.
Punch St Antoniesbreestraat 73 (Old Centre)
☎020/626 6673. Doc Martens and Lonsdale.
Rodolfo's Magna Plaza mall (Old Centre)
☎020/623 1214; also at Sarphatistraat 59
(Amsterdam Oost). Huge collection of in-line
skates and skateboards and the latest fashion to go with them.
Robin en Rik Leemakers Runstraat 30
(Grachtengordel west) ☎020/627 8924. Handmade leather clothes and accessories to
suit every taste and both sexes.
Sissy Boy Leidsestraat 15 (Grachtengordel
south) ☎020/623 8949. Simply designed but
classy and affordably priced clothes for
men and women. A number of designer
labels are featured here. Also at Kalverstraat
199 (☎020/626 00 88; Old Centre). & Van
Baerlestraat 12 (☎020/672 02 47; Museum
Quarter and Vondelpark). Sun & Mon noon–
6pm; Tues–Sat 10am-6pm (Thurs till 9pm).

Solid Haarlemmerdijk 20 (Jordaan and the Westerdok) ☎020/627 4114. Interesting and hip womenswear from designers such as Moschino, Kenzo and Chlöe. Mon 1–6pm, Tues–Sat 10am–6pm (Thurs 7pm).

Secondhand clothes

Daffodil Jacob Obrechtstraat 41 (Museum Quarter and Vondelpark) ☎020/673 7237. Designer labels only in this posh secondhand shop down by the Vondelpark. Tues–Fri noon–6pm, sat noon–5pm.

Jojo Huidenstraat 23 ☎020/623 3476 (Grachtengordel west). Decent secondhand clothes from all eras. Particularly good for suit jackets and matching shirts. Mon noon–6pm, Tues–Sat 11am–6pm & Sun 2–6pm.

Lady Day Hartenstraat 9 (Grachtengordel west) ☎020/623 5820. Good-quality secondhand fashion at reasonable prices. Mon–Sat 11am–6pm (Thurs till 9pm) & Sun noon–5pm.

Laura Dols Wolvenstraat 6 & 7 (Grachtengordel west) ☎020/624 9066, ⊛www.lauradols.nl. Superb – and superbly creative – assortment of vintage clothing from dresses through to hats. Its forté is 1940s and 1950s gear. Mon–Sat 11am–6pm (Thurs till 9pm) & Sun 2–6pm.

Second Best Wolvenstraat 18 (Grachtengordel west) ☎020/422 0274. Classy cast-offs. Mon 1–6pm & Tues–Sat 11am–6pm.

Zipper Huidenstraat 7 (Grachtengordel west) ☎020/623 7302. Used clothes selected for style and quality – strong on jeans and flairs. Prices are high, but it's very popular, and everything is in good condition. Mon–Sat 11am–6pm & Sun 1–5pm. Also in the Old Centre at Nieuwe Hoogstraat 8 (same hours; ☎020/627 03 53).

▽ Zipper

Shoes and accessories

Big Shoe Leliegracht 12 (Grachtengordel west) ☎020/622 6645. All designs and styles for larger-sized feet for both male and female. Wed–Fri 10am–6pm & Sat 10am–5pm.

Body Sox Leidsestraat 35 (Grachtengordel south) ☎020/422 3544. Socks, tights and stockings in every conceivable colour and design. Mon–Sat 10am–6pm.

Dr Adam's Oude Doelenstraat 5 (Old Centre) ☎020/622 3734. One of the city's widest selections of trendy shoes. Also at Leidsestraat 24 (☎020/626 44 60; Grachtengordel south) and P.C. Hooftstraat 90 (☎020/662 38 35; Museum Quarter and Vondelpark). Mon noon–6pm, Tues–Sat 10am–6pm (Thurs till 9pm) & Sun noon–6pm.

The English Hatter Heiligeweg 40 (Old Centre) ☎020/623 4781. Ties, hats and various other accessories, alongside classic menswear from shirts to cricket sweaters.

Fred de la Bretonière St Luciensteeg 20 ☎020/623 4152 and Utrechtsetstraat 77 ☎020/626 9627 (both Grachtengordel south). Designer famous for his high-quality handbags and shoes, sold at reasonable – at least affordable – prices. Mon–Sat 10am–6pm.

De Grote Tas Oude Hoogstraat 6 (Old Centre) ☎020/623 0110. Family-run store now in the third generation, selling a wide selection of serious bags, briefcases and suitcases.

Hoeden M/V Herengracht 422 (Grachtengordel west) ☎020/626 3038. Pricey designer hats galore, from felt Borsalinos to straw Panamas. At Leidsestraat. Gloves and umbrellas too. Tues–Fri 11am–6pm (Thurs till 9pm), Sat 11am–5pm.

Jan Jansen Rokin 42 (Old Centre) ☎020/625 1350. Famous Dutch designer selling handmade shoes with frivolous designs.

Department stores and shopping malls

By and large, Amsterdam's **department stores** are really rather insipid and the same applies to most of the city's **shopping malls**, the bulk of which are consigned to the suburbs. An exception is **Magna Plaza**, a shopping mall imaginatively sited in the old neo–Gothic post office building behind Dam square at Nieuwezijds Voorburgwal 182, though frankly the shops – comprising the usual big–brand stuff – rarely live up to the setting.

De Bijenkorf Dam 1 (Old Centre) ☎020/621 8080. Dominating the northern corner of Dam square, this is the city's top shop, a huge bustling place (the name means bee-hive) that has an indisputably wide range. Departments to head for include household goods, cosmetics and kidswear; there's also a good choice of newspapers and magazines. Mon 11am–7pm, Tues & Wed 9.30am–7pm, Thurs & Fri 9.30am–9pm.

HEMA Nieuwendijk 174 (Old Centre) ☎020/623 4176; also in the Kalvertoren and branches out of the centre. A kind of Dutch Woolworth's, but of a better quality: good for stocking up on toiletries and other essentials, and occa-sional designer delights – it's owned by De Bijenkorf, and you can sometimes find the same items at knockdown prices. Surprises include wine and salami in the back of the shop, and sometimes a bakery and cheese counter. Their Fotoservice is convenient and gives same-day delivery.

Maison de Bonneterie Rokin 140 (Old Centre) ☎020/626 2162. Apart from the building, which rises through balustraded balconies to a high central dome, nothing special: very conservative and, on the whole, extremely expensive. Small lunch café as well. By appointment to Her Majesty. Mon 1–5.30pm, Tues–Sat 10am–5.30pm, Thurs until 9pm, Sun noon–5pm.

Metz & Co Leidsestraat 34 (Grachtengordel south) ☎020/520 7020. The complete depart-ment store with floor upon floor of clothing, furniture and household appliances. The rooftop café offers a particularly enjoyable view over the city centre. Mon 11am-6pm, Tues–Sat 9.30am-6pm (Thurs till 9pm) & Sun noon-5pm.

Peek & Cloppenberg Dam 20 (Old Centre) ☎020/623 2837. Less a department store than a multistorey clothes shop with some painfully middle-of-the-road styles. Nonethe-less, an Amsterdam institution. Mon 1–6pm, Tues–Sat 9.30am–6pm, Thurs until 9pm, Sun noon–6pm.

Vroom & Dreesmann Kalverstraat 203 (entrance also from Rokin; Old Centre) ☎020/622 0171. The main Amsterdam branch of a middle-ground nationwide chain, just near Munt-plein. It's pretty unadventurous, but take comfort from the fact that the restaurant is

quite outstanding (for a department store), and they bake fresh bread on the premises as well. Check out also the listening stands in the CD section on the top floor – the best place for a free Mozart recital with a canal view. Mon–Sat 11am–6.30pm, Tues–Sat 10am–6.30pm, Wed until 9pm, Sun noon–6pm.

Food and drink

While the city's supermarkets may not impress, there's a whole host of **speciality food stores** where you can buy anything from local fish to imported Heinz beans. We've also listed a selection of **wine and spir-its shops**, chosen for their location, specialities or simply because they're good value.

Supermarkets

Supermarkets are thin on the ground in central Amsterdam and most – apart from Albert Heijn's flag-ship store (see below) – are crowded and cramped. If you're buying fruit or vegetables, note you'll usually need to weigh and price them yourself (unless a price is given per item, *per stuk*) – put them on the scale, press the lit-tle picture, then press *BON* to get a sticky barcode. If you're buying beer, juice or water in **bottles** (glass or plastic), a deposit of €0.10–0.50 will be added on at the checkout; you get it back when you return the empties – to a different store if you like.

Albert Heijn Nieuwezijds Voorburgwal 226 (Old Centre) ☎020/421 8344. Located just behind Dam square, this is the biggest of the city's forty–odd Albert Heijn supermarkets. None of them take credit cards. It's open Mon–Sat 8am–10pm, Sun 11–7pm. There are other central branches at Koningsplein 4 (Grachtengordel south); Vijzelstraat 113 (Grachtengordel south); Westerstraat 79 (Jordaan and the Westerdok); Haarlemmerd-ijk 1 (Jordaan and the Westerdok); Overtoom 454 (Museum Quarter and Vondelpark).

De Natuurwinkel Weteringschans 133 (Grachtengordel south) ☎020/638 4083. Main branch of a chain selling only organic food. Much better tasting fruit and vegetables than anywhere else; also grains, pulses and Bon Bon Jeanette chocolates. Superb bread. Smaller branches around town. Mon–Sat 8am–8pm, Sun 11am–6pm.

Dirk van den Broek Heinekenplein 25 (De Pijp) ☎020/611 0812. Beats Albert Heijn hands down in everything except image. Cheaper across the board; bigger too. Trams #16, #24 or #25. Mon–Sat roughly 9am–9pm. More branches dotted around the suburbs.

Beer, wine and spirits

The **legal age** at which you can be sold beer is 16; for wines and spirits you need to be 18. The Dutch word for an off-licence (liquor store) is *slijterij*.

De Bierkoning Paleisstraat 125 (Old Centre) ☎020/625 2336. The "Beer King" is aptly named: 850 different beers, with matching glasses to drink them from. Mon 1-7pm, Tues–Fri 11am–7pm, Thurs until 9pm, Sat 11am–6pm, Sun 1–5pm.

Le Cellier Spuistraat 116 (Old Centre) ☎020/638 6573. The largest off-licence in the centre of the city. Very convenient with a huge selection of beers, wine and spirits.

Chabrol Haarlemmerstraat 7 (Jordaan and the Westerdok) ☎020/622 2781. All kinds of alcohol from (almost) every corner of the globe. A fine selection of wines, and an extremely knowledgeable staff. Mon–Sat 9.30am–7pm (Thurs & Fri 8pm), Sun noon–6pm.

Elzinga Wijnen Frederiksplein 1, corner of Utrechtsestraat (Grachtengordel south) ☎020/623 7270. High-quality wines from around the world. Wed–Sat 10am–6pm & Sun noon–6pm.

Gall & Gall Nieuw Zijds Voorburgwal 226 (Old Centre) ☎020/421 8370. Most central branch of the largest off-licence chain in Amsterdam; especially good for wine. Amongst others, there are also outlets at Jodenbreestraat 23 (☎020/428 70 60; Jewish Quarter and eastern docks); and Rozengracht 72 (☎020/624 46 66; Jordaan & the Westerdok).

Vintner Otterman Keizersgracht 300 (Grachtengordel west) ☎020/625 5088. Medium–sized, notably unpretentious store selling a first–rate selection of French wines. At Berenstraat. Mon 1–6pm, Tues–Fri 10.30am–6pm & Sat 10.30am–5.30pm.

Bread, pastries and chocolates

Amsterdam has a bevy of **bread and pastry shops**: a *warme bakkerij* sells bread and rolls baked on the premises, a *banketbakkerij* pastries and cream cakes. Specialist **chocolatiers** are much less common, but several of them are outstanding.

Bakkerij Paul Année Runstraat 25 (Grachtengordel west) ☎020/623 5322. The best wholegrain and sourdough breads in town, bar none – all made from organic grains. Mon–Sat 8am–5pm.

J.G.Beune Haarlemmerdijk 156 (Jordaan and the Westerdok) ☎020/624 8356. Handmade cakes and chocolates in antique premises. Mon–Fri 8.30am–6pm, Sat 8.30am–5pm.

Gary's Muffins Prinsengracht 454, at Berenstraat (Grachtengordel south) ☎020/420 1452. The best, most authentic New York bagels (and muffins) in town. Mon–Fri 9am–5pm, Sat & Sun 9am–5.30pm. Also branches at Marnixstraat 121 (Jordaan and the Westerdok) and Reguliersdwarsstraat 53 (Grachtengordel south).

Kwekkeboom Reguliersbreestraat 36 (Grachtengordel south) ☎020/623 6847. One of the city's most famous pastry shops, justly showered with awards. Mon–Fri 9am–5.45pm, Sat 9am–5.30pm & Sun noon–6pm. Also at Ferdinand Bolstraat 119 (Mon–Fri 9am–5.45pm, Sat 9am–5pm; ☎020/673 71 14) and Linnaeusstraat 80 (Mon–Fri 8.30am–5.30pm, Sat 8.30am–5pm; ☎020/665 04 43).

Lanskroon Singel 385 (Grachtengordel west) ☎020/623 7743. Another famously good pastry shop, with a small area for on-the-spot consumption. Near the south end of Spuistraat. Tues–Fri 8am–5.30pm, Sat 8am–5pm & Sun 9.30am–5pm.

Mediterrané Haarlemmerdijk 184 (Jordaan and the Westerdok) ☎020/620 3550. Well known for their croissants; also North African pastries and French bread. Daily 8am–8.30pm.

Pompadour Chocolaterie Huidenstraat 12 (Grachtengordel west) ☎020/623 9554. Delicious chocolates and lots of homemade pastries (usually smothered in or filled with chocolate). Mon–Fri 9am–6pm & Sat 8.30am–5pm.

Puccini Singel 184 ☎020/427 8341 (Grachtengordel west). Arguably the best chocolatier in town, selling a wonderfully creative range of chocs in all sorts of shapes and sizes.

This mini–chain has also abandoned the tweeness of the traditional chocolatier for brisk modern décor. At the junction of Oude Leliestraat. Tues–Sat 11am–6pm & Sun noon–5pm. Also at Staalstraat 17 (Old Centre), ☎020/626 5474, Mon noon–6pm, Tues–Sat 9am–6pm & Sun noon–5pm

Runneboom 1e van der Helststraat (De Pijp) ☎020/673 5941. Wonderful selection of breads from around the world – fitting, given its location in the multicultural Pijp district. Mon–Sat 7am–5pm.

Cheese

Arxhoek Damstraat 19 (Old Centre) ☎020/622 9118. Centrally situated general cheese shop. Mon–Fri 9am–6pm, Sat 9am–5pm, Sun noon–4pm.

Comestibles Kinders Westerstraat 189 (Jordaan and the Westerdok) ☎020/622 7983. Excellent selection of cheeses. Mon–Fri 8am–4.30pm, Sat 9am–4.30pm.

De Kaaskamer Runstraat 7 (Grachtengordel west) ☎020/623 3483. Friendly shop with a comprehensive selection of Dutch chesses plus international wines, cheeses and olives. Mon noon–6pm, Tues–Fri 9am–6pm, Sat 9am–5pm & Sun noon–5pm.

Coffee and tea

Geels & Co. Warmoesstraat 67 (Old Centre) ☎020/624 0683. Oddly situated among War-moesstraat's porn shops, this is one of the city's oldest and best-equipped specialists, with low prices on beans and utensils – and fantastically stocked with coffees and teas.

Levelt Prinsengracht 180 at Westermarkt (Grachtengordel west) ☎020/624 0823. This specialist tea and coffee company has occupied these premises for over 150 years, and much of the original decor remains. Now there are also branches scattered over almost every part of the city, including Centraal Station. Friendly service at all the shops. This branch open Mon noon–6pm, Tues–Fri 10am–6pm & Sat 10am–5pm.

Delis and imported foods

Eichholtz Leidsestraat 48 (Grachtengordel south) ☎020/622 0305. Old–fashioned store specialising in imported foods from Britain and the US. The only place to find Oreo cookies, Pop Tarts, Velveeta and Heinz beans. Mon 9am–6pm, Tues–Sat 9am–

6.30pm (Thurs till 9pm) & Sun noon–6pm.

La Tienda 1e Sweelinckstraat 21 (De Pijp) ☎020/671 2519. Musty old Spanish deli, with chorizos, hams and cheeses galore. Also all kinds of Latin American spices.

Meidi-Ya Beethovenstraat 18 (Nieuw Zuid) ☎020/673 7410. Comprehensively stocked Japanese deli, with a takeaway section and sushi bar.

Olivaria Hazenstraat 2a (Jordaan and the West-erdok) ☎020/638 3552. Olive oil, and nothing but. Incredible range of oils, all self-imported from small- and medium-sized concerns around the world. Expert advice and a well-stocked tasting table. Mon 2–6pm, Tues–Sat 11am–6pm.

Oriental Commodities Nieuwmarkt 27 (Old Centre) ☎020/626 2797. Large and warren-like Chinese supermarket. All sorts of stuff squirrelled away in corners – seaweed, water-chestnuts, spicy prawn crackers. Get there early for the handmade tofu.

Fish and seafood

Although there are lots of fresh herring and **seafood stalls** dotted around the city at strategic locations, including one or two excellent ones in the Albert Cuyp market, per-haps the best is the award-winning Bloemberg, on Van Baerlestraat, just along from the Van Gogh Museum. Others worth trying are on the cor-ner of Singel and Haarlemmerstraat, Singel and Raadhuisstraat, Utrech-tsestraat and Keizersgracht, and at Muntplein.

Organic and natural food

De Aanzet Frans Halsstraat 27 (De Pijp) ☎020/673 3415. Small organic supermarket co-operative, next to *De Waaghals* restau-rant in the Pijp.

De Belly Nieuwe Leliestraat 174 (Jordaan and the Westerdok) ☎020/330 94 83. Small and very friendly shop stocking all things organic, including beer. Mon–Fri 9am–6pm, Sat 9am–5pm.

Boerenmarkt See p.230. Weekly organic farm-ers' market.

De Groene Weg Huidenstraat 11 (Grachtengordel west) ☎020/627 91 32. Organic butcher. Mon–Fri 9am–6pm, Sat 9am–5pm.

De Natuurwinkel See p.223. By far the best selection.

Night shops

Most **night shops** (*avondwinkels*) open when everyone else is starting to think about closing up, and they stay open until well into the night – which sounds great, but you have to pay for the privilege: essentials can cost a barefaced three times the regular price. There are one or two exceptions, but most are located a fair walk from the city centre and may take time to seek out. For a complete list, see the *Gouden Gids* (Yellow Pages) under "*avondverkoop*". Bear in mind also that Albert Heijn supermarkets (see p.223) are mostly open until 10pm Monday through Saturday.

Big Bananas Leidsestraat 73 (Grachtengordel south) ☎020/627 70 40. Well stocked and convenient, but overly expensive and not known for politeness. Mon–Fri & Sun 10am–1am, Sat 10am–2am.

Dolf's Willemsstraat 79 (Jordaan and the Westerdok) ☎020/625 95 03. One of the better night shops: expensive, but reasonably central, tucked in a corner of the Jordaan. Mon–Sat 3pm–1am, Sun 10am–1am.

Sterk Waterlooplein 241 (Old Jewish Quarter and eastern docks) ☎020/626 50 97. Less a night shop than a city centre institution, with all kinds of fresh breads and pastries baked on the premises, a large fresh produce section, deli and friendly staff. Beats the pants off most regular supermarkets. Daily 8am–2am.

De Weegschaal Jodenbreestraat 20 (Old Jewish Quarter and eastern docks) ☎020/624 1765. Small, friendly natural food shop near the Waterlooplein flea market. Mon–Fri 9am–6pm, Sat 9am–5pm.

Music

The price of **CDs** in Amsterdam is higher than in Britain – and outrageous compared to the US. Where the city scores, however, is in its selection: there are lots of small, low-key independent shops specializing in one type of music, where you can turn up vintage items unavailable elsewhere. If it's **vinyl** you're after, however, you've come to the wrong country. Some places still sell records, but it's very much taken for granted that music comes on CDs. The main exception is the **Waterlooplein flea market** (see p.230), which has stacks of old records (and CDs) on offer.

Back Beat Records Egelantiersstraat 19 (Jordaan and the Westerdok) ☎020/627 1657. Small specialist in soul, blues, jazz, funk, etc, with a helpful and enthusiastic owner. Mon–Fri 11am–6pm, Sat 10am–6pm.

Boudisque Haringpakkersteeg 10–18, off Niuewendijk (Old Centre) ☎020/623 2603. One of the city's best record stores, with a good selection of metal, reggae, world music and dance – and reasonable rock and pop too.

Broekmans & Van Poppel Van Baerlestraat 92 (Museum Quarter and Vondelpark) ☎020/679 6575, ⊛www.broekmans.com/en. Specializes in classical music: historical recordings, small labels, opera, and sheet music. Mon–Fri 9am–6pm, Sat 9am–5pm.

Charles Weteringschans 193 (Grachtengordel south) ☎020/626 5538. Concentrates on classical and folk. Mon 1–6.30pm, Tues–Fri 10am–6.30pm (Thurs till 9pm) & Sat 10am–5.30pm.

Concerto Utrechtsestraat 54 (Grachtengordel south) ☎020/623 5228. New and used records and CDs in all categories; equally good on baroque as on grunge. The best all-round selection in the city, with the option to listen before you buy. Mon–Sat 10am–6pm & Sun noon–6pm.

Dance Tracks Nieuwe Nieuwestraat 69 (Old Centre) ☎020/639 0853. Imported dance music, hip-hop, jazz, dance, soul and house. Mon 1–7pm, Tues–Sat 11am–7pm, Thurs until 9pm, Sun 1–7pm.

Distortion Records Westerstraat 72 (Jordaan and the Westerdok) ☎020/627 0004. Secondhand independent with vinyl spilling all over the floor. Tues–Fri 11am–6pm (Thurs 9pm), Sat 10am–6pm.

Fame Kalverstraat 2 (Old Centre) ☎020/638 2525. The only large music warehouse in town; predictable selection of CDs and tapes. Books and computer games too.

Free Record Shop Kalverstraat 32 & 230 (Old Centre) ☏020/626 5808. Also at Leidsestraat 24 (Grachtengordel south), Centraal Station and Nieuwendijk 229 (both Old Centre). One of the better pop/rock chains. No records.

Get Records Utrechtsestraat 105 (Grachtengordel south) ☏020/622 3441. Sizeable selection of independent and alternative CDs, plus some vinyl. Check out also the deceptively small R&B section in the back of the shop. Tues–Sat 10am–6pm, Sun & Mon noon–6pm.

Killa Cutz Nieuwe Nieuwstraat 19 (Old Centre) ☏020/428 4040. Specializes in all the latest techno and electronic music. Mon 1–6pm, Tues–sat 11am–6pm, Sun 3–6pm.

Kuijper Klassiek Ferdinand Bolstraat 6 (De Pijp) ☏020/679 4634, ⊛www.kuijperklassiek .nl. Classical music and Royal Concertgebouw recordings on CD and DVD. Tues–Fri 10am–6pm, Sat 10am–5pm.

Phantasio 2e Tuindwarsstraat 53 (Jordaan and the Westerdok) ☏020/421 7110. Friendly shop with a good collection of mainstream alternative music, CDs only. Mon–Fri 11am–7pm (Thurs & Fri 8pm), Sat 10am–7pm, Sun noon–6pm.

The Sound of the Fifties Prinsengracht 669 (Grachtengordel south) ☏020/623 9745. Small place near the Leidsegracht with stacks of Fifties and Sixties pop and jazz. Mon 1–5pm & Tues–Sat noon–6pm.

South Miami Plaza Albert Cuypstraat 116 (De Pijp) ☏020/662 2817. Large hall specializing in Caribbean music, but plenty of other styles too. Good atmosphere.

Conscious Dreams Kokopelli Warmoestraat 12 (Old Centre) ☏020/421 7000, ⊛www .consciousdreams.nl. Everything you want to know about stimulants, with books, plants, aphrodisiacs etc. Very nicely set-up shop with Internet access and DJs on the weekend. Daily 11am–10pm.

Dreamlounge Kerkstraat 93 (Grachtengordel south) ☏020/626 6907, ⊛www .consciousdreams.nl. A small smart shop, with Internet facilities. Sun–Mon noon–6pm & Tues–Sat 11am–9pm.

The Magic Mushroom Gallery Spuistraat 249 (Old Centre) ☏020/427 5765; also at Singel 524 (Grachtengordel south). Mushroom mania.

When Nature Calls Keizersgracht 508 (Grachtengordel south) ☏020/330 0700, ⊛www .whennaturecalls.nl. Another shop selling cannabis products such as hemp chocolate and beer, plus seeds and, of course, mushrooms. At the corner of Leidsestraat. Mon–Sat 10am–10pm & Sun 11am–10pm.

Speciality shops

Perhaps more than any other city in Europe, Amsterdam is a great source of odd little shops devoted to one particular product or special interest. What follows is a selection of favourites.

3-D Holograms Grimburgwal 2 (Old Centre) ☏020/624 7225. All kinds of holographic art, big and small. Tues–Sat noon–6pm, Sun 1–5.30pm.

Absolute Danny O.Z. Achterburgwal 78 (Old Centre) ☏020/421 0915. A so-called "erotic lifestyle store", specializing in rubberwear, bondage gear, basques, etc.

Smart shops

Riding on the coat-tails of Amsterdam's liberal policy towards cannabis are a number of what have become known as "**smart shops**". Ostensibly established as outlets for "smart" drugs (memory enhancers, concentration aids, and so on), they do most of their business selling natural alternatives to hard drugs such as LSD, speed or ecstasy. These substitutes often have many or all of the effects of the real thing, but with greatly reduced health risks – and the added bonus of legality. A consistently popular alternative to LSD are psychotropic or "**magic**" **mushrooms**, which grow wild all over northern Europe, but when processed or dried are classified as hard drugs and thus illegal. Conscious Dreams (see above) was forced to fight a court case over its sale of magic mushrooms, but by reclassifying its business as a greengrocery it was permitted to continue its sale of fresh magic mushrooms (dried ones remain illegal). It also retains its role at the centre of a knowledgeable Amsterdam underground devoted to exploring altered states of consciousness.

Ajax Fan Shop Arena Boulevard 1–3. Official club shop selling the current strips and sportsgear, as well the usual hats and duvet covers. Mon–Sat 9.30am–6pm, last Sun in the month 10am–5pm, matchdays 10am until 30 minutes before kick-off. There's also an unofficial outlet at Kalverstraat 86 if you can't be bothered to schlep all the way out to the stadium.

Akkerman Kalverstraat 149 (Old Centre) ☎020/623 1649. Vast array of pens, inks and writing implements.

▽ Akkerman

Appenzeller Grimburgwal 3 (Old Centre) ☎020/616 6865. State-of-the-art designer jewellery, watches and spectacles. Tues–Sat 11am–5.30pm.

Condomerie Het Gulden Vlies Warmoesstraat 141 (Old Centre) ☎020/627 4174. Condoms of every shape, size and flavour imaginable. All in the best possible taste. Mon–Sat 11am–6pm.

Delftshop Rokin 44 ☎020/620 0000. If you love delftware, or are just searching for a present for someone you like a lot – real Delft isn't cheap! – then this is a very hand place to come. Other branches at Spiegelgacht 13 and Prinsengracht 440.

Coppenhagen Rozengracht 54 (Jordaan and the Westerdok) ☎020/624 3681. The only thing you'll find here is beads and beady accessories – including everything you need to make your own beady jewellery. Mon 1–5.30pm, Tues–Fri 10am–6pm, Sat 10am–5pm.

Demmenie Sports Marnixstraat 2 (Jordaan and the Westerdok) ☎020/624 3652, ⓦ www .demmeniesport.nl. Large sports shop spread over two floors, selling everything you could need for hiking, camping and wilderness survival. Mon 1–6pm, Tues–Fri 9.30am–6pm (Thurs 9pm) Sat 9.30am–5pm.

Peter Doeswijk Vijzelgracht 11 (Grachtengordel south) ☎020/420 3133, ⓦ www.peterdoeswijk .nl. Idiosyncratic, brightly–coloured, street–art style phones and toilet seats plus painted wooden canal houses in wobbly shapes – much, much better than the usual tourist stuff. Even better, the phones all work. Opening times vary.

Droog Design Staalstraat 7 (Old Centre) ☎020/523 50 50, ⓦ www.droogdesign.nl. Founded in 1993, Droog Design has made a serious contribution to the international reinvention of design. Some of their products, such as their milk bottle chandelier, have ended up in museum collections – this is the new location of their gallery and shop. Tues–Sat noon–6pm

Gamekeeper Hartenstraat 14 (Grachtengordel west) ☎020/638 1579. The place to go if you're into games. All kinds of "fantasy" games from Games Workshop to role-play games, collectible cards, backgammon, magic accessories etc. Mainly for adults. Mon noon–6pm, Tues–Fri 11am–7pm, Sat 10am–6pm & Sun noon–6pm.

Gerda's Runstraat 16 (Grachtengordel west) ☎020/624 2912. Amsterdam is full of flower shops, but this one is the most imaginative and sensual. Bouquets to melt the hardest of hearts. Mon–Fri 9am–6pm & Sat 9am–5pm.

P.G.C. Hajenius Rokin 92 (Old Centre) ☎020/623 7494. Old, established tobacconist selling its own and other brands of cigars, tobacco, smoking accessories, and every make of cigarette you can think of. There's also a room at the back where you can sit and smoke and have a coffee, view the amazing range of cigars, pipes and smoking accessories, and even leaf through a magazine or book from its library. Smoking heaven. Mon noon–6pm, Tues–Sat 9.30am–6pm, Thurs until 9pm, Sun noon–5pm.

The Head Shop Kloveniersburgwal 39 (Old Centre) ☎020/624 9061. Every dope-smoking accessory you could possibly need, along with assorted marijuana memorabilia. Mon–Sat 11am–6pm.

Hera Candles Overtoom 402 (Museum Quarter and Vondelpark) ☎020/616 2886. A wonderful little all-wood shop selling nothing but handmade candles of all shapes, sizes and scents. Tues–Fri 10am–6pm, Sat 11am–5pm.

Joe's Vliegerwinkel Nieuwe Hoogstraat 19 (Old Centre) ☎020/625 0139. Kites, frisbees, boomerangs, diabolos, yo-yos, juggling balls and clubs. Mon 1–6pm, Tue–Fri 11am–6pm, Sat 11am–5pm.

Kitsch Kitchen Rozengracht 8 (Jordaan and the Westerdok) ☎020/428 4969, ⓦwww .kitschkitchen.nl. Crammed full of chunky furniture, pots, bowls, spoons and other kitchen stuff in bright primary colours. Mon–Sat 10am–6pm.

▽ Kitsch Kitchen

't Klompenhuisje Nieuwe Hoogstraat 9a (Old Centre) ☎020/622 8100. Amsterdam's best and brightest array of clogs and kids' shoes. Mon–Sat 10am–6pm.

Kramer and Pontifex Reestraat 20 (Grachtengordel west) ☎020/626 5274. On one side of the shop, Mr Kramer repairs old broken dolls and teddies; on the other, Pontifex sells all kinds of candles, oils and incense. Mon–Fri 10am–6pm & Sat 10am–5pm.

Posthumus Sint Luciensteeg 23 (Old Centre) ☎020/625 5812. Posh stationery, cards and, best of all, a choice of hundreds of rubber stamps. By appointment to Her Majesty. Mon noon–5pm, Tues–Fri 9am–5pm, Sat 11am–5pm.

't Winkeltje Prinsengracht 228 (Grachtengordel south) ☎020/625 1352. Jumble of bargain–basement glassware and crockery, candle-

sticks, antique tin toys, kitsch souvenirs, old apothecaries' jars and flasks. Perfect for browsing. At Reestraat. Mon 1–5.30pm, Tues–Fri 10am–5.30pm & Sat 10am–5pm.

Witte Tandenwinkel Runstraat 5 (Grachtengordel west) ☎020/623 3443. The "White Teeth Shop" sells wacky toothbrushes and just about every dental hygiene accoutrement you could ever need and then some. Mon 1–6pm, Tues–Fri 10am–6pm & Sat 10am–5pm.

Ethnic shops

Baobab Elandsgracht 34 (Jordaan and the Westerdok) ☎020/626 8398. Textiles and ceramics from Indonesia and the Far East, plus a huge selection of well–priced silver jewellery. Mon–Sat 11am–6pm.

Fair Trade Shop Heiligeweg 45 ☎625 2245. Fair trade goods of all kinds – food products, household items, books and cards. Mon noon–6pm, Tues–Fri 10am–6pm, Thurs until 9pm, Sat 10am–5.30pm, Sun noon–5pm.

Santa Jet Prinsenstraat 7 (Grachtengordel west) ☎020/427 2070. Handmade Latin American items, from collectables to humorous knick-knacks, and plenty of religious icons, including hand–painted skulls. Mon–Fri 11am–6pm, Sat 10am–5pm & Sun noon–5pm.

Shalimar Utrechtsestraat 25 (Grachtengordel south) ☎020/639 2037. Tiny shop with a good selection of antique and modern Indian jewellery. Opening times vary – take pot luck or call ahead.

Tikal Hartenstraat 2a (Grachtengordel west) ☎020/623 2147. Colourful textiles and jewellery from Mexico and Guatemala. Mon 1–6pm, Tues–Fri 11am–6pm & Sat 11am–5.30pm

Tibet Winkel Spuistraat 185a (Old Centre) ☎020/420 4538. Books, music, jewellery and more, all made by Tibetan refugees in Nepal and India. The Tibet Support Group (☎020/623 7699) can give travel advice, information on Tibetan restaurants in Holland, and on anything else concerned with Tibet. Mon 1–6pm, Tues–Sat 10am–6pm, Sun noon–5pm.

New Age and natural remedies

Dela Rosa Staalstraat 10 (Old Centre) ☎020/421 1201. One of the better shops for vitamins and dietary supplements, with friendly, expert advice. Mon–Sat 11am–6pm.

Erica Centraal Station (Old Centre) ☎020/626 1842. Located in the unlikeliest of surroundings, this little shop is part of a chain selling a sizeable array of herbal remedies, teas, cosmetics and vitamins.

Himalaya Warmoesstraat 56 (Old Centre) ☎020/626 0899. Something of an oasis of calm in the midst of Warmoesstraat's porn shops, this cosy shop has a wide selection of books and magazines from around the world, with New Age music, tarot cards and bric-a-brac, as well as readings, a changing photo/art exhibit, and a marvellous café with a terrace and canal view out the back. Mon noon–6pm, Tues–Sat 10am–6pm, Thurs until 10pm, Sun noon–5.30pm.

Jacob Hooij Kloveniersburgwal 10–12 (Old Centre) ☎020/624 3041. In business at this address since 1778, and the shop and its stock are the same now as then. Homeopathic chemist with any amount of herbs and natural cosmetics, as well as a huge stock of *drop* (Dutch liquorice).

Kruiderij De Munt Vijzelstraat 1 (Grachtengordel south) ☎020/624 4533. A very wide range of herbal remedies, essential oils, teas and dietary supplements. Mon 1–6pm, Tues–Fri 11am–6pm & Sat 11am–5.30pm

De Roos P.C. Hooftstraat 183 (Museum Quarter and Vondelpark) ☎020/689 0081, ⓦwww.roos .nl. Delightful New Age centre, with a warm, intimate atmosphere. The bookshop has a wide selection of esoteric books, and the ground-floor café, with its own rambling garden, is the most peaceful in Amsterdam. A range of courses and workshops is available too, including daily open sessions in yoga and meditation.

Markets

Albert Cuypmarkt Albert Cuypstraat (see p.278) The city's principal general goods and food market, with some great bargains to be had – including slick fashionwear and shoes. Mon–Sat 9am–5pm.

Amstelveld Prinsengracht, near Utrechtsestraat (Grachtengordel south). Flowers and plants, but much less of a scrum than the Bloemenmarkt. Mon 10am–3pm.

Bloemenmarkt Singel, between Koningsplein and Muntplein (Grachtengordel south). Flowers and plants, ostensibly for tourists, but regularly frequented by locals. Bulbs for export (with health certificate). Some stalls open on Sunday as well. Mon–Sat 9am–5pm.

Boerenmarkt Noordermarkt, next to the Noorderkerk (Jordaan and the Westerdok). Organic farmers' market selling all kinds of organically grown produce, plus amazing fresh breads, exotic fungi, fresh herbs and homemade mustards. Sat 9am–3pm.

Kunstmarkt Spui (Old Centre) & Thorbeckeplein, south of Rembrandtplein (Grachtengordel south). Low-key but high-quality art market in two locations, with much lower prices than you'll find in the galleries; prints and occasional books as well. Neither operates during the winter. Sun 10am–3pm.

Lindengracht Lindengracht, south of Brouwersgracht (Jordaan and the Westerdok). Rowdy, raucous general household supplies market, a complete switch from the gentility of the neighbouring Boerenmarkt. Sat 8am–4pm.

Noordermarkt Noordermarkt, next to the Noorderkerk (Jordaan and the Westerdok). Junk lover's goldmine, with a general market on Mondays full of all kinds of bargains, tucked away beneath piles of useless rubbish. Get there early. There's also a farmers' produce market, Boerenmarkt (see above) and a bird market (Sat 8am–1pm). Main market Mon 9am–4pm, Sat 9am–4pm.

Waterlooplein Waterlooplein, behind the Stadhuis (Old Jewish Quarter and eastern docks). A real Amsterdam institution, and the city's best flea market by far. Sprawling and chaotic, it's the final resting place for many a pair of yellow corduroy flairs; but there are more wearable clothes to be found, and some wonderful antique/junk stalls to root through. Secondhand vinyl too. Mon–Sat 9am–5pm.

Westermarkt Westerstraat, from the Noorderkerk onwards (Jordaan and the Westerdok). Another general goods market, very popular with the Jordaan locals. Mon 9am–1pm.

▽ Albert Cutpmarkt

Gay and lesbian Amsterdam

n keeping with the Dutch reputation for tolerance, no other city in Europe accepts **gay people** as readily as Amsterdam, a liberalism that is displayed publicly at any of the gay events and festivals organized throughout the year: Amsterdam Pride is a huge occasion on the gay calendar as is Queen's Day and the many memorial days that take place around the **Homo Monument**. And, with the Dutch willingness to speak English, French and just about any other language, Amsterdam has become a magnet for the international gay scene – a city with a good network of advice centres, bars, clubs and cinemas. The COC (pronounced "say-oh-say"), the national gay and lesbian pressure group, will be celebrating its sixtieth birthday in 2006 – one of the longest-lived, and largest, groups of its kind in the world, and there are a number of smaller organizations representing the city's ethnic groups which also run regular workshops and events.

Homosexuality was decriminalized in the Netherlands as long ago as 1811; a century later – still sixty years ahead of the UK – the gay **age of consent** was reduced to 21, and in 1971 it was brought into line with that of heterosexuals at 16. The most recent legal development was in 2001, with the legalization of **same-sex marriages** with non-discriminatory adoption rights.

Gay couples have full legal rights, and it is maybe a mark of the level of acceptance of gay lifestyles in mainstream Dutch society that every year there is a party in Amsterdam for Holland's gay and lesbian civil servants. It also says much for the strength of the gay community that the arrival of **AIDS** was not accompanied by the homophobia seen in many other places. Rather than close down clubs and saunas, the city council funded education programmes, encouraged the use of condoms, and has generally conducted an open policy on the issue.

However, gay men in Amsterdam are much better catered for than **lesbians**. Although there is a sizeable lesbian community, there are no strictly women-only establishments in the city – even the *Saarein*, previously Amsterdam's solitary women-only café, has finally opened its doors to men. The lesbian scene is largely limited to a few women-only nights held in otherwise male or mixed clubs.

The city has four recognized gay areas: **Reguliersdwarsstraat** with its trendy bars and clubs is the best known and it attracts a young, lively and international crowd, while quieter **Kerkstraat** is populated as much by locals as visitors. The streets just north of **Rembrandtplein** and along the Amstel are a camp focus, as

△ *Gay & Night* magazine

well as being home to a number of rent-boy bars, while **Warmoesstraat**, in the heart of the Red Light District, is cruisey and mainly leather- and denim-oriented.

Same-sex couples holding hands and kissing in the streets are no more worthy of comment than straight couples. **Cruising** is generally tolerated in places where it's not likely to cause offence, and most bars and clubs have **darkrooms**, which are legally obliged to provide safe sex information and condoms.

If you want more information, get hold of a copy of the free and widely available visitor's **Amsterdam Gay Map**, published by the producers of the monthly magazine **Gay News**, both of which can be picked up from the COC (see below) or most bars and shops listed in this chapter. Their website ⓦwww.gayamsterdam .com is also a good resource for bar and club listings. Another free map is the **Columbia Fun Map**, produced by the *SAD-Schorerstichting* (see opposite), and available online at ⓦwww.gaymap.ws. You could also invest in a copy of *The Bent Guide To Amsterdam*, a small but practical and witty gay **guidebook** (in English) written by the volunteers of Pink Point (see below) and available from the bookshops listed on p.237. Among the many local gay **newspapers and magazines**, *Gay & Night* (ⓦwww.gay-night.nl), which appears monthly and costs €3.60 in newsagents (or free in a number of bars and shops) features interviews, news and film reviews. The fortnightly *Gay Krant* (€2.95) (ⓦwww.gaykrant.nl) has all the details you could conceivably need, including up-to-the-minute listings, though it is in Dutch only. You can also pick up flyers for parties and brochures and gay-orientated businesses such as clothes shops in most of the gay bars and businesses.

Resources and contacts

In addition to the organizations and centres listed below, two important sources of information on the gay and lesbian scenes are the **Gay and Lesbian Switchboard** (ⓉО20/623 6565; ⓦwww.switchboard.nl; daily 2–10pm), an English-speaking service which provides help and advice on all manner of things including where to go out in Amsterdam, and **MVS Radio** (ⓉО20/620 0247; ⓦwww.mvs.nl), Amsterdam's gay and lesbian radio station, which broadcasts Monday to Friday from 7pm to 8pm and Saturday & Sunday 6pm to 7pm on 106.8FM (or 88.1 via cable) – try and catch the English-language talk show *Alien*, at 6pm on Sunday.

COC Rozenstraat 14 (Jordaan and the Westerdok) ⓉО20/626 3087, ⓦwww.cocamsterdam .nl. Amsterdam branch of the national gay and lesbian organization, offering advice, contacts and social activities (office Mon, Tues, Thurs & Fri noon–5pm, Wed noon–8pm), plus a meeting point (Sat 1–5pm) and a large noticeboard. There's a general COC café (Wed & Thurs 8pm–midnight, Fri 8pm–3am) and a club, which is also the venue for more specific "themed" nights. One of the most popular women-only nights in Amsterdam, "Just Girls" (see p.234).

Gala Postbus 15815, 1001 NH Amsterdam ☎ 020/676 2317, ⓦ www.gala-amsterdam .nl. Organization responsible for Pink Point and the various Homomonument Festivals, including those on Queen's day and Liberation Day.

Homodok (The Documentation Centre for Lesbian and Gay Studies) Nieuwpoortkade 2a, 1055 RX Amsterdam ☎ 020/606 0712, ⓕ 020/606 0713, ⓦ www.ihlia.nl. A major archive of all forms of literature, as well as videos and photographs, relating to lesbian and gay studies, contemporary and historical. Prospective visitors should write several weeks ahead detailing areas of interest. See also the IIAV archive, p.255. Mon–Fri 10am–4pm.

Long Yang Club Holland PO Box 218, NL-3430 AE Nieuwegein ☎ 06/4538 8270, ⓦ www .longyangclubholland.nl. International organization for Asian gays, which holds regular parties and activities in Amsterdam, as well as publishing a bi-monthly magazine called *Oriental Express*. Meets every fourth Sunday, with an East/West Dance every second Sunday. Open to non-members (€4).

Pink Point Near to the Homomonument, Westermarkt (Jordaan and the Westerdok) ⓦ www

.pinkpoint.org. Daily noon–6pm. A free advice and information point run by a team of well-informed volunteers. Practical information about where to go and what to do in the city, including various flyers and brochures, as well as a range of souvenirs and T-shirts.

SAD Schorerstichting PC Hooftstraat 5 (Museum Quarter and Vondelpark) ☎ 020/662 4206, ⓦ www.sadschorer.nl. Gay and lesbian counselling centre offering professional and politically conscious advice on identity, sexuality and lifestyle (Mon–Fri 10am–4pm; July & Aug noon–4pm). Its clinic, held at the Municipal Health Department, provides STD examinations and treatment.

Sjalhomo ("Shalom-o") Postbus 2536, 1000 CM Amsterdam ☎ 023/531 2318, ⓦ www.sjalhomo .dds.nl. National organization for Jewish gays and lesbians.

Stichting Tijgertje Tijgertje 10521, 1001 EM Amsterdam ☎ 020/673 2458, ⓦ www.tijgertje.nl. Information on gay and lesbian sports clubs throughout Amsterdam.

Wild side Rozenstraat 14 (Jordaan and the Westerdok) ☎ 071/512 8632, ⓦ www.wildside .dds.nl. A lesbian S&M group which has regular open meetings, workshops and parties at the COC (see opposite page).

Accommodation

The city's **gay-friendly hotels** are reviewed below and, are marked on the colour maps at the back of the book. Prices are for the cheapest double in high season (see also p.163). There are no women-only hotels, although two unofficial, privately run bed-and-breakfasts – *Johanna's* (p.170) and *Liliane's Home* – cater for gay women, the latter exclusively so. *Quentin* (see p.169) is a particularly popular hotel with lesbians, though all the places listed below are lesbian-friendly. Note that it's illegal for a hotel to refuse entry to anyone on the grounds of sexual orientation.

Old Centre

Anco Oudezijds Voorburgwal 55 ☎ 020/624 1126, ⓦ www.ancohotel.nl; 10min walk from CS. Small and friendly hotel in the Red Light District, with a private bar catering exclusively to leather-wearing gay men. Three- and four-person dorms (€40) and studios with private bathroom and kitchenette Booking advised. (€135)

Centre Apartments Heintje Hoekssteeg 27; 5min walk from CS. ☎ 020/627 2503, ⓦ www .gayapartmentsamsterdam.com. Private self-catering studios and apartments for rent in the middle of the Old Centre. Higher

weekend rates; minimum three nights. From €97.50 for a studio, apartments from €107.50.

Stablemaster Warmoesstraat 23, ☎ 020/625 0148, ⓕ 020/638 9074. Small, exclusively male, gay hotel above a popular country and western bar in the heart of the Red Light action; the bar is known for its wild themed parties (see p.235). English-speaking staff. Doubles from €105.

Grachtengordel south

Aero Kerkstraat 45–49 ☎ 020/622 7728, ⓕ 020/638 8531. Tram #1, #2 or #5 to

Prinsengracht. Hotel linked to the *Camp Café* (see p.235), just off Leidsestraat. Eighteen modern rooms, most with shower. No single rooms. From €70.

Amistad Kerkstraat 42 ☎020/624 8074, ⒲www.amistad.nl. Tram #1, #2 or #5 to Koningsplein. Stylish and cosy gay hotel, conveniently located for the Kerkstraat area. Each room is equipped with soft lighting, and snug duvets, TV, fridge and a safe. Standard rooms come without shower, deluxe rooms have shower (and in some cases bathtub) and stereo (€135). Breakfast served 9am–1pm. (€85).

Golden Bear Kerkstraat 37 ☎020/624 4785, ⒲www.goldenbear.nl. Tram #1, #2 or #5 to Prinsengracht. Solid, well-managed budget option, with a good range of clean, comfortable rooms, some en suite. Booking essential. €70.

Greenwich Village Kerkstraat 25 ☎020/626 9746, ⒲www.greenwichvillage.nl. Tram #1, #2 or #5 to Prinsengracht. A well-kept, if slightly down-at-heel, two-star, gay-friendly hotel, situated next door to a karaoke bar. Rooms sleep from one to five people. Minimum three-night stay. Free pool in the downstairs bar. €40 per person.

Orfeo Leidsekruisstraat 14 ☎020/623 1347, ⒲www.hotelorfeo.com. Tram #1, #2 or #5 to Prinsengracht. Very pleasant gay and lesbian hotel linked to an Italian restaurant round the back of Leidseplein, with decent breakfasts served until 11am. You can opt for a cheaper room sharing a shower, but en-suite rooms are also available, as are some triples and quads. €75.

Waterfront Singel 458 ☎020/421 6621, ⒲www.waterfront.demon.nl. Tram #1, #2 or #5 to Koningsplein. Smart, value-for-money hotel with ten decent rooms on a major canal (you'll pay more for a canal view) close to the Flower Market, shopping and nightlife. Triples also available. En-suite doubles from €110.

The Old Jewish Quarter and the East

Liliane's Home Sarphatistraat 119 ☎020/627 4006. Metro Weesperplein. A privately run B&B for women only, Liliane runs the place herself, and doesn't have many rooms, so you'll need to call first. Plush singles (€50) as well as triples and quads available. She also rents out the second floor apartment for €100. Doubles from €80.

The Museum Quarter and Vondelpark

Sander Jacob Obrechtstraat 69 ☎020/662 7574, ⒲www.hotel-sander.nl. Tram #16 to Jacob Obrechtstraat. Right behind the Concertgebouw, a spacious, pleasant hotel with twenty en-suite rooms; welcoming to gay men and women, and everyone else too. Triples and quads available. Downstairs bar open to guests. En-suite doubles from €100.

Nightlife and entertainment

The main nightlife areas in the Old Centre and Grachtengordel are dotted with numerous **gay bars and clubs**. Some venues have both gay only and mixed gay/straight nights, as noted. Gay men should also check out posters and flyers for the regular Club Trash and Wasteland events, or get a copy of the monthly *SHARK* at the AUB at Leidseplein (see p.202). The Pink Point (see p.233), near the Homo Monument also has flyers and can provide good, reliable information about places to go in the city, as can the website ⒲www.nighttours.nl (in English), which features a guide to events, clubs and bars, as well as more general information on Amsterdam's gay scene. There are currently no clubs exclusively for lesbians, however lesbian-only nights are on the increase and we have also indicated which gay bars and clubs welcome women. At present, the most popular women–only night is "Just Girls" on Saturday at the COC. Further information on where to go for women in Amsterdam can be found from the Gay and Lesbian Switchboard (see p.232). All bars are marked on the colour maps.

The only **cinema** left that shows **gay films** on a regular basis is the Filmhuis Cavia which, in conjunction with De Balie (see p.214), hosts an annual event

in December called **De Roze Filmdagen** ("The Pink Film Days"; ⓦwww
.rozefilmdagen.nl), a mini-season of gay and lesbian movies. Call the Gay and
Lesbian Switchboard (see p.232) for details of gay movies showing around town,
or take a look at the AUB's *Uitlijst*.

Bars

Old Centre

Anco Oudezijds Voorburgwal 55. Late-night
hotel leather bar with a large darkroom.
Daily 9am–10pm.

Argos Warmoesstraat 95. Europe's oldest
leather bar, with two bars and a raunchy
cellar. Not for the faint-hearted. Mon–Thurs
& Sun 10pm–3am, Fri & Sat 10pm–4am.

Casa Maria Warmoesstraat 60. Mixed gay bar
in the heart of the Warmoesstraat scene.
Over-25s only. Mon–Thurs & Sun 11am–
1am, Fri & Sat 11am–3am.

Cuckoo's Nest Nieuwezijds Kolk 6. A cruisey
leather bar with a long reputation, this is
described as "the best place in town for
chance encounters". Vast and infamous
darkroom. Mon–Thurs & Sun 1pm–1am, Fri
& Sat 1pm–2am.

The Eagle Warmoesstraat 90. Long-established leather bar popular with men of all
ages. Gets very busy after 1am. Mon–Thurs
& Sun 10pm–4am, Fri & Sat 2pm–4am.

Le Shako's Gravelandseveer 2. Friendly bar in
a quiet street on the Amstel. Look out for
their monthly bear parties held on a Sunday,
for hairy or bearded men and their partners.
Mon–Thurs & Sun 10pm–3am, Fri & Sat
10pm–4am.

Stablemaster Warmoesstraat 23. A country
and western bar, well known for its regular
private Jack Off parties, also has a hotel
attached; English-speaking staff and a British following. Mon–Thurs & Sun 9am–1am,
Fri & Sat 9am–2am.

The Web St Jacobsstraat 6. Strict, but friendly
rubber, leather and denim bar with a dance
floor, darkrooms and a pool table. Mon–
Thurs & Sun 2pm–2am, Fri & Sat 2pm–3am.

Why Not Nieuwezijds Voorburgwal 28. Long-
standing, intimate bar with a porno cinema
and "boy's club" above. Terrace open in
summer. Live shows 10pm Thurs–Sat.
Mon–Thurs noon–1am, Fri & Sat noon–
2am.

Grachtengordel south

April Reguliersdwarsstraat 37. On the itinerary of almost every gay visitor to Amster-

dam. Lively and cosmopolitan, with a good
selection of foreign newspapers, cakes
and coffee, as well as three bars that offer
special 2-for-1 deals announced by flash-
ing lights and sirens. Small dance floor at
the back.

Arc Reguliersdwarsstraat 44. Trendy, mixed,
neon-lit club, with comfy couches and
friendly bar staff. Small fusion menu and
late-night dancing. Happy hour 5–7pm;
cocktails €5. Mon–Thurs & Sun 4pm–1am,
Fri & Sat 4pm–3am.

Camp Café Kerkstraat 45. Busy Dutch café
with a pleasant mix of friendly gay regulars
and foreign visitors. Daily 8am–1am.

Downtown Reguliersdwarsstraat 31. Popular
café that's a favourite with visitors as well as
locals. Relaxed and friendly, with inexpensive meals. Daily 11am–8pm.

Entre Nous Halvemaansteeg 14. Camp and
often outrageous small bar. Can be packed
at peak times, when everyone joins in the
singalongs. Mon–Thurs & Sun 8pm–3am,
Fri & Sat 8pm–4am.

Krokodil Amstelstraat 34. Amiable, noisy
bar close to the discos and clubs. Daily
4pm–2am.

Lellebel Utrechtsestraat 4. Small and popular
drag-show bar, with a lively and cheerful
atmosphere. Mon–Thurs & Sun 8pm–3am,
Fri & Sat 8pm–4am.

Mankind Weteringstraat 60. Quiet, non-scene,
traditional Dutch bar away from the usual
gay hangouts, with its own terrace beside
the canal attracting locals and visitors alike.
Inexpensive meals. Lovely in summer. Daily
noon–midnight.

Mix Café Amstel 50. Dutch *gezellig* bar, playing Top 40 and Europop. Mon–Thurs & Sun
8pm–3am, Fri & Sat 8pm–4am.

Montmartre de Paris Halvemaansteeg 17. A
convivial brown café, with the emphasis
on music and entertainment; voted best
gay bar by the readers of the *Gaykrant*.
Mon–Thurs & Sun 5pm –1am, Fri & Sat
5pm–3am. Happy hour 6–8pm.

Rouge Amstel 60. Welcoming bar, popular
with both tourists and locals. Mon, Thurs &
Sun 4pm–1am, Fri & Sat 2pm–3am. Closed
Tues & Wed.

De Spijker Kerkstraat 4. Leather and jeans bar showing porn movies. Pool table and upstairs darkroom. Happy hour 5–7pm. Women welcome. Open Mon–Thurs & Sun 1pm–1am, Fri & Sat 1pm–3am.

Vive la Vie Amstelstraat 7. Small, campy bar, patronized mostly, but not exclusively, by women and transvestites. Quiet during the week, it steams on the weekend.

Jordaan and the Westerdok

Saarein Elandsstraat 119. Notorious for years for its stringent women-only policy, *Saarein* has now opened its doors to men. Though some of the former glory of this café is gone, it's still a warm, relaxing place to take it easy, with a cheerful atmosphere. Also a useful starting point for contacts and information. Opens 5pm. Closed Mon.

Clubs

COC See p.232. Successful women-only disco and café for under-26s called "Just Girls", kicking off at 8pm every Saturday, with doors opening to all from 10pm onwards; disco till 4am. ClubCOC (for men and women) is pumping on Friday nights too, playing club classics and house from 11pm–4am; non-members €2.50. Every second Saturday is women over-30s disco from 10pm–4am.

Cockring Warmoesstraat 96 (Old Centre) ☎020/623 9604, ⓦwww.clubcockring.com. Currently Amsterdam's most popular – and very cruisey – gay men's disco with a small dance floor and bars on two levels. Strip shows Thurs, Sat & Sun. Also hosts Horsemen and Knights parties 3–7pm every third Saturday of the month. Get there early at the weekend to avoid queuing. Nightly 11pm–4am (Fri & Sat till 5am); entry Sat €5.

Exit Reguliersdwarsstraat 42 (Grachtengordel south) ☎020/625 8788, ⓦwww.discotheekexit .nl. A classic gay club in the centre of town, with four bars each playing different music from R&B to house to an upbeat, cruisey crowd. Predominantly male, though women

are admitted. 11pm–4am (Sat till 5am) Thurs–Sun. Entry Fri €5, Sat €7.

Getto Warmoestraat 51 (Old Centre) ☎020/421 5151, ⓦwww.getto.nl. Women-only night on Tuesdays at the *Getto* with plenty of music, plus a bar serving good food and cocktails. Tarot readings every Sunday. Daily 4pm–1am (Fri & Sat till 2am).

Habibi Ana Lange Leidsedwarsstraat 4 (Grachtengordel south) ☎020/620 1788, ⓦwww.habibiana.nl. A Mediterranean gay bar with a small dance floor, Arab music and belly dance shows every weekend. Mon–Thurs & Sun 7pm–1am, Fri & Sat 7pm–3am.

De Trut Bilderdijkstraat 165 (Jordaan and Westerdok). Housed in a former factory building, this popular squat venue holds a Sunday night, gay/lesbian only dance party: there's a large dance floor, cheap drinks, and a varied mix of music. Very popular with both men and women – the doors are closed at midnight and if you arrive after 11pm you may not get in. Gets very hot as it's in a basement. 11pm–3.30am; €1.50.

Vive la Vie Amstelstraat 7 (Grachtengordel south) ☎020/624 0114. Long-established café mainly for women, which shifts its tables at the weekend to make room for a dance space. Daily 4pm–1am (Fri & Sat till 3am).

Vrankrijk Spuistraat 216 ⓦwww.vrankrijk.org. Every Monday is "Blue Monday Queernight", in Amsterdam's most famous squat café playing funky, alternative music from 9pm–1am.

The Web St Jacobsstraat 6 (Old Centre) ☎020/623 6758. Somewhat underground leather and denim club that attracts an older crowd. Hosts Bear Hug nights every Saturday. Large upstairs darkroom. Mon–Thurs & Sun 2pm–2am, Fri & Sat 2pm–3am.

You II Amstel 178 (Grachtengordel south) ☎020/620 4754, ⓦwww.youii.nl. Amsterdam's first and long-awaited lesbian dance club, which first opened its doors in the summer of 1999. Men are in fact welcome, as long as they're under female supervision. Thurs 10pm–4am, Fri & Sat 10pm–5am; entry Sat €5.

Events

Three leading events in Amsterdam's gay calendar are **Remembrance Day** (May 4), the celebration of **Liberation Day** (May 5) and **World AIDS Day** (Dec 1). All of these prompt ceremonies and happenings around the Homomonument, the symbolic focus of the city's gay community (see p.231).

△ Amsterdam Pride

In addition, **Queen's Day** (April 30), when the whole town has a knees-up, sees gay parties and drag acts hosted throughout the city, culminating with The Pink Wester festival at the Homomonument. Other events include **Coming Out Day** (Sept 5), and **Leather Pride** (Ⓦwww.leatherpride.nl), held at the beginning of November with a number of organized fetish parties.

The first **Amsterdam Pride** (Ⓦwww.amsterdampride.nl) took place in 1996, organized by the Gay Business Association (Ⓣ020/620 8807), with street parties and performances, as well as a "Canal Pride" flotilla of boats parading along the Prinsengracht. If you're in the city in August, keep an eye out for parties at most bars and clubs around this annual event.

Finally, the old Amsterdam tradition of **Hartjesdag** ("Day of the Hearts"), which ceased to be observed just before World War II, was recently rediscovered and then popularized by a researcher in Gay and Lesbian Studies at the University of Amsterdam. At some time in August, it was once common for Amsterdammers to dress up in the clothes of the opposite sex and, although the majority of the population have hardly flocked to the cross-dressing banner, Amsterdam's nightclubs and bars, especially around the Zeedijk and Nieuwmarkt, often have themed drag weekends in August.

Shops and services

Bookstores

American Book Center Kalverstraat 185 (Old Centre) Ⓣ020/625 5537, Ⓦwww.abc.nl. Large general bookstore, with a fine gay and lesbian section. Mon–Sat 10am–8pm (Thurs till 9pm), Sun 11am–6.30pm.

Intermale Spuistraat 251 (Old Centre) Ⓣ020/625 0009, Ⓦwww.intermale.nl. Well-stocked gay bookshop, with a wide selection of English, French, German and Dutch literature, as well as cards, newspapers and magazines. They have a worldwide mail order service. Mon 11am–6pm, Tues–Sat 10am–6pm (Thurs till 9pm), Sun noon–5pm.

Vrolijk Paleisstraat 135 (Old Centre) Ⓣ020/623 5142, Ⓦwww.vrolijk.nu. "The largest gay and lesbian bookstore on the continent", with a vast stock of new and second-hand books and magazines, as well as music and videos. Mon 11am–6pm, Tues–Fri 10am–6pm (Thurs till 9pm), Sat 10am–5pm.

Xantippe Unlimited Prinsengracht 290 (Grachtengordel west) ☎020/623 5854, ⓦwww .xantippe.nl. Small, general bookstore with an impressively wide range of books and resources by, for and about women, including a large lesbian section. Mon 1–7pm, Tues–Fri 10am–7pm, Sat 10am–6pm, Sun noon–5pm.

Leather, rubber and sex shops

Adonis Warmoesstraat 92 (Old Centre) ☎020/627 2959, ⓦwww.adonis-4men.info. Longstanding gay video and DVD cinema; entry €7.50. Also stocks toys, books and videos. Mon–Thurs & Sun 10am–1am, Fri & Sat 10am–3am.

Black Body Lijnbaansgracht 292 (Grachtengordel south) ☎020/626 2553, ⓦwww .blackbody.nl. Huge selection of rubber and leather, plus toys and much more. Online ordering service available. Mon–Fri 10am–6.30pm, Sat 11am–6pm.

Bronx Kerkstraat 53–55 (Grachtengordel south) ☎020/623 1548, ⓦwww.bronx.nl. Strictly porno books, magazines and videos for men. Daily noon–midnight.

Demask Zeedijk 64 (Old Centre) ☎020/620 5603, ⓦwww.demask.com. Expensive rubber and leather fetish store for men and women. Mon–Fri 10am–7pm (Thurs till 9pm), Sun noon–5pm.

Drake's Damrak 61 (Old Centre) ☎020/627 9544. Gay porn cinema above a souvenir and sex shop. Entry €10, under-25s half price; free two unspecified months a year. Daily 9am–midnight.

Female and Partners Spuistraat 100 (Old Centre) ☎020/620 9152, ⓦwww.femaleandpartners .nl. Staffed by women, with an emphasis on products for women, this shop has a good selection of lingerie plus plain and erotic sex toys, with probably the best variety of vibrators in the city. Mon & Sun 1–6pm, Tues–Sat 11am–6pm (Thurs till 9pm).

Mantalk Reguliersdwarsstraat 39 (Grachtengordel south) ☎020/627 2525. Small shop with an enormous choice of quality underwear and T-shirts. Mon 1–6pm, Tues–Sat 10am–6pm (Thurs till 9pm).

Mister B Warmoesstraat 89 (Old Centre) ☎020/422 0003, ⓦwww.mrb.nl. Rubber and leather clothing and sex toys, spread over three floors. Piercing and tattoos by appointment. Mon–Fri 10am–6.30pm (Thurs till 9pm), Sat 11am–6pm, Sun 1–6pm.

RoB Amsterdam Weteringschans 253 (Grachtengordel south) ☎020/428 3000, ⓦwww.rob .nl. Top-quality made-to-measure leather wear, with a worldwide mail order service. Mon–Fri 11am–7pm (Thurs till 8pm), Sat 11am–6pm. Another smaller branch **RoB Accessories** (same hours plus Sun 1–6pm) is at Warmoesstraat 32 (Old Centre) ☎020/420 8548.

Robin and Rik Runstraat 30 (Grachtengordel west) ☎020/627 8924. Handmade leather clothes and accessories. Mon 2–6pm, Tues–Sat 11am–6.30pm.

Stout Berenstraat 9 (Grachtengordel west) ☎020/620 1676 ⓦwww.stoutinternational .com. A wide range of designer underwear and erotica for women in a smart environment and with helpful (female) staff. Mon–Fri noon–7pm, Sat 11am–6pm, Sun 11am–5pm.

Saunas, beauty and fitness

Cybersalon Gravenstraat 22 ☎020/330 0662, ⓦwww.cyberhairsalon.nl. Gay-friendly salon offering hair, beauty and a solarium, all under one white, stylish roof. Mon–Wed & Fri 9.30am–7pm, Thurs 9.30am–8pm, Sat 9.30pm–5.30pm, Sun 12.30–6.30pm (hair) & 10am–6pm (beauty).

Sauna Damrak Damrak 54 (Old Centre) ☎020/622 6012. Centrally located gay men's sauna; €13.50, including towels. You can also get a private sauna for two for €33 per hour; towels extra. Mon–Fri 10am–11pm, Sat & Sun noon–8pm.

Splash Looiersgracht 26 (Jordaan and the Westerdok) ☎020/624 8404. Gay-friendly gym. Daily 7am–midnight. See p.246.

Thermos Day Sauna Raamstraat 33 (Jordaan and the Westerdok) ☎020/623 9158 ⓦwww .thermos.nl. Modern gay men's sauna, with steam room, swimming pool, cinema, and café and bar spread out over five floors. Mon–Fri noon–11pm, Sat & Sun 11am–10pm; day pass €18.

Thermos Night Sauna Kerkstraat 58–60 (Grachtengordel south) ☎020/623 4936 ⓦwww .thermos.nl. Much the same facilities as the day sauna, with the addition of a Jacuzzi and dark steam room. Cruisey atmosphere. Nightly 11pm–8am (Sat till 10am); night pass €18.

Kids' Amsterdam

W ith its canals, tiny cobbled alleys and – expecially – trams, Amsterdam in itself can be entertaining enough for some kids. There's also a multitude of attractions specifically aimed at children, ranging from circuses, puppet theatres and urban farms to one of the best zoos in Europe, with a planetarium attached, as well as plenty of opportunities for play – practically all the city's parks and most patches of green have some form of playground, and the play area in the Vondelpark is heaven for kids and parents alike.

You'll find that most places are pretty child-friendly. If museums don't allow prams then they provide snugglies to carry small children in; most restaurants have highchairs and special children's menus (though they're not always that great); and bars don't seem to mind accompanied kids, as long as they're well under control. In short, it's rare that having a small child in your care will close doors to you.

Some hotels, however, don't welcome young children (they'll make this clear when you book), but many of those that do also provide a **babyminding** service. If yours doesn't, try contacting **Oppascentrale Kriterion** (℡020/624 5848, ⓦwww.kriterionoppas.org; 4.30–8pm), a long-established agency with a good reputation.

Parks, playgrounds and farms

The city's most central park, the leafy and lawned **Vondelpark** (ⓦwww .vondelpark.nl), has an excellent playground, as well as sandpits, paddling pools, ducks and a couple of cafés where you can take a break. *De Vondeltuin*, a pancake house on the Amstelveen side of the park, rents out skates and is perfectly situated opposite the playground – see p.185. During the summer there's always some free entertainment put on for kids – mime, puppets, acrobats and the like.

Most other city parks offer something to keep children entertained, the best being the **Gaasperpark**, outside the centre (metro stop Gaasperplas; buses #59, #60, #174), which has a play area and paddling pools. In the **Amsterdamse Bos** (ⓦwww.amsterdamsebos.nl; see p.134) you'll find playgrounds, lakes, and a nature reserve with bison and sheep, and you can also rent canoes and pedaloes to explore the waterways, or visit the **Geitenhouderij Ridammerhoeve** (℡020/645 5034, ⓦwww. geitenhouderij.nl; March–Oct daily except Tues 10am–5pm; Nov–Feb also closed Mon), an entertaining mini-farm with a herd of goats and their kids. The new visitors' centre near the Bosbaan entrance has a kids' area and exhibitions about the park.

One area where Amsterdammers fall flat on their face is in keeping **dog shit** off the streets and parks. They just don't seem able to do it, and the stuff is a major hazard, especially for kids. Although there are teams of street-cleaners armed with high-power hoses to regularly blast it off the pavement, wait another hour or two and there'll be more to replace it. Any patch of green space is obviously susceptible too, and unless an area is marked as being dog-free, you'd do well to keep one eye on your offspring and the other on your next step.

There are also plenty of **urban farms** dotted around the city – look in the phone book under *Kinderboerderij* for a full list, but one of the best is the **Artis Zoo Children's Farm**, which can easily be visited as part of an Artis day out; see below for details of the zoo itself.

Activities

For older children, a good introduction to Amsterdam might be one of the **canal trips** that start from Centraal Station or Damrak. Much more fun, though, is a ride on a **canal bike**. This can get tiring, but jetties where boats can be picked up and dropped off are numerous, and it's quite safe; see p.32 for details. If your kids enjoy being on the water, you could also take them on a **free ferry ride** to Amsterdam North (only 5–10min away). The best ferry to take is the *IJveer 51*, a small tug-like craft with a partly exposed deck, which leaves every 10min or so from Pier 8 behind Centraal Station (daily 24hr). On the other side, you can either come straight back, or walk a few hundred metres west along the riverfront and take the larger *IJveer 50* back to Centraal Station. For more details on the city's **canal cruises and bus tours**, see p.33.

For a panoramic **view** of the city, try a trek up the **tower** of the Westerkerk (summer only; see p.71).

It's possible to take the kids along when you're **cycling** around the city, by renting either a bike with a child seat attached, or a tandem, depending on the size of the child. Bike City at Bloemgracht 70 (℡020/626 3721) rents both types and gives friendly advice too.

In the winter, there's **ice skating** at the Sporthal Jaap Eden (see p.247), which has indoor and outdoor rinks, open at different times. If the canals are frozen and you don't have any skates, just teeter along on the ice with everybody else. Alternatively you could go **bowling**, the centre near the RAI complex has 18 lanes and a café (see p.244).

The best **swimming pool** for kids is the indoor, tropical-style Mirandabad, De Mirandalaan 9 (℡020/546 4444; tram #25), which has all sorts of gimmicks such as wave machines, slides and whirlpools; there's also a separate toddlers' pool, and every Sunday (9am–4pm) is family day (children aged 1–10). In summer, the most popular outdoor pool is in the Flevopark; for details of this and other outdoor pools, see p.248.

Finally, **TunFun** (Mr Visserplein 7 ℡020/689 4300, ⓦ www.tunfun.nl; tram #9 or #14) is a large underground playground, near the Portuguese Synagogue, for children aged 1 to 12. Activities range from parties, films, gymnastics and football, and there's lots of equipment to clamber into, under and over. It's open daily from 10am to 7pm, and entry is adult accompanied and costs €7.50 for 1–12-year-olds, free for under-1s.

The zoo and museums

A trip to the **Artis Zoo** is one of the best days out in the city. The ticket includes entry to the zoo and its gardens, the Zoological Museum, the Geological Museum, the Aquarium and the Planetarium. You can also combine an Artis day out with a canal cruise: the Artis Express runs daily 10am–5.30pm every 30min between Centraal Station and the zoo, including a half-hour detour through the city on the return journey (return €19 including zoo entry, 3- to 9-year-olds €16.75; information on ☎020/530 1090).

Artis Zoo Plantage Kerklaan 38–40 (Old Jewish Quarter and the eastern docks; metro Waterplein, tram #6, #9 or #14) ☎020/523 3400. Opened in 1838, this is the oldest zoo in the country, and it's now one of the city's top tourist attractions, though thankfully its layout and refreshing lack of bars and cages mean that it never feels overcrowded. The huge aquariums are one of its main features. In addition to the usual lions, monkeys and creepy-crawlies there is also a Children's Farm where kids can come nose-to-nose with sheep, calves, goats, etc. Feeding times – always popular – are as follows: 11am birds of prey; 11.30am and 3.45pm seals and sea lions; 2pm pelicans; 2.30pm crocodiles (Sun only); 3pm lions and tigers (not Fri); 3.30pm penguins. The on-site Planetarium has five or six shows daily, all in Dutch – you can pick up a leaflet with an English translation from the desk. An English guidebook to the whole complex costs €2.50. No dogs. Daily: April–Oct 9am–6pm; Oct–March 9am–5pm. Adults €14.50, 3- to 9-year-olds €11; during September admission is reduced by thirty percent.

Madame Tussaud's Dam 20 (Old Centre) ☎020/522 1010, ⊛ www.madame-tussauds .nl. Large waxworks collection with the usual smattering of famous people and rock stars, plus some Amsterdam peasants and merchants thrown in for local colour. Hardly the high point of anyone's trip to the city, but there are parts that might interest teenagers such as the Pop Idols Experience or Models Zone. Daily 10.30am–6.30pm. Adults €23; 5- to 15-year-olds €17.50, over-65s €20; family tickets available.

NEMO Oosterdok 2 ☎020/531 3233, ⊛ www .e-nemo.nl (Old Jewish Quarter and eastern docks; bus #22 to Kadijksplein). A 10min walk from CS, the whopping great green building that marks the entrance to the IJ tunnel is home to NEMO, a large, three-floor science and technology centre, whose interactive exhibits are geared up for children. The first

▽ Artis Zoo

deck is devoted to "Fenomenen" (Phenomena), housing displays on light, sound and static energy, while deck two deals with technology and looks at the properties of metal and water treatment, with a lab where visitors can make their own key ring or purify tap water. Other exhibits explore the human mind. Labelling is in Dutch and English. Tues–Sun 10am–5pm, Mon 10am–5pm July, Aug & school hols). €11, under-4s free.

Tropenmuseum Junior In the Tropenmuseum, Linnaeusstraat 2 (Amsterdam Oost; tram #9, #10 or #14) ☎020/568 8233, ⊛ www .tropenmuseumjunior.nl. Designed especially for children between the ages of 6 and 12, the museum's aim is to promote international understanding through exhibitions on other cultures. It's nowhere near as dry as it sounds, and although the show is in

Dutch only, this is more than compensated for by the lively exhibits, which are expertly presented, incorporating art and music and dance performances, all designed to fascinate children (which they do). There are lots of things for kids to get their hands on and exhibits tend to have a two-year run. Shows Sat, Sun & school hols 3–4.30pm, plus Sun 12.30–2pm; call to reserve. Adults €7.50, children (under 12s) €5.75.

Theatres, circuses and funfairs

A number of **theatres** put on inexpensive (around €2–3) entertainment for children most afternoons. Furthermore, a fair proportion get around the (English) language problem by being **mime**- or **puppet**-based: check the children's section ("Jeugdagenda") of the monthly *Uitkrant* (see p.202), and look for the words *mimegroep* and *poppentheater*. Public holidays and the summer season bring touring **circuses** and the occasional mobile **funfair** (*kermis*) to the city, the latter usually setting up on Dam square and thus hard to miss. Lastly, check out the **festivals** listings in Chapter Fifteen; many of them, such as the Queen's Birthday celebrations, can be enjoyable for kids.

Circustheater Elleboog Passeerdersgracht 32 **(Jordaan and the Westerdok)** ☎020/623 5326, ✉info@elleboog.nl. A club running regular courses for children aged 6 to 12 on how to juggle, tightrope walk, unicycle and do conjuring tricks. Half-day workshops also available for around €10 during school holidays. Students also put on shows at various venues around the city. Phone or email for full details of times and prices.
Deridas Hobbemakade 68 **(Museum Quarter and Vondelpark)** ☎020/662 1588. Excellent weekly puppet theatre, wonderful for the under-6s.

The shows are every Saturday at 3pm (4- to 12-year-olds) and Sunday at 11am & noon (2- to 6-year-olds). Also the first Friday of the month 10.30am (2- to 6-year-olds) & 11.30am (4- to 9-year-olds). Shows from €2.50. Booking essential.
De Krakeling Nieuwe Passeerdersstraat 1 **(Jordaan and the Westerdok)** ☎020/624 5123, ⊛www.krakeling.nl. Permanent children's theatre, with shows for youngsters up to the age of 18. The emphasis is often on full-scale audience participation. Phone for a schedule.

Restaurants

KinderKookKafé Vondelpark 6 **(Museum Quarter and Vondelpark)** ☎020/625 3257, ⓦwww .kinderkookkafe.nl. A restaurant run entirely by children aged 6- to 12-years, who cook, waiter and dishwash (though there are adult staff on hand). The food is simple but well done, and the whole experience is worth it just for the novelty. Mon–Fri 10am–3pm for brunch. Parties Wed–Sun tea (6yrs+) 12.30pm, dinner (8yrs+) 3.30pm; booking essential. Children are expected to bring 2 guests each. Adults €10, 6- to 12-year-olds €5 (€10 if cooking), under-6s €2.50.
The Pancake Bakery Prinsengracht 191 **(Grachtengordel west)** ☎020/625 1333. Well-known busy pancake and omelette house that caters especially well for children. Delicious pancakes, and kids are kept entertained at the table with pens and paper and free novelty toys. Children's pancakes

start at around €4.90 with toy, adults' pancakes start from €4.75 – no toy. Mon–Fri noon–9.30pm.

▽ KinderKookKafé

Shops

Azzurro Kids P.C. Hooftstraat 122 (Museum Quarter and Vondelpark) ☎020/673 0457, ⓦwww.azzurrokids.nl. Perhaps the city's chicest kids' clothes store, stocking labels such as Diesel, Replay, Armani and Tommy Hilfiger. Mon 1–6pm, Tues–Sat 10am–6pm, Sun noon–5pm.

De Beestenwinkel Staalstraat 11 (Old Centre) ☎020/623 1805, ⓦwww.beestenwinkel.nl. Stuffed toy animals, in all shapes and sizes. Mon noon–6pm, Tues–Fri 10am–6pm, Sat 10am–5.30pm, Sun noon–5.30pm.

De Bijenkorf Dam 1 (Old Centre) ☎020/552 1700. This department store has one of the best (and most reasonably priced) toy sections in town. Mon 11am–7pm, Tues & Wed 9.30am–7pm, Thurs & Fri 9.30am–9pm, Sat 9.30am–6pm, Sun noon–6pm.

Broer & Zus Rozengracht 104 (Jordaan and the Westerdok) ☎020/422 9002, ⓦwww .broerenzus.nl. Quality clothes and gifts with a funky twist for babies and toddlers. The range includes T-shirts with logos, cute bags and bright knitwear. Mon noon–6pm, Tues–Fri 10.30am–6pm, Sat 10am–6pm.

Carla C Leliegracht 42 (Grachtengordel west) ☎020/620 6020, ⓦwww.carla-c.com. Fashionable and stylish designer maternity wear, which also has an outlet in London.

De Geboortewinkel Bosboom Toussaintstraat 22 (Museum Quarter and Vondelpark) ☎020/683 1806, ⓦwww.degeboortewinkel.nl. Specialists in all kinds of stuff for new or expectant parents, from quality clothes to prams and bedding.

Intertoys Heiligeweg 26 (Old Centre) ☎020/638 3356, ⓦwww.intertoys.nl. Amsterdam's largest toy shop, with branches throughout the city. Mon 11am–6pm, Tues–Fri 9.30am–6pm, Sat 9.30am–5.30pm, Sun noon–5pm.

De Kinderbrillenwinkel Nieuwezijds Voorburgwal 129–131 (Old Centre) ☎020/626 4091, ⓦwww.kinderbrillenwinkel.com. Shop specializing in spectacles for children with a selection of stylish frames for teenagers available next door at Marcel Barlag Visuals. Wed–Fri 11am–6pm, Sat 11am–5pm.

Kleine Nicolaas Cornelis Schuytstraat 19 (Oud Zuid) ☎020/676 9661. Good selection of handmade dolls and wooden toys. Mon–Fri 10am–6pm, Sat 10am–5pm.

Tinkerbell Spiegelgracht 10 (Grachtengordel south) ☎020/625 8830, ⓦwww.tinkerbelltoys .nl. A wonderful shop full of old-fashioned toys, mobiles, models and kids' books, with everything beautifully gift-wrapped. Mon 1–6pm, Tues–Sat 10am–6pm.

⑬

KIDS' AMSTERDAM | Shops

Sports and activities

Most visitors to Amsterdam tend to confine their exercise to walking around the major sights, but if you do get the urge to stretch your muscles, there's a wide range of sports to enjoy. In winter, if it's cold enough, skating on the frozen waterways is the most popular and enjoyable activity; other winter sports are mostly based in private, health or sports clubs, to which you can usually get a day pass, though many are well outside the city centre.

The chief **spectator sport** is football. Amsterdam is home to the legendary Ajax (pronounced "eye-axe") who play in the ArenA stadium out in the suburbs – though you'll be hard pressed to get a ticket. Less mainstream offerings include Holland's own *korfbal* and the weird spectacle of pole sitting. For details on all sporting activities in the city, call the sport infoline ☎020/530 6870.

Baseball

The local team is the **Amsterdam Pirates**, based at Sportpark Jan van Galenstraat (☎020/616 2151; tram #17, then bus #19). Matches take place on Saturday and Sunday afternoons in the summer, and cost €3.75. The Pirates are in the top baseball division. To **play**, you need only wander into the Vondelpark on any summer afternoon – impromptu baseball games are commonplace.

Beaches

The Netherlands has some great **beaches**, although the weather is unreliable and the North Sea is pretty murky and often littered with stray jellyfish. For swimming or sunbathing, the nearest resort is Zandvoort (see p.148), a short train ride from Amsterdam. Although the beach here is fine – it's a long strip of golden sand – Zandvoort is a large and rather untidy place and there are much more appealing places further afield near Haarlem (see pp.148–149).

Bowling

The closest bowling alley to the city centre is Knijn Bowling Centre, Scheldeplein 3, opposite the RAI complex (☎020/664 2211; Mon–Fri 10am–midnight, Sat noon–1am, Sun noon–10pm; tram #25), with eighteen lanes and a bar. Lanes cost between €16.20 and €25 per hour, depending on when you go,

with a maximum of six people per lane. Reservations recommended. Fridays
and Saturdays have "twilight bowling" from 11pm, accompanied by a DJ playing club music.

Chess and draughts

There are two **cafés** in Amsterdam where chess and draughts are played to the
exclusion of (almost) everything else: *Gambit* at Bloemgracht 20 where boards
are laid out until midnight, and *Het Hok* at Lange Leidsedwarsstraat 134 (see
p.183). There's a small charge for a board. In addition, a number of cafés may
have a board behind the bar if you ask – for instance, *The Jolly Joker* at Nieuw-
market 4A allows customers to play for free.

Football

It's a mark of the dominance of Amsterdam's **Ajax**, Rotterdam's **Feyenoord**
and Eindhoven's **PSV** that most foreigners would be hard pushed to name any
other Dutch football teams. More generally familiar perhaps is the Dutch style
of play – based on secure passing with sudden, decisive breaks – which has made
Dutch players highly sought-after all over Europe. Nevertheless, with the building of Ajax's extravagant all-seater ArenA stadium in the suburbs of Amsterdam
(see p.138), it's actually become more than a little difficult to get to see Ajax
play. You can't buy a ticket without a "club card", and although these only cost
€6 for two years, you must apply in advance (☏020/3111 444) and wait up
to five weeks for your application to be processed. Having done all that, ticket
prices are between €12 and €40 – and it's more or less the same situation for
Feyenoord and PSV, whose grounds are both within easy striking distance of
Amsterdam by public transport. Tickets for all matches can be bought online
at ⊛www.ticketbox.nl. The football season runs from September to May, and
matches are generally on Sunday at 12.30pm or 2.30pm, with occasional games
at 8pm on Wednesday. Your best bet is to catch a game on screen in a bar. Try
the *The Globe* hostel at Oudezijds Voorburgwal 3.

Ajax Amsterdam ArenA, Bijlmer ☏020/311
1444, ⊛www.ajax.nl. Metro Bijlmer.
Feyenoord Olympiaweg 50, Rotterdam
☏010/292 3888, ⊛www.feyenoord.nl. Stadion
Rotterdam or Rotterdam CS then tram #23.

PSV Eindhoven Frederiklaan 10a, Eindhoven
☏040/250 5505, ⊛www.psv.nl. Eindhoven CS
then bus #16 or #17 to Mathildelaan

Gyms, saunas, yoga and flotation

Dancestreet 1e Rozendwarsstraat 10 (Jordaan
and the Westerdok) ☏020/489 7676, ⊛www
.dancestreet.net. Dance and yoga centre
offering a wide range of classes from contemporary to tango, for all levels; also offers
various forms of yoga, as well as Pilates
and Tai Chi. Classes from €6. Sauna and
massage available. Café overlooking the
main studio. Mon–Fri 9am–10pm, Sat &
Sun 9am–6pm.

Deco Herengracht 115 (Grachtengordel west)
☏020/623 8215. Built in 1920, this is definitely in the running for Amsterdam's most
stylish sauna and steam bath, with a magnificent Art Deco interior and a small, but
pleasant café. A great place to hang out
for the day without a stitch on. Highly recommended. Entry costs €14.50. Mon–Sat
noon–11pm, Sun 1–6pm.

Eastern Bathhouse Hammam Zaanstraat 88 (Near Westerpark bus #22) ☏020/681 4818. A unique and wonderful institution, for women only. Comprises hot and cold rooms and top-to-toe washing; other treatments such as full body scrub and massage also available. Emerge feeling cleaner and more alive than you ever thought possible. Last admission 2.5hr before closing. Tues–Fri noon–10pm, Sat & Sun noon–8pm; closed Aug. Day pass €11.

Garden Gym Jodenbreestraat 158 (Old Jewish Quarter and the eastern docks) ☏020/626 8772, ⓦwww.thegarden.nl. Weight-training and dance-workout studio, with saunas, solarium, and massage. Mainly, but not exclusively, for women. A sauna costs €11; a day pass for all activities €12.50. Mon, Wed & Fri 9am–11pm, Tues noon–11pm, Thurs noon–10pm, Sat 9am–4pm, Sun 9am–5pm.

Koan Float Herengracht 321 (Grachtengordel west) ☏020/555 0333, ⓦwww.koan-float.com. Currently the only flotation centre in Amsterdam. There are three lockable individual floating cabins, each with its own shower; once you're inside, lights, music and clothing are optional. Advance reservations are essential. Current charges are €30 per 45min or €37.50 for an hour, and there are discounts for return visits. The centre also offers massage. Towels and bathrobes are provided. Daily 9.30am–11pm.

Splash Looiersgracht 26 (Jordaan and the Westerdok) ☏020/624 8404, ⓦwww.thehealthupclub.com. Very popular hi-tech fitness centre with sauna, tanning salon and Turkish bath. A range of daily aerobic classes from €9 for non-members. Day pass €16 including towel and a drink; week's pass €40. Daily 7am–midnight.

Horse riding

Amsterdamse Manege Nieuwe Kalfjeslaan, Amstelveen (Outer districts; bus #63 or #74) ☏020/643 1342. The place for a ride in the Amsterdamse Bos – but only with supervision. An hour's lesson costs €18.50 for adults and €15 for children, with free hire of boots and a riding hat. You must reserve ahead. English-speaking class Sun at noon.

Hollandsche Manege Vondelstraat 140 (Museum Quarter and Vondelpark) ☏020/618 0942, ⓦwww.dehollandschemanege.nl. Stables built in 1882 in neo-Renaissance style on the rim of the Vondelpark, offering classes in Dutch only. The upstairs bar and café has a viewing area overlooking the indoor school. A lesson costs €18.50 for adults, €15.50 for 11- to 17-year-olds, and €13.50 for under-11s. You will need your own boots.

Ice skating

Whenever the city's canals and waterways freeze over, local **skaters** are spoiled for choice with almost every stretch of water utilized, providing an exhilarating way to whizz round the city – much more fun than a rink. Surprisingly, canal cruises continue even when the ice is solid, with the boats crunching their way up and down the Prinsengracht, but they leave the Keizersgracht well alone – to be occupied by bundled-up Amsterdammers, who take to the ice in droves. Most Amsterdammers have their own skates, and there are surprisingly few places where you can **rent** a pair. **Buying** a pair from a department store or sports shop will cost close to €100; one option is to look out for a second-hand pair often advertised on notice boards in bars.

Before you venture out on the ice, however, take note of a few **safety points**:

• If no one's on the ice, don't try skating – locals have a better idea of its thickness.
• To gain confidence, start off on the smaller ponds in the Vondelpark.
• Be careful under bridges, where the ice takes longest to freeze.
• If the ice gives way and you find yourself underneath, head for the darkest spot you can see in the ice above – that's the hole.

△ In-line skating, Vondelpark

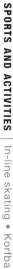

Probably the easiest and safest option is to head for **Jaap Eden**, Radioweg 64 (☎020/694 9652; €4.90; tram #9), a large ice-skating complex, to the east of the city centre, with indoor and outdoor rinks. You can rent skates for €5 from Waterman Sport next door (☎020/694 9884), but you can only use them at Jaap Eden, and you must leave your passport or driving licence as a deposit. Outdoor rink: Oct–March Mon, Wed & Fri 8am–4pm & 9–11pm (closed Fri evening), Sat 2–4pm, Sun 11am–4pm; indoor rink: daily, hours vary, phone for details; Sat 9–11pm "disco skate".

One of the great events in Holland's sporting calendar is the annual **Elfst-edentocht**, a race across eleven towns and 200km of frozen waterways in Fries-land, in the north of the Netherlands (see p.249). If you're around in January and the ice is good, you'll hear talk of little else.

In-line skating

If you're equipped with **skates**, the parks have plenty of smooth cycle tracks to let loose on or there's also the free Friday Night Skate (ⓦ www.fridaynightskate. nl), a fifteen-kilometre tour around Amsterdam, which takes place – weather permitting – every week from 8.30pm at the Roemer Visscherstraat entrance of the Vondelpark. For the more experienced skater there is a free public ramp at the northeastern edge of Museumplein. One place to **rent** skates and gear is *De Vondeltuin* at the Amstelveen entrance in the Vondelpark (see p.185). If you're renting to skate around town, take care not to get stuck in the tram-tracks.

Korfbal

This is a home-grown sport, cobbled together from netball, basketball and volleyball, and played with mixed teams and a high basket. To watch a game,

Amsterdam's team, **Blauw Wit**_(ⓦ www.akcblauw-wit.nl) play at the Sportpark Joos Banckersweg, off Jan van Galenstraat (ⓣ020/616 0894; east of the centre; tram #12), on Sunday, usually around 2.30pm, from September to June.

Pole sitting

Every year in July or early August, there's the chance to witness the offbeat spectator sport of pole sitting. In Noorderwijkerhout, just north of Scheveningen on the coast near The Hague, there's a **pole-sitting marathon** that lasts about five days. Although hardly a dynamic sport, it generates a fair amount of excitement as some fifteen brave souls sit it out on poles perched in the North Sea. The last one left is the winner.

Snooker and carambole

There are plenty of bars and cafés across the city where you can find a game of **pool**, although you will have go to a hall to play **snooker**. A popular local variation on billiards (*biljart*) is **carambole**, played on a table without pockets. You score by making cannons – striking the white and red ball of your opponent in a single stroke, and the skill of some of the locals, often spinning the ball through impossible angles, is unbelievable in a misspent sort of way. You'll find tables in a number of cafés, and get plenty of advice on how to play if you so much as look at a ball.

Snooker and Pool Centre Bavaria Van Ostadestraat 97 (Oud Zuid; tram #25). The first, third and fourth floors comprise the pool centre (Mon–Thurs 2pm–1am, Fri, Sat & Sun 2pm–2am; ⓣ020/676 7903), with 26 tables costing a flat rate of €7.50 per hour. The second floor is the snooker centre (Mon–Fri 1pm–1am, Sat & Sun 1pm–2am; ⓣ020/676 4059), which has seven tables at €8 per hour. There's also one carambole table, charged at €7.50 per hour.

Snooker Centre Rokin 28 (Old Centre) ⓣ020/620 4974, ⓦ www.snookerrokin.nl. Nine snooker tables and thirteen pool tables at €9 per hour, plus €10 deposit. Mon–Thurs & Sun 11am–1am, Fri & Sat 11am–3am.
Snooker Centre de Keizer Keizersgracht 256 (Grachtengordel west) ⓣ020/623 1586. Eight high-quality tables in a seventeenth-century canal house. Both snooker and pool cost €8 per hour. Mon–Fri 6pm–1am, Sat & Sun 1pm–1am.

Swimming pools

Flevoparkbad Zeeburgerdijk 630 (Amsterdam Oost; tram #14.) ⓣ020/692 5030. The best outdoor pool in the city; gets very busy on sunny days. May to early Sept.
Jan van Galenbad Jan van Galenstraat 315 (Amsterdam West; metro Jan van Galenbad) ⓣ020/612 8001. Outdoor pool in the west of the city. May–Sept.
De Mirandabad De Mirandalaan 9 (Nieuwe Zuid; tram #25) ⓣ020/546 4444, ⓦ www .mirandabad.nl. Superbly equipped swimming centre (outdoor and indoor pools),

with wave machine, whirlpools and slides. You should call before you set out, since certain times are set aside for small children, family groups, etc. Admission €3.25.
Zuiderbad Hobbemastraat 26 (Museum Quarter and Vondelpark) ⓣ020/678 1390. Lovely old pool dating from the nineteenth century and refreshingly free of the gimmicks that clutter up the others. Naturist hour on Sunday from 4.30 to 5.30pm. Adults €3, under-12s €2.70.

⑭

⑮

Festivals and events

Most of Amsterdam's festivals are music and arts events, supplemented by a sprinkling of religious celebrations and, as you might expect, the majority take place in the summer. The **Queen's Birthday** celebration at the end of April is the city's most touted and exciting annual event, with a large portion of the city given over to an impromptu flea market and lots of street-partying. On a more cultural level, the art extravaganza, the **Holland Festival**, held throughout June, attracts a handful of big names. Check with the VVV (see p.28) for further details, and remember that many other interesting events, such as the Easter performance of Bach's *St Matthew Passion* in Grote Kerk Naarden and the North Sea Jazz Festival in The Hague (ⓦ www .northseajazz.nl*)*, are only a short train ride away.

January

Elfstedentocht (Eleven Cities' Journey)
Although a fair distance from Amsterdam, you may wish to take part in this annual ice-skating marathon, held across eleven towns and frozen rivers, in Friesland, starting and finishing in Leeuwarden. It happens, weather permitting, sometime in January, though a lack of ice meant the race had to be suspended for a number of years. For more details, call the organizers, De Friese Elfsteden, in the town of Leeuwarden (ⓣ058/215 5020 ⓦ www.elfstedentocht.nl).

February

Chinese New Year Depends on lunar calendar: first or second week, or last week Jan (2006). Dragon dance and fireworks, held at Nieuwmarkt.
Februaristaking (Commemoration of the February Strike) February 25. ⓦ www.februaristaking .nl. Speeches and wreath-laying at the Docker Statue on J.D. Meijerplein (see p.103).

March

Stille Omgang (Silent Procession) Sunday closest to March 15 ⓦ w ww.stille-omgang.nl. Procession by local Catholics commemorat-

ing the Miracle of Amsterdam, starting and finishing at Spui and passing through the Red Light District.

April

Nationaal Museumweekend Second weekend ⓣ 020/670 1111, ⓦ www.museumweekend .nl. Free entrance to most of the museums in the Netherlands. Contact VVV for more information.
Koninginnedag (the Queen's Birthday) April 30. This is one of the most popular dates in the Dutch diary, a street event par excellence, which seems to grow annually and is almost worth planning a visit around, despite some claiming it has become too commercialized over recent years. Celebrations for Queen Beatrix take place throughout the whole of Holland, though festivities in Amsterdam tend to be somewhat wilder and larger in scale. Special club nights and parties are held both the night before and the night after; however, to gain entry you'll need to book in advance either from the club itself or from selected record stores, such as Boudisque and Get Records (see p.226). The next day sees the city's streets and canals lined with people, most of whom are dressed in ridiculous costumes (not surprisingly, Queen's Day is one

of the most flamboyant events on the gay calendar as well). Anything goes, especially if it's orange – the Dutch national colour. A fair is held on the Dam, and music blasts continuously from huge sound systems set up across most of the major squares. This is also the one day of the year when goods can be bought and sold tax-free to anyone on the streets, and numerous stalls are set up in front of people's houses.

World Press Photo Annual competition ☎020/676 6096, ⓦ www.worldpressphoto.nl. Open to photographers from all over the world. Judging and award days take place towards the end of April, marking the beginning of the exhibition, which is held at the Oude Kerk until the end of middle of June.

May

Herdenkingsdag (Remembrance Day) May 4. There's a wreath-laying ceremony and two-minute silence at the National Monument in Dam square, commemorating the Dutch dead of World War II, as well as a smaller event at the Homomonument in Westermarkt in honour of the country's gay soldiers who died.

Bevrijdingsdag (Liberation Day) May 5. The country celebrates the 1945 liberation from Nazi occupation with bands, speeches and impromptu markets around the city.

Oosterparkfestival First week. Held in the large park near the Tropenmuseum, this free festival celebrates the mix of cultures living in the area, with live music and numerous food stands.

National Windmill Day Second Saturday. On this day over half the country's remaining windmills and watermills are opened to the public. Contact Vereniging De Hollandsche (☎020/623 8703, ⓔdhm@molens.nl) or the VVV for further details.

KunstRAI First week ☎020/549 1212, ⓦ www .kunstrai.nl. The annual mainstream contemporary arts fair, held in the RAI conference centre, south of the centre, featuring work from over 120 galleries. A less commercial alternative is the Kunstvlaai (ⓦwww .kunstvlaai.nl) at the Westergasfabriek, always held the week before or after KunstRAI.

June

Amsterdam Roots Festival Third Sunday. ⓦ www.amsterdamroots.nl. Week long world music and film festival that opens with a free open air concert in Oosterpark with stalls, workshops and a parade. The festival continues throughout the week with a program of acts performing in the Concertgebouw, Melkweg and Tropentheater.

Holland Festival Throughout June ☎020/530 7110, ⓦ www.hollandfestival.nl. The largest music, dance and drama event in the Netherlands, aimed at making the dramatic arts more accessible. Showcasing around thirty productions, it features a mix of established and new talent. See "Entertainment and Nightlife" chapter (p.10) for more details.

International Theatre School Festival Third week ☎020/530 5566, ⓦ www.itsfestival.nl. Ten day program of events showcasing aspiring actors, dancers, musicians and opera singers in theatres on Nes, off Dam square, culminating in an award night with the prize presented to the most promising director.

July

Beachbop Last Sunday; June, July and August ⓦ www.beachbop.info. Live percussion, dance acts and plenty of beach parties held at the Bloemendaal beach cafés (close to Zandvoort). Friendly, low-key atmosphere, but extremely popular. (4–11pm).

Over het IJ Festival First one or two weeks ☎020/624 6380, ⓦ www.overhetij.nl. Modern theatre and dance festival held at the NDSM wharf (ⓦwww.ndsm.nl) in Amsterdam-Noord, across the river from the city centre. A festival boat runs there from behind Centraal Station.

Kwakoe Festival Weekends only from second week of July to second week of August ⓦ www .kwakoe.nl. A Surinamese and Antillian festival held at a playground close to the Amsterdam ArenA in the southeastern suburbs, featuring lots of music, dance acts and stand-up comedy. There are also workshops, and even prayer services on Sunday morning. In the middle of the festival there's a football competition between several "tropical" teams. Caribbean delicacies such as *roti* and the Surinamese *bakabana*, baked banana with peanut sauce, are widely available from stalls around the festival.

Vondelpark Open Air Theatre June– Aug ☎020/523 7790, ⓦ www.openluchttheater.nl. Free theatre, dance and music performances throughout the summer, showcasing anything from jazz and classical concerts through to stand-up comedy. (Wed–Sun only).

August

Amsterdam Pride First or second weekend ⓦwww.amsterdampride.nl. The city's gay community celebrates, with street parties and performances held along the Amstel, Warmoesstraat and Reguliersdwarsstraat. The Canal Parade takes place the first Saturday between 2–6pm; a flotilla of up to 75 boats cruising along the Prinsengracht watched by over 200,000 people.
Dance Valley First week ⓦwww.dancevalley.nl. Huge international dance event held over a weekend at a natural amphitheatre in the hills of Spaarnwoude, just north of Haarlem, with all the techno, drum-and-bass, house and ambient DJs you could possibly wish for. Also hosts an winter event in 's Hertogenbosch (see "December").
The Parade First two weeks ⓣ033/465 4555, ⓦwww.mobilearts.nl. An excellent travelling theatrical fair with various short theatre performances given in or in front of the artists' tents (they all work independently). Held in the Martin Luther King Park, next to the River Amstel (from CS tram #25 to Hunzestraat), with a special kids' parade in the afternoons.
Uitmarkt Last week ⓦwww.uitmarkt.nl. A weekend where every cultural organization in the city advertises itself with free preview performances either on Museumplein or by the Amstel.
Grachtenfestival Third week ⓣ020/421 4542, ⓦwww.grachtenfestival.nl. International musicians perform classical music at twenty historical locations around the three main canals. Includes the Prinsengracht Concert, one of the world's most prestigious free open-air concerts, held opposite the *Pulitzer Hotel*.

September

Bloemencorso (Flower Parade) First week ⓦwww.bloemencorsoaalsmeer.nl. The Aalsmeer–Amsterdam flower pageant in the city centre, celebrating every kind of flower except tulips, which are out of season. Each year has a different theme. Vijzelstraat is the best place to see things, since the events in Dam square are normally packed solid.
Chinatown Festival Second weekend. Tong and Soeng musicians, acrobatics, kung-fu and tai-chi demonstrations at the Nieuwmarkt.

Open Monument Day First or second weekend ⓣ020/552 4887. Monuments throughout the Netherlands that are normally closed or have restricted opening times throw open their doors to the public for free.
Jordaan Festival Second or third week ⓣ020/626 5587, ⓦwww.jordaanfestival.nl. A street festival in the Jordaan. There's a commercial fair on Palmgracht, talent contests on Elandsgracht, a few street parties and a culinary fair on the Sunday afternoon at the Noordermarkt.

October

Amsterdam City Marathon Mid to late October, usually the third weekend ⓦwww.amsterdammarathon.nl. A 42-kilometre course around Amsterdam starting at and finishing inside the Olympic Stadium, passing through the old city centre along the way.

November

Crossing Border First or second week ⓣ070/346 2355, ⓦwww.crossingborder.nl. Four-day festival held at the Royal and National theatres in The Hague that explores and crosses artistic boundaries, with performances by over a hundred international acts presenting the spoken word in various forms, from rap to poetry. Last day is children's day.
Parade of Sint Nicolaas Second or third week. The traditional parade of *Sinterklaas* (Santa Claus) through the city on his white horse, starting from behind Centraal Station where he arrives by steam boat, before parading down the Damrak towards Rembrandtplein accompanied by his helpers the *Zwarte Pieten* ("Black Peters") – so called because of their blackened faces– who hand out sweets and little presents. It all finishes in Leidseplein on the balcony of the Stadsschouwburg.
Cannabis Cup Late November ⓦwww.hightimes.com. Five-day harvest festival organized by *High Times* magazine at the Melkweg (see p.204), with speeches, music and a competition to find the best cultivated seed. Judging is open to the general public, but the entrance fee is pricey.

December

Dance Valley First week ⓦwww.dancevalley.nl. Winter party hosted by the same organizers

FESTIVALS AND EVENTS

△ Cannabis Cup, November

of the hugely popular outdoor summer event (see August), with over fifty international DJs, eight stages and live acts. Held in the Brabanthallen in 's Hertogenbosch, north of Eindhoven, which has a capacity of 40,000.

Pakjesavond (Present Evening) Dec 5. Though it tends to be a private affair, Pakjesavond, rather than Christmas Day, is when Dutch kids receive their Christmas presents. If you're here on that day and have Dutch friends, it's worth knowing that it's traditional to give a present together with an amus-

ing poem you have written caricaturing the recipient.

New Year's Eve Dec 31. New Year's Eve is big in Amsterdam, with fireworks and celebrations everywhere. Most bars and discos stay open until morning – make sure you get tickets in advance. This might just qualify as the wildest and most reckless street partying in Europe, but a word of warning: Amsterdammers seem to love the idea of throwing lit fireworks around and won't hesitate to send one careering into the crowd.

16

Directory

Addresses These are written as, for example, "Kerkstr. 79 II", which means the second-floor apartment at Kerkstraat 79. The ground floor is indicated by **hs** (*huis*, house) after the number; the basement is **sous** (*sousterrain*). In some cases, especially in the Jordaan, streets have the same name and to differentiate between them, **1e**, **2e**, **3e** and even occasionally **4e** are placed in front. These are abbreviations for *Eerste* (first), *Tweede* (second), *Derde* (third), and *Vierde* (fourth). Thus, "1e Vogelstraat 10" is a completely different address from "2e Vogelstraat 10". In addition, many **side streets** take the name of the main street they run off, with the addition of the word *dwars*, meaning "crossing"; for instance, Palmdwarsstraat is a side street off Palmstraat. Furthermore, and for no apparent reason, some dead-straight cross-streets change their name – so that, for example, in the space of about 300m, 1e Bloemdwarsstraat becomes 2e Leliedwarsstraat and then 3e Egelantiersdwarsstraat. As for boats, **T/O** (*tegenover*, or "opposite") in an address shows that the address is a boat: hence "Prinsengracht T/O 26" would indicate a boat to be found opposite Prinsengracht 26. Incidentally, the main Grachtengordel canals begin their **numbering** at Brouwersgracht and increase as they progress counter-clockwise. By the time they reach the Amstel, Herengracht's house numbers are in the 600s, Keizersgracht's in the 800s and Prinsengracht's in the 900s.

Airlines All at Schiphol airport: Aer Lingus ☎020/517 4747; Alitalia ☎0900/202 2622; British Airways ☎020/346 9559; British Midland ☎020/346 9211; Delta Airlines ☎020/201 3536; easyJet ☎023/568 4880;

KLM ☎020/474 7747; United Airlines ☎020/201 3708.

Bike rental You can rent bikes at the following outlets: Bike City, Bloemgracht 70 (Jordaan and the Westerdok) ☎020/626 3721; Damstraat Rent-a-Bike, Damstraat 20 (Old Centre) ☎020/625 5029; Holland Rent-a-Bike, Damrak 247 (Old Centre) ☎020/622 3207; Koenders Take-a-Bike, Stationsplein 12 (Old Centre) ☎020/624 8391; MacBike, Mr Visserplein 2 (Old Jewish Quarter and the East) ☎020/620 0985; Macbike Too, Marnixstraat 220 (Jordaan and the Westerdok) ☎020/626 6964.

Car parks The following are all 24-hour city-centre car parks: De Bijenkorf, Dam 1, off Damrak; Byzantium, near Leidseplein; De Kolk, Nieuwezijds Kolk 20; Muziektheater, Waterlooplein (under City Hall); ANWB Parking Amsterdam Centraal, Prins Hendrikkade 20a, east of Centraal Station. Expect to pay €3–3.50 per hour with a maximum of €36–47.50 for 24hr.

Car rental Selected car rental agencies (*auto-verhuur*) all in the Oud West just north of the Vondelpark include: Avis, Nassaukade 380 ☎020/683 6061; Budget, Overtoom 121 ☎0900/1576; Europcar, Overtoom 197 ☎020/683 2123; Hertz, Overtoom 333 ☎020/612 2441.

Concessions Concessionary rates are applied at every city sight and attraction as well as on the public transport system. Rates vary, but usually seniors (65+) get in free, as do children under 5. Concessionary cut-off points for children over 5 and under 18 vary; family tickets are common too. For details of visitors' passes and the Museum-kaart (museum year-card), see p.29.

Consulates UK, Koningslaan 44 (Museum Quarter and Vondelpark) ☎020/676 4343;

USA, Museumplein 19 (Museum Quarter and Vondelpark) ☎020/575 5309.

Contraceptives Condoms are widely available from *drogists* or the Condomerie (see p.228). To get the pill you need a prescription.

Diamonds Currently around twenty diamond firms operate in Amsterdam. All are working factories, but several open their doors to the public for viewing the cutting, polishing and sorting practices, and (most importantly) for buying. The best one to visit is Gassan Diamonds (see p.99).

Doctors and dentists Your hotel or the VVV should be able to provide the address of an English-speaking doctor or dentist (*tandarts*) if you need one. If you're seeking treatment under EU health agreements, double-check that the doctor is seeing you as a patient of the public health care system. This being the case, you'll need to pay upfront for treatment and medicines; you'll then be able to reclaim a proportion of the cost by applying to the local Health Service Office (ask the doctor for details) with your E111 form.

Electric current 220v AC – effectively the same as British, although with round two- (or occasionally three-) pin plugs. British equipment will need either an adaptor or a new plug; American requires both a transformer and a new plug.

Emergencies Police, fire service and ambulance ☎112.

Hospitals The main hospital is situated out of the city centre; Academic Medical Centre (AMC), Meibergdreef 9 (☎020/566 9111). The closest medical centre is at Prinsengracht 769 (☎020/599 4100).

Laundry (wassalons) The Clean Brothers, Kerkstraat 56 (Grachtengordel south; daily 7am–9pm), is the city's best self-service laundry, with a sizeable load currently €4 to wash, €1 per 30min in the drier and soap for €0.50; they also do service washes, dry-cleaning, ironing, and so on; there is also a branch at Jacob van Lennepkade 179 (Oud West). Other laundries are to be found at: Elandsgracht 59 (Jordaan and the Westerdok), Warmoesstraat 30 and Oude Doelenstraat 12 (Old Centre).

Left luggage Centraal Station has both coin-operated luggage lockers (daily 7am–11pm) and a staffed left-luggage office (daily 7am–11pm). Small coin-operated lockers cost €3.50, the larger ones €5.50 per 24 hours; left luggage costs €8 per item.

Libraries The main public library, Centrale Bibliotheek, is at Prinsengracht 587, just north of Leidsegracht (Mon 1–9pm, Tues–Thurs 10am–9pm, Fri & Sat 10am–5pm; Oct–March also Sun 1–5pm). There's no problem about using its books for reference purposes, but to borrow them you'll need to show proof of residence and pay €21 for a year's membership (less for under-18s & over-65s).

Lost property For items lost on the trams, buses or metro, contact GVB Head Office, Prins Hendrikkade 108–114 (Mon–Fri 9am–4pm; ☎020/460 5858). For property lost on a train, go to the Gevonden Voorwerpen office at the nearest station; Amsterdam's is at Centraal Station, near the left-luggage lockers (☎020/557 8544; 24hr). After three days all unclaimed property goes to the Central Lost Property Office at 2e Daalsedijk 4, Utrecht (☎030/235 3923), and costs €10 per item to pick up. If you lose something in the street or a park, try the police lost property at Stephensonstraat 18 (Mon–Fri noon–3.30pm; ☎020/559 3005). Schiphol airport's lost and found number is ☎0900/7244 7465 (Mon–Fri 7.30am–5.30pm, Sat & Sun 9am–5pm).

Pharmacies Minor ailments can be remedied at a drugstore (*drogist*). These sell non-prescription drugs as well as toiletries, tampons, condoms and the like. A pharmacy or *apotheek* (usually open Mon–Fri 9.30am–6pm, but often closed Mon mornings) also handle prescriptions. There aren't any 24-hour pharmacies, but the 24-hour Afdeling Inlichtingen Apotheken helpline (☎020/694 8709) will supply addresses of ones that are open late. Most of the better hotels will have these details too.

Public transport See "Basics" p.31. Information on ☎0900/9292, ⦿www.gvb.nl.

Time One hour ahead of Britain, six hours ahead of New York, nine hours ahead of Los Angeles. Daylight-saving operates from the end of March to the end of October.

Tipping Although you're not obliged to do so, a ten- to fifteen-percent tip is expected by taxi drivers and anticipated in most restaurants.

Toilets Public toilets are invariably spotlessly clean and well maintained; many cost

DIRECTORY

€0.25 or €0.50. For men, there are also free, al-fresco pissoirs located all over the city centre.

Women's contacts Amsterdam has an impressive feminist infrastructure: there are support groups, health centres and businesses run by and for women. A good starting point to find out what's going on is Het Vrouwenhuis, Nieuwe Herengracht 95 (☎020/625 2066, ⓦwww .vrouwenhuis.nl; Mon–Fri 11am–4pm), a centre which organizes women's activities and cultural events. IIAV at Obiplein 4 (☎020/665 0820, ⓦwww.iiav.nl; Mon noon–5pm, Tues–Fri 10am–5pm) houses the International Archives of the Women's Movement and has a wealth of literature of all kinds detailing the history of the feminist movement in the Netherlands.

Working EU nationals (prior to 2003) are entitled to work without a work permit. For stays longer than three months a resident's permit (MVV permit) is required, obtainable from your Dutch Embassy or in Amsterdam at the Vreemdelingenpolitie (Foreign Police), Johan Huizingalaan 757 (☎020/559 6300, ⓦwww.immigratiedienst.nl). Non-EU and new EU members will need a work permit, issued on application by the potential employer.

Contexts

Contexts

A brief history of Amsterdam

To a large degree, a **history of Amsterdam** is a history of the whole of the Netherlands, which in turn was an integral part of the Low Countries – today's Belgium, Luxembourg and the Netherlands – until the late sixteenth century. It was then that the Dutch broke with their Habsburg masters and, ever since, Amsterdam has been at the centre of Dutch events. The city was the country's most glorious cultural and trading centre throughout its seventeenth-century heyday, the so-called Golden Age, and, after a brief downturn in the eighteenth century, picked itself up to emerge as a major metropolis in the nineteenth. In the 1960s Amsterdam was galvanized by its youth, who took to hippy culture with gusto; their legacy is a social progressiveness – most conspicuously over drugs and prostitution – that still underpins the city's international reputation, good and bad, today.

Medieval foundations

Amsterdam's earliest history is as murky as the marshes from which it arose. Legend asserts that two Frisian fishermen were the first inhabitants and, true or not, it is indeed likely that the city began as a fishing village at the mouth of the **River Amstel**. Previously, this area had been a stretch of peat bog and marsh, but a modest fall in the sea-level permitted settlement on the high ground along the riverside. The village was first given some significance when the local lord built a castle here around 1204, and then, some sixty years later the Amstel was dammed – hence Amstelredam – and it received its municipal **charter** from a new feudal overlord, Count Floris V, in 1275. Designating the village a toll port for beer imported from Hamburg, the charter led to Amsterdam's flourishing as a trading centre from around 1300, when it also became an important transit port for Baltic grain, destined for the burgeoning cities of the Low Countries (modern-day Belgium and the Netherlands).

As Amsterdam grew, its **trade** diversified. In particular, it made a handsome profit from English **wool**: the wool was imported into the city, barged onto Leiden and Haarlem – where it was turned into cloth – and then much of it returned to Amsterdam to be exported. The cloth trade drew workers into the town to work along Warmoesstraat and the Amstel, and ships were able to sail right up to Dam square to pick up the finished work and drop off imported wood, fish, salt and spices.

Though the city's **population** rose steadily in the early sixteenth century, to around 12,000 souls, Amsterdam was still small compared to Antwerp or London: building on the waterlogged soil was difficult and slow, requiring timber piles to be driven into the firmer sand below. And with the extensive use of timber and thatch, **fires** were a frequent occurrence. A particularly disastrous blaze in 1452 resulted in such destruction that the city council made building with slate, brick and stone obligatory – one of the few wooden houses that survived the fire still stands today in the Begijnhof (see p.62). In the mid-sixteenth century the city underwent its first major **expansion**, as burgeoning trade with the Hanseatic towns of the Baltic made the city second only to Antwerp as a marketplace and warehouse for northern and western Europe. The trade in cloth, grain and wine brought craftspeople to the city, and its merchant fleet grew: by the 1550s three-quarters of all grain cargo out of the Baltic was carried in Amsterdam vessels. The foundations were being laid for the wealth of the Golden Age.

The rise of Protestantism

At the beginning of the sixteenth century the superstition, corruption and elaborate ritual of the established (Catholic) **Church** found itself under attack throughout northern Europe. First, Erasmus of Rotterdam promoted ideas of reformation and then, in 1517, **Martin Luther** went one step – or rather, leap – further, producing his 95 theses against the Church practice of indulgences, a prelude to his more comprehensive assault on the entire institution. Furthermore, when Luther's works were disseminated his ideas gained a European following amongst a range of reforming groups branded as **Lutheran** by the Church, whilst other reformers were drawn to the doctrines of **John Calvin** (1509–64). Luther asserted that the Church's political power was subservient to that of the state; Calvin emphasized the importance of individual conscience and the need for redemption through the grace of Christ rather than the confessional. Luther's writings and Bible translations were printed in the Netherlands, but the doctrines of Calvin proved more popular in Amsterdam, setting the seal on the city's religious transformation. Calvin was insistent on the separation of church and state, but the lines were easily fudged in Amsterdam by the church's ruling council of ministers and annually elected elders, who soon came to exercise considerable political clout. The council also had little time for other (more egalitarian) Protestant sects and matters came to a head when, in 1535, one of the radical splinter groups, the **Anabaptists**, occupied Amsterdam's town hall, calling on passers-by to repent. Previously the town council had tolerated the Anabaptists but, prompted by the Calvinists, it acted swiftly when civic rule was challenged: the town hall was besieged and the leaders of the Anabaptists were executed on the Dam.

The revolt of the Netherlands

In 1555, the fanatically Catholic **Philip II** succeeded to the Spanish throne. Through a series of marriages the Spanish monarchy – and **Habsburg** family – had come to rule over the Low Countries, and Philip was determined to rid his empire of its heretics, regardless of whether they were Calvinists or Anabaptists. Philip promptly garrisoned the towns of the Low Countries with Spanish mercenaries, imported the **Inquisition** and passed a series of anti-Protestant edicts. However, other pressures on the Habsburg Empire forced him into a tactical withdrawal and he transferred control of the Low Countries to his sister **Margaret of Parma** in 1559. Based in Brussels, the equally resolute Margaret implemented the policies of her brother with gusto. In 1561 she reorganized the church and created fourteen new bishoprics, a move that was construed as a wresting of power from civil authority, and an attempt to destroy the local aristocracy's powers of religious patronage. Right across the Low Countries, **Protestantism** – and Protestant sympathies – spread to the nobility, who now formed the "League of the Nobility" to counter Habsburg policy. The League petitioned Margaret for moderation but were dismissed out of hand by one of her (French–speaking) advisers, who called them "ces geux" (those beggars), an epithet that was to be enthusiastically adopted by the rebels. In 1565 a harvest failure caused a winter famine among the urban workers of the region and, after years of repression, they struck back. In 1566, a Protestant sermon in the tiny Flemish textile town of Steenvoorde incited the congregation to purge the local church of its "papist" idolatry. The crowd smashed up the church's reliquaries and shrines, broke the stained glass windows and terrorized the priests, thereby igniting what is commonly called the **Iconoclastic Fury**. The rioting spread like wild fire and within ten days churches had been ransacked from one end of the Low Countries to the other, nowhere more so than in Amsterdam – hence the plain whitewashed interiors of many of the city's churches today.

The ferocity of this outbreak shocked the upper classes into renewed support for Spain, and Margaret regained the allegiance of most nobles – with the principal exception of the country's greatest landowner, Prince William of Orange-Nassau, known as **William the Silent**, who prudently slipped away to his estates in Germany. Meanwhile, Philip II was keen to capitalize on the increase in support for Margaret and, in 1567, he dispatched the **Duke of Albe**, with an army of ten thousand men, to the Low Countries to suppress his religious opponents absolutely. One of Albe's first acts was to set up the Commission of Civil Unrest, which was soon nicknamed the "**Council of Blood**", after its habit of executing those it examined. No fewer than 12,000 citizens were polished off, mostly for taking part in the Fury. Initially the repression worked: in 1568, when William attempted an invasion from Germany, the towns, including Amsterdam, offered no support. William withdrew and conceived other means of defeating Albe, sponsoring the Protestant privateers, the so-called **Waterguezen** or sea-beggars, who took their name from the epithet provided by Maragaret's advisor. In April 1572, the Waterguezen entered Brielle on the Maas and captured it from the Spanish in the first of several commando-style attacks. At first, the Waterguezen were obliged to operate from England, but it was soon possible for them to secure bases in the Netherlands, whose citizens had grown to loathe the autocratic Albe and his Spanish army.

After the success at Brielle, the revolt spread rapidly. By June the rebels controlled all of the province of Holland except for Amsterdam, which steadfastly refused to come off the fence. Albe and his son Frederick fought back, but William's superior naval power frustrated him and a mightily irritated Philip replaced Albe with **Luis de Resquesens**. Initially, Resquesens had some success in the south, where the Catholic majority were more willing to compromise with Spanish rule than their northern neighbours, but the tide of war was against him – most pointedly in William's triumphant relief of Leiden in 1574. Two years later, Resquesens died and the (unpaid) Habsburg garrison in Antwerp mutinied and attacked the town, slaughtering some eight thousand of its people in what was known as the **Spanish Fury**. Though the Habsburgs still held several towns, the massacre alienated the south and pushed its peoples – including the doubting Thomases of Amsterdam – into the arms of William, whose troops now swept into Brussels, the heart of imperial power. Momentarily, it seemed possible for the whole region to unite behind William and all signed the **Union of Brussels**, which demanded the departure of foreign troops as a condition for accepting a diluted Habsburg sovereignty.

Philip was, however, not inclined to compromise, especially when he realized that William's Calvinist sympathies were giving his newly found Walloon and Flemish allies the jitters. The king bided his time until 1578, when, with his enemies arguing amongst themselves, he sent another army from Spain to the Low Countries under the command of Alessandro Farnese, the **Duke of Parma**. Events played into Parma's hands. In 1579, tiring of all the wrangling, seven northern provinces agreed to sign the **Union of Utrecht**, an alliance against Spain that was to be the first unification of the Netherlands as an identifiable country – the **United Provinces**. It was then that Amsterdam formally declared for the rebels and switched from Catholicism to Calvinism in what became known as the "**Alteratie**" of 1578. The rebels had conceded freedom of religious belief, but in Amsterdam as elsewhere this did not extend to freedom of worship. Nonetheless, a pragmatic compromise was reached in which a blind eye was turned to the celebration of Mass if it was done privately and inconspicuously. It was this ad hoc arrangement that gave rise to "clandestine" Catholic churches (*schuilkerken*) like that of the Amstelkring on Oudezijds Voorburgwal (see p.56).

The assembly of these United Provinces was known as the **States General**, and met at Den Haag (The Hague); it had no domestic legislative authority, and could only carry out foreign policy by unanimous decision, a formula designed to reassure the independent-minded merchants of every Dutch city. The role of **Stadholder** was the most important in each province, roughly equivalent to that of governor, though the same person could occupy this position in any number of provinces. Meanwhile, in the south – and also in 1579 – representatives of the southern provinces signed the **Union of Arras**, a Catholic-led agreement that declared loyalty to Philip II and counter-balanced the Union of Utrecht in the north. Thus, the Low Countries were, de facto, divided into two – the Spanish Netherlands and the United Provinces – beginning a separation that would lead, after many changes, to the creation of Belgium, Luxembourg and the Netherlands. With the return of more settled times, Amsterdam was now free to carry on with what it did best – trading and making money.

The Golden Age

The brilliance of Amsterdam's explosion onto the European scene is as difficult to underestimate as it is to detail. The size of its **merchant fleet** carrying Baltic grain into Europe had long been considerable. Even the Spaniards had been unable to undermine Dutch **maritime superiority** and, with the commercial demise of Antwerp, Amsterdam became the emporium for the products of northern and southern Europe as well as the East and West Indies. The city didn't prosper from its market alone, though, as Amsterdam ships also carried produce, a cargo trade that greatly increased the city's wealth. Dutch **banking and investment** brought further prosperity, and by the middle of the seventeenth century Amsterdam's wealth was spectacular. The Calvinist bourgeoisie indulged themselves in fine canal houses, and commissioned images of themselves in group portraits. Civic pride knew no bounds as great monuments to self-aggrandizement, such as the new **town hall** (now the Royal Palace, see p.51), were hastily erected and, if some went hungry, few starved, as the poor were cared for in municipal almshouses.

The arts flourished and **religious tolerance** was extended even to the traditional scapegoats, the Jews, and in particular the Sephardic Jews, who had been hounded from Spain by the Inquisition but were guaranteed freedom from religious persecution under the terms of the Union of Utrecht. By the end of the eighteenth century, Jews accounted for ten percent of the city's population. Guilds and craft associations thrived, and in the first half of the seventeenth century Amsterdam's population quadrupled: the relatively high wages paid by the city's industries attracted agricultural workers from every part of the country and Protestant refugees arrived from every corner of Catholic Europe.

To accommodate its growing populace, Amsterdam **expanded** several times during the seventeenth century. The grandest and most elaborate plan to enlarge the city was begun in 1613, with the building of the western stretches of the Herengracht, Keizersgracht and Prinsengracht, the three great canals of the **Grachtengordel** (literally "girdle of canals") that epitomized the wealth and self-confidence of the Golden Age. In 1663 this sweeping crescent was extended beyond the River Amstel, but by this time the population had begun to stabilize, and the stretch that would have completed the ring of canals around the city was left only partially developed – an area that would in time become the Jewish Quarter.

One organization that kept the city's coffers brimming throughout the Golden Age was the **East India Company** (Verenigde Oost Indische, VOC). Formed in 1602, this Amsterdam-controlled enterprise sent ships to Asia, Indonesia and as far away as China to bring back spices, wood and other assorted plunder. Given a trading monopoly in all lands east of the Cape of Good Hope, it also had unlimited military powers over the lands it controlled, and was effectively the occupying government in Malaya, Ceylon and Malacca. Twenty years later the **West Indies Company** (Westindische Compagnie, WIC) was inaugurated to protect new Dutch interests in the Americas and Africa. It never achieved the success of the East India Company, expending its energies in waging war on Spanish and Portuguese colonies from a base in Surinam, but it did make handsome profits until the 1660s. The company was dismantled in 1674, ten years after its small colony of New Amsterdam had been ceded to the British – and renamed **New York**. Elsewhere, the Dutch held on to their colonies for as long as possible – Indonesia, its principal possession, only secured its independence in 1949.

Decline – 1660 to 1795

Although the economics of the Golden Age were dazzling, the **political climate** was dismal. The United Provinces were dogged by interminable wrangling between those who hankered for a central, unified government under the pre-eminent **House of Orange-Nassau** and those who championed provincial autonomy. Frederick Henry, the powerful head of the House of Orange-Nassau, died in 1647 and his successor, William II, lasted just three years before his death from smallpox. A week after William's death, his wife bore the son who would become William III of England, but in the meantime the leaders of the province of Holland, with the full support of Amsterdam, seized their opportunity. They forced measures through the States General abolishing the position of Stadholder, thereby reducing the powers of the Orangists and increasing those of the provinces, chiefly Holland itself. Holland's foremost figure in these years was **Johan de Witt**, Council Pensionary (chief minister) to the States General. He guided the country through wars with England

and Sweden, concluding a triple alliance between the two countries and the United Provinces in 1668. This was a striking reversal of policy: the economic rivalry between the United Provinces and England had already precipitated two **Anglo–Dutch wars** (1652–54 and 1665–67) and there was much bitterness in Anglo–Dutch relations – a popular English pamphlet of the time was titled "*A Relation Shewing How They [the Dutch] Were First Bred and Descended from a Horse–Turd Which Was Enclosed in a Butter–Box*". Much of the ill feeling came from an embarrassing defeat in the second Anglo–Dutch war, when **Admiral Michiel de Ruyter** had sailed up the Thames and caught the Englisg fleet napping. This infuriated England's Charles II, who was quite willing to break with his new-found allies and join a French attack on the Provinces in 1672. The republic was now in deep trouble – previous victories had been at sea, and the army, weak and disorganized, could not withstand the onslaught. In panic, the country turned to **William III** of Orange for leadership and Johan de Witt was brutally murdered by a mob of Orangist sympathizers in Den Haag. By 1678 William had defeated the French and made peace with the English – and was rewarded (along with his wife Mary, the daughter of Charles I of England) with the English crown ten years later.

Though King William had defeated the French, **Louis XIV** retained designs on the United Provinces and the pot was kept boiling in a long series of dynastic wars that ranged across northern Europe. In 1700, Charles II of Spain, the last of the Spanish Habsburgs, died childless, bequeathing the Spanish throne and control of the Spanish Netherlands (now Belgium) to Philip of Anjou, Louis' grandson. Louis promptly forced Philip to cede the latter to France, which was, with every justification, construed as a threat to the balance of power by France's neighbours. The **War of the Spanish Succession** ensued with the United Provinces, England and Austria forming the **Triple Alliance** to thwart the French king. The war itself was a haphazard, long-winded affair distinguished by the spectacular victories of the Duke of Marlborough at Blenheim, Ramillies and Malplaquet. It dragged on until the **Treaty of Utrecht** of 1713 in which France finally abandoned its claim to the Spanish Netherlands.

However, the fighting had drained the United Provinces' reserves and a slow economic decline began, accelerated by a reactive trend towards conservatism. This in turn reflected the development of an increasingly socially static society, with power and wealth concentrated within a small elite. Furthermore, with the threat of foreign conquest effectively removed, the Dutch ruling class divided into two main camps – the Orangists and the pro-French "Patriots" – whose interminable squabbling soon brought political life to a virtual standstill. The situation deteriorated even further in the latter half of the century and the last few years of the United Provinces present a sorry state of affairs.

French occupation

In 1795 the **French**, aided by the Patriots, invaded, setting up the **Batavian Republic** and dissolving the United Provinces – along with many of the privileges of the richer Dutch merchants. Now part of the Napoleonic empire, the Netherlands were obliged to wage unenthusiastic war with England, and in 1806 Napoleon appointed his brother **Louis** as their king in an attempt to unite the rival Dutch groups under one (notionally independent) ruler. **Louis** was installed in Amsterdam's town hall, giving it its title of Koninklijk Paleis

(Royal Palace; see p.51). Louis, however, wasn't willing to allow the Netherlands to become a simple satellite of France; he ignored Napoleon's directives and after just four years of rule was forced to abdicate. The country was then formally incorporated into the French Empire, and for three gloomy years suffered occupation and heavy taxation to finance French military adventures.

Following Napoleon's disastrous retreat from Moscow, the **Orangist faction** surfaced to exploit weakening French control. In 1813, Frederick William, son of the exiled William V, returned to the country and eight months later, under the terms of the **Congress of Vienna**, was crowned King William I of the **United Kingdom of the Netherlands**, incorporating both the old United Provinces and the Spanish (Austrian) Netherlands. A strong-willed man, he spent much of the later part of his life trying to control his disparate kingdom, but he failed primarily because of the Protestant north's attempt – or perceived attempt – to dominate the Catholic south. The southern provinces revolted against his rule and in 1830 the separate Kingdom of **Belgium** was proclaimed. During the years of the United Kingdom, Amsterdam's status was dramatically reduced. Previously, the self-governing city, made bold by its wealth, could (and frequently did) act in its own self-interest, at the expense of the nation. From 1815, however, it was integrated within the country, with no more rights than any other city. The seat of government (and the centre for all decision-making) was Den Haag (The Hague), and so it remained after the southern provinces broke away.

The nineteenth century

In the first decades of the nineteenth century the erosion of Amsterdam's pre-eminent position among Dutch cities was largely camouflaged by its profitable colonial trade with the East Indies (Indonesia). This trade was however hampered by the character of the **Zuider Zee**, whose shallows and sandbanks presented all sorts of navigational problems given the increasing size of merchant ships. The **Noordhollandskanaal** (North Holland Canal), completed in 1824 to bypass the Zuider Zee, made little difference, and it was Rotterdam, strategically placed on the Rhine inlets between the industries of the Ruhr and Britain, that prospered at Amsterdam's expense. Even the 1876 opening of the **Nordzeekanaal** (North Sea Canal), which provided a direct link west from Amsterdam to the North Sea, failed to push Amsterdam's trade ahead of rival Rotterdam's, though the city did hold on to much of the country's **shipbuilding industry**, remnants of which can still be seen at the 't Kromhout shipyard (see p.111). The city council was also slow to catch on to the possibilities of rail, but finally, in 1889, the opening of **Centraal Station** put the city back on the main transport routes. Nonetheless, Amsterdam was far from being a backwater: in the second half of the nineteenth century, its industries boomed, attracting a new wave of migrants, who were settled outside of the centre in the vast tenements of De Pijp and the Oud Zuid (Old South). These same workers were soon to radicalize the city, supporting a veritable raft of Socialist and Communist politicians. One marker was a reforming **Housing Act** of 1901 that pushed the city council into a concerted effort to clear the city's slums. Even better, the new municipal housing was frequently designed to the highest specifications, no more so than under the guidance of the two leading architects of the (broadly

Expressionist) **Amsterdam School**, Michael de Klerk (1884–1923) and Piet Kramer (1881–1961). The duo were responsible for the layout of much of the Nieuw Zuid (New South; see p.131–135).

Nationally, **Jan Rudolph Thorbecke**, the outstanding political figure of the times, formed three ruling cabinets (1849–53, 1862–66 and 1872, in the year of his death) and steered the Netherlands through a profound attitudinal change. The political parties of the late eighteenth century had wished to resurrect the power and prestige of the seventeenth-century Netherlands; Thorbecke and his liberal allies resigned themselves to the country's reduced status as a small power and eulogized its advantages. For the first time, from about 1850, liberty was seen as a luxury made possible by the country's very lack of power, and the malaise that had long disturbed public life gave way to a positive appreciation of the very narrowness of its national existence. One of the results of Thorbecke's liberalism was a gradual extension of the franchise, culminating in the **Act of Universal Suffrage** in 1917.

The war years

The Netherlands remained neutral during **World War I** and although it suffered privations from the Allied blockade of German war materials, this was offset by the profits many Dutch merchants made by trading with both sides. Similar attempts to remain neutral in **World War II** however, failed: the **Germans invaded** on May 10, 1940, and the Netherlands was quickly overrun. Queen Wilhelmina fled to London to set up a government-in-exile, and members of the **NSB**, the Dutch fascist party, which had welcomed the invaders, were rewarded with positions of authority. Nevertheless, in the early months of the occupation, life for ordinary Amsterdammers went on pretty much as usual. Even when the first roundups of the **Jews** began in late 1940, many managed to turn a blind eye, though in February 1941 Amsterdam's newly outlawed Communist Party did organize a widely supported strike, spearheaded by the city's transport and refuse workers, shipbuilders and dockers (see p.103). It was a gesture rather than a move to undermine German control, but an important one all the same. Interviewed after the war, one of the leaders summarized it thus: "If only one of Amsterdam's Jews did not feel forgotten and abandoned as he was packed off in a train, then the strike was well worth it."

As the war progressed, so the German grip got tighter and the Dutch **Resistance** stronger, its activities – primarily industrial and transportation sabotage as well as the forgery of identity papers, a real Dutch speciality – trumpeted by underground newspapers such as *Het Parool* (The Password), which survives in good form today. The Resistance paid a heavy price with some 23,000 of its fighters and sympathizers losing their lives, but the city's Jews (see box on p.100) took the worst punishment. In 1940, the city's Jewish population, swollen by refugees from Hitler's Germany, was around 140,000, but when the Allies liberated the city in May 1945 only a few thousand were left. The Old Jewish Quarter (see Chapter Four) lay deserted, a rare crumb of comfort being the survival of the diary of a young Jewish girl – **Anne Frank**.

Reconstruction – 1945 to 1960

The **post-war years** were spent patching up the damage of occupation, though at first progress was hindered by a desperate shortage of food, fuel and building materials. Indeed, things were in such short supply and the winter of 1945–6 so cold that hundreds of Amsterdammers died of hunger and/or hypothermia, their black cardboard coffins being trundled to mass graves. Neither did it help that the retreating Germans had blown up all the dykes and sluices on the North Sea coast at Ijmuiden, at the mouth of the Nordzeekanaal. Nevertheless, Amsterdam had not received an aerial pounding of the likes dished out to Rotterdam and Arnhem and the reconstruction soon built up a head of steam. One feature of the reconstruction was the creation of giant suburbs like **Bijlmermeer**, to the southeast of the city, the last word in early 1960s large-scale residential planning, with low-cost modern housing, play areas and traffic-free foot and cycle paths.

Two events were, however, to mar Dutch reconstruction in the late 1940s and early 1950s. The former **Dutch colonies** of Java and Sumatra, taken by the Japanese at the outbreak of the war, were now ruled by a nationalist Republican government that refused to recognize Dutch sovereignty. Following the failure of talks between Den Haag and the islanders in 1947, the Dutch sent the troops in, a colonial enterprise that soon became a bloody debacle. International opposition was intense and, after much condemnation and pressure, the Dutch reluctantly surrendered their most important Asian colonies, which were ultimately incorporated as **Indonesia** in 1950. Back at home, tragedy struck on February 1, 1953 when an unusually high tide was pushed over Zeeland's sea defences by a westerly gale, flooding 160 square kilometres of land and drowning over 1800 people. The response was the **Delta Project**, which closed off the western part of the Scheldt and Maas estuaries with massive sea dykes, thereby ensuring the safety of cities to the south of Amsterdam, though Amsterdam itself had already been secured by the completion of the **Afsluitdijk** in 1932. This dyke closed off the Zuider Zee, turning it into the freshwater Ijsselmeer and Markermeer (see box on p.151).

The Provos and the 1960s

The radical and youthful mass movements that swept through the West in the 1960s transformed Amsterdam from a middling, rather conservative city into a turbo-charged hotbed of **hippy action**. In 1963, one-time window cleaner and magician extraordinaire **Jasper Grootveld** won celebrity status by painting "K" – for *kanker* ("cancer") – on cigarette billboards throughout the city. Two years later, he proclaimed the statue of the *Lieverdje* ("Loveable Rascal") on the Spui (see p.62) the symbol of "tomorrow's addicted consumer" – since it had been donated to the city by a cigarette manufacturer – and organized large-scale gatherings there once a week. His actions enthused others, most notably **Roel van Duyn**, a philosophy student at Amsterdam University, who assembled a Left-wing-cum-anarchist movement known as the **Provos** – short for *provocatie* ("provocation"). The Provos participated in Grootveld's meetings and then proceeded to organize their own street "happenings", which proved to be fantastically popular among young Amsterdammers. The number of

Provos never exceeded about thirty and the group had no coherent structure, but they did have one clear aim – to bring points of political or social conflict to public attention by spectacular means. More than anything they were masters of publicity, and pursued their "games" with a spirit of fun rather than grim political fanaticism. The reaction of the police, however, was aggressive: the first two issues of the Provos' magazine were confiscated and, in July 1965, they intervened at a Saturday night "happening", setting a pattern for future confrontations. The magazine itself contained the Provos' manifesto, a set of policies which later appeared under the title "**The White Plans**". These included the famously popular **white bicycle plan**, which proposed that the council ban all cars in the city centre and supply 20,000 bicycles (painted white) for general public use.

There were regular police-Provo confrontations throughout 1965, but it was the **wedding of Princess Beatrix** to Claus von Amsberg on March 10, 1966, that provoked the most serious unrest. Amsberg had served in the German army during World War II and many Netherlanders were deeply offended by the marriage. Consequently, when hundreds took to the streets to protest, pelting the wedding procession with smoke bombs, a huge swath of Dutch opinion supported them – to some degree or another. Amsberg himself got no more than he deserved when he was jeered with the refrain "Give us back the bikes", a reference to the commandeering of hundreds of bikes by the retreating German army in 1945. The wedding over, the next crisis came in June when, much to the horror of the authorities, it appeared that students, workers and Provos were about to combine. In panic, the Hague government ordered the dismissal of Amsterdam's police chief, but in the event the Provos had peaked and the workers proved far from revolutionary, settling for arbitration on their various complaints.

The final twist in the Provos tale was the formation of a splinter group called the **Kabouters**, named after a helpful gnome in Dutch folklore. Their manifesto described their form of socialism as "not of the clenched fist, but of the intertwined fingers, the erect penis, the escaping butterfly…" – appealing perhaps, but never massively popular.

The 1970s and 1980s – and the squatters

In 1967, the Provos formally dissolved their movement at a happening in the Vondelpark, but many of their supporters promptly moved on to **neighbourhood committees**, set up to oppose the more outlandish development plans of the city council. The most hated scheme by a long chalk was the plan to build a **metro line** through the Nieuwmarkt to the new suburb of Bijlmermeer as this involved both wholesale demolitions and compulsory relocations. For six months, there were regular confrontations between the police and the protestors and, although the council eventually had its way, the scene was set for more trouble. In particular, the council seemed to many to be unwilling to tackle Amsterdam's acute **housing shortage**, neglecting the needs of its poorer citizens in favour of business interests. It was this perception that fuelled the **squatter movement**, which coalesced around a handful of symbolic squats. The first major incident came in March 1980 when several hundred police evicted squatters from premises on **Vondelstraat**. Afterwards, there was widespread rioting, but this was small beer in comparison with the protests of April 30, 1980 – the **coronation day of Queen Beatrix** – when a mixed bag of squatters and leftists vigorously protested both the lavishness of the proceedings and the expense of refurbishing Beatrix's palace in Den Haag. Once again there was widespread rioting and this time it spread to other Dutch cities, though the unrest was short-lived.

Now at its peak, Amsterdam's squatting movement boasted around ten thousand activists, many of whom were involved in two more major confrontations with the police – the first at the **Lucky Luyk** squat, on Jan Luykenstraat, the second at the **Wyers** building, when, in February 1984, the squatters were forcibly cleared to make way for a Holiday Inn, now the Crowne Plaza Hotel (see p.50). The final show-down – the **Stopera** campaign – came with the construction of the **Muziektheater/Stadhuis** complex on Waterlooplein (see p.101). Thereafter, the movement faded away, at least partly because of its repeated failure to stop the developers, who now claim, with some justification, to be more sensitive to community needs.

The present

The street protests and massive squats of Amsterdam's recent past now seem a distant memory, but some of the old ideas – and ideals – have been carried forward by the **Greens**, who attract a small but significant following in every municipal – and national – election. The much larger Labour Party – the Pvda – has picked up on some of these issues too, though it has a problem with **Schiphol airport**, which needs to be expanded, but is an environmental minefield. Politically, one of the problems is that the city's finely balanced system of **proportional representation** brings little rapid change and often mires in interminable compromise and debate. The same is true nationally, where politics has long seemed a bland if necessary business conducted between the three main parties, the **Protestant–Catholic CDA** coalition, the **Liberal VVD** and the **Socialist Pvda**. However, the entire political class received a jolt in the national elections of May 2002 when a brand-new Rightist grouping – **Leefbaar Neederlands** (Liveable Netherlands) – led by **Pim Fortuyn** swept to second place behind the CDA, securing seventeen percent of the national vote. Stylish and witty, openly gay and a former Marxist, Fortuyn managed to cover several popular bases at the same time, from the need for law and order through to tighter immigration controls. Most crucially, he also attacked the liberal establishment's espousal of multi-culturalism even when the representatives of minority groups were deeply reactionary, anti-gay and sexist. Politically, it worked a treat, but a year later Fortuyn was assassinated and his party rapidly unravelled, losing most of its seats in the general election of January 2003 (see below).

One of the reasons for Fortuyn's electoral success reflected the other shock to the Dutch system, which came with the publication of a damning report on the failure of the Dutch army to protect the Bosnian Muslims ensconced in the UN safe-haven of **Srebrenica** in 1995. Published in April 2002, the report told a tale of extraordinary incompetence: the UN's Dutch soldiers were inadequately armed, but still refused American assistance, and watched as Serb troops separated Muslim men and women in preparation for the mass executions, which the Dutch soldiers then did nothing to stop (though they were never involved). In a country that prides itself on its internationalism, the report was an especially hard blow and the whole of the Pvda-led government, under **Wim Kok**, resigned in April 2002.

The general election of 2003 was a close run thing, and perhaps against the odds there was a revival in Pvda fortunes, but a **Rightist alliance** – consisting of the VVD, the CDA and the Lijst Pim Fortuyn (formerly Leefbaar Neederlands) – managed to cobble together an administration that is in power at time of writing under the leadership of Jan Peter Balkenende. Superficially, with the Fortuyn representatives reduced to a rump, it seemed that normal political service had been resumed, but although the CDA, the Pvda and the VVD were once again the largest parties, there was an uneasy undertow. In truth, Fortuyn's popularity had pushed certain sorts of social debate, particularly on **immigration**, to the right both in Amsterdam and the country as a whole and the situation got much worse – and race relations much tenser – when, in late 2004, the filmmaker Theo van Gogh was shot dead on an Amsterdam street by a Moroccan who objected to a film Gogh had made – Submission – about Islamic violence against women. Shown on Dutch TV, the film had been scripted by an MP, Ayaan Hirsi Ali, a Somali refugee and current Dutch citizen, who herself had fled an arranged marriage and now travels everywhere with armed bodyguards. With polls indicating that many Dutch feel apprehensive if not actually hostile to the Muslims in their midst, it will take all of Balkenende's skills to keep the lid on the inter–communal pot.

National events aside, the majority of Amsterdammers have readily accepted the city council's recent attempt to recast the city as a dynamic, go-ahead metropolis with the drugs and the hippies as a byline. Redevelopment has become the name of the game, particularly of the old docklands bordering the River Ij, and yet Amsterdam still retains its idiosyncratic character, of houseboats and sky-rises, and its historic centre is now recognized as too valuable a tourist attraction to be placed under threat.

Dutch art

Designed to serve only as a quick reference, the following outline is the very briefest of introductions to a subject that has rightly filled volumes. Inevitably, it covers artists that lived and worked in both the Netherlands and Belgium, as these two countries have – along with Luxembourg – been bound together as the "**Low Countries**" for most of their history. For in-depth and academic studies, see the recommendations in "Books" on p.286. For a list of where to find some of the paintings mentioned here, turn to the box on p.282.

Beginnings – the Flemish Primitives

Throughout the medieval period, **Flanders**, in modern-day Belgium, was one of the most artistically productive parts of Europe and it was here that the solid realist base of later Dutch painting developed. Today the works of these early Flemish painters, the **Flemish Primitives**, are highly prized and although examples are fairly sparse in the Netherlands, all the leading museums – especially Amsterdam's Rijksmuseum and Den Haag's Mauritshuis – have fine examples, though those of the Rijksmuseum are not on display during the museum's refurbishment (see p.116).

Jan van Eyck (1385–1441) is generally regarded as the first of the Flemish Primitives, and has even been credited with the invention of oil painting – though it seems more likely that he simply perfected a new technique by thinning his paint with (the then newly discovered) turpentine, thus making it more flexible. The most famous of his works still in the Low Countries is the altarpiece in Belgium's Ghent cathedral, which was revolutionary in its realism, for the first time using elements of native landscape in depicting Biblical themes. Van Eyck's style and technique were to influence several generations of the region's artists.

Firmly in the Eyckian tradition were the **Master of Flemalle** (1387–1444) and **Rogier van der Weyden** (1400–64), one-time official painter to the city of Brussels. The Flemalle master is a shadowy figure: some believe he was the teacher of Van der Weyden, others that the two artists were in fact the same person. There are differences between the two, however: the Flemalle master's paintings are close to Van Eyck's, whereas Van der Weyden shows a greater degree of emotional intensity in his religious works. Van der Weyden also produced serene portraits of the bigwigs of his day that were much admired across a large swath of western Europe. His style, never mind his success, influenced many painters with one of the most talented of these being **Dieric Bouts** (1415–75). Born in Haarlem but active in Leuven, Bouts is recognizable by his stiff, rather elongated figures and horrific subject matter, all set against carefully drawn landscapes. **Hugo van der Goes** (d. 1482) was the next Ghent master after Van Eyck, most famous for the Portinari altarpiece in Florence's Uffizi gallery. After a short painting career, he died insane, and his late works have strong hints of his impending madness in their subversive use of space and implicit acceptance of the viewer's presence.

Few doubt that **Hans Memling** (1440–94) was a pupil of Van der Weyden. Active in Bruges throughout his life, he is best remembered for the pastoral charm of his landscapes and the quality of his portraiture, much of which survives on the rescued side panels of triptychs. **Gerard David** (1460–1523) was a native of Oudewater, near Gouda, but he moved to Bruges in 1484, becoming the last of the great painters to work in that city, before it was outstripped by Antwerp, producing formal religious works of traditional bent. Strikingly different, but broadly contemporaneous, was **Hieronymus Bosch** (1450–1516), who lived for most of his life in Holland, though his style is linked to that of his Flemish contemporaries. His frequently reprinted religious allegories are filled with macabre visions of tortured people and grotesque beasts, and appear at first faintly unhinged, though it's now thought that these are visual representations of contemporary sayings, idioms and parables. While their interpretation is far from resolved, Bosch's paintings draw strongly on subconscious fears and archetypes, giving them a lasting, haunting fascination.

The sixteenth century

At the end of the fifteenth century, Flanders was in economic and political decline and the leading artists of the day were drawn instead to the booming port of **Antwerp**, also in present–day Belgium. The artists who worked here soon began to integrate the finely observed detail that characterized the Flemish tradition with the style of the Italian painters of the Renaissance. **Quentin Matsys** (1464–1530) introduced florid classical architectural details and intricate landscapes to his works, influenced perhaps by the work of Leonardo da Vinci. As well as religious works, he painted portraits and genre scenes, all of which have recognizably Italian facets – and paved the way for the Dutch genre painters of later years. **Jan Gossaert** (1478–1532) made the pilgrimage to Italy too, and his dynamic works are packed with detail, especially finely drawn classical architectural backdrops. He was the first Low Countries artist to introduce the subjects of classical mythology into his paintings, part of a steady trend through the period towards secular subject matter, which can also be seen in the work of **Joachim Patenier** (d.1524), who painted small landscapes of fantastical scenery.

The middle of the sixteenth century was dominated by the work of **Pieter Bruegel the Elder** (c.1525–69), whose gruesome allegories and innovative interpretations of religious subjects are firmly placed in Low Countries settings. Pieter also painted finely observed peasant scenes, though he himself was well-connected in court circles in Antwerp and, later, Brussels. **Pieter Aertsen** (1508–75) also worked in the peasant genre, adding aspects of still life: his paintings often show a detailed kitchen scene in the foreground, with a religious episode going on behind. Bruegel's two sons, **Pieter Bruegel the Younger** (1564–1638) and **Jan Bruegel** (1568–1625), were lesser painters: the former produced fairly insipid copies of his father's work, while Jan developed a style of his own – delicately rendered flower paintings and genre pieces that earned him the nickname "Velvet". Towards the latter half of the sixteenth century highly stylized Italianate portraits became the dominant fashion, with **Frans Pourbus the Younger** (1569–1622) the leading practitioner. Frans hob-nobbed across Europe, working for the likes of the Habsburgs and the Médicis.

Meanwhile, there were artistic rumblings in the province of Holland. Leading the charge was **Geertgen tot Sint Jans** (Little Gerard of the Brotherhood of St John; d. 1490), who worked in Haarlem, initiating – in a strangely naive style – an artistic vision that would come to dominate the seventeenth century. There was a tender melancholy in his work very different from the stylized paintings produced in Flanders and, most importantly, a new sensitivity to light – and lighting. **Jan Mostaert** (1475–1555) took over after Geertgen's death, developing similar themes, but the first painter to effect real changes in northern painting was **Lucas van Leyden** (1489–1533). Born in Leiden, his bright colours and narrative technique were refreshingly novel, and he introduced a new dynamism into what had become a rigidly formal treatment of devotional subjects. There was rivalry, of course. Carel van Mander (see below) claimed Alkmaar native **Jan van Scorel** (1495–1562) as the better painter, complaining, too, of Van Leyden's dandyish ways. Certainly Van Scorel's influence should not be underestimated. Like many of his contemporaries, Van Scorel hot-footed it to Italy to view the works of the Renaissance, but in Rome his career went into over-drive when he found favour with Pope Hadrian VI, one-time bishop of Utrecht, who installed him as court painter in 1520. Van Scorel stayed in Rome for four years and when he returned to Utrecht, armed with all that papal prestige, he combined the ideas he had picked up in Italy with those underpinning Haarlem realism, thereby modifying what had previously been an independent artistic tradition once and for all. Amongst his several students, probably the most talented was **Maerten van Heemskerck** (1498–1574), who went off to Italy himself in 1532, staying there five years before returning to Haarlem.

The Golden Age

The seventeenth century begins with **Karel van Mander**, Haarlem painter, art impresario and one of the few contemporary chroniclers of the art of the Low Countries. His *Schilderboek* of 1604 put Flemish and Dutch traditions into context for the first time, and in addition specified the rules of fine painting. Examples of his own work are rare – though Haarlem's Frans Hals Museum (see p.144) weighs in with a couple – but his followers were many. Among them was **Cornelius Cornelisz van Haarlem** (1562–1638), who produced elegant renditions of biblical and mythical themes; and **Hendrik Goltzius** (1558–1616), who was a skilled engraver and an integral member of Van Mander's Haarlem academy. These painters' enthusiasm for Italian art, combined with the influence of a late revival of Gothicism, resulted in works that combined Mannerist and Classical elements. An interest in realism was also felt, but, for them, the subject became less important than the way in which it was depicted: biblical stories became merely a vehicle whereby artists could apply their skills in painting the human body, landscapes, or copious displays of food. All of this served to break religion's stranglehold on art, and make legitimate a whole range of everyday subjects for the painter.

In Holland (and this was where the north and the south finally diverged) this break with tradition was compounded by the **Reformation**: the austere Calvinism that had replaced the Catholic faith in the United (ie northern) Provinces had no use for images or symbols of devotion in its churches. Instead, painters catered to the burgeoning middle class, and no longer visited Italy to learn their craft. Indeed, the real giants of the seventeenth century – Hals, Rembrandt, Vermeer – stayed in the Netherlands all their lives. Another innovation was that painting split into more distinct categories – genre, portrait, landscape – and artists tended (with notable exceptions) to confine themselves to one field throughout their careers. So began the greatest age of Dutch art.

Historical and religious painting

The artistic influence of Renaissance Italy may have been in decline, but Italian painters still had clout with the Dutch, most notably **Caravaggio** (1571–1610), who was much admired for his new realism. Taking Caravaggio's cue, many artists – Rembrandt for one – continued to portray classical subjects, but in a way that was totally at odds with the Mannerists' stylish flights of imagination. The Utrecht artist **Abraham Bloemaert** (1564–1651), though a solid Mannerist throughout his career, encouraged these new ideas, and his students – **Gerard van Honthorst** (1590–1656), **Hendrik Terbrugghen** (1588–1629) and **Dirck van Baburen** (1590–1624) – formed the nucleus of the influential **Utrecht School**, which followed Caravaggio almost to the point of slavishness. Honthorst was perhaps the leading figure, learning his craft from Bloemaert and travelling to Rome, where he was nicknamed "Gerardo delle Notti" for his ingenious handling of light and shade. In his later paintings, however, this was to become more routine technique than inspired invention, and though a supremely competent artist, Honthorst is somewhat discredited among critics today. Terbrugghen's reputation seems to have aged rather better: he soon forgot Caravaggio and developed a more individual style, his later, lighter work having a great influence on the young Vermeer. After a jaunt to Rome, Baburen shared a studio with Terbrugghen and produced some fairly original work – work which also had some influence on Vermeer – but today he is the least studied member of the group and few of his paintings survive.

Above all others, **Rembrandt** (1606–1669) was the most original historical artist of the seventeenth century, also chipping in with religious paintings throughout his career. In the 1630s, the poet and statesman Constantijn Huygens procured for him his greatest commission – a series of five paintings of the Passion, beautifully composed and uncompromisingly realistic. Later, however, Rembrandt drifted away from the mainstream, ignoring the smooth brushwork of his contemporaries and choosing instead a rougher, darker and more disjointed style for his biblical and historical subjects. This contributed to a decline in his artistic fortunes and it is significant that while the more conventional Jordaens, Honthorst and Van Everdingen were busy decorating the Huis ten Bosch near Den Haag for the Stadholder Frederick Henry, Rembrandt was having his monumental *Conspiracy of Julius Civilis* – painted for the new Amsterdam Town Hall – thrown out. The reasons for this rejection have been hotly debated, but it seems probable that Rembrandt's rendition was thought too pagan an interpretation of what was an important event in Dutch history – Julius had organized a revolt against the Romans, which had obvious resonance in a country just freed from the Habsburgs. Even worse, perhaps, Rembrandt had shown Julius to be blind in one eye, which was historically accurate but not at all what the city's burghers had in mind for a Dutch hero.

Finally, **Aert van Gelder** (1645–1727), Rembrandt's last pupil and probably the only one to concentrate on historical painting, followed the style of his master closely, producing shimmering biblical scenes well into the eighteenth century.

Genre painting

Often misunderstood, the term **genre painting** was initially applied to everything from animal paintings and still lifes through to historical works and landscapes, but later – from around the middle of the seventeenth century – came to be applied only to scenes of everyday life. Its target market was the region's burgeoning middle class, who had a penchant for non-idealized portrayals of common scenes, both with and without symbols – or subtly disguised details – making one moral point or another. One of its early practitioners was Antwerp's **Frans Snijders** (1579–1657), who took up still-life painting where Aertsen (see p.272) left off, amplifying his subject – food and drink – to even larger, more sumptuous canvases. Snijders also doubled up as a member of the Rubens art machine (see p.279), painting animals and still-life sections for the master's works. In the north, in Utrecht, Hendrik Terbrugghen and Gerard van Honthorst adapted the realism and strong chiaroscuro learned from Caravaggio to a number of tableaux of everyday life, though they were more concerned with religious works (see opposite), whilst Haarlem's Frans Hals dabbled in genre too, but is better known as a portraitist. The opposite is true of one of Hal's pupils, **Adriaen Brouwer** (1605–38), whose riotous tavern scenes were well received in their day and collected by, among others, Rubens and Rembrandt. Brouwer spent only a couple of years in Haarlem under Hals before returning to his native Flanders, where he influenced the inventive **David Teniers the Younger** (1610–1690), who worked in Antwerp, and later in Brussels. Teniers' early paintings are Brouwer-like peasant scenes, although his later work is more delicate and refined, including *kortegaardje* – guardroom scenes that show soldiers carousing. **Adriaen van Ostade** (1610–85), on the other hand, stayed in Haarlem most of his life, skilfully painting groups of peasants and tavern brawls – though his later acceptance by the establishment led him to water down the realism he had learnt from Brouwer. He was teacher to his brother **Isaak** (1621–49), who produced a large number of open-air peasant scenes, subtle combinations of genre and landscape work.

The English critic E.V. Lucas dubbed Teniers, Brouwer and Ostade "coarse and boorish" compared with **Jan Steen** (1625–79) who, along with Vermeer, is probably the most admired Dutch genre painter. You can see what he had in mind: Steen's paintings offer the same Rabelaisian peasantry in full fling, but they go their debauched ways in broad daylight, and nowhere do you see the filthy rogues in shadowy hovels favoured by Brouwer and Ostade. Steen offers more humour, too, as well as more moralizing, identifying with the hedonistic mob and reproaching them at the same time. Indeed, many of his pictures are illustrations of well-known proverbs of the time – popular epithets on the evils of drink or the transience of human existence that were supposed to teach as well as entertain.

Leiden's **Gerrit Dou** (1613–75) was one of Rembrandt's first pupils. It's difficult to detect any trace of the master's influence in his work, however, as Dou initiated a style of his own: tiny, minutely realized and beautifully finished views of a kind of ordinary life that was decidedly more genteel than Brouwer's – or even Steen's for that matter. He was admired, above all, for his painstaking attention to detail: and he would, it's said, sit in his studio for hours waiting for the dust to settle before starting work. Among his students, **Frans van Mieris** (1635–81) continued the highly finished portrayals of the Dutch bourgeoisie, as did **Gabriel Metsu** (1629–67) – perhaps Dou's most talented pupil – whose pictures often convey an overtly moral message. Another pupil of Rembrandt's, though a much later one, was **Nicholas Maes** (1629–93), whose early works were almost entirely genre paintings, sensitively executed and again with an obvious didacticism. His later paintings show the influence of a more refined style of portraiture, which he had picked up in France.

As a native of Zwolle, well to the east of Amsterdam, **Gerard ter Borch** (1619–81) found himself far from all these Leiden/Rembrandt connections; despite trips abroad to most of the artistic capitals of Europe, he remained very much a provincial painter. He depicted Holland's merchant class at play and became renowned for his curious doll-like figures and his ability to capture the textures of different cloths. His domestic scenes were not unlike those of **Pieter de Hooch** (1629–after 1684), whose simple depictions of everyday life are deliberately unsentimental, and have little or no moral commentary. De Hooch's favourite trick was to paint darkened rooms with an open door leading through to a sunlit courtyard, a practice that, along with his trademark rusty red colour, makes his work easy to identify and, at its best, exquisite. That said, his later pictures reflect the encroaching decadence of the Dutch Republic: the rooms are more richly decorated, the arrangements more contrived and the subjects far less homely.

It was, however, **Jan Vermeer** (1632–75) who brought the most sophisticated methods to painting interiors, depicting the play of natural light on indoor surfaces with superlative skill – and the tranquil intimacy for which he is now famous the world over. Another observer of the better-heeled Dutch household and, like De Hooch, without a moral tone, he is regarded (with Hals and Rembrandt) as one of the big three Dutch painters – though he was, it seems, a slow worker. As a result, only about forty paintings can be attributed to him with any certainty. Living all his life in Delft, to the south of Amsterdam, Vermeer is perhaps the epitome of the seventeenth-century Dutch painter – rejecting the pomp and ostentation of the High Renaissance to record quietly his contemporaries at home, painting for a public that demanded no more than that – bourgeois art at its most complete.

Portraits – and Rembrandt

Predictably enough, the ruling bourgeoisie of Holland's flourishing mercantile society were keen to record and celebrate their success, and consequently portraiture was a reliable way for a young painter to make a living. **Michiel Jansz Miereveld** (1567–1641), court painter to Frederick Henry of Orange–Nassau in Den Haag, was the first real portraitist of the Dutch Republic, but it wasn't long before his stiff and rather conservative figures were superseded by the more spontaneous renderings of **Frans Hals** (1585–1666). Hals is perhaps best known for his "corporation pictures" – portraits of the members of the Dutch civil guard regiments that were formed in most of the larger towns during the war with Spain, but subsequently becoming social clubs. These large group pieces demanded superlative technique, since the painter had to create a collection of individual portraits while retaining a sense of the group, and accord prominence based on the relative importance of the sitters and the size of the payment each had made. Hals was particularly good at this, using innovative lighting effects, arranging his sitters subtly, and putting all the elements together in a fluid and dynamic composition. He also painted many individual portraits, making the ability to capture fleeting and telling expressions his trademark; his pictures of children are particularly sensitive. Later in life, however, his work became darker and more akin to Rembrandt's, spurred – it's conjectured – by his penury.

Jan Cornelisz Verspronck (1597–1662) and **Bartholomeus van der Helst** (1613–70) were the other great Haarlem portraitists after Frans Hals – Verspronck recognizable by the smooth, shiny glow he always gave to his sitters' faces, Van der Helst by a competent but unadventurous style. Of the two,

Van der Helst was the more popular, influencing a number of later painters and leaving Haarlem as a young man to begin a solidly successful career as portrait painter to Amsterdam's burghers.

The reputation of **Rembrandt van Rijn** (1606–69) is still relatively recent – nineteenth-century connoisseurs preferred Gerard Dou – but he is now justly regarded as one of the greatest and most versatile painters of all time. Born in Leiden, the son of a miller, he was a boy apprentice to Jacob van Swanenburgh, a then quite important, though singularly uninventive, local artist. Rembrandt shared a studio with Jan Lievens, a promising painter and something of a rival, though now all but forgotten, before venturing forth to Amsterdam to study under the fashionable Pieter Lastman. Soon he was painting commissions for the city elite and became an accepted member of their circle. The poet and statesman Constantijn Huygens acted as his agent, pulling strings to obtain all of Rembrandt's more lucrative jobs, and in 1634 the artist married Saskia van Ulenborch, daughter of the burgomaster of Leeuwarden and quite a catch for a relatively humble artist. His self-portraits from this period show the confident face of security – on top of things and quite sure of where he's going.

Rembrandt would not always be the darling of the Amsterdam burghers, but his fall from grace was still some way off when he painted *The Night Watch*, a group portrait often – but inaccurately – associated with the artist's decline in popularity. Indeed, although Rembrandt's fluent arrangement of his subjects was totally original, there's no evidence that the military company who commissioned the painting was anything but pleased with the result. More likely culprits are the artist's later pieces, whose obscure lighting and psychological insights took the conservative Amsterdam merchants by surprise, and his irascibility. Whatever the reason, his patrons were certainly not sufficiently enthusiastic about his later work to support his taste for art collecting and his expensive house on Jodenbreestraat (see p.98), and in 1656 he was declared bankrupt. Rembrandt died thirteen years later, a broken and embittered old man – as his last self-portraits show. Throughout his career he maintained a large studio, and his influence pervaded the next generation of Dutch painters. Some – Dou and Maes – more famous for their genre work, have already been mentioned. Others turned to portraiture.

Govert Flinck (1615–60) was perhaps Rembrandt's most faithful follower, and he was, ironically enough, given the job of decorating Amsterdam's new Town Hall after his teacher had been passed over. Unluckily for him, Flinck died before he could execute his designs and Rembrandt took over, but although the latter's *Conspiracy of Julius Civilis* (see p.274) was installed in 1662, it was discarded a year later for reasons that remain obscure. The early work of **Ferdinand Bol** (1616–80) was also heavily influenced by Rembrandt, so much so that for centuries art historians couldn't tell the two apart, though Bol's later paintings are readily distinguishable, blandly elegant portraits, which proved very popular with the well-heeled. At the age of 53, Bol married a wealthy widow and promptly stopped painting – perhaps because he knew how emotionally tacky his work had become. Most of the pitifully slim extant work of **Carel Fabritius** (1622–54) was portraiture, but he too died young, before he could properly realize his promise as perhaps the most gifted of all Rembrandt's students. Generally regarded as the teacher of Vermeer, he forms a link between the two masters, combining Rembrandt's technique with his own practice of painting figures against a dark background, prefiguring the lighting and colouring of the Delft painter.

Landscapes

Aside from **Pieter Bruegel the Elder** (see p.272), whose depictions of his native surroundings make him the first true Low Countries landscape painter, **Gillis van Coninxloo** (1544–1607) stands out as the earliest Dutch landscapist. He imbued his native scenery with elements of fantasy, painting the richly wooded views he had seen on his travels around Europe as backdrops to biblical scenes. In the early seventeenth century, **Hercules Seghers** (1590–1638), apprenticed to Coninxloo, carried on his mentor's style of depicting forested and mountainous landscapes, some real, others not: his work is scarce but is believed to have had considerable influence on the landscape work of Rembrandt. **Esaias van der Velde**'s (1591–1632) quaint and unpretentious scenes show the first real affinity with the Dutch countryside, but while his influence was likewise considerable, he was soon overshadowed by his pupil **Jan van Goyen** (1596–1656). A remarkable painter, who belongs to the so-called "tonal phase" of Dutch landscape painting, Van Goyen's early pictures were highly coloured and close to those of his teacher, but it didn't take him long to develop a marked touch of his own, using tones of green, brown and grey to lend everything a characteristic translucent haze. His paintings are, above all, of nature, and if he included figures it was just for the sake of scale. A long neglected artist, Van Goyen only received recognition with the arrival of the Impressionists, when his fluid and rapid brushwork was at last fully appreciated.

Another "tonal" painter, Haarlem's **Salomon van Ruysdael** (1600–70) was also directly affected by Esaias van der Velde, and his simple and atmospheric, though not terribly adventurous, landscapes were for a long time consistently confused with those of Van Goyen. More esteemed is his nephew, **Jacob van Ruysdael** (1628–82), generally considered the greatest of all Dutch landscapists, whose fastidiously observed views of quiet flatlands dominated by stormy skies were to influence European landscapists right up to the nineteenth century. Constable, certainly, acknowledged a debt to him. Ruysdael's foremost pupil was **Meindert Hobbema** (1638–1709), who followed the master faithfully, sometimes even painting the same views as in his his *Avenue at Middelharnis*.

Nicholas Berchem (1620–83) and **Jan Both** (1618–52) were the "Italianizers" of Dutch landscapes. They studied in Rome and were influenced by the Frenchman Claude Lorraine, taking back to Holland rich, golden views of the world, full of steep gorges and hills, picturesque ruins and wandering shepherds. **Allart van Everdingen** (1621–75) had a similar approach, but his subject matter stemmed from travels in Norway, which, after his return to the Netherlands, he reproduced in all its mountainous glory. **Aelbert Cuyp** (1620–91), on the other hand, stayed in Dordrecht all his life, painting what was probably the favourite city skyline of Dutch landscapists. He inherited the warm tones of the Italianizers, and his pictures are always suffused with a deep, golden glow.

Of a number of specialist seventeenth-century painters who can be included here, **Paulus Potter** (1625–54) is rated as the best painter of **domestic animals**. He produced a surprisingly large number of paintings in his short life, the most reputed being his lovingly executed pictures of cows and horses. The accurate rendering of **architectural** features also became a specialized field, in which **Pieter Saenredam** (1597–1665), with his finely realized paintings of Dutch church interiors, is the most widely known exponent. **Emanuel de Witte** (1616–92) continued in the same vein, though his churches lack the spartan crispness of Saenredam's. **Gerrit Berckheyde** (1638–98) worked in Haarlem soon after, but he limited his views to the outside of buildings, producing variations on the same scenes around town. **Nautical scenes** in praise of the Dutch navy were, on the other hand, the speciality of **Willem van der Velde II** (1633–1707), whose melodramatic canvases, complete with their churning seas and chasing skies, are displayed to greatest advantage in the Nederlands Scheepvaartsmuseum in Amsterdam (see p.108).

A further thriving category of seventeenth-century painting was the **still life**, in which objects were gathered together to remind the viewer of the transience of human life and the meaninglessness of worldly pursuits. Thus, a skull would often be joined by a book, a pipe or a goblet, and some half-eaten food. Again, two Haarlem painters dominated this field: **Pieter Claesz** (1598–1660) and **Willem Heda** (1594–1680), who confined themselves almost entirely to such carefully arranged groups of objects.

Rubens and his followers

Back down to the south, in Antwerp, **Pieter Paul Rubens** (1577–1640) was easily the most important exponent of the Baroque in northern Europe. Born in Siegen, Westphalia, he was raised in Antwerp, where he entered the painters' Guild in 1598. Two years later, he became court painter to the Duke of Mantua and thereafter he travelled extensively in Italy, absorbing the art of the High Renaissance and classical architecture. By the time of his return to Antwerp in 1608 he had acquired an enormous artistic vocabulary – and like his Dutch contemporaries (see p.275), the paintings of Caravaggio were to greatly influence his work. His first major success was *The Raising of the Cross*, painted in 1610 and displayed today in Antwerp cathedral. A large, dynamic work, caused a sensation at the time, establishing Rubens' reputation and leading to a string of commissions that enabled him to set up his own studio.

The division of labour in Rubens' studio, and the talent of the artists working there (who included Anthony van Dyck and Jacob Jordaens – see p.280) ensured an extraordinary output of excellent work. The degree to which Rubens personally worked on a canvas would vary – and would determine its price. From the early 1620s onwards he turned his hand to a plethora of themes and subjects – religious works, portraits, tapestry designs, landscapes, mythological scenes, ceiling paintings – each of which was handled with supreme vitality and virtuosity. From his Flemish antecedents he inherited an acute sense of light, and used it not to dramatize his subjects (a technique favoured by Caravaggio and other Italian artists), but in association with colour and form. The drama in his works comes from the vigorous animation of his characters. His large-scale allegorical works, especially, are packed with heaving, writhing figures that appear to tumble out from the canvas.

The energy of Rubens' paintings was reflected in his private life. In addition to his career as an artist, he also undertook diplomatic missions to Spain and England, and used these opportunities to study the works of other artists and – as in the case of Velázquez – to meet them personally. In the 1630s gout began to hamper his activities, and from this time his painting became more domestic and meditative. Hélène Fourment, his second wife, was the subject of many portraits and served as a model for characters in his allegorical paintings, her figure epitomizing the buxom, well-rounded women found throughout his work.

Rubens' influence on the artists of the period was enormous. The huge output of his studio meant that his works were universally seen and also widely disseminated by the engravers he employed to copy his work. Chief among his followers was the portraitist **Anthony van Dyck** (1599–1641), who worked in Rubens' studio from 1618, often taking on the depiction of religious figures in his master's works that required particular sensitivity and pathos. Like Rubens, van Dyck was born in Antwerp and travelled widely in Italy, though his initial work was influenced less by the Italian artists than by Rubens himself. Eventually van Dyck developed his own distinct style and technique, establishing himself as court painter to Charles I in England, and creating portraits of a nervous elegance that would influence the genre there for the next hundred and fifty years. **Jacob Jordaens** (1593–1678) was also an Antwerp native who studied under Rubens. Although he was commissioned to complete several works left unfinished by Rubens at the time of his death, his robustly naturalistic works have an earthy – and sensuous – realism that is quite different and distinct in style and technique.

The eighteenth and nineteenth centuries

Accompanying Holland's economic decline was a gradual deterioration in the quality and originality of Dutch painting. The delicacy of some of the classical seventeenth-century painters was replaced by finicky still lifes and minute studies of flowers, or finely finished portraiture and religious scenes, as in the work of **Adrian van der Werff** (1659–1722). Of the era's big names, **Gerard de Lairesse** (1640–1711) spent most of his time decorating a rash of brand-new civic halls and mansions, but, like the buildings he worked on, his style and influences were French. **Jacob de Wit** (1695–1754) continued where Lairesse left off, painting burgher ceiling after ceiling in flashy style. He also benefited from a relaxation in the laws against Catholics, decorating several of their (newly legal) churches. The period's only painter of any true renown was **Cornelis Troost** (1697–1750) who, although he didn't produce anything really original, painted competent portraits and some neat, faintly satirical pieces that have since earned him the title of "The Dutch Hogarth". Cosy interiors also continued to prove popular and the Haarlem painter **Wybrand Hendriks** (1744–1831) satisfied demand with numerous proficient examples.

Johann Barthold Jongkind (1819–91) was the first important artist to emerge in the nineteenth century, painting landscapes and seascapes that were to influence Monet and the early Impressionists. He spent most of his life in France and his work was exhibited in Paris with the Barbizon painters, though he owed less to them than to Van Goyen and the seventeenth-century "tonal" artists. Jongkind's work was a logical precursor to the art of the **Hague School**. Based in and around Den Haag between 1870 and 1900, this prolific group of painters tried to re-establish a characteristically Dutch national school of painting. They produced atmospheric studies of the dunes and polders around Den Haag, nature pictures that are characterized by grey, rain-filled skies, windswept seas, and silvery, flat beaches – pictures that, for some, verge on the sentimental. **J.H. Weissenbruch** (1824–1903) was a founding member, a specialist in low, flat beach scenes dotted with stranded boats. The banker-turned-artist **H.W. Mesdag** (1831–1915) did the same but with more skill than imagination, while **Jacob Maris** (1837–99), one of three artist brothers, was perhaps the most typical with his rural and sea scenes heavily covered by grey, chasing skies. His brother **Matthijs** (1839–1917) was less predictable, ultimately tiring of his colleagues' interest in straight observation and going to London to design windows, while the youngest brother **Willem** (1844–1910) is best known for his small, unpretentious studies of nature.

Anton Mauve (1838–88) is better known, an exponent of soft, pastel landscapes and an early teacher of Van Gogh. Profoundly influenced by the French Barbizon painters – Corot, Millet et al – he went to Hilversum near Amsterdam in 1885 to set up his own group, which became known as the "Dutch Barbizon". **Jozef Israëls** (1826–1911) has often been likened to Millet, though it's generally agreed that he had more in common with the Impressionists, and his best pictures are his melancholy portraits and interiors. Lastly, **Johan Bosboom**'s (1817–91) church interiors may be said to sum up the romanticized nostalgia of the Hague School: shadowy and populated by figures in seventeenth-century dress, they seem to yearn for Holland's Golden Age.

Vincent van Gogh (1853–90), on the other hand, was one of the least "Dutch" of Dutch artists, and he spent most of his relatively short painting career in France. After countless studies of Dutch peasant life – studies which culminated in the sombre *Potato Eaters* (see p.123) – he went to live in Paris with his art-dealer brother Theo. There, under the influence of the Impressionists, he lightened his palette, following the pointillist work of Seurat and "trying to render intense colour and not a grey harmony". Two years later he went south to Arles, the "land of blue tones and gay colours", and, struck by the brilliance of Mediterranean light, his characteristic style began to develop. A disastrous attempt to live with Gauguin, and the much-publicized episode when he cut off part of his ear and presented it to a local prostitute, led to his committal in an asylum at St-Rémy. Here he produced some of his most famous, and most Expressionistic, canvases – strongly coloured and with the paint thickly, almost frantically, applied. Now one of the world's most popular – and popularized – painters, Amsterdam's Van Gogh Museum has the world's finest collection of his work (see p.122–124).

Like Van Gogh, **Jan Toorop** (1858–1928) went through multiple artistic changes, though he did not need to travel to do so; he radically adapted his technique from a fairly conventional pointillism through a tired Expressionism to Symbolism with an Art Nouveau feel. Roughly contemporary, **George Hendrik Breitner** (1857–1923) was a better painter, and one who refined his style rather than changed it. His snapshot-like impressions of his beloved Amsterdam figure among his best work and offered a promising start to the new century.

The twentieth century

Each of the major modern art movements has had – or has – its followers in the Netherlands and each has been diluted or altered according to local taste. Of many lesser names, **Jan Sluyters** (1881–1957) stands out as the Dutch pioneer of Cubism, but this is small beer when compared with the one specifically Dutch movement – **De Stijl** (The Style). **Piet Mondriaan** (1872–1944) was De Stijl's leading figure, developing the realism he had learned from the Hague School painters – via Cubism, which he criticized for being too cowardly to depart totally from representation – into a complete abstraction of form which he called **Neo-Plasticism**. He was something of a mystic, and this was to some extent responsible for the direction that De Stijl – and his paintings – took:

canvases painted with grids of lines and blocks made up of the three primary colours and white, black and grey. Mondriaan believed this freed the work of art from the vagaries of personal perception, making it possible to obtain what he called "a true vision of reality".

De Stijl took other forms too: there was a magazine of the same name, and the movement introduced new concepts into every aspect of design, from painting to interior design and architecture. But in all these media, lines were kept simple, colours bold and clear. **Theo van Doesburg** (1883–1931) was a De Stijl co-founder and major theorist. His work is similar to Mondriaan's except for the noticeable absence of thick, black borders and the diagonals that he introduced into his work, calling his paintings "contra-compositions" – which, he said, were both more dynamic and more in touch with twentieth-century life. **Bart van der Leck** (1876–1958) was the third member of the circle, identifiable by white canvases covered by seemingly randomly placed interlocking coloured triangles. Mondriaan split with De Stijl in 1925, going on to attain new artistic extremes of clarity and soberness before moving to New York in the 1940s and producing atypically exuberant works such as *Victory Boogie Woogie* – named for the artist's love of jazz.

During and after De Stijl, a number of other movements flourished in the Netherlands, though their impact was not so great and their influence was largely regional. The Expressionist **Bergen School** was probably the most localized, its best-known exponent **Charley Toorop** (1891–1955), daughter of Jan, developing a distinctively glaring but strangely sensitive realism. **De Ploeg** (The Plough), centred in Groningen, was headed by **Jan Wiegers** (1893–1959) and influenced by Kirchner and the German Expressionists; the group's artists set out to capture the uninviting landscapes around their native town, and produced violently coloured canvases that hark back to Van Gogh. Another group, known as the **Magic Realists**, surfaced in the 1930s, painting quasi-surrealistic scenes that, according to their leading light, **Carel Willink** (1900–83), revealed "a world stranger and more dreadful in its haughty impenetrability than the most terrifying nightmare."

Postwar Dutch art began with **CoBrA**: a loose grouping of like-minded painters from Denmark, Belgium and Holland, whose name derives from the initial letters of their respective capital cities. Their first exhibition at Amsterdam's Stedelijk Museum in 1949 provoked a huge uproar, at the centre of which was **Karel Appel** (b.1921), whose brutal Abstract Expressionist pieces, plastered with paint inches thick, were, he maintained, necessary for the era

---

Amsterdam galleries: a hit list

Of the galleries in Amsterdam, the **Rijksmuseum** (see p.116–122) owns a fabulous and wonderfully comprehensive collection of Dutch/Low Countries art, but much of it is out of sight during a major refurbishment which is scheduled to last until 2008. In the meantime, one wing of the museum remains open and features the major artists of the Golden Age, most memorably Rembrandt. The **Van Gogh Museum** (see p.122–124) is best for the Impressionists and, of course, Van Gogh, and for contemporary Dutch art, there's both the inventive **De Appel** (see p.81) and the impressive **Stedelijk Museum** (see p.111), which has been moved to the old postal tower block near Centraal Station. In the city's southern suburbs, the **CoBrA Museum** (see p.135) is dedicated to the CoBrA art movement of the 1950s and 60s, and the neighbouring town of Haarlem possesses the excellent Frans Hals Museum (see p.144–146), which holds some of the best work of Hals, his predecessors and successors.

– indeed, inevitable reflections of it. "I paint like a barbarian in a barbarous age," he claimed. In the graphic arts the most famous twentieth-century Dutch figure was **Maurits Cornelis Escher** (1898–1972), whose Surrealistic illusions and allusions were underpinned by his fascination with mathematics.

As for today, there's as vibrant a contemporary art scene as there ever was, best exemplified in Amsterdam by the rotating exhibitions of De Appel (see p.81) and the Stedelijk Museum (see p.111), and by the dozens of galleries and exhibition spaces dotted across the city. Among contemporary Dutch artists, look out for the abstract work of **Edgar Fernhout** and **Ad Dekkers**, the reliefs of **Jan Schoonhoven**, the multimedia productions of **Jan Dibbets**, the glowering realism of **Marlene Dumas**, the imprecisely coloured geometric designs of **Rob van Koningsbruggen**, the smeary Expressionism of **Toon Verhoef**, and the exuberant figures of **Rene Daniels** – to name just eight of the more important figures.

Books

T he following **books** should be readily available in the UK, US, Canada, Australia and New Zealand, apart from those few titles we mention which are currently out of print, signified o/p. Titles marked with the ✶ symbol are especially recommended.

Travel and general

A. Burton et al *Smokers Guide to Amsterdam.* Exactly what it says – a dope-smokers' guide to the city with no leaf unturned. Regularly updated – the last edition was published in 2004.

Richard Huijing (ed & trans.) *The Dedalus Book of Dutch Fantasy.* A fun and artfully selected collection of stories that contains contributions from some of the greats of Dutch literature, including a number whose work does not as yet appear in translation anywhere else.

Simon Kuper *Ajax, the Dutch, the War: Football in Europe in the Second World War.* A tad cumbersome in its execution, but some intriguing details – and disappointments – regarding the extent of collaboration during the German occupation: for starters, one of the Dutch policeman who arrested Anne Frank worked in the police until 1980. Ajax football team have long been associated with the city's Jewish community.

Sir William Temple *Observations upon the United Provinces of The Netherlands.* An entertaining and evocative account of the country written by a seventeenth-century English diplomat. (o/p)

Tim Webb *Good Beer Guide to Belgium & Holland.* Detailed and enthusiastic guide to the best bars, beers

and breweries, including a strong showing for Amsterdam. A good read, and extremely well informed to boot. Undoubtedly, the best book on its subject on the market. The last edition was published in 2002, but a new, updated version is promised in 2005.

David Winner *Brilliant Orange – The Neurotic Genius of Dutch Football.* Great title; great cover and great idea – zeroing in on the fine Dutch footballers of the 1960s and 1970s, including super-talented Johan Cruyff, and the way they – and their style of play – reflect Dutch culture and history. The problem is that sometimes the inferences and conclusions seem too obtuse, or at least unconvincing.

Manfred Wolf (ed) *Amsterdam: A Traveler's Literary Companion.* Published by an independent American press, Whereabout Press, these anthologies aim to get to the heart of the modern cities they cover, and this well-chosen mixture of travel pieces, short fiction and reportage does exactly that, uncovering a low-life aspect to the city of Amsterdam that exists beyond the tourist brochures. A high-quality – and evocative – selection, and often the only chance you'll get to read some of this material in translation. Published in 2001.

History and politics

Leo Akveld et al *The Colourful World of the VOC.* Beautifully illustrated, coffee–table size book on the VOC – the

East India Company. The subject is dealt with in a series of intriguing essays on the likes of the uses of

Eastern spices, Indonesian fashion and furniture, rituals and beliefs.

J. C. H. Blom (ed) *History of the Low Countries*. Dutch history books are fairly thin on the ground, so this heavyweight volume fills a few gaps, though it's hardly sun-lounge reading. A series of historians weigh in with their specialities, from Roman times onwards. Taken as a whole, its forte is in picking out those cultural, political and economic themes that give the region its distinctive character.

Mike Dash *Tulipomania*. An examination of the introduction of the tulip into the Low Countries at the height of the Golden Age, and the extraordinarily inflated and speculative market in the many varieties of bulbs and flowers that ensued. There's a lot of padding and scene-setting, but it's an engaging enough read, and has nice detail on seventeenth-century Amsterdam, Leiden and Haarlem.

Pieter Geyl *The Revolt of The Netherlands 1555–1609*. Geyl presents a detailed account of the Netherlands during its formative years, chronicling the uprising against the Spanish and the formation of the United Provinces. First published in 1932, it has long been regarded as the classic text on the subject, though it is a hard and often ponderous read.

Christopher Hibbert *Cities and Civilisation*. Includes a diverting chapter on Amsterdam in the age of Rembrandt. Hibbert, one of the UK's best historians, is always a pleasure to read.

Carol Ann Lee *Roses from the Earth: the Biography of Anne Frank*. Amongst a spate of recent publications trawling through and over the life of the young Jewish diarist, this is probably the best, written in a straightforward and insightful manner without sentimentality. Working the same mine is the same author's *The Hidden Life of Otto Frank* – clear, lucid and equally as interesting – plus her *Anne Frank's Story*.

Geert Mak *Amsterdam: A Brief Life of the City*. First published in 1995, this infinitely readable trawl through the city's past is a simply wonderful book – amusing and perceptive, alternately tart and indulgent. It's more a social history than anything else so – for example – it's here you'll find out quite why Rembrandt lived in the Jewish Quarter and why the city's merchant elite ossified in the eighteenth century. It's light and accessible enough to read from cover to cover, but its index of places makes it easy to dip into. Highly recommended.

Geoffrey Parker *The Dutch Revolt*. Compelling account of the struggle between the Netherlands and Spain. Quite the best thing you can read on the period. Also *The Army of Flanders and the Spanish Road 1567–1659*. The title may sound academic, but this book gives a fascinating insight into the Habsburg army which occupied the Low Countries for well over a hundred years – how it functioned, was fed and moved from Spain to the Low Countries along the so-called Spanish Road.

Simon Schama *The Embarrassment of Riches: An Interpretation of Dutch Culture in the Golden Age*. Long before his reinvention on British TV, Schama had a reputation as a specialist in Dutch history and this chunky volume draws on a huge variety of archive sources. Also by Schama, *Patriots and Liberators: Revolution in the Netherlands 1780–1813* focuses on one of the less familiar periods of Dutch history and is particularly good on the Batavian Republic set up in the Netherlands under French auspices. Both are heavyweight tomes and leftists might well find Schama too reactionary by half. See also Schama's *Rembrandt's Eyes* (p.286).

Andrew Wheatcroft *The Habsburgs*. Excellent and well-researched trawl through the family's history, from eleventh-century beginnings to its eclipse at the end of World War I. Enjoyable background reading.

Art and architecture

Svetlana Alpers *Rembrandt's Enterprise*. Intriguing 1980s study of Rembrandt, positing the theory – in line with findings of the Leiden-based Rembrandt Research Project – that many previously accepted Rembrandt paintings are not his at all, but merely the products of his studio. Bad news if you own one.

★ **Anthony Bailey** *A View of Delft*. Startlingly well-researched and clearly written book on Vermeer with thoughtful commentary on all his paintings plus a well-considered exploration of his milieu.

★ **R.H. Fuchs** *Dutch Painting*. As complete an introduction to the subject – from Flemish origins to the present day – as you could wish for in just a couple of hundred pages.

R.H. Fuchs et al *Flemish and Dutch Painting (from Van Gogh, Ensor, Magritte and Mondrian to Contemporary)*. Excellent, lucid account giving an overview of the development of Flemish and Dutch painting. o/p

Walter S. Gibson *Bosch* and *Bruegel*. Two wonderfully illustrated Thames & Hudson titles on these most famous allegorical painters. The former contains everything you wanted to know about Hieronymus Bosch, his paintings and his late fifteenth-century milieu, while the latter takes a detailed look at Pieter Bruegel the Elder's art, with nine well-argued chapters investigating its various components.

H.L.C. Jaffe *De Stijl 1917–1931: Visions of Utopia*. A good, informed introduction to the twentieth-century movement and its philosophical and social influences. Well illustrated too.

Melissa McQuillan *Van Gogh*. Extensive, in-depth look at Vincent's paintings, as well as his life and times. Superbly researched and illustrated.

Simon Schama *Rembrandt's Eyes*. Published in 1999, this erudite work received good reviews, but it's very long – and often very long-winded. Some judicious pruning would have helped.

Irving Stone *Lust for Life: the Life of Vincent van Gogh*. Everything you ever wanted to know about Van Gogh in a pop genius-is-pain biography.

★ **Mariet Westerman** *The Art of the Dutch Republic 1585–1718*. This excellently written, well-illustrated and enthralling book tackles its subject thematically, from the marketing of works to an exploration of Dutch ideologies. Similarly classy – and equally recommendable – is Westerman's *Rembrandt*.

★ **Christopher White** *Rembrandt and his world*. This is the most widely available – and wide-ranging – study of the painter and his work. Well illustrated, as you would expect of a Thames & Hudson publication, plus a wonderfully incisive and extremely detailed commentary. Also by White is *Peter Paul Rubens: Man and Artist*, a beautifully illustrated introduction to both Rubens' work and social milieu.

Literature

Tracey Chevalier *Girl with a Pearl Earring*. Chevalier's book is a fanciful piece of fiction, building a story around the subject of one of Vermeer's most enigmatic paintings. It's an absorbing read, if a tad too detailed and slow-moving for some tastes, and it paints a convincing picture of seventeenth-century Delft and Holland, exploring its social structures and values. Has proved a popular novel.

Anne Frank *The Diary of a Young Girl*. Lucid and moving, the most revealing thing you can read on the plight of Amsterdam's Jews during the war years.

Nicolas Freeling ★ *Over the High Side; Love in Amsterdam; Dwarf Kingdom; A City Solitary; Strike Out Where Not Applicable; A Long Silence.* Freeling specialised in detective novels and his most famous creation was the rebel Amsterdam cop, Van der Valk. The author turned out a number of Van der Valk stories – including these six – and each is a light, carefully crafted tale, with just the right amount of twists to make them classic cops 'n' robbers reading – and with good Amsterdam (and Dutch) locations. London-born, Freeling evoked Amsterdam (and Amsterdammers) as well as any writer ever has, subtly and unsentimentally using the city and its people as a vivid backdrop to his fast-moving action, though he did get fed up with writing the Van der Valk series and killed his detective off in 1972.

Etty Hillesum *An Interrupted Life: the Diaries and Letters of Etty Hillesum, 1941–1943.* The Germans transported Hillesum, a young Jewish woman, from her home in Amsterdam to Auschwitz, where she died. As with Anne Frank's more famous journal, penetratingly written – though a tad less readable. Also in print as *Etty: A Diary 1941–43.*

Arthur Japin ★ *The Two Hearts of Kwasi Boachi.* Inventive recreation of a true story in which the eponymous Ashanti prince was dispatched to the court of King William of the Netherlands in 1837. Kwasi and his companion Kwame were ostensibly sent to Den Haag to further their education, but there was a strong colonial subtext and this is subtly explored. Intriguing descriptions of Ashanti-land in its pre-colonial pomp.

Sylvie Matton *Rembrandt's Whore.* Taking its cue from Chevalier's *Girl with a Pearl Earring* (see previous page), this slim novel tries hard to conjure Rembrandt's life and times with limited success. Matton certainly knows her Rembrandt onions – she worked for two years on a film of his life.

Marga Minco *The Fall; An Empty House; The Glass Bridge; Bitter Herbs;* and *Vivid Memories of a Fugitive Jewish girl in Nazi-occupied Holland* (o/p). One of the best known of Amsterdam's modern writers, the prolific Margo Minco has written widely and well about the city's Jewish community, particularly during the German occupation. She herself was a Holocaust survivor, spending several years in hiding – unlike the rest of her family, who were dispatched to concentration camps where they all died. One of Minco's favourite hideaways was Kloveniersburgwal 49, which served as a safe house for various Dutch artists and later as the inspiration for *An Empty House.* Published in 1991, *Bitter Herbs* is her testament.

Deborah Moggach *Tulip Fever.* At first Deborah Moggach's novel seems no more than an attempt to build a story out of her favourite domestic Dutch interiors, genre scenes and still-life paintings. But ultimately the story is a basic one – of lust, greed, mistaken identity and tragedy. The Golden Age backdrop is well realized, but almost incidental.

Marcel Moring *In Babylon.* Best–selling Dutch author with an intense style and thought–provoking, philosophical content. *In Babylon* has an older Jewish man and his niece trapped in a cabin in the eastern Netherlands and here they ruminate on their family's history. Moring's *Dream Room* is also gracefully nostalgic in its concentration on the family of Boris and his son, David, while Moring's latest novel, *Dis*, is set in the town of Assen, again in the east of the country, during the annual Dutch TT motorbike races.

Harry Mulisch *The Assault.* Set part in Haarlem, part in Amsterdam, this novel traces the story of a young boy who loses his family in a reprisal raid by the Nazis. A powerful tale, made into an excellent and effective film.

Also, *The Discovery of Heaven,* a gripping yarn of adventure and happenstance, and *The Procedure,* featuring a modern-day Dutch scientist investigating strange goings-on in sixteenth-century Prague. 2004's paperback offering is *Siegfried: A Black Idyll* kicks off in Vienna and is all about guilt and responsibility, secrets and truth with the tentacles of Hitler reaching out from the past.

Multatuli *Max Havelaar, or, The Coffee Auctions of a Dutch Trading Company.* Classic nineteenth-century Dutch satire on colonial life in the East Indies. Eloquent and intermittently amusing. If you have Dutch friends, they should be impressed (dumbstruck) if you have read it, especially as it's 352 pages long. For more on Multatuli, see p.69.

Cees Nooteboom *Rituals.* Cees Nooteboom is one of Holland's best-known writers. He published his first novel in 1955, but only really came to public attention after the publication of his third novel, *Rituals,* in 1980. The central theme of all his work is the phenomenon of time: *Rituals* in particular is about the passing of time and the different ways of controlling the process. Inni Wintrop, the main character, is an outsider, a well-heeled, antique-dabbling "dilettante" as he describes himself. The book is almost entirely set in Amsterdam, and although it describes the inner life of Inni himself, it also paints a strong picture of the decaying city. Bleak but absorbing. Born in Den Haag in 1933, Nooteboom lives by turn in Germany, Spain and the Netherlands. If you like this one, try *All Souls' Day*, which is set in contemporary Berlin.

Stav Sherez *The Devil's Playground.* Fast-paced debut thriller that makes good use of Amsterdam locations and the city's Jewish history. A good read, and, if you like crime, the perfect contemporary Amsterdam novel for your trip.

David Veronese *Jana.* A hip thriller set in the druggy underworld of Amsterdam and London.

Jan Wolkers *Turkish Delight.* Wolkers is one of the Netherlands' best-known artists and writers, and this is one of his early novels, a close examination of the relationship between a bitter, working-class sculptor and his young, middle-class wife.

Language

Language

Dutch

t's unlikely that you'll need to speak anything other than English while you're in **Amsterdam**: the Dutch have a seemingly natural talent for languages, and your attempts at speaking theirs may be met with some bewilderment – though this can have as much to do with your pronunciation (Dutch is very difficult to get right) as their surprise that you're making an effort. Outside Amsterdam, people aren't quite as cosmopolitan, but even so the following Dutch words and phrases should be the most you'll need to get by. We've also included a basic food and drink glossary, though menus are nearly always multilingual and where they aren't, ask and one will almost invariably appear.

Dutch is a Germanic language – the word "Dutch" itself is a corruption of Deutsche, a label inaccurately given by English sailors in the seventeenth century. Though the Dutch are at pains to stress the differences between the two languages, if you know any German you'll spot many similarities. As for **phrasebooks**, the *Rough Guide's Dutch Dictionary and Phrasebook* has a perfectly adequate dictionary section and a menu reader; it also provides a useful introduction to grammar and pronunciation.

Pronunciation

Dutch is pronounced much the same as English. However, there are a few Dutch sounds that don't exist in English, which can be difficult to pronounce without practice.

Consonants

Double-consonant combinations generally keep their separate sounds in Dutch – kn, for example, is never like the English "knight". Note also the following consonants and consonant combinations:

v like the English f in **f**ar

w like the v in **v**at

j like the initial sound of **y**ellow

ch and g are considerably harder than in English, enunciated much further back in the throat. They become softer the further south towards Dutch–speaking Belgium you go, where they're more like the Scottish lo**ch**.

ng is as in bri**ng**

nj as in o**nio**n

Vowels and diphthongs

Doubling the letter lengthens the vowel sound.

a is like the English **a**pple

aa like c**a**rt

e like l**e**t

ee like l**a**te

o as in p**o**p

oo in p**o**pe

u is like the French t**u** if preceded by a consonant; it's like w**oo**d if followed by a consonant

uu the French t**u**

au and ou like h**ow**

ei and ij as in f**i**ne, though this varies strongly from region to region; sometimes it can sound more like l**a**ne

oe as in s**oo**n

eu is like the diphthong in the French l**eu**r

ui is the hardest Dutch diphthong of all, pronounced like h**ow** but much further forward in the mouth, with lips pursed (as if to say "oo")

Words and phrases

Basics and greetings

yes	ja	goodbye	tot ziens
no	nee	see you later	tot straks
Please	alstublieft	do you speak English?	spreekt u Engels?
(no) thank you	(nee) dank u or bedankt	I don't understand	Ik begrijp het niet
hello	hallo or dag	women/men	vrouwen/mannen
good morning	goedemorgen	children	kinderen
good afternoon	goedemiddag	push/pull	duwen/trekken
good evening	goedenavond		

Getting around

how do I get to… ?	hoe kom ik in… ?	left/right	links/rechts
where is… ?	waar is… ?	straight ahead	rechtuit gaan
how far is it to… ?	hoe ver is het naar… ?	platform	spoor or perron
when?	wanneer?	ticket office	loket
far/near	ver/dichtbij	here/there	hier/daar

Ordering, shopping and money

I want…	Ik wil…	cash desk	kassa
I don't want…	Ik wil niet… (+verb)	good/bad	goed/slecht
	Ik wil geen… (+noun)	big/small	groot/klein
how much is… ?	wat kost… ?	new/old	nieuw/oud
post office	postkantoor	cheap/expensive	goedkoop/duur
stamp(s)	postzegel(s)	hot/cold	heet or warm/koud
money exchange	geldwisselkantoor	with/without	met/zonder

Useful cycling terms

tyre	band	pedal	trapper
puncture	lek	pump	pomp
brake	rem	handlebars	stuur
chain	ketting	broken	kapot
wheel	wiel		

Signs and abbreviations

A.U.B.	*Alstublieft*: please (also shown as S.V.P., from French)	K	*kelder*: basement
		let op!	attention!
		heren/dames	men's/women's toilets
BG	*Begane grond*: ground floor	open	open
		T/M	*Tot en met*: up to and including
BTW	*Belasting Toegevoegde Waarde*: VAT		
		toegang	entrance
geen toegang	no entry	uitgang	exit
gesloten	closed	Z.O.Z.	please turn over (page, leaflet etc)
ingang	entrance		

Days of the week

Monday	Maandag	today	vandaag
Tuesday	Dinsdag	tomorrow	morgen
Wednesday	Woensdag	tomorrow morning	morgenochtend
Thursday	Donderdag	year	jaar
Friday	Vrijdag	month	maand
Saturday	Zaterdag	week	week
Sunday	Zondag	day	dag
yesterday	gisteren		

Months of the year

January	januari	July	juli
February	februari	August	augustus
March	maart	September	september
April	april	October	oktober
May	mei	November	november
June	juni	December	december

Time

hour	uur	it's…	het is…
minute	minuut	3.00	drie uur
what time is it?	hoe laat is het?	3.05	vijf over drie

3.10	tien over drie	3.45	kwart voor vier
3.15	kwart over drie	3.50	tien voor vier
3.20	tien voor half vier	3.55	vijf voor vier
3.25	vijf voor half vier	8am	acht uur 's ochtends
3.30	half vier	1pm	een uur 's middags
3.35	vijf over half vier	8pm	acht uur 's avonds
3.40	tien over half vier	1am	een uur 's nachts

Numbers

When saying a number, the Dutch generally transpose the last two digits: for example, €3.25 is drie euros vijf en twintig.

0	nul	18	achttien
1	een	19	negentien
2	twee	20	twintig
3	drie	21	een en twintig
4	vier	22	twee en twintig
5	vijf	30	dertig
6	zes	40	veertig
7	zeven	50	vijftig
8	acht	60	zestig
9	negen	70	zeventig
10	tien	80	tachtig
11	elf	90	negentig
12	twaalf	100	honderd
13	dertien	101	honderd een
14	veertien	200	twee honderd
15	vijftien	201	twee honderd een
16	zestien	500	vijf honderd
17	zeventien	1000	duizend

Food and drink terms

Basics

boter	butter	hoofdgerechten	main courses
boterham/broodje	sandwich/roll	kaas	cheese
brood	bread	koud	cold
dranken	drinks	nagerechten	desserts
eieren	eggs	peper	pepper
gerst	barley	pindakaas	peanut butter
groenten	vegetables	sla/salade	salad
honing	honey	smeerkaas	cheese spread

stokbrood	French bread	voorgerechten	starters/hors d'oeuvres
suiker	sugar	vruchten	fruit
vis	fish	warm	hot
vlees	meat	zout	salt

Starters and snacks

erwtensoep/snert	thick pea soup with bacon or sausage
huzarensalade	potato salad with pickles
Kkoffietafel	a light midday meal of cold meats, cheese, bread and perhaps soup
patates/frites	chips/French fries
soep	soup
uitsmijter	ham or cheese with eggs on bread

Meat and poultry

biefstuk (hollandse)	steak	kip	chicken
biefstuk (duitse)	hamburger	kroket	spiced veal or beef in hash, coated in breadcrumbs
eend	duck		
fricandeau	roast pork		
fricandel	frankfurter-like sausage	lamsvlees	lamb
gehakt	minced meat	lever	liver
ham	ham	rookvlees	smoked beef
kalfsvlees	veal	spek	bacon
kalkoen	turkey	worst	sausages
karbonade	chop		

Fish

forel	trout	oesters	oysters
garnalen	prawns	paling	eel
haring	herring	schelvis	haddock
haringsalade	herring salad	schol	plaice
kabeljauw	cod	tong	sole
makreel	mackerel	zalm	salmon
mosselen	mussels		

Vegetables

aardappelen	potatoes	knoflook	garlic
bloemkool	cauliflower	komkommer	cucumber
bonen	beans	prei	leek
champignons	mushrooms	rijst	rice
erwten	peas	sla	salad, lettuce
hutspot	mashed potatoes and carrots	stampot andijvie	mashed potato and endive

| stampot boerenkool | mashed potato and cabbage | wortelen | carrots |
| uien | onions | zuurkool | sauerkraut |

Cooking terms

belegd	filled or topped, as in *belegde broodjes* – bread rolls topped with cheese, etc	gekookt	boiled
		geraspt	grated
		gerookt	smoked
		gestoofd	stewed
doorbakken	well-done	half doorbakken	medium-done
gebakken	fried/baked	hollandse saus	hollandaise (a milk and egg sauce)
gebraden	roasted		
gegrild	grilled	rood	rare

Indonesian dishes and terms

ajam	chicken	nasi rames	rijsttafel on a single plate
bami	noodles with meat/chicken and vegetables	pedis	hot and spicy
		pisang	banana
daging	beef	rijsttafel	collection of different spicy dishes served with plain rice
gado gado	vegetables in peanut sauce		
goreng	fried	sambal	hot, chilli-based sauce
ikan	fish	satesaus	peanut sauce to accompany meat grilled on skewers
katjang	peanut		
kroepoek	prawn crackers		
loempia	spring rolls	seroendeng	spicy shredded and fried coconut
nasi	rice		
nasi goreng	fried rice with meat/chicken and vegetables	tauge	bean sprouts

Sweets and desserts

appelgebak	apple tart or cake	pannekoeken	pancakes
drop	Dutch liquorice, available in *zoet* (sweet) or *zout* (salted) varieties – the latter an acquired taste	pepernoten	Dutch ginger nuts
		poffertjes	small pancakes, fritters
		(slag)room	(whipped) cream
		speculaas	spice and honey-flavoured biscuit
gebak	pastry		
IJs	ice cream	stroopwafels	waffles
koekjes	biscuits	taai-taai	Dutch honey cake
oliebollen	doughnuts	vla	custard

Fruits and nuts

aardbei	strawberry	**hazelnoot**	hazelnut
amandel	almond	**kers**	cherry
appel	apple	**kokosnoot**	coconut
appelmoes	apple purée	**peer**	pear
citroen	lemon	**perzik**	peach
druiven	grape	**pinda**	peanut
framboos	raspberry	**pruim**	plum/prune

Drinks

anijsmelk	anis	**melk**	milk
appelsap	apple juice	**met ijs**	with ice
bessenjenever	blackcurrant gin	**met slagroom**	with whipped cream
chocomel	chocolate milk	**pils**	Dutch beer
citroenjenever	lemon gin	**proost!**	cheers!
droog	dry	**sinaasappelsap**	orange juice
frisdranken	soft drinks	**thee**	tea
jenever	Dutch gin	**tomatensap**	tomato juice
karnemelk	buttermilk	**vruchtensap**	fruit juice
koffie	coffee	**wijn**	wine
koffie verkeerd	coffee with warm milk	**(wit/rood/rosé)**	(white/red/rosé)
kopstoot	beer with a jenever chaser	**vieux**	Dutch brandy
		zoet	sweet

Glossary of Dutch words and terms

abdij abbey

amsterdammertje phallic-shaped objects placed alongside Amsterdam streets to keep drivers off pavements – and out of the canals

beiaard carillon chimes

belfort belfry

begijnhof similar to a *hofje* (alms house) but occupied by Catholic women (*begijns*) who lead semi-religious lives without taking full vows – also see box on p.63.

beurs stock exchange

botermarkt butter market

brug bridge

burgher member of the upper or mercantile classes of a town, usually with certain civic powers

fietspad bicycle path

gasthuis hospital for the sick or infirm

gemeente municipal, as in *Gemeentehuis* (town hall)

gerechtshof law courts

gevel gable

gezellig a hard term to translate – something like "cosy", "comfortable" and "inviting" all in one – but one which is often said to lie at the heart of the Dutch psyche. A long, relaxed meal in a favourite restaurant with friends is *gezellig*; grabbing a quick snack is not. The best brown cafés ooze *gezelligheid*; Kalverstraat on a Saturday afternoon definitely doesn't.

gilde guild

gracht canal

groentenmarkt vegetable market

grote kerk literally "big church" – the main church of a town or village

hal hall

hijsbalk pulley beam, often decorated, fixed to the top of a gable to lift goods, furniture etc. They are essential in canal houses whose staircases were – and still are – narrow and steep.

hof courtyard

hofje almshouse, usually for elderly women, who could look after themselves but needed small charities such as food and fuel; usually a number of buildings centred around a small, enclosed courtyard.

huis house

jeugdherberg youth hostel

kasteel castle

kerk church

koning king

koningin queen

koninklijk royal

kunst art

kursaal casino

lakenhal cloth hall – the building in medieval weaving towns where cloth would be weighed, graded and sold

luchthaven airport

markt central town square and the heart of most Dutch communities, normally still the site of weekly markets

mokum A Yiddish word meaning "city", originally used by the Jewish community to indicate Amsterdam; now in general usage as a nickname for the city

molen windmill

nederland the Netherlands

nederlands Dutch

noord north

ommegang procession

oost east

paleis palace

plein square or open space.

polder an area of land reclaimed from the sea

poort gate

raadhuis town hall

randstad literally "rim-town", this refers to the urban conurbation that makes up much of North and South Holland, stretching from Amsterdam in the north down to Rotterdam and Dordrecht in the south

rijk state

schepenzaal alderman's hall

schone kunsten fine arts

schouwburg theatre

sierkunst decorative arts

spionnetje small mirror on a canal house enabling the occupant to see who is at the door without descending the stairs.

spoor train station platform

stadhuis the most common word for a town hall

stedelijk civic, municipal

steeg alley

steen stone

stichting institute or foundation

straat street

toren tower

tuin garden

vleeshuis meat market

volkskunde folklore

VVV Dutch tourist information office

waag old public weighing-house, a common feature of most towns

weg way

west west

wijk district (of a city)

zuid south

Art and architecture glossary

ambulatory Covered passage around the outer edge of the choir of a church.

apse Semicircular protrusion (usually) at the east end of a church.

Art Deco Geometrical style of art and architecture popular in the 1930s.

Art Nouveau Style of art, architecture and design based on highly stylized vegetal forms. Especially popular in the early part of the twentieth century.

balustrade An ornamental rail, running, almost invariably, along the top of a building.

Baroque The art and architecture of the Counter-Reformation, dating from around 1600 onwards. Distinguished by extreme ornateness, exuberance and by the complex but harmonious spatial arrangement of interiors.

carillon A set of tuned church bells, either operated by an automatic mechanism or played by a keyboard.

caryatid A sculptured (female) figure used as a column.

chancel The eastern part of a church, often separated from the nave by a screen (see "rood screen"). Contains the choir and ambulatory.

Classical Architectural style incorporating Greek and Roman elements – pillars, domes, colonnades, etc – at its height in the seventeenth century and revived, as Neo-classical, in the nineteenth century.

clerestory Upper storey of a church, incorporating the windows.

diptych Carved or painted work on two panels. Often used as an altarpiece – both static and, more occasionally, portable.

Expressionism Artistic style popular at the beginning of the twentieth century, characterized by the exaggeration of shape or colour; often accompanied by the extensive use of symbolism.

Flamboyant Florid form of Gothic.

fresco Wall painting – durable through application to wet plaster.

gable The triangular upper portion of a wall – decorative or supporting a roof – which is a feature of many Amsterdam canal houses. Initially fairly simple, they became more ostentatious in the late seventeenth century, before turning to a more restrained if imposing classicism in the eighteenth and nineteenth centuries.

genre painting In the seventeenth century the term "genre painting" applied to everything from animal paintings and still lifes through to historical works and landscapes. In the eighteenth century the term came only to be applied to scenes of everyday life.

Gothic Architectural style of the thirteenth to sixteenth centuries, characterized by pointed arches, rib vaulting, flying buttresses and a general emphasis on verticality.

grisaille A technique of monochrome painting in shades of grey.

misericord Bracket on the underside of a hinged choir stall seat, which, when the seat was upright, could help a worshipper keep on his feet; they were often carved with secular subjects as bums were not thought worthy of religious carvings.

nave Main body of a church.

Neoclassical A style of classical architecture revived in the nineteenth century, popular in the Low Countries during and after the Napoleonic occupation.

Neo-Gothic Revived Gothic style of architecture popular between the late eighteenth and nineteenth centuries.

pediment Feature of a gable, usually triangular and often sporting a relief.

pilaster A shallow rectangular column projecting, but only slightly, from a wall.

Renaissance The period of European history marking the end of the medieval period and the rise of the modern world. Defined, amongst many criteria, by an increase in classical scholarship, geographical discovery, the rise of secular values and the growth of individualism. Began in Italy in the fourteenth century. Also the art and architecture of the period.

retable Altarpiece.

Rococo Highly florid, light and graceful eighteenth-century style of architecture, painting and interior design, forming the last phase of Baroque.

Romanesque Early medieval architecture distinguished by squat forms, rounded arches and naive sculpture.

rood screen Decorative screen separating the nave from the chancel. A rood loft is the gallery (or space) on top of it.

stucco Marble-based plaster used to embellish ceilings, etc.

transept Arms of a cross-shaped church, placed at ninety degrees to nave and chancel.

triptych Carved or painted work on three panels. Often used as an altarpiece.

tympanum Sculpted, usually recessed, panel above a door.

vault An arched ceiling or roof.

Rough
Guides
advertiser

Rough Guides travel...

...music & reference

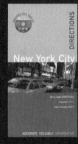

STAYOKAY HOSTELS

Stayokay, part of Hostelling International, has 30 comfortable hostels in the Netherlands. The atmosphere is informal and relaxed.

HOSTELS IN AMSTERDAM

Stayokay has 2 hostels in the centre of Amsterdam. From the hostels you can walk easily to attractions, like the Van Gogh Museum. So you can make the very most of your visit and see all the highlights.

Stayokay Amsterdam Vondelpark is located in the beautiful Vondelpark and is one of Europe's largest and most modern hostels. Downtown Amsterdam you find the international and exciting Stayokay Amsterdam Stadsdoelen.

MORE INFORMATION OR RESERVATIONS

Stayokay Amsterdam Vondelpark
Zandpad 5, Amsterdam
tel +31 (0)20 589 89 961

Stayokay Amsterdam Stadsdoelen
Kloveniersburgwal 97, Amsterdam
tel +31 (0)20 624 68 32

www.stayokay.com   **30 hostels in the Netherlands**

Don't bury your head in the sand!

Take cover!

with Rough Guide Travel Insurance

Worldwide cover, for Rough Guide readers worldwide

Check the web at
www.roughguidesinsurance.com

UK: 0800 083 9507
US: 1-800 749-4922
Australia: 1 300 669 999
Worldwide: **(+44) 870 890 2843**

ROUGH GUIDES

small print and

Index

A Rough Guide to Rough Guides

In the summer of 1981, Mark Ellingham, a recent graduate from Bristol University, was travelling round Greece and couldn't find a guidebook that really met his needs. On the one hand there were the student guides, insistent on saving every last cent, and on the other the heavyweight cultural tomes whose authors seemed to have spent more time in a research library than lounging away the afternoon at a taverna or on the beach.

In a bid to avoid getting a job, Mark and a small group of writers set about creating their own guidebook. It was a guide to Greece that aimed to combine a journalistic approach to description with a thoroughly practical approach to travellers' needs —a guide that would incorporate culture, history and contemporary insights with a critical edge, together with up-to-date, value-for-money listings. Back in London, Mark and the team finished their Rough Guide, as they called it, and talked Routledge into publishing the book.

That first *Rough Guide to Greece*, published in 1982, was a student scheme that became a publishing phenomenon. The immediate success of the book – with numerous reprints and a Thomas Cook prize shortlisting – spawned a series that rapidly covered dozens of destinations. Rough Guides had a ready market among low-budget backpackers, but soon also acquired a much broader and older readership that relished Rough Guides' wit and inquisitiveness as much as their enthusiastic, critical approach. Everyone wants value for money, but not at any price.

Rough Guides soon began supplementing the "rougher" information about hostels and low-budget listings with the kind of detail on restaurants and quality hotels that independent-minded visitors on any budget might expect, whether on business in New York or trekking in Thailand.

These days the guides – distributed worldwide by the Penguin group – offer recommendations from shoestring to luxury and cover more than 200 destinations around the globe, including almost every country in the Americas and Europe, more than half of Africa and most of Asia and Australasia. Our ever-growing team of authors and photographers is spread all over the world, particularly in Europe, the USA and Australia.

In 1994, we published the *Rough Guide to World Music* and *Rough Guide to Classical Music*; and a year later the *Rough Guide to the Internet*. All three books have become benchmark titles in their fields – which encouraged us to expand into other areas of publishing, mainly around popular culture. Rough Guides now publish:

- Travel guides to more than 200 worldwide destinations
- Dictionary phrasebooks to 22 major languages
- History guides ranging from Ireland to Islam
- Maps printed on rip-proof and waterproof Polyart™ paper
- Music guides running the gamut from Opera to Elvis
- Restaurant guides to London, New York and San Francisco
- Reference books on topics as diverse as the Weather and Shakespeare
- Sports guides from Formula 1 to Man Utd
- Pop culture books from *Lord of the Rings* to Cult TV
- World Music CDs in association with World Music Network

Visit **www.roughguides.com** to see our latest publications.

Rough Guide credits

Text editor: Andy Turner
Layout: Dan May
Cartography: Karobi Gogoi
Picture editor: Harriet Mills
Photography: Neil Setchfield/Anthony Cassidy
Proofreader: Tamara Colloff-Bennett
Cover design: Chloë Roberts

Editorial: **London** Kate Berens, Claire
Saunders, Geoff Howard, Ruth Blackmore,
Gavin Thomas, Polly Thomas, Richard Lim,
Clifton Wilkinson, Alison Murchie, Sally Schafer,
Karoline Densley, Andy Turner, Ella O'Donnell,
Keith Drew, Edward Aves, Nikki Birrell, Chloë
Thomson, Helen Marsden, Joe Staines, Duncan
Clark, Peter Buckley, Matthew Milton, Daniel
Crewe; **New York** Andrew Rosenberg, Richard
Koss, Steven Horak, AnneLise Sorensen, Amy
Hegarty, Hunter Slaton
Design & Pictures: **London** Simon Bracken,
Dan May, Diana Jarvis, Mark Thomas, Jj
Luck, Harriet Mills, Chloë Roberts; **Delhi**
Madhulita Mohapatra, Umesh Aggarwal, Ajay
Verma, Jessica Subramanian, Amit Verma
Production: Julia Bovis, Sophie Hewat,

Katherine Owers
Cartography: **London** Maxine Repath, Ed
Wright, Katie Lloyd-Jones; **Delhi** Manish
Chandra, Rajesh Chhibber, Jai Prakash
Mishra, Ashutosh Bharti, Rajesh Mishra,
Animesh Pathak, Jasbir Sandhu, Karobi
Gogoi
Online: **New York** Jennifer Gold, Suzanne
Welles; **Delhi** Manik Chauhan, Narender
Kumar, Shekhar Jha, Rakesh Kumar
Marketing & Publicity: **London** Richard
Trillo, Niki Hanmer, David Wearn, Demelza
Dallow; **New York** Geoff Colquitt, Megan
Kennedy, Milena Perez; **Delhi** Reem Khokhar
Custom publishing and foreign rights:
Philippa Hopkins
Finance: Gary Singh
Manager India: Punita Singh
Series editor: Mark Ellingham
Reference Director: Andrew Lockett
PA to Managing and Publishing Directors:
Megan McIntyre
Publishing Director: Martin Dunford
Managing Director: Kevin Fitzgerald

Publishing information

This 8th edition published July 2005 by **Rough
Guides Ltd**,
80 Strand, London WC2R 0RL.
345 Hudson St, 4th Floor,
New York, NY 10014, USA.
Distributed by the Penguin Group
Penguin Books Ltd,
80 Strand, London WC2R 0RL
Penguin Putnam, Inc.
375 Hudson Street, NY 10014, USA
Penguin Group (Australia)
250 Camberwell Road, Camberwell
Victoria 3124, Australia
Penguin Books Canada Ltd,
10 Alcorn Avenue, Toronto, Ontario,
Canada M4V 1E4
Penguin Group (New Zealand)
Cnr Rosedale and Airborne Roads
Albany, Auckland, New Zealand
Typeset in Bembo and Helvetica to an original
design by Henry Iles.

Printed in Italy by LegoPrint S.p.A

© Martin Dunford, Phil Lee, Rough Guides 2005

No part of this book may be reproduced in any
form without permission from the publisher
except for the quotation of brief passages in
reviews.

320pp includes index
A catalogue record for this book is available from
the British Library

ISBN 1-84353-460-6

The publishers and authors have done their best
to ensure the accuracy and currency of all the
information in **The Rough Guide to Amsterdam**,
however, they can accept no responsibility for
any loss, injury, or inconvenience sustained by
any traveller as a result of information or advice
contained in the guide.

1   3   5   7   9   8   6   4   2

Help us update

We've gone to a lot of effort to ensure that
the eighth edition of **The Rough Guide
to Amsterdam** is accurate and up-to-
date. However, things change – places get
"discovered", opening hours are notoriously
fickle, restaurants and rooms raise prices or
lower standards. If you feel we've got it wrong
or left something out, we'd like to know, and if
you can remember the address, the price, the
time, the phone number, so much the better.

We'll credit all contributions, and send a
copy of the next edition (or any other Rough

Guide if you prefer) for the best letters.
Everyone who writes to us and isn't already
a subscriber will receive a copy of our full-
colour thrice-yearly newsletter. Please mark
letters: "**Rough Guide Amsterdam Update**"
and send to: Rough Guides, 80 Strand,
London WC2R 0RL, or Rough Guides, 4th
Floor, 345 Hudson St, New York, NY 10014.
Or send an email to **mail@roughguides.com**
  Have your questions answered and tell
others about your trip at
www.roughguides.atinfopop.com

Acknowledgements

Martin: thanks to Caroline, Peggy and Daisy for tramping around Amsterdam in the rain, and to Andy Turner for another meticulous editing job.

Phil: a special thanks to Els Wamsteeker of the Amsterdam Tourism and Convention Board and to the ever helpful Malijn Maat.

Karoline: thanks to Phil Lee for his continuous help and support, Sarah Rogan for her patience and understanding and Richard, without whom the evenings would have seemed much longer. Thanks also to Andy Turner for his diligent editing.

The editor: special thanks to Maxine Repath and Karobi Gogoi for a great set of maps, Harriet Mills for good-humoured picture editing, Dan May for his patience and layout skills and Geoff Howard for helpful advice.

Readers' letters

Thanks to all the following for their letters and emails:

Tim Adams; Caroline Baurdoux; A C Berridge; Sian Beusch; Victor Blease; Diederik von Bonninghausen; Bram Bos; Adrian Brown; M Brown; Craig Bryant; Andy Coates; Alan and Anita Cohen; Adam Cook; Máire Corbett; Kelly Cross; Peter Deeley; Nathalie Delorme; Marie Doney; Julian Dorling; Paul Duggan; Michael Farr; G. C. Francis; Steven Goldberg; John Gordon; Leah Gourley; Patricia Griffin; Carol Hakins; Annmarie Hanlon; Caroline Harmeer; Birgit Hartmann; R. E. Harvard; Frederik Hemmes; Dominic Herrington; Chris Jackson; Tushar Jiwarajka; Alan Jolly; Peter de Koning; Joep Koperdraat; Tiny and Riana Ligthart; Pieter van Litsenburg; Wendy Lloyd; Betty McCall; Margot McCarthy; Craig MacDonald; Caroline McElwee; Dolores Mateo; Edward Mayor; Constance Messer; Abby Miller; Norman Miller; P. Moffat; Ronald Moor; Boris de Munnick; Janey Napier; Jay Nemes; Judith Orford; Jill Pearson; Valentina Pennazio; Elizabeth Plummer; Jim Vander Putten; Nick Reeves; Eleanor Renwick; Naomi Robinson; Amy Ryan; Sumitra Sankar; Toby Screech; Amy Shields; Douglas Smith; Phyllis Snyder; Keith Spanner; Dave Sutton; K Tan; Kiran Thomson; Kenneth Thosteman; M A Turnbull; R Vos; Charles Wass; Birgit Westhawk; Lesley White; David Wilson; J. Wood; Alison Wright; and Alison Young.

Photo credits

All photographs © Rough Guides except the following:

Cover

Main picture: Canal at night © Alamy
Small front top picture: Traditional clogs © Corbis
Small front lower picture: Tram © Alamy
Back top picture: Bike © Alamy
Back lower picture: Canal houses © Alamy

Introduction

Ice skaters © Anthony Cassidy

Things Not To Miss

09 "Self Portrait with Straw Hat" (1887) by Vincent van Gogh © Bridgeman Art Library/Rijksmuseum/J.P. Zenobel
10 Queen's Day © Netherlands Tourism
18 Vondelpark © Anthony Cassidy
25 Anne Frankhuis © Netherlands Tourism

Black and white pictures

Visitors looking at *The Night Watch* by Rembrandt van Rijn in the Rijksmuseum © Adam Woolfit/Corbis (p.120)
Interior of the Van Gogh Museum © John Van Hasselt/Corbis (p.123)
Amsterdam Arena © Amsterdam Arena (p.138)
Houses along the River Spaarne, Haarlem © DK Images (p.143)
Edam townhall © Florian Monheim/Alamy (p.155)
Alkmaar Cheese Market © DK Images (p.159)
Bulldog Hotel © Anthony Cassidy (p.173)
Hans Brinker Budget Hotel © Anthony Cassidy (p.174)
Melkweg © DK Images (p.204)
Paradiso © The Cover Story/Corbis (p.207)
Amsterdam Pride © Richard Wareham/Sylvia Cordaiy (p.237)
Cannabis Cup © Jeffrey L. Rottman/Corbis (p.252)

Index

Map entries are in colour.

INDEX

INDEX

C

D

E

INDEX

Map symbols

maps are listed in the full index using coloured text

▰▰▰	Motorway	✡	Synagogue
═══	Major road	⊙	Statue/memorial
───	Minor road	⊤	Gardens
▒▒▒	Pedestrianized road	⌣	Bridge
⋯⋯⋯	Tunnel	⊠—⊠	Gate
– – –	Footpath	▬	Boat
═▶═	Railway	▨	Building
▓▓▓	Waterway	▦	Church
— —	Ferry route	▢	Market
✈	Airport	⬭	Stadium
Ⓜ	Metro station	⊞	Cemetery
ⓘ	Information office	▨	Park/National park
⊠	Post office		

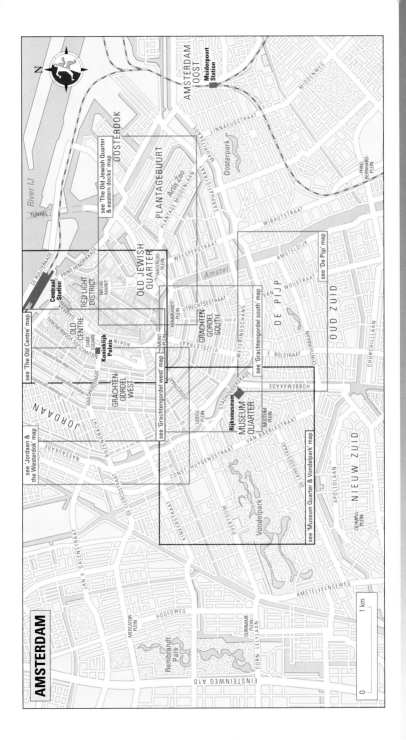

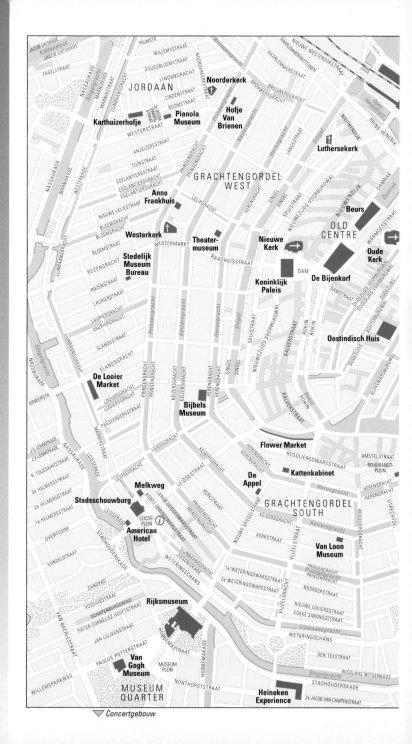

JACOB CATSKADE
Kattensloot
JACOB CATSKADE
FAGELSTRAAT
NASSAUKADE
MARNIXKADE
Singelgracht
MARNIXKADE
PALMSTR
WILLEMSSTRAAT
GOUDSBLOEMSTRAAT
LINDENGRACHT
LINDENSTRAAT
BOOMSTRAAT
WESTERSTRAAT
ANJELIERSSTRAAT

JORDAAN

Noorderkerk

Hofje Van Brienen

Karthuizerhofje **Pianola Museum**

WESTERSTRAAT

TUINSTRAAT
EGELANTIERSSTRAAT
EGELANTIERSGRACHT
EGELANTIERSGRACHT

NASSAUKADE
MARNIXKADE
WESTERKADE

NIEUWE LELIESTRAAT
BLOEMGRACHT
BLOEMGRACHT
BLOEMSTRAAT
ROZENGRACHT
ROZENSTRAAT
LAURIERGRACHT
LAURIERGRACHT
LAURIERGRACHT
LAURIERSTRAAT
ELANDSSTRAAT

LIJNBAANSGRACHT
LIJNBAANSGRACHT

Anne Frankhuis

Westerkerk

Stedelijk Museum Bureau

WESTERMARKT

Theater-museum

GRACHTENGORDEL WEST

LELIEGRACHT

RAADHUISSTRAAT

Nieuwe Kerk

Koninklijk Paleis

DAM

De Bijenkorf

PRINSENGRACHT
KEIZERSGRACHT
HERENGRACHT
SINGEL
SPUISTRAAT
NIEUWEZIJDS VOORBURGWAL

Luthersekerk

Beurs

OLD CENTRE

Oude Kerk

WARMOESSTRAAT
DAMRAK
DAMRAK
PRINS HENDRIK
NIEUWENDIJK
NIEUWENDIJK

DAMSTRAAT
OUDEZIJDS VOORBURGWAL
OUDEZIJDS VOORBURGWAL
OUDEZIJDS ACHTERBURGWAL
OUDEZIJDS

Oostindisch Huis

ROKIN
ROKIN
KALVERSTRAAT
KALVERSTRAAT

ELANDSGRACHT

De Looier Market

LODIERGRACHT
LODIERGRACHT
PASSEERDERSGRACHT

KINKERSTR.
NASSAUKADE
Singelgracht
MARNIXSTRAAT

PRINSENGRACHT
PRINSENGRACHT
KEIZERSGRACHT
KEIZERSGRACHT
HERENGRACHT
HERENGRACHT
SINGEL
SINGEL

Bijbels Museum

LEIDSEGRACHT

J.V. LENNEPKADE
J.V. LENNEPKADE
R. TOUSSAINTSTRAAT
3e HELMERSSTRAAT
2e HELMERSSTRAAT
1e HELMERSSTRAAT
OVERTOOM

LEIDSEKADE

Melkweg

Stadsschouwburg

American Hotel

LEIDSE-PLEIN ℹ

LEIDSEKADE

Flower Market

REGULIERSDWARSSTRAAT

Kattenkabinet

De Appel

Herengracht

HERENGRACHT
HERENGRACHT

AMSTELSTRAAT
REMBRANDT-PLEIN

HERENGRACHT
HERENGRACHT
UTRECHTSE-

LANGE LEIDSEDWARSSTRAAT
KORTE LEIDSEDWARSSTRAAT
PRINSENGRACHT
PRINSENGRACHT
KERKSTRAAT
NIEUWE SPIEGELSTRAAT
KEIZERSGRACHT
KEIZERSGRACHT
KERKSTRAAT
VIJZELSTRAAT
VIJZELGRACHT

GRACHTENGORDEL SOUTH

Van Loon Museum

PRINSENGRACHT
PRINSENGRACHT

REGULIERSGRACHT

LIJNBAANSGRACHT
LIESGRACHT
WETERINGSCHANS

1e WETERINGDWARSSTRAAT
2e WETERINGDWARSSTRAAT

NOORDERSTRAAT

NIEUWE LOOIERSSTRAAT
FOKKE SIMONSZSTRAAT

Lijnbaansgracht

WETERINGSCHANS

ZANDPAD
VOSSIUSSTRAAT
SCHAPENBURGERPAD
PIETER CORNELISZ HOOFTSTRAAT
STADHOUDERSKADE
VAN BAERLESTRAAT

Rijksmuseum

HOBBEMASTRAAT
HOBBEMAKADE

DEN TEXSTRAAT

NICOLAAS WITSENKADE
Singelgracht
STADHOUDERSKADE

JAN LUIJKENSTRAAT
PAULUS POTTERSTRAAT

Van Gogh Museum

MUSEUM PLEIN

MUSEUM QUARTER

WILLEMSPARKWEG

NONTHORSTSTRAAT

Heineken Experience

2e JACOB VAN CAMPENSTRAAT

▽ Concertgebouw

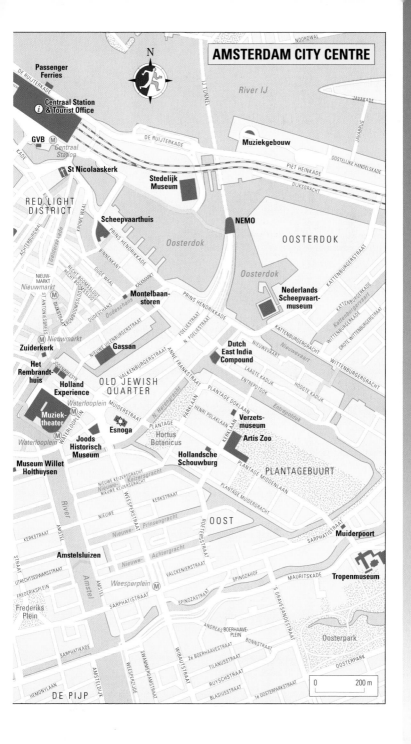

AMSTERDAM CITY CENTRE

NOORDWAL

River IJ

JAVAKADE

Passenger
Ferries

DE RUIJTERKADE

Centraal Station
& Tourist Office

DE RUIJTERKADE

Muziekgebouw

OOSTELIJKE HANDELSKADE

IJ TUNNEL

AJAXBRUG

GVB Ⓜ
Centraal
Station

PIET HEINKADE

KADE

St Nicolaaskerk

Stedelijk
Museum

DIJKSGRACHT

RED LIGHT
DISTRICT

Scheepvaarthuis

NEMO

OOSTERDOK

ACHTERBURGWAL

Oosterdok

Geldersekade

KATTENBURGERSTRAAT

KROMME WAAL

PRINS HENDRIKKADE

BINNENKANT

OUDE WAAL

KALKMARKT

Oosterdok

Nederlands
Scheepvaart-
museum

KATTENBURGERKADE

NIEUW-
MARKT
Nieuwmarkt

RECHT BOOMSSLOOT

KROMBOOMSSLOOT

OUDESCHANS

Montelbaan-
storen

PRINS HENDRIKKADE

Kattenburgervaart

WITTENBURGERKADE

GROTE WITTENBURGERSTRAAT

ST ANTONIESBREE

FOELIESTRAAT

NIEUWE WITTENBURGERSTRAAT

Ⓜ Nieuwmarkt

Oudeschans

KATTENBURGERGRACHT

Nieuwevaart

Zuiderkerk

Gassan

NIEUWE WITTENBURGERSTRAAT

Dutch
East India
Compound

NIEUWEVAART

WITTENBURGERGRACHT

JODENBREESTR

ANNE FRANKSTRAAT

LAAGSTE KADIJK

Het
Rembrandt-
huis

Holland
Experience

OLD JEWISH
QUARTER

VALKENBURGERSTRAAT

PLANTAGE DOKLAAN

ENTREPOTDOK

HOOGTE KADIJK

PARKLAAN

Entrepotdok

Waterlooplein

MUIDERSTRAAT

N. Herengracht

HENRI POLAKLAAN

Verzets-
museum

KERKLAAN

Muziek-
theater

Esnoga

PLANTAGE

Hortus
Botanicus

Artis Zoo

Waterlooplein

WATERLOOPLEIN

Joods
Historisch
Museum

Hollandsche
Schouwburg

PLANTAGE MIDDENLAAN

PLANTAGEBUURT

Museum Willet
Holthuysen

NIEUWE KEIZERSGRACHT

Nieuwe Keizersgracht

PLANTAGE MUIDERGRACHT

River

NIEUWE

KERKSTRAAT

Nieuwe- Prinsengracht

OOST

Amstel

KERKSTRAAT

Nieuwe- Achtergracht

ROETERSSTRAAT

SARPHATISTRAAT

Muiderpoort

Amstelsluizen

VALCKENIERSTRAAT

MAURITSKADE

UTRECHTSEDWARSSTRAAT

Weesperplein Ⓜ

SPINOZAHOF

Tropenmuseum

STRAAT

Amstel

SARPHATISTRAAT

SPINOZASTRAAT

'S GRAVESANDESTRAAT

FREDERIKSPLEIN

Frederiks
Plein

ANDREAS BOERHAAVE-
PLEIN

Oosterpark

SARPHATIKADE

2e BOERHAAVESTRAAT

BONNSTRAAT

AMSTELDIJK

SWAMMERDAMSTRAAT

WIBAUTSTRAAT

TILANUSSTRAAT

OOSTERPARK

HEMONYLAAN

DE PIJP

WEESPERZIJDE

RUYSCHSTRAAT

BLASIUSSTRAAT

1e OOSTERPARKSTRAAT

0   200 m

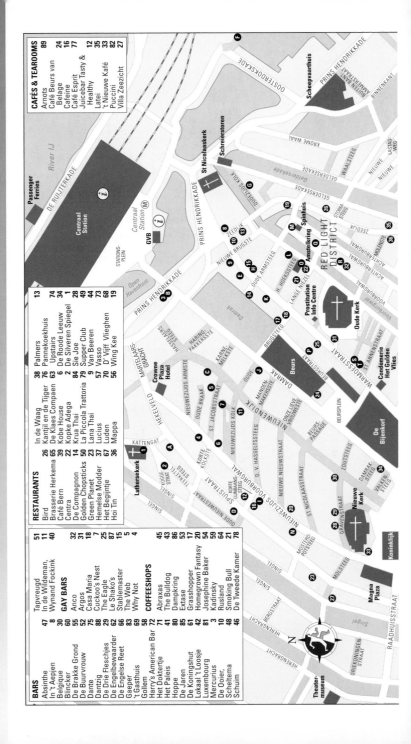

CAFÉS & TEAROOMS	
Arnots	89
Café Beurs van	
Belage	24
Cafeine	16
Café Esprit	77
Juicebar Tasty &	
Healthy	12
Latei	35
't Nieuwe Kafé	33
Puccini	82
Villa Zeezicht	27

BARS	
Absinthe	51
In 't Aepjen	11
Belgique	40
Blincker	60
De Brakke Grond	32
De Buurvrouw	31
Dante	18
Dantzig	75
De Drie Fleschjes	88
De Engelbewaarder	29
De Engelse Reet	62
Gaeper	66
't Gasthuis	83
Gollem	69
Harry's American Bar	58
Het Doktertje	72
Het Paleis	41
Hoppe	80
De Jaren	85
De Koningshut	61
Lokaal 't Loosje	42
Luxembourg	81
Mercurius	3
De Ooier,	10
Scheltema	48
Schuim	46

Tapvreugd	47
In de Wildeman,	8
Wynand Fockink	30

GAY BARS	
Anco	55
Argos	52
Casa Maria	75
Cuckoo's Nest	7
The Eagle	25
Le Shako's	87
Stablemaster	15
The Web	5
Why Not	4

COFFEESHOPS	
Abraxas	45
The Bulldog	43
Dampkring	86
Extase	53
Grasshopper	17
Homegrown Fantasy	20
Josephine Baker	54
Kadinsky	59
Rusland	64
Smoking Bull	48
De Tweede Kamer	78

RESTAURANTS	
Bird	13
Brasserie Herkema	26
Café Bern	74
Centra	39
De Compagnon	34
Golden Chopsticks	14
Green Planet	50
Hemelse Modder	23
Het Begijntje	37
Hoi Tin	67

In de Waag	38
Kantjil en de Tiger	36
De Klaes Compaen	76
Kobe House	65
Kopke Adega	22
Krua Thai	6
La Piccola Trattoria	84
Lana Thai	49
Lucius	23
Luden	9
Mappa	57

Palmers	13
Pannekoekhuis	74
Upstairs	34
De Roode Leeuw	1
De Silveren Spiegel	28
Sie Joe	44
Supper Club	73
Van Beeren	79
Vasso	57
D' Vijff Vlieghen	70
Wing Kee	56

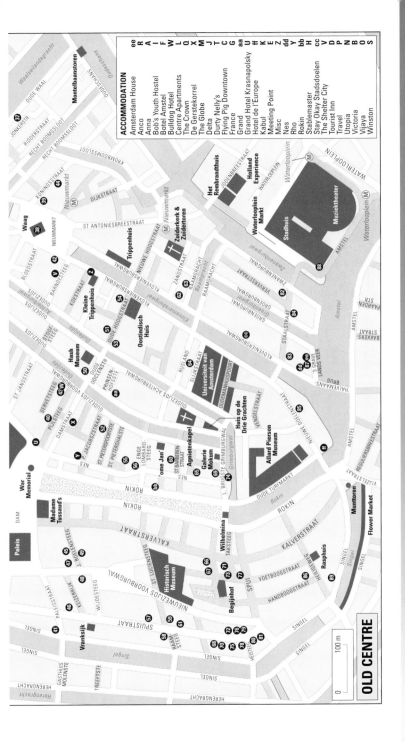

ACCOMMODATION

Amsterdam House	ee
Anco	R
Anna	A
Bob's Youth Hostel	I
Botel Amstel	F
Bulldog Hotel	W
Centre Apartments	L
The Crown	Q
De Gerstekorrel	X
The Globe	M
Delta	J
Durty Nelly's	T
Flying Pig Downtown	C
France	G
Grand	aa
Grand Hotel Krasnapolsky	U
Hotel de l'Europe	ff
Kabul	K
Meeting Point	E
Misc	N
Nes	Z
Rho	dd
Rokin	Y
Stablemaster	bb
Stay Okay Stadsdoelen	H
The Shelter City	cc
Tourist Inn	V
Travel	D
Utopia	P
Victoria	N
Vijaya	B
Winston	O
	S

OLD CENTRE

0 100 m

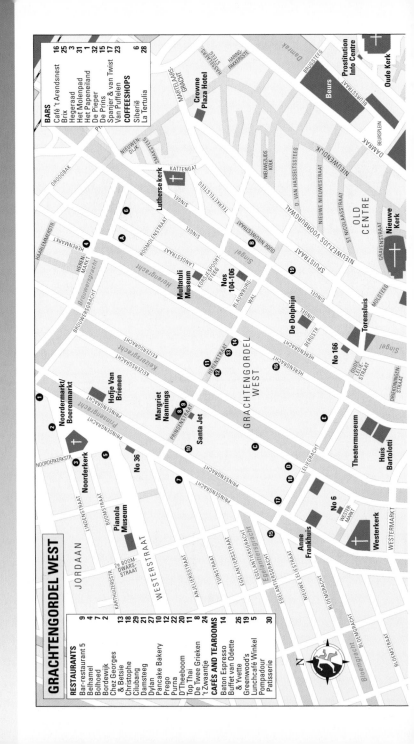

GRACHTENGORDEL WEST

JORDAAN

Noordermarkt/
Boerenmarkt

Noorderkerk

Pianola Museum

Hofje Van Brienen

Multatuli Museum

Nos 104–106

Margriet Nannings

Santa Jet

No 36

Lutherse kerk

GRACHTENGORDEL WEST

De Dolphijn

Torensluis

No 166

Theatermuseum

Huis Bartolotti

Westerkerk

WESTERMARKT

Anne Frankhuis

No 6

Crowne Plaza Hotel

Beurs

Prostitution Info Centre

Oude Kerk

Nieuwe Kerk

OLD CENTRE

Damrak

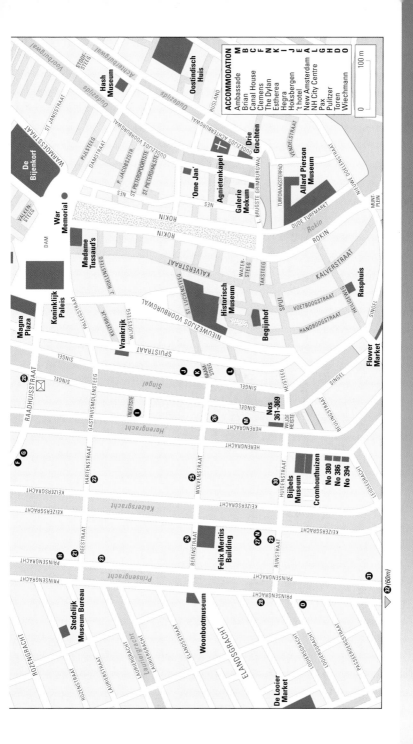

ACCOMMODATION
Ambassade M
Brian B
Canal House C
Clemens F
The Dylan K
Estherea N
Hegra J
Hoksbergen E
't hotel I
New Amsterdam A
NH City Centre L
Pax G
Pulitzer H
Toren D
Wiechmann O

0   100 m

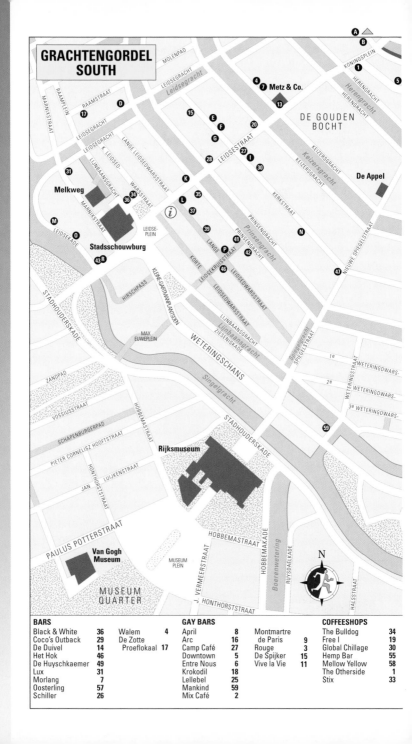

GRACHTENGORDEL SOUTH

MOLENPAD

LEIDSEGRACHT / *Leidsegracht*

KONINGSPLEIN

HERENGRACHT / *Herengracht*

Metz & Co.

DE GOUDEN BOCHT

RAAMPLEIN

RAAMSTRAAT

MARNIXSTRAAT

LEIDSEGRACHT

LANGE LEIDSEDWARSSTRAAT

K. LEIDSED.

WARMOESSTRAAT

LEIDSESTRAAT

KEIZERSGRACHT / *Keizersgracht*

KERKSTRAAT

De Appel

LIJNBAANSGRACHT

Melkweg

MARNIXSTRAAT

LEIDSEKADE

Stadsschouwburg

LEIDSE-PLEIN

PRINSENGRACHT / *Prinsengracht*

NIEUWE SPIEGELSTRAAT

KLEINE-GARTMANPLANTSOEN

HIRSCHPASS

KORTE LEIDSEKRUISSTRAAT

LANGE LEIDSEDWARSSTRAAT

LEIDSEDWARSSTRAAT

STADHOUDERSKADE

MAX EUWEPLEIN

LIJNBAANSGRACHT

ZIESENISKADE

WETERINGSCHANS

Singelgracht

SPIEGELGRACHT

SPIEGELSTRAAT

1e WETERINGDWARS-

2e WETERINGDWARS-

3e WETERINGDWARS-

ZANDPAD

VOSSIUSSTRAAT

SCHAPENBURGERPAD

PIETER CORNELISZ HOOFTSTRAAT

HOBBEMASTRAAT

STADHOUDERSKADE

Rijksmuseum

JAN LUIJKENSTRAAT

HONTHORSTSTRAAT

PAULUS POTTERSTRAAT

Van Gogh Museum

MUSEUM PLEIN

HOBBEMASTRAAT

HOBBEMAKADE

Boerenwetering

RUYSDAELKADE

HALLSTRAAT

J. VERMEERSTRAAT

J. HONTHORSTSTRAAT

MUSEUM QUARTER

N

BARS		GAY BARS				COFFEESHOPS	
Black & White	36	April	8	Montmartre		The Bulldog	34
Coco's Outback	29	Arc	16	de Paris	9	Free I	19
De Duivel	14	Camp Café	27	Rouge	3	Global Chillage	30
Het Hok	46	Downtown	5	De Spijker	15	Hemp Bar	55
De Huyschkaemer	49	Entre Nous	6	Vive la Vie	11	Mellow Yellow	58
Lux	31	Krokodil	18			The Otherside	1
Morlang	7	Lellebel	25			Stix	33
Oosterling	57	Mankind	59				
Schiller	26	Mix Café	2				
Walem	4						
De Zotte							
Proeflokaal	17						

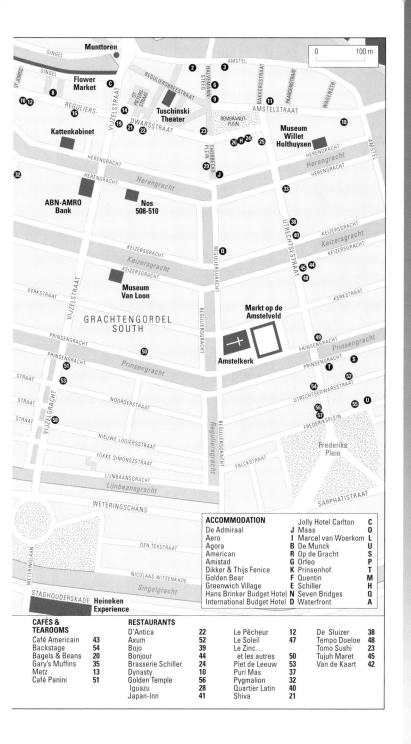

ACCOMMODATION

De Admiraal	**J**	Jolly Hotel Carlton	**C**
Aero	**I**	Maas	**O**
Agora	**B**	Marcel van Woerkom	**L**
American	**R**	De Munck	**U**
Amistad	**G**	Op de Gracht	**S**
Dikker & Thijs Fenice	**K**	Orfeo	**P**
Golden Bear	**F**	Prinsenhof	**T**
Greenwich Village	**E**	Quentin	**M**
Hans Brinker Budget Hotel	**N**	Schiller	**H**
International Budget Hotel	**D**	Seven Bridges	**Q**
		Waterfront	**A**

CAFÉS & TEAROOMS

Café Americain	43
Backstage	54
Bagels & Beans	20
Gary's Muffins	35
Metz	13
Café Panini	51

RESTAURANTS

D'Antica	22	Le Pêcheur	12	De Sluizer	38
Axum	52	Le Soleil	47	Tempo Doeloe	48
Bojo	39	Le Zinc…		Tomo Sushi	23
Bonjour	44	et les autres	50	Tujuh Maret	45
Brasserie Schiller	24	Piet de Leeuw	53	Van de Kaart	42
Dynasty	10	Puri Mas	37		
Golden Temple	56	Pygmalion	32		
Iguazu	28	Quartier Latin	40		
Japan-Inn	41	Shiva	21		

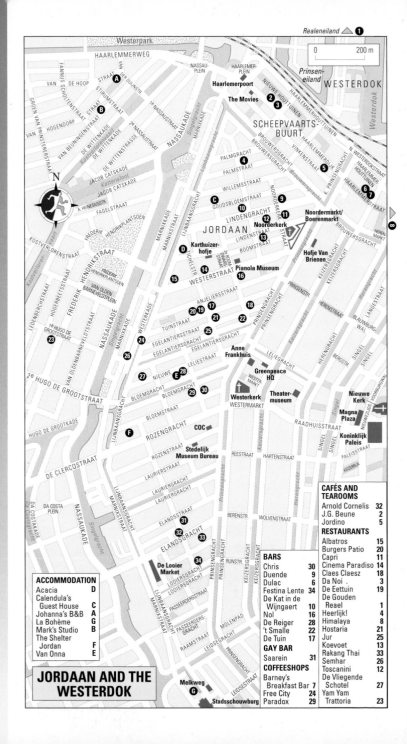

Realeneiland △ ①

Westerpark

HAARLEMMERWEG

Prinsen-
eiland

WESTERDOK

NASSAU-
PLEIN

HAARLEMER-
PLEIN

Haarlemerpoort

The Movies ② ③

SCHEEPVAARTS-
BUURT

PALMGRACHT ④

PALMSTRAAT

⑤

WILLEMSSTRAAT

GOUDSBLOEMSTRAAT ⑨

LINDENGRACHT ⑩

Noorderkerk ⑫ ⑪

Noordermarkt/
Boerenmarkt

JORDAAN

LINDENSTRAAT ⑬

BOOMSTRAAT

Karthuizer-
hofje Ⓓ

WESTERSTRAAT ⑭

Pianola Museum ⑯

**Hofje Van
Brienen**

ANJELIERSSTRAAT ⑰

⑮

⑳ ⑲ ㉑ ⑱

TUINSTRAAT

㉒

⑳

EGELANTIERSSTRAAT ㉕

㉔

EGELANTIERSGRACHT

**Anne
Frankhuis**

⑳

LELIEGRACHT

㉗ Ⓔ ㉘

NIEUWE

**Greenpeace
HQ**

BLOEMGRACHT

㉙ ㉚

BLOEMGRACHT

Westerkerk

WESTERMARKT

**Theater-
museum**

**Nieuwe
Kerk**

BLOEMSTRAAT

**Magna
Plaza**

ROZENGRACHT

COC ▬

RAADHUISSTRAAT

**Koninklijk
Paleis**

ROZENGRACHT

**Stedelijk
Museum Bureau**

REESTRAAT

HARTENSTRAAT

PALEISSTRAAT

DE CLERCQSTRAAT

LAURIERSTRAAT

LAURIERGRACHT

DA COSTA
PLEIN

BERENSTR.

WOLVENSTRAAT

ELANDSSTRAAT ㉛

㉜

ELANDSGRACHT ㉝

**De Looier
Market** ㉞

LOOIERSGRACHT

Melkweg Ⓖ

Stadsschouwburg

JORDAAN AND THE
WESTERDOK